Clinical research in Asia

Woodhead Publishing Series in Biomedicine

1 Practical leadership for biopharmaceutical executives
J. Y. Chin

2 Outsourcing biopharma R&D to India
P. R. Chowdhury

3 Matlab® in bioscience and biotechnology
L. Burstein

4 Allergens and respiratory pollutants
Edited by M. A. Williams

5 Concepts and techniques in genomics and proteomics
N. Saraswathy and P. Ramalingam

6 An introduction to pharmaceutical sciences
J. Roy

7 Patently innovative: How pharmaceutical firms use emerging patent law to extend monopolies on blockbuster drugs
R. A. Bouchard

8 Therapeutic protein drug products: Practical approaches to formulation in the laboratory, manufacturing and the clinic
Edited by B. K. Meyer

9 A biotech manager's handbook: A practical guide
Edited by M. O'Neill and M. H. Hopkins

10 Clinical research in Asia: Opportunities and challenges
U. Sahoo

11 Therapeutic antibody engineering: Current and future advances driving the strongest growth area in the pharma industry
W. R. Strohl and L. M. Strohl

12 Commercialising the stem cell sciences
O. Harvey

Published by Woodhead Publishing Limited, 2012

13

14 Human papillomavirus infections: From the laboratory to clinical practice
F. Cobo

15 Annotating new genes: From *in silico* to validations by experiments
S. Uchida

16 Open-source software in life science research: Practical solutions in the pharmaceutical industry and beyond
Edited by L. Harland and M. Forster

17 Nanoparticulate drug delivery: A perspective on the transition from laboratory to market
V. Patravale, P. Dandekar and R. Jain

18 Bacterial cellular metabolic systems: Metabolic regulation of a cell system with ^{13}C-metabolic flux analysis
K. Shimizu

19 Contract research and manufacturing services (CRAMS) in India
M. Antani, G. Gokhale and K. Baxi

20 Bioinformatics for biomedical science and clinical applications
K-H. Liang

21 Deterministic versus stochastic modelling in biochemistry and systems biology
P. Lecca, I. Laurenzi and F. Jordan

22 Protein folding *in silico*: Protein folding versus protein structure prediction
I. Roterman-Konieczna

23 Computer-aided vaccine design
T. J. Chuan and S. Ranganathan

24 An introduction to biotechnology
W. T. Godbey

25 RNA interference: Therapeutic developments
T. Novobrantseva, P. Ge and G. Hinkle

26 Patent litigation in the pharmaceutical and biotechnology industries
G. Morgan

27 Clinical research in paediatric psychopharmacology: A practical guide
P. Auby

28 The application of SPC in the pharmaceutical and biotechnology industries
T. Cochrane

Published by Woodhead Publishing Limited, 2012

29 Ultrafiltration for bioprocessing
  H. Lutz

30 Therapeutic risk management of medicines
  A. K. Banerjee and S. Mayall

31 21st century quality management and good management practices: Value added compliance for the pharmaceutical and biotechnology industry
  S. Williams

32

33 CAPA in the pharmaceutical and biotech industries
  J. Rodriguez

34 Process validation for the production of biopharmaceuticals: Principles and best practice
  A. R. Newcombe and P. Thillaivinayagalingam

35 Clinical trial management: An overview
  U. Sahoo and D. Sawant

36 Impact of regulation on drug development
  H. Guenter Hennings

37 Lean biomanufacturing
  N. J. Smart

38 Marine enzymes for biocatalysis
  Edited by A. Trincone

39 Ocular transporters and receptors in the eye: Their role in drug delivery
  A. K. Mitra

40 Stem cell bioprocessing: For cellular therapy, diagnostics and drug development
  T. G. Fernandes, M. M. Diogo and J. M. S. Cabral

41

42 Fed-batch fermentation: A practical guide to scalable recombinant protein production in *Escherichia coli*
  G. G. Moulton and T. Vedvick

43 The funding of biopharmaceutical research and development
  D. R. Williams

44 Formulation tools for pharmaceutical development
  Edited by J. E. A. Diaz

Published by Woodhead Publishing Limited, 2012

45 Drug-biomembrane interaction studies: The application of calorimetric techniques
R. Pignatello

46 Orphan drugs: Understanding the rare drugs market
E. Hernberg-Ståhl

47 Nanoparticle-based approaches to targeting drugs for severe diseases
J. L. A. Mediano

48 Successful biopharmaceutical operations
C. Driscoll

49 Electroporation-based therapies for cancer
Edited by R. Sundarajan

50 Transporters in drug discovery and development
Y. Lai

51 The life-cycle of pharmaceuticals in the environment
R. Braund and B. Peake

52 Computer-aided applications in pharmaceutical technology
Edited by J. Petrović

53 From plant genomics to plant biotechnology
Edited by P. Poltronieri, N. Burbulis and C. Fogher

54 Bioprocess engineering: An introductory engineering and life science approach
K. G. Clarke

55 Quality assurance problem solving and training strategies for success in the pharmaceutical and life science industries
G. Welty

56 Nanomedicine: Prognostic and curative approaches to cancer
K. Scarberry

57 Gene therapy: Potential applications of nanotechnology
S. Nimesh

58 Controlled drug delivery: The role of self-assembling multi-task excipients
M. Mateescu

59 *In silico* protein design
C. M. Frenz

60 Bioinformatics for computer science: Foundations in modern biology
K. Revett

61 Gene expression analysis in the RNA world
J. Q. Clement

Published by Woodhead Publishing Limited, 2012

62 Computational methods for finding inferential bases in molecular genetics
Q-N. Tran

63 NMR metabolomics in cancer research
M. Čuperlović-Culf

64 Virtual worlds for medical education, training and care delivery
K. Kahol

I dedicate this book to my parents,
Jatindra Mohan Sahoo and Harapriya Sahoo,
and my in-laws, Dr Padmanav Nayak and Sumati Nayak

Published by Woodhead Publishing Limited, 2012

Woodhead Publishing Series in Biomedicine: Number 10

Clinical research in Asia

Opportunities and challenges

Umakanta Sahoo

Oxford   Cambridge   Philadelphia   New Delhi

Published by Woodhead Publishing Limited, 2012

Woodhead Publishing Limited, 80 High Street, Sawston, Cambridge, CB22 3HJ, UK
www.woodheadpublishing.com
www.woodheadpublishingonline.com

Woodhead Publishing, 1518 Walnut Street, Suite 1100, Philadelphia, PA 19102-3406, USA

Woodhead Publishing India Private Limited, G-2, Vardaan House, 7/28 Ansari Road,
Daryaganj, New Delhi – 110002, India
www.woodheadpublishingindia.com

First published in 2012 by Woodhead Publishing Limited
ISBN: 978-1-907568-00-8 (print) and ISBN: 978-1-908818-13-3 (online)
Woodhead Publishing Series in Biomedicine ISSN 2050-0289 (print); ISSN 2050-2097 (online)

© U. Sahoo, 2012

The right of U. Sahoo to be identified as author(s) of this Work has been asserted by them in
accordance with sections 77 and 78 of the Copyright, Designs and Patents Act 1988.

British Library Cataloguing-in-Publication Data: A catalogue record for this book is available from
the British Library.

Library of Congress Control Number: 2012939579

All rights reserved. No part of this publication may be reproduced, stored in or introduced
into a retrieval system, or transmitted, in any form, or by any means (electronic, mechanical,
photocopying, recording or otherwise) without the prior written permission of the Publishers. This
publication may not be lent, resold, hired out or otherwise disposed of by way of trade in any
form of binding or cover other than that in which it is published without the prior consent of the
Publishers. Any person who does any unauthorised act in relation to this publication may be liable
to criminal prosecution and civil claims for damages.

Permissions may be sought from the Publishers at the above address.

The use in this publication of trade names, trademarks, service marks, and similar terms, even if
they are not identified as such, is not to be taken as an expression of opinion as to whether or not
they are subject to proprietary rights. The Publishers are not associated with any product or vendor
mentioned in this publication.

The Publishers and author(s) have attempted to trace the copyright holders of all material
reproduced in this publication and apologise to any copyright holders if permission to publish in
this form has not been obtained. If any copyright material has not been acknowledged, please write
and let us know so we may rectify in any future reprint. Any screenshots in this publication are the
copyright of the website owner(s), unless indicated otherwise.

Limit of Liability/Disclaimer of Warranty
The Publishers and author(s) make no representations or warranties with respect to the accuracy or
completeness of the contents of this publication and specifically disclaim all warranties, including
without limitation warranties of fitness of a particular purpose. No warranty may be created or
extended by sales of promotional materials. The advice and strategies contained herein may not be
suitable for every situation. This publication is sold with the understanding that the Publishers are
not rendering legal, accounting or other professional services. If professional assistance is required,
the services of a competent professional person should be sought. No responsibility is assumed by the
Publishers or author(s) for any loss of profit or any other commercial damages, injury and/or damage
to persons or property as a matter of products liability, negligence or otherwise, or from any use or
operation of any methods, products, instructions or ideas contained in the material herein. The fact
that an organisation or website is referred to in this publication as a citation and/or potential source
of further information does not mean that the Publishers nor the author(s) endorse the information
the organisation or website may provide or recommendations it may make. Further, readers should
be aware that internet websites listed in this work may have changed or disappeared between when
this publication was written and when it is read. Because of rapid advances in medical sciences, in
particular, independent verification of diagnoses and drug dosages should be made.

Typeset by Domex e-Data Pvt. Ltd., India
Printed in the UK and USA

Published by Woodhead Publishing Limited, 2012

Contents

List of figures and tables	*xxi*
Acknowledgments	*xxvii*
List of abbreviations	*xxix*
Preface	*xxxiii*
About the author	*xxxvii*

1 Clinical research in Asia: a brief overview   **1**

1.1	Background	1
1.2	Global pharmaceutical market	2
1.3	Clinical research business – a global overview	5
1.4	CRO services mix	8
1.5	The clinical research boom in Asia	8
1.6	Asian country segmentation analysis	15
1.7	Clinical trials in Asia	17
1.8	Inspection and data quality	19
1.9	Clinical research in Asia – SWOT analysis	22
	1.9.1 Strengths	22
	1.9.2 Weaknesses	23
	1.9.3 Opportunities	24
	1.9.4 Threats	25

2 Clinical research in Japan   **27**

2.1	Background and history	27
2.2	Clinical research industry in Japan	29
2.3	The regulatory environment in Japan	32
2.4	Evolution of Japanese good clinical practice	38
2.5	Global clinical trials in Japan	44
	2.5.1 Basic principles	45
2.6	Emerging outsourcing models in Japan	46

Published by Woodhead Publishing Limited, 2012

xii Clinical Research in Asia: Opportunities and Challenges

		2.6.1	Model 1: global pharma with global CRO	47

2.6.1 Model 1: global pharma with global CRO — 47
2.6.2 Model 2: global pharma with global CRO and its allied local CRO — 48
2.6.3 Model 3: global pharma's local affiliate and CRO — 49
2.6.4 Model 4: in-country clinical caretaker — 51
2.7 Japan's international strategic outlook — 51
2.7.1 Strategy 1: strengthening international collaboration — 51
2.7.2 Strategy 2: strengthening international harmonisation — 52
2.7.3 Strategy 3: promotion of personnel exchange programmes — 53
2.7.4 Strategy 4: creation of world-class human resources — 53
2.7.5 Strategy 5: international publicity and information sharing — 53
2.8 Future outlook — 54

3 Clinical research in India — 55

3.1 Pharmaceutical industry background — 55
3.2 History of clinical research in India — 60
3.3 Evolution of clinical research in India — 61
3.3.1 Drug discovery and chemistry business — 62
3.3.2 Clinical research business — 63
3.3.3 BABE/Phase I and pre-clinical business — 64
3.3.4 IT and ITES life science business — 65
3.3.5 Centralised laboratory/ECG business — 66
3.3.6 Clinical research training — 67
3.3.7 Clinical trials undertaken in India — 67
3.4 Regulatory environment in India — 73
3.4.1 The Drugs and Cosmetics Act — 73
3.4.2 Ethical guidelines for biomedical research on human subjects — 73
3.4.3 Good clinical practice guidelines — 74
3.4.4 Salient features of Indian GCP — 75
3.5 Clinical trial approval — 81
3.5.1 Import permission and processing time — 81
3.5.2 Export of biological samples – the formalities — 82
3.6 Difference between ICH-GCP and Indian GCP — 83
3.6.1 Regulatory standards for Phase I and Phase 0 trials — 84
3.7 Regulatory inspections in India — 85
3.8 Clinical research in India: PESTLE analysis — 86

Published by Woodhead Publishing Limited, 2012

	3.8.1 Political factors	86
	3.8.2 Economic factors	93
	3.8.3 Socio-economic-cultural factors	95
	3.8.4 Cultural factors	97
	3.8.5 Technology factors	99
	3.8.6 Environmental factors	101
	3.8.7 Legal factors	103
3.9	Future outlook	105

4 Clinical research in China — 107

4.1	Pharmaceutical market	107
4.2	Pharmaceutical investments in China	109
4.3	China's healthcare system	111
	4.3.1 Population factors	114
	4.3.2 Ageing and healthcare	114
	4.3.3 Political situation	115
	4.3.4 Disease burden	116
4.4	Healthcare delivery system	118
4.5	The importance of traditional medicine in modern healthcare	120
4.6	China's CRO market	122
4.7	Clinical trials in China	125
4.8	Accreditation of clinical trial sites in China	128
4.9	Clinical research in China – environmental analysis	130
	4.9.1 Political environment	130
	4.9.2 Economic environment	132
	4.9.3 Regulatory environment	134
	4.9.4 Overview of regulation in China	135
	4.9.5 Evolution of GCP	135
	4.9.6 Monitoring adverse drug reactions	139
	4.9.7 Application and approval of new drugs	141
	4.9.8 Clinical trials for new drugs	143
4.10	Future outlook	147

5 Clinical research in South Korea — 149

5.1	Pharmaceutical industry overview	149
	5.1.1 New drugs marketed in South Korea	152
5.2	CRO market in South Korea	153

Published by Woodhead Publishing Limited, 2012

		5.2.1	Government initiatives	153
5.3		Clinical trial environment		154
5.4		Evolution of GCP in South Korea		155
		5.4.1	IND review process	156
		5.4.2	IRB review process	157
		5.4.3	Study start-up timeline	159
		5.4.4	Import, storage and labelling requirements of the investigational product	159
		5.4.5	Insurance	160
		5.4.6	Safety reporting	160
		5.4.7	Recruitment modalities	161
		5.4.8	Interim report submission	161
		5.4.9	Discontinuation/termination of trial	161
		5.4.10	Final study report	162
		5.4.11	Drug accountability/disposal report	162
5.5		Clinical trials in South Korea		162
5.6		Accreditation of medical centres		165
		5.6.1	Therapeutic focus	166
5.7		Environmental analysis		168
		5.7.1	Hospital infrastructure	169
		5.7.2	Other infrastructure	169
		5.7.3	Quality investigator	169
		5.7.4	Regional cooperation and data acceptance between Japan, China, South Korea and Taiwan	170
		5.7.5	Compliance	170
		5.7.6	Language barrier	172
		5.7.7	Shortage of skilled professionals	172
		5.7.8	Cultural barriers	173
5.8		Future outlook		173

6 Clinical research in Taiwan 175

6.1		Pharmaceutical industry overview		175
6.2		Biotech industry in Taiwan		177
6.3		Healthcare system in Taiwan		178
6.4		CRO market in Taiwan		180
6.5		Evolution of GCP in Taiwan		181
		6.5.1	IND review process	182
		6.5.2	Bridging study evaluation	185
		6.5.3	Consultations: online application	185

Contents

	6.5.4	Institutional review board approval process	186
	6.5.5	Regulatory approval process	187
	6.5.6	Study start-up timeline	188
	6.5.7	Safety reporting	189
	6.5.8	Recruitment modalities	190
6.6		Clinical trials in Taiwan	190
	6.6.1	General clinical research centres	192
	6.6.2	Environmental analysis	194
	6.6.3	Infrastructure and facilities	194
	6.6.4	Quality investigators	194
	6.6.5	Regional cooperation and data acceptance between Japan, China, South Korea and Taiwan	195
	6.6.6	Language barriers	195
	6.6.7	Shortage of skilled professionals	196
	6.6.8	Cultural barriers	196
6.7		Future outlook	196

7 Clinical research in Singapore — 199

7.1		Overview of the pharmaceutical industry in Singapore	199
7.2		Pharmaceutical investments in Singapore	200
7.3		Governing authority and regulatory structure	203
	7.3.1	Drug Administration Division	203
	7.3.2	Chinese Proprietary Medicine Unit	204
	7.3.3	Good Manufacturing Practices and Licensing Unit	204
	7.3.4	Cosmetic Control Unit	204
	7.3.5	Adverse Drug Reaction Monitoring Unit	205
7.4		Healthcare system in Singapore	205
	7.4.1	Primary healthcare	206
	7.4.2	Intermediate and long-term care	206
	7.4.3	Health research	207
7.5		Clinical research in Singapore	207
7.6		CRO market	208
	7.6.1	Focus on specialised therapeutics	209
7.7		Clinical trials in Singapore	211
	7.7.1	Clinical trial approval	213
	7.7.2	Application for CTC	215
	7.7.3	Import of clinical trial material	216
7.8		Evolution of GCP in Singapore	217

Published by Woodhead Publishing Limited, 2012

xvi Clinical Research in Asia: Opportunities and Challenges

7.8.1	Salient features of the SGGCP	217
7.8.2	Medical Clinical Research Committee	218
7.8.3	Hospital ethics committee	219
7.8.4	Other salient features of the SGGCP	222
7.9	Role of clinical trial resource centre	224
7.10	Environmental analysis	225
7.10.1	Political and economic environment	225
7.10.2	Public–private partnership	226
7.10.3	Socio-cultural environment	229
7.10.4	Regulatory and legal environment	230
7.11	Clinical trial challenges	232
7.11.1	Competition for experienced investigators	232
7.11.2	Competition for patient database	232
7.11.3	Advanced healthcare and medical practice	233
7.11.4	Cosmopolitan society	233
7.11.5	Financial stability and social security	233
7.11.6	Widespread awareness	234
7.11.7	Cultural outlook	234
7.11.8	Ethnic limitations	234
7.11.9	Traditional medicine practices	234
7.11.10	Higher cost of medical practice and technology	235
7.11.11	The widening gap of demand-supply for quality resources	235
7.12	Future outlook	235

8 Clinical research in Thailand   **237**

8.1	Pharmaceutical industry in Thailand	237
8.2	The pharmaceutical regulatory environment	239
8.3	Pharmaceutical market	240
8.3.1	Demography	241
8.4	Clinical research in Thailand	242
8.5	CRO market in Thailand	242
8.5.1	Major CROs operating in Thailand	243
8.5.2	Clinical trial conduct in Thailand	243
8.5.3	Patient recruitment/willingness to participate in clinical trials	245
8.6	Hospital systems in Thailand	246

Published by Woodhead Publishing Limited, 2012

Contents

	8.6.1	Compliance with 21 CFR Part 11	247
	8.6.2	Economic advantages	247
	8.6.3	Qualified site staff	247
	8.6.4	Therapeutic areas	248
	8.6.5	Monitoring sites in Asia	248
	8.6.6	Biomedical research – ethical issues in Thailand	249
	8.6.7	Reduction in steps and resource loss	251
	8.6.8	World-class research standards	251
	8.6.9	Motivation for sponsors	252
	8.6.10	Opportunities for Thai researchers	252
	8.6.11	Opportunities for patients	252
8.7		Conducting clinical trials in Thailand	252
	8.7.1	Marketing approval for new drugs and generics	254
	8.7.2	Compulsory licensing	254
	8.7.3	Clinical trial approval process and timelines	256
	8.7.4	Study start-up timeline	257
	8.7.5	Import, storage and labelling requirements of investigational product	259
	8.7.6	Insurance	259
	8.7.7	Suspected unexpected serious adverse reaction reports for investigational drugs under pre-marketing clinical trials	259
	8.7.8	Recruitment modalities	260
	8.7.9	Interim report submission	260
	8.7.10	Discontinuation/termination of trial	260
	8.7.11	Final study report	261
	8.7.12	Drug accountability/disposal report	261
8.8		Clinical trials in Thailand	261
8.9		Environmental analysis	263
	8.9.1	Shortage of skilled professionals	264
	8.9.2	Cultural barrier	264
8.10		Future outlook	265
	8.10.1	Personal data protection	265
	8.10.2	Pro-generic policies	265
	8.10.3	Drug registration process	266
	8.10.4	New drug registration process	266
	8.10.5	Generic process approval	267
	8.10.6	A level playing field	267

xviii Clinical Research in Asia: Opportunities and Challenges

9	**Clinical research in Malaysia**	**269**
	9.1 Pharmaceutical industry overview	269
	9.2 Pharmaceutical market	270
	9.3 Pharmaceutical regulation	271
	9.4 Healthcare systems in Malaysia	273
	9.5 Clinical trial environment	274
	9.6 Regulatory environment in Malaysia	275
	9.7 Evolution of Malaysian GCP	276
	9.7.1 Clinical trial permission	277
	9.7.2 Regulatory, ethics committee approval and start-up timeline	280
	9.7.3 Safety reporting	281
	9.7.4 Interim report	283
	9.7.5 Discontinuation/termination of trial	283
	9.7.6 Final study report	284
	9.7.7 Drug accountability and disposal	284
	9.8 CRO market in Malaysia	284
	9.9 Clinical trials in Malaysia	286
	9.10 Registration of clinical trials	288
	9.10.1 Value proposition and challenges	289
	9.11 Challenges and future outlook	290
10	**Clinical research in Hong Kong**	**293**
	10.1 Background and history	293
	10.2 Pharmaceutical industry in Hong Kong	295
	10.3 Healthcare system in Hong Kong	296
	10.4 Clinical trials in Hong Kong	299
	10.5 The regulatory environment	301
	10.5.1 Ethics committees	303
	10.5.2 Regulatory and ethics committee approval	303
	10.5.3 Import and export permission	303
	10.5.4 Study start-up timeline	305
	10.5.5 Clinical trial insurance	306
	10.5.6 Safety reporting	308
	10.5.7 Recruitment modalities	308
	10.5.8 Progress report submission	309
	10.6 Clinical trials in Hong Kong	309

Published by Woodhead Publishing Limited, 2012

| Contents | xix |

10.7 Environmental analysis | 311
 10.7.1 Regional cooperation and data acceptance | 312
 10.7.2 Shortage of skilled professionals | 312
 10.7.3 Cultural barrier | 312
10.8 Future outlook | 313

11 Clinical research in the Philippines, Indonesia and Vietnam | 315

11.1 Clinical research in the Philippines | 315
 11.1.1 Background and history | 315
 11.1.2 Regulatory environment | 316
 11.1.3 Ethics committee approval | 318
 11.1.4 Clinical trials in the Philippines | 319
 11.1.5 Challenges and future outlook | 320
11.2 Clinical research in Indonesia | 321
 11.2.1 Background and history | 321
 11.2.2 The regulatory environment | 322
 11.2.3 Evolution of GCP | 323
 11.2.4 Ethics committee | 324
 11.2.5 Clinical trials in Indonesia | 324
 11.2.6 Challenges and future outlook | 326
11.3 Clinical research in Vietnam | 327
 11.3.1 Background and history | 327
 11.3.2 Pharmaceutical industry in Vietnam | 328
 11.3.3 The regulatory environment | 329
 11.3.4 Regulatory approval | 330
 11.3.5 Safety reporting in Vietnam | 331
 11.3.6 Clinical trials in Vietnam | 332
 11.3.7 Challenges and future outlook | 334

12 Conclusions | 335

12.1 PESTLE analysis | 335
12.2 Political environment | 336
 12.2.1 Regulatory environment | 336
 12.2.2 Intellectual property protection norms | 338
 12.2.3 Improved infrastructure and processes | 339
 12.2.4 Government incentives | 340

Published by Woodhead Publishing Limited, 2012

12.3	Economic environment	340
	12.3.1 Cost-effectiveness	340
	12.3.2 Human resources cost	341
12.4	Socio-cultural forces	342
	12.4.1 Language barrier	343
	12.4.2 Ethnicity	345
12.5	Technological factors	345
12.6	Legal environment	346
12.7	Other environmental factors	347
	12.7.1 Patient pool and doctors	347
	12.7.2 Local partners	348
12.8	Strategic issues for the CRO industry	349
	12.8.1 Organic growth vs mergers and acquisitions	350
	12.8.2 Generic innovation	351
	12.8.3 Increased competition	351
	12.8.4 Competitive research	352
	12.8.5 Western trial design	352
	12.8.6 Changing geo-political environment	352
12.9	Future outlook	353

Bibliography   **355**

Index   **361**

Published by Woodhead Publishing Limited, 2012

List of figures and tables

Figures

1.1	Drug development life-cycle	2
1.2	The growing contract research market	7
1.3	Overall country attractiveness index	13
1.4	Country segmentation	15
1.5	Number of clinical trials in the Asia region	18
1.6	Number of industry-sponsored trials in the Asia region	18
2.1	Global pharmaceutical industry – an overview	28
2.2	Projections of total public health and long-term care expenditure (% GDP)	29
2.3	Japanese CRO industry revenue and staff numbers	30
2.4	Clinical development revenue by phase in Japan (2010)	31
2.5	Local and global CROs in Japan	32
2.6	Evolution of PMDA	34
2.7	Consultation and review system for drugs and devices	37
2.8	Global clinical trial consultations	37
2.9	Evolution of GCP in Japan	38
2.10	Global clinical trials in Japan	47
2.11	Model 1: global pharma with global CRO	48
2.12	Model 2: global pharma with global CRO and its allied local CRO	49
2.13	Model 3: global pharma's local affiliate and CRO	50
2.14	Model 4: in-country clinical caretaker	50
2.15	Tripartite cooperations to study ethnic factors	52
3.1	India's share of abbreviated new drug approvals granted in the USA (2008)	56
3.2	Percentage of drug master filings in the USA (2008), by country	57
3.3	Leading service providers in clinical research business	63

Published by Woodhead Publishing Limited, 2012

xxii Clinical Research in Asia: Opportunities and Challenges

3.4	Process flow-chart for BABE trials	65
3.5	Growth of clinical trials in India	68
3.6	Clinical trials in India, by phase	69
3.7	Healthcare resources in India: (a) absolute numbers, 2009; (b) average population served by one professional	93
3.8	Health Investment outlays, 1992–2012	94
4.1	Pharmaceutical market size: world vs China – in 2010 and 2015	108
4.2	Government of China's spending on education, healthcare and social security (% GDP)	112
4.3	Population of China by age group (%), 1964, 2000, 2035	115
4.4	China's urban population (%), 1970, 2000, 2030	115
4.5	China's CRO market	123
4.6	Clinical research players in China	125
4.7	Growth of industry-sponsored clinical trials in China	126
4.8	Clinical trials in China, by phase	126
4.9	Number of SFDA accredited study sites in China	129
4.10	Review and approval process for Drug Clinical Trial Approval	145
5.1	New chemical entities in the LG Life Sciences pipeline	154
5.2	The IND review process in South Korea	157
5.3	Growth of industry-sponsored clinical trials in South Korea	163
5.4	Industry-sponsored clinical trials in South Korea, by phase	163
6.1	IND review process in Taiwan	183
6.2	IND review process	184
6.3	Bridging study – current evaluation process	185
6.4	Online application consultation process flow	186
6.5	Regulatory approval process in Taiwan	188
6.6	Study start-up timelines in Taiwan	189
6.7	Growth of industry-sponsored clinical trials in Taiwan	191
6.8	Industry-sponsored clinical trials in Taiwan, by phase	191
7.1	Clinical trials in Singapore by therapeutic area	210
7.2	Clinical research players in Singapore	211
7.3	Growth of clinical trials in Singapore	212
7.4	Clinical trials in Singapore, by phase	212
8.1	Study start-up timelines in Thailand	258
8.2	Growth of clinical trials in Thailand	262
8.3	Industry-sponsored clinical trials in Thailand, by phase	262

Published by Woodhead Publishing Limited, 2012

List of figures and tables xxiii

9.1	Safety reporting process for drugs in clinical trial in Malaysia	282
9.2	Growth of clinical trials in Malaysia	287
9.3	Industry-sponsored clinical trials in Malaysia, by phase	288
9.4	Malaysia value proposition	289
10.1	Hong Kong's healthcare system	297
10.2	Overall structure of the healthcare system in Hong Kong	298
10.3	Flow chart for ethics committee and regulatory submissions	307
10.4	Study start-up timelines in Hong Kong	307
10.5	Growth of clinical trials in Hong Kong	310
10.6	Clinical trials in Hong Kong, by phase	310
11.1	Growth of clinical trials in the Philippines	319
11.2	Clinical trials in the Philippines, by phase	320
11.3	Growth of clinical trials in Indonesia	325
11.4	Clinical trials in Indonesia, by phase	325
11.5	Growth of clinical trials in Vietnam	333
11.6	Clinical trials in Vietnam, by phase	333

Tables

1.1	Global pharmaceutical market analysis	3
1.2	Pharmaceutical market size in select Asian countries	3
1.3	Health expenditure in select Asian countries	4
1.4	Top 15 global pharmaceutical players and their clinical research, 2009	5
1.5	Developed vs emerging Asian pharmaceutical markets	6
1.6	Global CROs and their financials	8
1.7	CRO services mix	9
1.8	Big pharma R&D investment in Asia	10
1.9	Global CRO offerings in Asia	14
1.10	Key economic indicators in Asia-Pacific	17
1.11	Number of industry-sponsored clinical trials in Asia by phase	19
1.12	US FDA inspections in Asia	20
1.13	Deficiency codes	21

Published by Woodhead Publishing Limited, 2012

xxiv Clinical Research in Asia: Opportunities and Challenges

2.1	Japanese pharma companies' industry-sponsored trials in Asia (December 2009)	31
2.2	Regulatory requirements for IRB and PMDA	43
3.1	Pharma partnerships in India	58
3.2	Global pharma R&D and outsourcing by 2010	58
3.3	Drug development pipeline of key Indian companies	59
3.4	US FDA approved new drugs – data generated from India	62
3.5	Pharma companies undertaking trials in India	69
3.6	Research institutes in India	90
3.7	Healthcare infrastructure in India (March 2008)	91
3.8	Healthcare education infrastructure in India, 2009–10	92
3.9	Health expenditure in India	95
3.10	A comparison of drug prices, USA vs India	95
3.11	Languages in India	98
3.12	Technology-driven service providers in India	100
4.1	Investments by major multinational pharma companies in China	110
4.2	Mergers and acquisitions in the Chinese CRO industry, 2000–2010	124
4.3	Pharma companies undertaking GCP trials in China	127
4.4	Most active clinical trial sponsors in mainland China	127
4.5	Most common therapeutic areas under clinical trial in mainland China	128
4.6	Comparison of investigational new drug review process between the US FDA and Chinese SFDA	146
5.1	Top 10 local and foreign companies in South Korea	150
5.2	South Korean companies' investigational new drugs and new drug applications	151
5.3	New drugs being marketed in South Korea	152
5.4	ICH-GCP vs Korean GCP	156
5.5	Documents required for IND submission	158
5.6	Study start-up timeline in South Korea	159
5.7	Industry-sponsored trials in South Korea	164
5.8	Institution/hospital sponsored trials in South Korea, July 2011	165
5.9	Number of industry-sponsored study sites in South Korea by city (trials registered 2005–08)	167
5.10	Therapeutic areas of industry-sponsored trials in South Korea	168

Published by Woodhead Publishing Limited, 2012

List of figures and tables

5.11	Drop-out and compliance rates of trials in South Korea	171
6.1	Hospital infrastructure in Taiwan	179
6.2	Industry-sponsored trials undertaken in Taiwan	192
6.3	Hospitals/institutions undertaking clinical trials in Taiwan	193
7.1	Investments by multinational companies in Singapore	201
7.2	CRO market size in Singapore, 2009–10	208
7.3	Industry-sponsored trials in Singapore, 2011	213
7.4	Hospital/institution initiated trials in Singapore	214
7.5	Number of CTCs issued	216
7.6	Summary of health authorities, acts and guidelines in Singapore	230
8.1	Health insurance coverage	245
8.2	Numbers of medical graduate students	248
8.3	Trials undertaken in Thailand by major players	263
9.1	Accredited CRCs in Malaysia	285
9.2	Trials undertaken in Malaysia by major players	287
10.1	Ethics committees in Hong Kong	304
10.2	Trials undertaken in Hong Kong by major players	311
11.1	Causes of morbidity in the Philippines	316
11.2	Causes of mortality in the Philippines	317
11.3	Trials undertaken in the Philippines by major players	321
11.4	Major causes of death in Indonesia, 2007	322
11.5	Trials undertaken in Indonesia by major players	326
11.6	Trials undertaken in Vietnam by major players	334
12.1	Regulatory requirements in Asia	337
12.2	Languages in Asia	344
12.3	Regional CROs in Asia	348

Published by Woodhead Publishing Limited, 2012

Acknowledgments

First, I express my deepest thanks to those colleagues and industry professionals in the pharmaceutical and contracts research industry who freely shared their knowledge and experience, helping me to focus on the dynamic and evolving clinical research environments in Asia. My sincere thanks go to Nishant Kumar, who supported me in the collection of the data and literature which are invaluable for this book.

List of abbreviations

ADR	adverse drug reaction
ANDA	abbreviated new drug application
APEC	Asia-Pacific Economic Cooperation
ASEAN	Association of Southeast Asian Nations
BABE	bioanalytical and bioequivalence
BPA	Bureau of Pharmaceutical Affairs
CAGR	compound annual growth rate
CDSCO	Central Drug Standard Control Organization
CFR	Code of Federal Regulations
CIA	Central Intelligence Agency
CMC	Christian Medical College
COA	certificate of approval
CRA	clinical research associate
CRC	clinical research coordinator
CRF	case report form
CRO	contract research organisation
CTA	Clinical Trial Approval
CTC	clinical trial certificate
CTIL	clinical trial import licence
CTM	clinical trial material
CTRC	clinical trial resource centre
CTX	clinical trial exemption

Published by Woodhead Publishing Limited, 2012

DCGI	Drugs Controller General of India
DMF	drug master file
DSCI	Data Security Council of India
ECG	electrocardiogram
EDB	Economic Development Board
EDC	electronic data capture
EMEA	European Medicines Agency
FDA	Food & Drug Administration
FERCAP	Forum for Ethical Review Committees in the Asian and Western Pacific Region
GCP	good clinical practice
GHTF	Global Harmonisation Task Force
GLP	good laboratory practice
GMP	good manufacturing practice
HSA	Health Science Authority
ICCC	in-country clinical caretaker
ICF	informed consent form
ICH	International Conference on Harmonisation
ICH-GCP	International Conference on Harmonisation Guidelines for Good Clinical Practice
ICMR	Indian Council of Medical Research
IEC	institutional ethics committee
IMP	investigational medicinal product
IND	investigational new drug
IRB	institutional review board
ITeS	IT enabled services
IVRS	interactive voice recognition system
JCROA	Japan CRO Association
MCRC	Medical Clinical Research Committee

Published by Woodhead Publishing Limited, 2012

List of abbreviations

MDR-TB	multidrug-resistant tuberculosis
MHRA	Medicines & Healthcare Products Regulatory Agency
MOH	Ministry of Health
NAI	no action indicated
NCE	new chemical entity
NDA	new drug application
NIHS	National Institute of Health Sciences
NMRC	National Medical Research Council
NPA	National Pharmaceutical Administration
NPC	National People's Congress
OAI	official action indicated
OECD	Organization for Economic Cooperation and Development
OHRP	Office for Human Research Protections
OPSR	Organization for Pharmaceutical Safety and Research
OTC	over the counter
PCHRD	Philippine Council for Health Research and Development
PHREB	Philippine Health Research Ethics Board
PICS	Pharmaceutical Inspection Cooperation Scheme
PMDEC	Pharmaceuticals and Medical Devices Evaluation Center
PNHRS	Philippine National Health Research System
QA	quality assurance
QMS	quality management system
R&D	research and development
RDC	remote data capture
SAE	serious adverse event
SDA	State Drug Administration
SFDA	State Food & Drug Administration
SGGCP	Singapore Guidelines for Good Clinical Practice
SOP	standard operating procedure

Published by Woodhead Publishing Limited, 2012

SUSAR	suspected unexpected serious adverse reaction
TABA	Taiwan-America Biotechnology Association
TBP	Tuas Biomedical Park
TRIPS	Trade-Related Aspects of Intellectual Property Rights
VAI	voluntary action indicated
WHO	World Health Organization
WTO	World Trade Organization
XDR-TB	extensively drug-resistant tuberculosis

Preface

Fifteen years ago, the drug development and clinical research activities of global pharmaceutical, biotech and medical devices companies were concentrated in North America and Western Europe. At this time, companies had no incentive to look beyond these territories as the global research community had very little confidence in other potential destinations as the prevailing regulatory environment was not well developed, the infrastructure to support quality clinical research was inadequate, and there was a lack of experience or inclination for scientific research.

With rapid commercialisation in the last decade, major pharma companies expanded their operations in Asian countries. The initial objective had a clear-cut commercial mandate: to enter these emerging economies to market their products. While these big pharmaceutical and biotech companies saw a huge patient pool with Western-style diseases, their commercial objectives compelled them, for regulatory reasons and otherwise, to undertake clinical research on a low scale and help develop the regulatory environment. Again, the thinking was tied to commercial objectives: if physicians gained experience with company compounds during the various stages of clinical trials, it would enhance the chances of success for that company's products on the market.

The tide began to change. The pharma companies became less inclined to continue clinical research in North America and Western Europe as generating the additional data required by regulators was leading to slow patient recruitment and rocketing clinical trial costs. With growing competition from rivals to bring products to market, companies were further incentivised to explore new markets.

Published by Woodhead Publishing Limited, 2012

xxxiv Clinical Research in Asia: Opportunities and Challenges

The last decade has therefore seen a significant rise in clinical research in Asia. Indeed, it is clear that companies have moved far beyond the exploratory stage and are engaged in markets in many Asian countries as a core part of their clinical development plans. Far from serving simply as a reserve option due to competition in other markets, sponsors are proactively conducting trials in the region.

The experience of the pharma companies to date has demonstrated that Asia can generate high-quality clinical data that can satisfy even the most stringent regulatory demands and that the general environment is most welcoming to global clinical research in the region.

Since the start of the twenty-first century, pharmaceutical industry professionals in Asian countries have made numerous attempts to attract clinical trials to the region. However, there remains much to do in order to increase awareness about Asia and to win the confidence of pharmaceutical innovators and researchers worldwide. While the region offers significant opportunities for quality clinical research, the rapid growth of clinical research in the region has also posed many challenges due to the diverse nature of the population, racial profile, and multiple regulatory environments and cultures. To this end, the present book focuses on the potential for clinical research in Asian countries and offers a guide to the opportunities and challenges for clinical research in the region.

The book aims to serve as a reliable guide and to give the reader an overall viewpoint on how the clinical trial environment in Asia has developed to date and where it is likely to head over the next decade. The book delves into the top 12 Asian countries and discusses the clinical research environment of each country separately. The tables and figures in the book have been compiled from various public domain sources and web links or from newsletters/news items from pharma dailies and media presentations, footnoted as 'media reports'. Most of the facts and figures about clinical trials were compiled using the clinicaltrial.gov registry, which is again available in the public domain.

This book should prove useful to a wide audience – many of whom will be looking at Asia as the future power centre for clinical research. The book offers a detailed introduction for those who are

Published by Woodhead Publishing Limited, 2012

new to the business environment in this area. It gives an understanding of the key business segments and discusses key factors in the environment surrounding the business. In today's scenario, many entrepreneurs are considering venturing into this business, looking into the potential of the region. This book will help them understand the business and regulatory environments, thus helping them to undertake clinical research activities in Asia more effectively.

This book will also help practising entry-level professionals, such as clinical research associates, medical research associates and business development professionals, to gain an insight into the clinical research industry in Asia, which will facilitate their career development. This book works both as a student's guide and a reference book for trainers in the classroom. It will also be of benefit for those wanting to hone their knowledge and skills in clinical research.

This book is likely to be of interest to:

- corporate pharma companies, contract research organisations, site management organisations and medical colleges/hospitals conducting clinical research, in both the private and public sector;
- public and private academic/research institutions;
- students and researchers in clinical research, pharmaceutical management and hospital management courses;
- persons working in regulatory bodies in government both at state and national level as well as non-government organisations dealing with experimental studies.

Published by Woodhead Publishing Limited, 2012

About the author

Dr Umakanta Sahoo is Executive Director, Asia-Pacific and Managing Director, India for Chiltern, a full-service global contract research organisation. He is a bioscience graduate with an MBA and PhD from India, and over 18 years of experience in the pharmaceutical industry and contract research sector. He has worked in various positions in clinical operations, project management, regulatory affairs and data management functions in his assignments with companies such as Core Healthcare, Quintiles, Sterling (now PRA International), ClinInvent and Chiltern. He has experience of handling clinical trial projects for international pharmaceutical companies in different therapeutic areas and their quality assurance/third-party audits. He provides leadership and direction to local staff and contributes to the management and development of the global business. He has also been awarded a diploma in management and marketing with special emphasis on the biopharmaceutical industry by the Kriger Research Institute, Canada. The award is further recognition of his growing contribution to the burgeoning clinical research sector in India. He is a frequent speaker at industry conferences and academic institutions and has authored a number of publications and books regarding the environment for clinical trials in India.

The author may be contacted at:

> ZARA 107, Nahar Amritshakti
> Chandivalli Farm Rd
> Chandivalli, Andheri (E)
> Mumbai – 400 072
> India
> E-mail: *sahoou@yahoo.com*

Published by Woodhead Publishing Limited, 2012

1

Clinical research in Asia: a brief overview

Abstract: Starting with a brief background of the drug development cycle, Chapter 1 delves into the global pharmaceutical market and key global pharmaceutical players in terms of market size and their clinical research initiatives. This chapter briefly discusses the clinical research business, the global market and key players and contract research organisations (CROs). It further narrows down to describe the clinical research boom and key players in Asia and undertakes a country segmentation analysis of Asia. This chapter summarises the number of trials undertaken in Asia, inspections and audits performed in Asia and outlines a SWOT analysis.

1.1 Background

Clinical research forms the backbone of new product development in pharmaceutical business. It involves the testing of new drugs or new chemical entities for safety and efficacy in human beings and could pose risks to human life. It is always based on scientific rationale and highly regulated by government bodies. Clinical trials for a drug can cost up to $1 billion and can take as long as 12 years from discovery phase to marketing phase (Figure 1.1).

Until recently, most new pharmaceutical products were due largely to the sincere efforts and investments of the global pharma companies. Most of these companies have invested a lot of time and

Published by Woodhead Publishing Limited, 2012

2 Clinical Research in Asia: Opportunities and Challenges

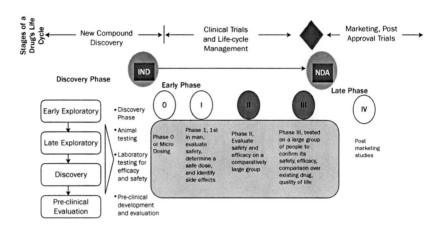

Figure 1.1 Drug development life-cycle

money to undertake clinical studies in the USA and Western Europe. Their success is due to increased public awareness for research and development, driven by relevant expertise among government bodies to implement regulations to protect the interests of human subjects. These regulations also safeguard the commercial interests of the pharma companies in terms of protecting their intellectual property.

1.2 Global pharmaceutical market

According to IMS Report, the global pharmaceutical market is presently worth $808 billion, and is estimated to grow at a compound annual growth rate (CAGR) of 5–8 per cent during 2009–14. The same analysis also forecasts that while developed markets such as the USA, Europe and Japan will grow at a CAGR of 2–6 per cent, the emerging countries of Asia, Africa, Australia and Latin America will grow at a CAGR of 12–15 per cent (Table 1.1).

Despite the similarity in environmental and disease traits, there are striking differences between the various Asian countries as far as pharmaceutical market size and health expenditure are concerned; this is primarily due to differences in regulatory and business environments. Table 1.2 highlights these differences across the Asian countries. Note that the Japanese and Chinese pharmaceutical markets are huge and hence attract significant investment.

Clinical research in Asia

Table 1.1 Global pharmaceutical market analysis

	2009			2008	2004–2009	2010	2009–2014
	Mkt Size US$bn	Mkt Size Const. US$	% Growth Const. US$	% Growth Const. US$	CAGR % Const. US$	Forecast % Growth Const. US$	CAGR % Const. US$
Total unaudited and audited global market							
	$808.3	$837.3	7.0%	5.5%	6.7%	4–6%	5–8%

Total unaudited and audited global market by region							
North America	$322.1	$323.8	5.5%	1.9%	5.2%	3–5%	3–6%
Europe	$247.6	$263.9	4.8%	7.0%	6.6%	3–5%	3–6%
Asia/Africa/ Australia	$102.6	$106.6	15.9%	15.0%	13.9%	13–15%	12–15%
Japan	$90.3	$95.0	7.6%	2.1%	3.9%	0–2%	2–5%
Latin America	$45.8	$47.9	10.6%	12.7%	10.9%	10–12%	12–15%

Source: IMS Health Market Prognosis, March 2010

Table 1.2 Pharmaceutical market size in select Asian countries

Country	Market size ($)
Japan	60bn
China	20bn
India	6bn
Taiwan	2.5bn
Hong Kong	1.5bn
Thailand	1.5bn
Singapore	400m
Indonesia	350m
Philippines	300m
Malaysia	210m

Source: World Bank, World Development Indicators 2006

Again, per capita health expenditure between different countries in Asia varies significantly, from $27 in India to $2,662 in Japan (Table 1.3). Considering the huge population base in Asian countries,

Published by Woodhead Publishing Limited, 2012

4 Clinical Research in Asia: Opportunities and Challenges

Table 1.3 Health expenditure in select Asian countries

Country	Health expenditure per capita ($)	Health expenditure (% of GDP)	Physicians per 1,000 people	Hospital beds per 1,000 people
Japan	2,662	7.9	2.0	14.3
Singapore	964	4.5	1.4	2.9
Taiwan	743	5.6	7.4	5.7
Korea	705	5.6	1.6	7.1
Malaysia	163	3.8	0.7	1.9
Thailand	76	3.3	0.4	2.2
China	61	5.6	1.6	2.5
Philippines	31	3.2	1.2	1.0
Indonesia	30	3.1	0.1	6.0
India	27	4.8	0.6	0.9
Vietnam	26	5.4	0.5	2.4

Source: World Bank, World Development Indicators 2006

the region offers huge value propositions for pharmaceutical companies to undertake clinical trials and market their products in Asian countries.

Global pharmaceutical players contribute significantly in providing healthcare medicine for mankind. From Table 1.4 it is evident that the main multinational pharma companies have a robust product portfolio that yields a huge sales revenue. These companies invest large sums of money in research and development. Their objective is to develop new drugs and devices to fight advanced chronic or rare diseases. In the process, pharmaceutical and biotech companies undertake a number of trials to prove not only that their products are safe, but also that they are more efficacious than what exists in the market already. These trials are undertaken in preclinical and clinical phases from Phase I to IV, which is time-consuming and very cost-intensive. As shown in Table 1.4, these 15 global pharmaceutical players were undertaking some 16,428 clinical trials in 2009, representing 46 per cent of the industry-sponsored clinical trials registered globally.

Published by Woodhead Publishing Limited, 2012

Table 1.4 Top 15 global pharmaceutical players and their clinical research, 2009

Rank	Company	Sales ($m)	No. of clinical trials
1	Pfizer	57,024	2,422
2	Merck and Co	38,963	1,715
3	Novartis	38,460	2,400
4	Sanofi-Aventis	35,524	1,420
5	Glaxo	34,973	2,820
6	AstraZeneca	34,434	1,754
7	Roche	32,763	1,018
8	J&J	26,783	681
9	Lilly	20,310	1,122
10	Abbott	19,840	872
11	Teva	15,947	368
12	Bayer	15,711	832
13	Boehringer	15,275	643
14	Amgen	15,038	543
15	Takeda	14,352	304

Source: IMS Health Midas December 2009 and *www.clinicaltrials.gov* (August 2010)

Over the last two decades, pharma companies have been increasingly exploring emerging Asian markets to supplement their primary clinical trials, with the goal of improving speed to market and cost-effectiveness. Table 1.5 summarises the key features of the emerging Asian markets versus the developed markets.

1.3 Clinical research business – a global overview

Clinical research is a drawn-out labour and capital-intensive regulated business. It requires financial as well as human power. It is dependent on multiple uncontrollable variables such as regulatory bureaucracy in different countries and unpredictable drug behaviour

Published by Woodhead Publishing Limited, 2012

6   Clinical Research in Asia: Opportunities and Challenges

Table 1.5   Developed vs emerging Asian pharmaceutical markets

Key features	Developed markets	Emerging Asian markets
Countries	USA, UK, Germany, France, Italy, Spain, Japan, Australia, New Zealand, Canada	India, China, Taiwan, South Korea, other Asian countries
Market size	$700bn	$70bn
Market growth rate	3–6%	12–15%
Regulatory environment	Structured and well laid regulatory system, robust inspection mechanism	Evolving regulatory system and inspections mechanism
Healthcare system	USA – more privately owned medical institutions; other countries – state-owned state-of-the-art facilities	China – state-owned facilities; India – a mixed bag of private hospitals and clinics and public hospitals (primary, secondary and tertiary care centres) Huge patient load
Patient demography	Ageing patient population; superior living conditions; chronic disease conditions requiring long-term treatment	Young population; comparatively inferior-quality living; acute disease conditions requiring short-term treatment
Insurance	Private insurance for all in USA; government social security cover for other developed markets	China promotes cooperative insurance; in other countries, mostly private insurance dominates
Standards of good clinical practice	Established	Still evolving
Infrastructure	Best physical infrastructure in hospitals set up for research; modern technology infrastructure prevalent (e.g. internet connectivity, video conferencing and 3G connectivity)	World-class physical infrastructure in major cities and private hospitals, with smaller cities and hospitals gearing up; technological infrastructures are improving, with much still to do to catch up with the developed market

Fictitious data, for illustration purposes only

Published by Woodhead Publishing Limited, 2012

due to drug–drug or drug–disease interactions. It needs thorough supervision and control at every level. To make research more cost-effective, many pharmaceutical and biotechnology companies depend on the contract research organisation (CRO) industry. More than 1,000 CROs around the world provide outsourced research and clinical-trial services. According to an August 2009 report by London-based market analysts Business Insights, CROs accounted for 20 per cent of the global pharmaceutical and biotechnology research and development budget in 2008. Revenues were expected to reach US$24 billion in 2010, doubling 2004 earnings (Figure 1.2).

Many CROs are large privately held companies and their financial figures are not available in the public domain. For example, Quintiles, the global leader in CRO space, is reported to have more than 25,000 staff globally. Table 1.6 describes the key financials of a few publicly listed global CROs with market capitalisation greater than $1 billion and at least 8,000 staff working globally.

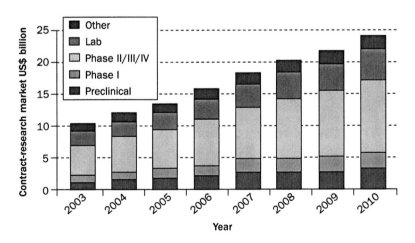

Figure 1.2 The growing contract research market

Source: Business Insight, available from: http://www.nature.com/news/2010/100602/full/465530a.html

8   Clinical Research in Asia: Opportunities and Challenges

Table 1.6   Global CROs and their financials

	ICON	Covance	PPDI	Charles River	PRXL
Market capital ($)	1.39bn	2.63bn	2.83bn	1.87bn	1.17bn
Employees	7,170	9,491	10,860	8,000	9,275
Quarterly revenue growth yoy (%)	1.70	2.30	4.30	−5.20	10.80
Revenue ttm ($)	890.64m	2.01bn	1.41bn	1.18bn	1.28bn
Gross margin ttm (%)	41.54	29.41	48.00	35.24	31.17
EBITDA ttm ($)	147.13m	314.55m	218.82m	252.06m	138.52m
Operating margin ttm (%)	12.63	10.77	10.61	13.16	6.22
Net income ttm ($)	99.90m	163.40m	95.39m	83.50m	34.95m
EPS ttm ($)	1.66	2.52	0.8	1.32	0.60

yoy, year-on-year; ttm, trailing twelve months; EBITDA, earnings before interest, taxes, depreciation, and amortisation; EPS, earnings per share

Source: www.finance.yahoo.com

1.4   CRO services mix

Most CROs offer a broad range of services to the pharmaceutical, biotech and medical device companies (Table 1.7). They customise their services to the requirements of these companies.

1.5   The clinical research boom in Asia

Asia is increasingly being recognised as a hub for clinical trial activities. Besides being an important growing market, many multinational pharma companies are beginning to see Asia's potential in contributing to drug development. Several pharma companies have established their research and development facilities in Asia to undertake basic and advanced research to international standards. Table 1.8 shows that in the last decade, Asia has been a key area for many big pharma firms to establish new research and development (R&D) centres as well as to expand their existing centres.

Published by Woodhead Publishing Limited, 2012

Clinical research in Asia

Table 1.7 CRO services mix

Service category	Service mix
Pre-clinical	Animal studies Toxicology Molecular biology Chemistry In-vitro services In-vivo services Histology
Clinical	Phase 0, I, II, III, IV (early and late phase) Clinical monitoring Project management Quality assurance Safety monitoring Pharmacovigilance Medical affairs/medical monitoring Regulatory affairs Site management
Biometrics	Data entry Data management Biostatistics Medical writing
Laboratory services	Centralised laboratory services
Consulting service	Planning clinical research programmes Product development Study design and protocol development Scientific/medical consultations Data safety monitoring boards Regulatory and quality consulting Market intelligence
Electronic data capture (EDC) services	EDC 24/7 call centre EDC training EDC management EDC licence support EDC data management

Besides this, CROs, global and regional have made big moves in the region by expanding their operations to different countries in Asia and opening multiple offices. They have expanded their reach either through acquisitions or organic growth. Many have chosen the preferred partnership and alliance routes. All these growth stories make it amply clear that the next decade of clinical research

Published by Woodhead Publishing Limited, 2012

10   Clinical Research in Asia: Opportunities and Challenges

Table 1.8   Big pharma R&D investment in Asia

Company	Country	Major locations	Main focus
Pfizer	China	Dalian, Suzhou and Wuxi	Mfg. facilities
	India	Thane (Mumbai) and Bangalore	Mfg. facilities – Pfizer to develop India as hub for Asian clinical trials
	South Korea	Kwangiang-dong (East Seoul)	Production and packaging
	Singapore	Tuas Pharma Park	Chemical bulk actives manufacturing facility
GlaxoSmith-Kline	China	Beijing, Chongqing, Tianjin, Suzhou and Pudong	Mfg. facilities and joint ventures
	India	Mumbai, Gurgaon and Bangalore	Mfg. and clinical data management facilities
	South Korea	Seoul	Production facility and nationwide sales network
	Singapore	Gateway West	Basic R&D, process development, clinical development and API mfg.
AstraZeneca	China	Shanghai and Wuxi	Clinical development and mfg. facilities
	India	Bangalore	Research and mfg. facilities. India will become the company's center for tuberculosis research
	South Korea	Seoul	Commercial operations
	Singapore		Clinical development
Merck & Co	China	Beijing, Shanghai, Hangzhou, Guangzhou	Mfg. and possible joint development projects
	India		
	South Korea	Seoul, Shihung Kyunggi-Du	Mfg. and possible joint development projects
	Singapore	Tuas Pharma Park	Mfg. and marketing operations

Published by Woodhead Publishing Limited, 2012

Clinical research in Asia

Table 1.8 Big pharma R&D investment in Asia (*cont'd*)

Company	Country	Major locations	Main focus
Novartis	China	Beijing	Mfg. facilities
	India	Mumbai	Research and mfg. facilities
	South Korea	Seoul	Commercial and mfg. operations
	Singapore	Biopolis	R&D for tropical diseases
Roche	China	Shanghai and Wuxi	R&D and mfg. facilities
	India	Mumbai	Research and commercial operations; plans to set up clinical development facilities
	South Korea	Seoul	Mfg. facilities
	Singapore		Mfg. facilities
Aventis	China	Shenzhen and Beijing	Mfg. and joint ventures importation and distribution
	India	Goa, Ankleshwar, Delhi, Mumbai, Lucknow, Kolkata, Hyderabad, Chennai	Mfg. facilities (Goa, Ankleshwar) and a network of commercial regional offices
	Singapore	Jurong Island	Mfg. and commercial operations
BMS	China	Minghang (Shanghai)	Joint venture mfg. facilities
	India		Exited India in 1996, but filed an application with the Foreign Investment Promotion Board in early 2004 to set up R&D and production facilities over next three years
	Singapore		Clinical development operations

Source: Contract Pharma, *www.contractpharma.com*

Published by Woodhead Publishing Limited, 2012

12   Clinical Research in Asia: Opportunities and Challenges

history belongs to Asia. Certainly, during the past decade, Asia has laid the groundwork to overtake Central and Eastern Europe in global clinical trial participation. For example, many countries in Asia-Pacific, most notably China, India and Japan, have made regulatory changes to foster participation in global drug development programmes and bring cutting-edge therapies sooner to their respective populations.

Due to the slow pace of recruitment, clinical trials in developed regions, such as the USA, Western Europe and Japan, are very costly and time-consuming, and delays in the recruitment of suitable patients have a significant impact on trial budget. In fact, according to *Data Monitor* (22 July 2008), almost 90 per cent of clinical trials experience an unexpected delay, with recruitment being the number one reason for these delays. With rapid and easy patient recruitment supported by a huge pool of potential patients exposed to few or no medications, Asia offers significant cost-effectiveness. Not only are the costs for trial-related tests and procedures in Asian hospitals comparatively cheaper than in the USA or Europe, but the per capita cost (i.e. the investigator fee) is also lower due to the comparatively low cost of living and base salary.

While looking for alternative destinations for clinical research, many pharma companies focus on the emerging countries as their huge population, disease spread and improved regulatory mechanisms make them an ideal destination for clinical research initiatives. To aid the outsourcing of clinical trials, consulting companies have developed structured country attractiveness indices for evaluating geographical locations. For example, the instrument of AT Kearney (Figure 1.3) analyses countries based on size, diversity and geographical distribution, and ranks them on a scale of 1 to 10, where a higher score corresponds to a higher level of attractiveness vis-à-vis a number of key indicators, including:

- patient pool;
- cost efficiencies;
- regulatory conditions;
- relevant skill/expertise;
- infrastructure and environments.

Published by Woodhead Publishing Limited, 2012

Clinical research in Asia

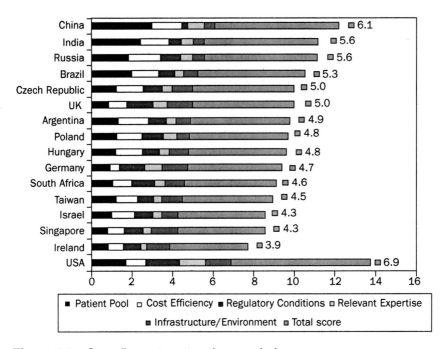

Figure 1.3 Overall country attractiveness index
Source: AT Kearney

The data in Figure 1.3 suggest that countries such as India, China, Japan, Korea, Taiwan and Singapore are among the most attractive locations for pharmaceutical, biotech and medical device companies to conduct clinical trials, with China and India clearly front-runners in attracting clinical research business to Asia.

This trend has resulted in the mushrooming growth of local and global CROs in emerging countries in Asia. Globally, most CROs grow an average of 10–14 per cent per annum. From 2010 to 2015, however, the CRO industry in Asia is expected to grow by 25–30 per cent each year, thus increasing Asia's contribution to global clinical trials from 5 per cent in 2010 to 10 per cent in 2015. Such trends have been highlighted by leading CROs such as Quintiles, PPD, Covance, I3 and Research Pharmaceutical Services, with many other global CROs also expanding their operations in Asian countries. Table 1.9 summarises the key information of a few global CROs.

14 Clinical Research in Asia: Opportunities and Challenges

Table 1.9 Global CRO offerings in Asia

CRO	Offerings in Asia
Quintiles	*Staff:* 5,000 in Asia *Offices:* India, China, Hong Kong, Indonesia, Japan, South Korea, Philippines, Singapore, Taiwan, Thailand, Malaysia and Vietnam *Service mix:* clinical development, biometrics, central laboratory services, central imaging, central pharmacovigilance, site management
PPD	*Staff:* 1,400 in Asia (of which 1,000 in China) *Offices:* China, Hong Kong, India, Indonesia, Japan, South Korea, Philippines, Singapore, Taiwan, Thailand and Vietnam *Service mix:* preclinical, clinical, biometrics, central laboratory services, vaccine research, registration studies *Note:* Acquired Excel PharmaStudies and Bioduro in 2009
I3 (an Ingenix Group Company)	*Offices:* Singapore, Thailand, Taiwan, Hong Kong, South Korea, Japan, Philippines and India *Service mix:* contract staffing (Asia), data management and biostatistics (Mumbai, India), drug safety (Pune, India), clinical research (Delhi, India); focuses on oncology, central nervous system, respiratory, infectious and pulmonary diseases and endocrinology *Note:* Operation in Asia for last 10 years; acquired Singapore CRO Pacific Pharma Partners in 2006
Covance	*Offices:* Singapore, South Korea, India, China, Japan and Hong Kong *Service mix:* pre-clinical, central laboratory, clinical development *Note:* 20 years of operations
Research Pharmaceutical Services	*Staff:* More than 100 people *Offices:* China and South Korea *Note:* Acquired China-based CRO Paramax International in 2009
Parexel	*Offices:* India, China, Indonesia, Japan, South Korea, Philippines, Singapore, Taiwan, Thailand and Malaysia *Service mix:* clinical development, biometrics
ICON	*Offices:* India, China, Japan, South Korea, Singapore, Taiwan, Thailand and Hong Kong *Service mix:* clinical development, biometrics
Pharmanet	*Offices:* India, China, Singapore, Malaysia, Philippines, South Korea and Taiwan *Service mix:* clinical development, biometrics
Kendle	*Offices:* India, China, Singapore, Thailand, Hong Kong, Malaysia and Philippines *Service mix:* clinical development, biometrics
Chiltern	*Offices:* India, Singapore, Taiwan. Office in South Korea to be opened. Working with partner CROs in Japan, China and other Asian countries *Service mix:* clinical development, biometrics, electronic data capture training *Note:* Started operations in Asia in 2004–05

Source: Media reports

Published by Woodhead Publishing Limited, 2012

1.6 Asian country segmentation analysis

Informed by their research objectives and experiences, global pharma companies have expanded their outsourcing activities beyond the USA and Europe. Besides the parameters that determine the overall country attractiveness index, many have been attracted by the operational efficiencies in Asia, including (1) ease of timely regulatory approval; (2) potential to recruit patients quickly; (3) availability of patients with particular disease profiles; (4) advancement in infrastructure and technology; and (5) the ultimate aim of marketing the product in the region. Based on these additional operational parameters, clinical trial destinations in Asia can be divided into three tiers (Figure 1.4).

The first tier in the country segmentation analysis is Japan, which is a mature developed pharmaceutical market. Japan is very sensitive with respect to research quality, as the medical community is very inclusive and conservative. Clinical research in Japan is approached slightly differently, being more resource-focused and hence more

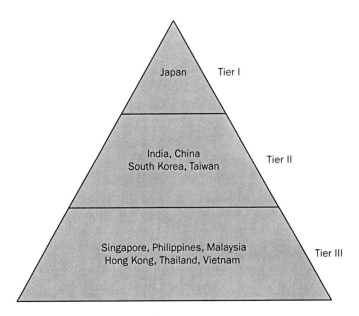

Figure 1.4 Country segmentation

Published by Woodhead Publishing Limited, 2012

16 Clinical Research in Asia: Opportunities and Challenges

expensive in comparison with the trials in the West. The CRO industry in Japan is no more than two decades old. As Japan is a significant pharmaceutical market, more and more companies are now entering the country. The need for global and local trials has increased. Japanese companies have started looking at selectively accepting data from other countries with a similar racial profile and have broadened their country-focused clinical trial initiatives to adopt a globalised approach. Now that the health ministers of China, Korea and Japan have agreed to accept clinical research data from one another's countries, most global pharma companies are adapting their Asia strategy to include more regional bridging studies.

The second tier includes India, China, Taiwan and South Korea. India and China offer a great advantage for clinical research due to the sheer size of their population base. Some 37 per cent of the global population live in these two countries. Nonetheless, in terms of global industry-sponsored trials, South Korea and Taiwan have performed extremely well in comparison with India and China. Patient recruitment in these countries is quite rapid, which significantly reduces the cost of drug development in comparison with Japan and Western countries. The countries in this tier offer significant advantage as the resources they provide are rigorously tested and comparatively cheaper. A high level of quality research is performed in these countries, and their economies are growing consistently, making them a highly significant market for the pharmaceutical industry. Table 1.10 describes key economic indicators in the Asia-Pacific region.

The third tier includes Singapore, Malaysia, Hong Kong, Thailand, Vietnam, the Philippines and Thailand. As a central location with very well developed infrastructure and connectivity, Singapore is perceived as another hub of clinical research activities. Many pharma companies and CROs have their Asian headquarters in Singapore. The other countries in this tier are catching up with the other Asian countries with good quality clinical research at a significantly lower cost.

On the face of it, the countries in all three tiers look very promising for clinical trials, although there are issues, challenges and concerns surrounding each of them. Subsequent chapters will explore these countries further and will discuss various aspects of clinical trials.

Published by Woodhead Publishing Limited, 2012

Table 1.10 Key economic indicators in Asia-Pacific

Country	Population	Population growth	GDP (PPP)	Per capita income (PPP)
Australia	21,262,641	1.195%	$802.9 billion	$38,200
China	1,338,612,968	0.655%	$7.992 trillion	$6,000
Hong Kong	7,055,071	0.504%	$307.3 billion	$43,800
India	1,166,079,217	1.548%	$3.304 trillion	$2,900
Indonesia	240,271,522	1.136%	$916.7 billion	$3,900
Japan	127,078,679	<0.191%>	$4.34 trillion	$34,100
Malaysia	25,715,819	1.723%	$385.2 billion	$15,200
New Zealand	4,213,418	0.935%	$116.6 billion	$27,900
Philippines	97,976,603	1.957%	$318.2 billion	$3,300
South Korea	48,508,972	0.266%	$1.338 trillion	$27,700
Singapore	4,657,542	0.998%	$237.9 billion	$51,600
Taiwan	22,974,347	0.227%	$713.7 billion	$31,100
Thailand	65,905,410	0.615%	$548.7 billion	$8,400
Vietnam	86,967,524	0.977%	$242.3 billion	$2,800

Source: 2009 CIA Factbook

1.7 Clinical trials in Asia

Further analysis of clinical studies in the Asia region suggests that Taiwan, Korea, China, India, Thailand and Singapore are undertaking a significant number of clinical trials. Although one might expect China to be the leading destination for clinical trials, the majority of trials in China are limited to local registration trials. With 2,612 clinical trials, South Korea tops the list of clinical trial participation, while the number of clinical trials registered in China is 2,294.

These 12 countries participate in 18 per cent of the industry-sponsored clinical trials globally. Of the 8,120 industry-sponsored trials undertaken in Asia in July 2011, 55 per cent were Phase III and 23 per cent are Phase II. Due to limited exposure in first-in-man studies and the lack of proper regulatory mechanisms in Asia, industry sponsors greatly prefer to perform Phase I trials in Europe.

Published by Woodhead Publishing Limited, 2012

18 Clinical Research in Asia: Opportunities and Challenges

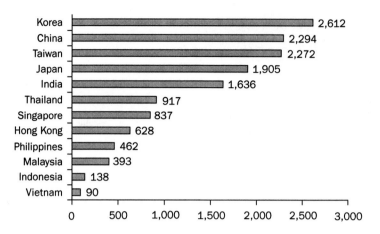

Figure 1.5 Number of clinical trials in the Asia region

Source: www.clinicaltrials.gov (accessed 20 July 2011)

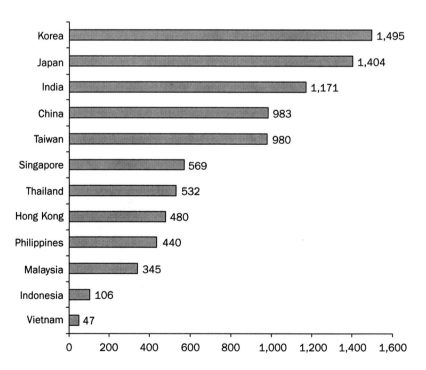

Figure 1.6 Number of industry-sponsored trials in the Asia region

Source: www.clinicaltrials.gov (accessed 20 July 2011)

Clinical research in Asia

Table 1.11 Number of industry-sponsored clinical trials in Asia by phase

Country	Phase I	Phase II	Phase III	Phase IV	Total
Korea	156	329	654	252	1,391
Japan	273	384	658	66	1,381
India	116	283	639	99	1,137
Taiwan	42	222	567	106	937
China	81	132	486	176	875
Singapore	112	123	268	45	548
Thailand	14	110	319	70	513
Hong Kong	31	108	288	48	475
Philippines	7	75	272	63	417
Malaysia	7	49	238	38	332
Indonesia	0	9	57	18	84
Vietnam	1	5	19	5	30
Total	840	1,829	4,465	986	8,120

Source: www.clinicaltrials.gov (accessed 20 July 2011)

Phase IV or post-marketing studies, though undertaken for the marketed products, are not generally outsourced to CROs but rather managed by pharmaceutical field staff. Many of these post-marketing studies are not available in the clinical trial registry.

Due to Asia's strong financial growth, however, more and more investments are being channelled into the region's life-science industry, in parallel with large investments by international companies in facilities for both pre-clinical and clinical drug discovery and drug development research. A rise in CRO business in Asia is therefore possible.

1.8 Inspection and data quality

Over the last two decades, Asian sites have shown positive contributions to global clinical trials and have always demonstrated good quality. This has been confirmed by several sponsors/CROs during their internal quality assurance audits and independent third-party audit

Published by Woodhead Publishing Limited, 2012

20 Clinical Research in Asia: Opportunities and Challenges

programmes. Insufficient data are available to showcase the efforts of local regulatory authorities to inspect data quality in Asian trials. The US Food & Drug Administration (US FDA) has conducted 67 data audits in nine Asian countries, as shown in Table 1.12.

US FDA classifies its inspection findings into three major codes:

- *No action indicated (NAI)*: No objectionable conditions or practices were found during the inspection.
- *Voluntary action indicated (VAI)*: Objectionable conditions were found but the problems do not justify further regulatory action. Any corrective action is left to the investigator to take voluntarily.
- *Official action indicated (OAI)*: Objectionable conditions were found and regulatory and/or administrative sanctions by the FDA are indicated.

During the 67 inspections, the US FDA has not issued a single OAI notification, which indicates that data generated from Asian sites meet the acceptable global standard. In fact, 29 inspections have had NAI notifications, meaning that no objectionable conditions or

Table 1.12 US FDA inspections in Asia

Country	Years	No. of data audits	Classifications	Deficiency codes
Japan	1988–2009	7	NAI(4) VAI2(3)	03,05,06
India	2005–10	17	NAI(9) VAI(7) VAI2(1)	04, 05, 06
China	2004–09	11	NAI (4) VAI (7)	04, 06, 16
Korea	2007–09	8	NAI(3) VAI(5)	05, 06
Taiwan	2002–06	3	NAI(2) VAI(1)	16
Singapore	2006	1	NAI(1)	0
Hong Kong	1998–2009	8	NAI(1) VAI(7)	03,04,05,06,12,15,16
Philippines	1997–2009	7	NAI(5) VAI(2)	06
Malaysia	1984–2009	5	NAI(1) VAI(1) VAI2(3)	03,04,05,06,15

Source: Compiled from US FDA site

Published by Woodhead Publishing Limited, 2012

Table 1.13 Deficiency codes

Code	Deficiency	Code of Federal Regulations
00	No deficiencies noted	n/a
01	Records availability	21 CFR 312.62
02	Failure to obtain and/or document subject consent	21 CFR 312.60, 50.20, 50.27
03	Inadequate informed consent form	21 CFR 50.25
04	Inadequate drug accountability	21 CFR 312.60, 312.62
05	Failure to follow investigational plan	21 CFR 312.60
06	Inadequate and inaccurate records	21 CFR 312.62
07	Unapproved concomitant therapy	21 CFR 312.60
08	Inappropriate payment to volunteers	21 CFR 50.20
09	Unapproved use of drug before investigational new drug submission	21 CFR 312.40(d)
10	Inappropriate delegation of authority	21 CFR 312.7, 312.61
11	Inappropriate use/commercialisation of investigational new drug	21 CFR 312.7, 312.61
12	Failure to list additional investigators on Form 1572	21 CFR 312.60
13	Subjects receiving simultaneous investigational drugs	21 CFR 312.60
14	Failure to obtain or document institutional review board approval	21 CFR 312.60, 62, 66; 56.103
15	Failure to notify institutional review board of changes, failure to submit progress reports	21 CFR 312.66
16	Failure to report adverse drug reactions	21 CFR 312.64, 312.66
17	Submission of false information	21 CFR 312.70
18	Other	n/a
19*	Failure to supervise or personally conduct the clinical investigation	21 CFR 312.60
20*	Failure to protect the rights, safety and welfare of subjects	21 CFR 312.60
21*	Failure to permit FDA access to records	21 CFR 312.68

*Codes 19–21 became effective 1 October 2005.

22   Clinical Research in Asia: Opportunities and Challenges

practices were found. The minor observations that were reported as VAI were due to minor deficiencies at the sites which did not require any regulatory actions. Deficiencies during the US FDA inspections are coded giving special reference to Code of Federal Regulations (CFR) guidelines, as described in Table 1.13.

During the US FDA inspections, the most common deficiencies observed and reported under VAI were: inadequate informed consent form, inadequate drug accountability, failure to follow investigational plan, inadequate and inaccurate records, failure to list additional investigators on Form 1572, failure to notify institutional review board of changes, failure to submit progress reports and failure to report adverse drug reactions.

1.9   Clinical research in Asia – SWOT analysis

1.9.1 Strengths

- Huge treatment-naïve patient population across all disease profiles
- High enrolment rates (2–5 times higher than USA and Western Europe)
- Predominantly clinical research hub for extended Phase II and Phase III programmes for new chemical entities and volunteer studies (bio-analytical and bioequivalence studies) for marketed generic drugs
- Large, well-qualified, young and English-speaking resource base
- Highly-qualified and western-educated doctors practising modern advanced medicines who are inclined to work in global clinical trials
- Cost effectiveness – low per patient cost due to comparatively low investigator fees and cheaper tests and procedures
- Most Asian countries have brought their national good clinical practice recommendations in line with global standards, namely the International Conference on Harmonisation Guidelines for Good Clinical Practice (ICH-GCP)

Published by Woodhead Publishing Limited, 2012

Clinical research in Asia

- Government initiatives have helped to improve good clinical practice awareness; for example the Chinese government helped establish good clinical practice centres to provide training to investigators and staff, while the Indian government offered similar training programmes to site staff and ethics committee members
- Recently adopted intellectual property protection and patent laws to win the confidence of global sponsors with respect to confidentiality and data exclusivity
- Strong IT background, secured leased line and VPN connectivity facilitate easy data transfer
- Committed and cost-effective workforce
- Substantial presence of pharma multinationals in major Asian countries
- Initial positive feedback on data quality during US FDA inspections

1.9.2 Weaknesses

- Cultural factors such as illiteracy, differences in the practice of medicine and socio-economic conditions pose inherent weakness in the system
- Regulatory differences across countries may impact timing and cost of clinical trials
- Regulatory systems across Asian countries are not harmonised
- Hospital infrastructure is not standardised
- Multiple countries and the large number of languages form a critical operational barrier – data often recorded in local languages need translation into English and vice versa
- Mandatory toxicology tests after Phase II completion require six-month delay before start of Phase III
- Coordination with local physicians and hospitals is mandatory as some hospitals and investigators are very capable but do not have enough experience
- Investigators are less experienced with ICH-GCP and global standards and hence site operations are not efficient

Published by Woodhead Publishing Limited, 2012

24   Clinical Research in Asia: Opportunities and Challenges

- Phase I tests/first-in-man studies are not allowed for drugs that have not originated in India
- Asian countries are not ready to undertake Phase 0/Phase I programmes due to lack of expertise and infrastructure
- Clinical research is limited to large cities and large hospitals
- Lack of central institutional review board; some areas have no organised institutional review board process
- Each country has its own process for systems and permits, which are very difficult to standardise; this requires substantial resources for pharma companies/CROs/vendors
- Cost advantage eroding due to competition, increased investigator expectations and rising salary costs
- Higher attrition rates; poaching leads to loss of knowledge and quality outcome
- Unrealistic career expectations regarding rapid promotions and salary growth

1.9.3 *Opportunities*

- Some Asian countries are expected to be significant players in the global commercial pharma market in the next five years
- The growing drug market is also a reason for conducting clinical trials in China and India
- Strong overall economic growth will lead to improvements in general and healthcare infrastructure
- The increased number of CROs and other service providers will help pharma companies increase manufacturing and testing in India
- Expanding private health insurance services is also a consideration for conducting clinical trials in many countries in Asia
- Expansion in early-phase capabilities (Phase 0 and Phase I) with the growth of the business
- More and more late-phase (Phase IV studies) will be conducted as new drugs become affordable for the Asian public at large and pharmacovigilance resources and capabilities are in place

Published by Woodhead Publishing Limited, 2012

Clinical research in Asia

- Opportunities for high-end CRO services, consulting and business solutions, new areas of research possible based on increased domain knowledge over time

1.9.4 Threats

- Limited enforcement of intellectual property protection and the legacy of reverse engineering is a dragging force, being watched globally
- Bureaucracy and government regulations require trials to be approved, with drug import licences required for every shipment
- Ethnicity in Asia may impact trial results due to different metabolic rates and other genetic effects
- Differences in the practice of medicine may impact trial results or affect trial execution
- Perception of political instability and other geopolitical risks may jeopardise investments in clinical research
- Limited local R&D initiatives by local pharma companies
- Overdependence on US pharma companies for clinical trial outsourcing
- Growing resistance to outsourcing from USA
- Talent availability not in sync with growth potential, leading to growth of low-end labour-intensive work
- Media sensitivity and misleading messages
- Exchange rate fluctuation
- Competition from IT/IT enabled services in the life-science domain acts as a potential threat for the CRO industry in Asia

Published by Woodhead Publishing Limited, 2012

2

Clinical research in Japan

Abstract: After the USA and Europe, Japan is the most important market for global pharmaceutical and research and development companies. This chapter discusses trends in the Japanese pharmaceutical market, as well as the state of the CRO market. Also considered are the key players and clinical research environments. The chapter goes on to analyse the market environment, emerging outsourcing models and the key challenges faced by market players. Finally, it provides an outlook for the future of the Japanese pharmaceutical market.

2.1 Background and history

After the USA and Europe, Japan is the most important market for global pharmaceutical and research and development (R&D) companies. The Japanese pharmaceutical industry is worth $81 billion (Figure 2.1). All the major multinational pharma companies have well established marketing and R&D operations in the country. There is a growing demand for effective pharmaceutical products in Japan, but the current government emphasis on slowing rising healthcare expenditure has made the business environment problematic for the pharmaceutical industry.

Japan is presently suffering from the outstanding success of its past investment in healthcare. As Faiz Kermani has reported, figures from the Japanese Ministry of Health, Labour and Welfare indicate that national healthcare expenditure as a proportion of GDP rose

Published by Woodhead Publishing Limited, 2012

28   Clinical Research in Asia: Opportunities and Challenges

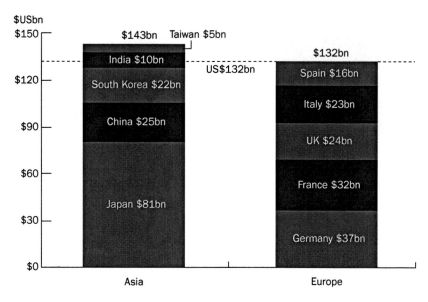

Figure 2.1 Global pharmaceutical industry – an overview
Source: IMS and Biospectrum, China Trial 2009

from 2.78 per cent in 1955 to 6.25 per cent in 2001. Over the same period, average life expectancy rose from 64 years to 78 years for men and from 68 years to 85 years for women. Japanese citizens expect their government to provide quality healthcare, and patients routinely seek access to the latest medical technologies. Ageing populations are not the only pressure on healthcare spending – advances in medical technology and the rapid spread in health services also push up costs.

As Faiz Kermani has also reported, the World Health Organization (WHO) has estimated that by 2020, more than one-quarter of the Japanese population will be classed as elderly, and that a high proportion of these will be over 80 years of age. Kermani points to figures from the Organization for Economic Cooperation and Development (OECD) that indicate that the over-65 age group accounts for 40–50 per cent of healthcare spending in industrialised nations and that per capita healthcare costs for this group are three to five times higher than for those under 65.

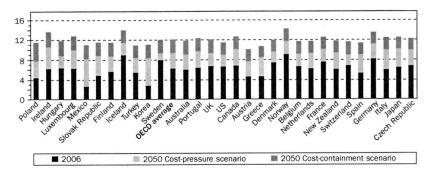

Figure 2.2 Projections of total public health and long-term care expenditure (% GDP)

Source: OECD

Kermani has also shown that according to a new OECD report, the public cost of health and long-term care in OECD countries will double by 2050 if current trends continue. In Japan, the rising medical demands of ageing and wealthier populations could push average health costs from 6.9 per cent to 10.9 per cent (Figure 2.2).

Furthermore, in terms of research, many pharma companies view conditions in Japan as less than ideal and have called upon the government to provide incentives for the pharmaceutical industry to invest in R&D operations in the country.

2.2 Clinical research industry in Japan

Contract research organisations in Japan began their clinical research business in the early 1990s; since then, the business has been growing steadily. According to the Japan CRO Association (JCROA), CROs in Japan generated total revenues of approximately $645 million (¥71 billion) in 2005, rising to about $872 million (¥96 billion) in 2007. It is estimated that the figure for 2011 will exceed $1.5 billion (¥120 billion) (Figure 2.3).

In 2010, the majority of CRO sales in Japan were clinical monitoring services (approximately 86 per cent). Pre-clinical services accounted for 8 per cent, while the final 6 per cent was comprised

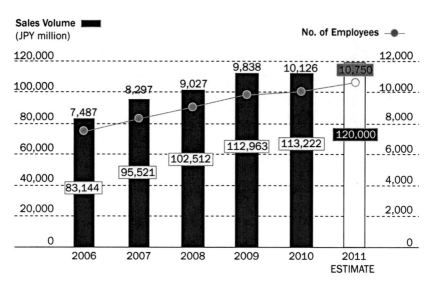

Figure 2.3 Japanese CRO industry revenue and staff numbers
Source: JCROA

of such functions as medical devices; food and supplements; site management organisations and site services; bioanalytics and bioequivalence; laboratory work; electronic data capture; quality control and training etc. For sponsor classification, Japanese pharma companies accounted for 66 per cent, while foreign pharma companies accounted for 34 per cent, with the latter increasing over the years. According to the JCROA Annual Report 2010, Phase III studies accounted for 42 per cent of clinical development revenue, post marketing study and surveillance accounted for 19 per cent, Phase II accounted for 16 per cent, and Phase I studies accounted for 6 per cent (Figure 2.4).

In the last decade, the Japanese pharmaceutical industry has been more active in pursuing research and development activities. Previously, Japanese pharma companies were mostly limiting their clinical research to the Japanese population. In the last decade, however, they have moved out of Japan and are undertaking clinical trials in other countries too. Table 2.1 shows that 264 trials are being sponsored by Japanese pharma companies in other Asian countries.

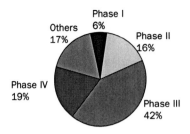

Figure 2.4 Clinical development revenue by phase in Japan (2010)
Source: JCROA

Table 2.1 Japanese pharma companies' industry-sponsored trials in Asia (December 2009)

Pharma company	Korea	Taiwan	China	Hong Kong	India	Australia
Astella	22	18	9	1	1	15
Daiichi	4	5	8		6	4
Dainippon Sumitomo	1	1	1		3	
Esai	7	7	6	1	8	23
Otsuka	36	5	16	2	5	4
Taiho	1	2	2	1		
Takeda	4	3	1	1	13	17
Kowa					1	
Mitsubishi						1
Total	75	41	43	6	37	64

Source: www.clinicaltrials.gov (accessed December 2009)

While clinical research activities are increasingly being undertaken by pharma companies, the CROs have also set up operations in Japan. Several domestic CROs, such as EPS, CMIC, Tokyo CRO etc., have commenced operations in Japan to address the cultural barriers of language, race etc. and to meet the specific requirements of local regulatory authorities.

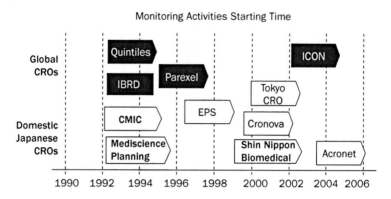

Figure 2.5   Local and global CROs in Japan

During the late 1990s, several global CROs including Quintiles, Parexel etc. expanded their operations to set up offices in Japan to coordinate global multicentric clinical trials as a part of their drug development support to multinational companies.

2.3   The regulatory environment in Japan

In the wake of the thalidomide disaster, the Fund for Adverse Drug Reactions Suffering Relief was established in October 1979. The fund, based on stipulations in the Adverse Drug Reaction Suffering Relief Fund Law (Law No. 55 of 1979), was established for the purpose of providing prompt relief to patients suffering from adverse drug reactions. In 1987, the fund started R&D-promoting operations under the name of the Fund for Adverse Drug Reaction Relief and R&D Promotion; it was subsequently reorganised into the Organization for Pharmaceutical Safety and Research (OPSR) in 1994 to play a role in equivalency reviews of generic drugs. Later, in 1997, the organisation started to provide advice on clinical trials and conduct conformity audits on applications for drug approval.

In 1997, the Pharmaceuticals and Medical Devices Evaluation Center (PMDEC) was established at the National Institute of Health Sciences (NIHS) in order to develop a full-scale approval review system and to make the contents of the review more advanced. It was decided that reviews at the centre should be conducted by teams of experts specialising in pharmaceutical science, medical science, biostatistics, etc. In addition, the Japan Association for the Advancement of Medical Equipment (JAAME) began operations in 1995 to conduct equivalence reviews of medical devices as a designated investigative body under the Pharmaceutical Affairs Law.

From 1997 to 1999, there was a systematic increase in the number of staff engaging in reviews and post-marketing safety measures at the former Ministry of Health and Welfare and the three abovementioned organisations (from 121 staff members in 1996 to 241 in 1999). This growth was curtailed, however, when in December 2001, the cabinet adopted the Special Service Agency Restructuring Plan. In this plan, it was decided that to further enhance reviews and post-marketing safety measures, the OPSR should be dissolved and replaced with the new Pharmaceuticals and Medical Devices Agency (PMDA), which would be founded by consolidating the operations previously allocated to PMDEC, OPSR and JAAME. In 2002, a legislative bill for the Law for the Pharmaceuticals and Medical Devices Agency was discussed and passed at the 155th extraordinary session of the Diet. As a result, PMDA was established on 1 April 2004 in accordance with the Law for the Pharmaceuticals and Medical Devices Agency (Law No. 192 of 2002) (Figure 2.6).

PMDA's objective is to contribute to improvement in public health by providing the following services:

- *Relief for adverse health effects*:
  - PMDA offers relief services for those suffering from adverse drug reactions as well as adverse health effects resulting from infections derived from biological products.
- *Consultation and review services*:
  - *evaluation services* – in accordance with the Pharmaceutical Affairs Law, PMDA reviews the efficacy, safety and quality of drugs and medical devices for which regulatory approval applications have been submitted based on the current scientific and technological standards;

Published by Woodhead Publishing Limited, 2012

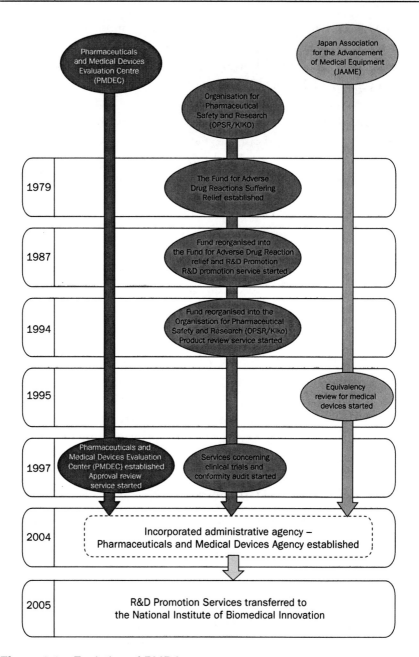

Figure 2.6 Evolution of PMDA

- *approval review services* – PMDA conducts re-examinations/ re-evaluations of drugs and medical devices and reviews of applications for confirmation of the quality and safety of cell and tissue-based products prior to the first-in-man study (hereinafter referred to as 'application for pre-clinical quality and safety confirmation') as well as reviews of applications for confirmation of clinical use of genetically-modified biological entities in accordance with the Law Concerning the Conservation and Sustainable Use of Biological Diversity through Regulations on the Use of Living Modified Organisms (Law No. 97 of 2003);

- *face-to-face consultation services* – in response to requests from clinical trial sponsors, PMDA provides face-to-face guidance and consultations on clinical trials of new drugs and medical devices as well as on clinical trials for re-examinations/re-evaluations of approved products;

- *conformity audit services* – for items for which applications have been made for approval reviews and re-examinations/ re-evaluations, on-site and document inspections are implemented to determine whether documents attached to approval applications conform to good laboratory practice (GLP), good clinical practice (GCP), and conformity standards for application documents;

- *good manufacturing practices (GMP)/quality management system (QMS) inspection services* – on-site and document inspections are conducted to determine whether manufacturing equipment and manufacturing control methods for new drugs and medical devices etc., conform with the requirements of the Ministerial Ordinance on Good Manufacturing Practices, and whether there is a system for manufacturing products of appropriate quality.

- *Post-marketing safety measures*:
  - PMDA cooperates with the Ministry of Health, Labour and Welfare (MHLW) on the following services:

Published by Woodhead Publishing Limited, 2012

36   Clinical Research in Asia: Opportunities and Challenges

- *safety* – improving the safety of marketed drugs and medical devices as well as enabling patients and healthcare professionals to use drugs and medical devices appropriately and with peace of mind;

- *collection and organisation of information* – services for centrally collecting and organising information on the post-marketing safety of drugs and medical devices from a broad range of sources, such as reports from the private sector, information from medical institutions, information from foreign regulatory agencies, and presentations at academic conferences, relating to adverse drug reactions, malfunctions and infections;

- *research and review services* – services for conducting research and reviews relating to safety measures based on the information collected above;

- *consultation services* – services for giving guidance and advice to marketing authorisation holders as well as providing advice in response to consultations from consumers;

- *information provision services* – services to provide safety information on drugs and medical devices widely to healthcare professionals, patients, private companies etc. in a timely manner;

- *standards development-related survey services* – surveys related to developing various standards, such as the Japanese Pharmacopoeia, as stipulated in the Pharmaceutical Affairs Law.

Figure 2.7 summarises the consolidated consultation and review system for drugs and devices.

Over the last six years, PMDA has been actively involved in the consultation and review of global clinical trial applications as the use of foreign clinical data in Japanese new drug applications has increased, contributing to reduced clinical development times (Figure 2.8). Although PMDA's overall review times have declined since it was

Published by Woodhead Publishing Limited, 2012

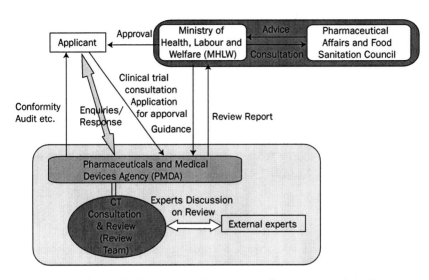

Figure 2.7 Consultation and review system for drugs and devices

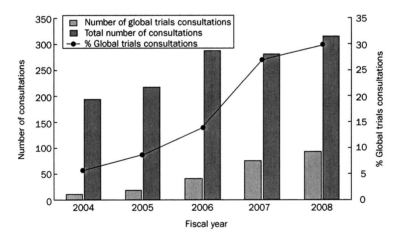

Figure 2.8 Global clinical trial consultations

Source: JCROA

established in April 2004, there has been no improvement in the time between submission of responses to the first set of queries after the interview meeting and subsequent queries to the expert meeting, which account for two-thirds of the review time.

2.4 Evolution of Japanese good clinical practice

Japan's first GCP standards for the conduct of ethical and scientific clinical trials on drugs were issued as Notification No. 874, dated 2 October 1989. The GCP standards were implemented as administrative guidance from 1 October 1990. The MHLW has since undertaken various studies to improve the quality of clinical studies in Japan in accordance with changes in the international regulatory standards. On 27 March 1997, amended GCP standards were issued as MHLW Ordinance No. 28, based on the report of the Central Pharmaceutical Affairs Council dated 13 March 1997. The new and legally binding GCP standards came into effect from 1 April 1997. While the old GCP consisted mainly of provisions concerning pharma companies as the sponsors of clinical studies, the new GCP clarified and reinforced the role and responsibilities of sponsors, and also included provisions concerning the medical institutions and investigators (physicians) performing the clinical studies.

The revised GCP standards were enacted by the ordinance for partial revision of the standards for the conduct of clinical trials on drugs (Notification No. 106 issued by the MHLW on 12 June 2002) and enforced on 1 April 2005 by the ordinance for partial revision

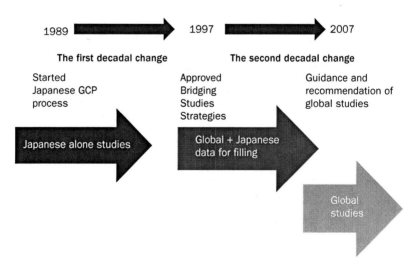

Figure 2.9 Evolution of GCP in Japan

of the standards for the conduct of clinical trials on drugs (Notification No. 172 issued by the MHLW on 21 December 2004). The GCP standards were further revised to improve the quality and function of the investigational review board by the ordinance for partial revision of the standards for the conduct of clinical trials on drugs (Notification No. 72 issued by the MHLW on 31 March 2006). On 19 September 2007, a report was compiled by the MHLW Council for ideal registration-directed clinical trials.

Though the latest Japanese GCP guidelines are in line with the requirements of the International Conference on Harmonisation Guidelines for Good Clinical Practice (ICH-GCP), some of the salient features of Japanese GCP are described below. The Japanese GCP standards consist of six chapters and 59 articles, with three main parts:

- standards for the sponsoring of clinical studies;
- standards for the management of clinical studies which are related to sponsors;
- standards for the conduct of clinical studies in medical institutions.

Chapter 1 describes the general provisions in form of Articles 1 to 3, which consist of outline, definitions of terms and standards for review of data respectively. The chapter specifies the following standards:

- standards to be followed by prospective sponsors in the collection and preparation of data related to results of clinical trials on drugs to be attached to approval applications;
- standards to be followed by prospective sponsors of clinical trials, institutions or persons performing clinical trials and sponsors of clinical trials to conduct or manage clinical trials which are both ethically and scientifically sound;
- standards to be followed by sponsors in the collection and preparation of data from post-marketing clinical trials for the re-examination or re-evaluation of drugs.

Published by Woodhead Publishing Limited, 2012

40 Clinical Research in Asia: Opportunities and Challenges

Chapter 2 describes the following provisions or standards for sponsoring clinical trials in Articles 4 to 15:

- provisions to be followed when clinical trials are sponsored or managed in medical institutions by persons who wish to sponsor clinical trials (sponsor initiated trials);
- provisions to be followed when clinical trials are prepared or managed by persons from the medical institutions who wish to conduct clinical trials by themselves (investigator-initiated trials).

This chapter clearly specifies that prospective sponsors must prepare standard operating procedures so that all work related to sponsoring (or preparation) and management of the clinical trial, such as preparation of the clinical trial protocol, selection of a medical institution(s) and investigator(s) to perform the trial, control of the investigational product, collection of information on adverse reactions and retention of records, can always be performed properly.

The clinical trial protocol and an investigator's brochure based on information concerning the quality, efficacy and safety of the investigational product must be prepared.

A contract must be executed between the sponsor and clinical research organisation when all or part of the clinical trial management is contracted out. When persons or participating medical institutions perform clinical trials on their own and outsource part of the work related to preparation or conduct or management of clinical trials, a contract must be executed with the third party showing that the work was outsourced to a site management organisation. Insurance coverage and other measures required for compensation in cases of trial-related injury must be clearly documented.

Persons who wish to sponsor clinical trials may with the prior approval of the other stakeholders. To do so, they must submit documents to the director of the participating medical institutions, and conclude contracts for outsourcing work or contracts for clinical trials by electronic methods.

Chapter 3 discusses the standards concerning the management of clinical trials and provisions to be followed by the sponsor for the scientific and ethical conduct of clinical trials. To maintain the scientific and ethical conduct, the following standards are maintained:

Published by Woodhead Publishing Limited, 2012

Clinical research in Japan

- The specified items must be included on the labels of the investigational products.
- Manufacturing records, quality test records and other records related to the investigational product must be prepared.
- Investigational products manufactured in factories fulfilling the investigational product GMP requirements must be supplied to or used by the medical institutions that perform the clinical trial.
- The status of all patients with unknown serious adverse drug reactions in Japan and overseas and patients with adverse drug reactions known or thought to be linked with deaths in Japan and overseas must be reported to medical institutions performing clinical trials every six months.
- Standard operating procedures (SOP) concerning monitoring must be prepared and monitoring must be performed on the basis of these SOPs.
- Monitors must confirm that the trial is being performed properly and that reliability of the data is adequately maintained by visits to the medical institutions performing the trial and direct access to the source data, and they must submit a monitoring report to the sponsor, the person who performs the trial, or the director of the medical institution involved.
- An audit plan and audit SOP must be prepared and the audit must be performed in accordance with these documents. The auditor must prepare an audit report and an audit certificate proving that the audit has been performed, and these documents must be submitted to the sponsor, the person who performs the trial, or the director of the medical institutions involved.
- When the trial is completed or discontinued, the results obtained must be compiled in a clinical trial report. If the study results collected from the trial concerned are not attached to the application form as application data, this fact and the reason for it must be notified in writing to the directors of the medical institutions performing the trial.
- Records related to the clinical trial must be retained for the specified period.

Chapter 4 describes the standards and provisions to be followed by the medical institutions while performing clinical trials scientifically

Published by Woodhead Publishing Limited, 2012

42 Clinical Research in Asia: Opportunities and Challenges

and ethically. These include provisions concerning the institutional review boards (IRBs), their functions, compositions and review of clinical trial data for the ethical and scientific appropriateness for the clinical trial. The medical institutions are not allowed to conduct a clinical trial without the IRB's approval.

When there is no established IRB in the medical institution, Japanese GCP permits – at the discretion of the director of the medical institution performing the clinical trials – either a new IRB to be established as per GCP guidelines, or the selection of an alternative IRB either within or outside of the medical institution performing the clinical trials. The IRB can publish information related to IRBs to improve transparency and assure the quality of reviews.

Subsequent chapters describe the provisions related to medical institutions performing clinical trials:

- The guidelines specify that medical institutions performing clinical trials must have the facilities and personnel to undertake adequate clinical observations and laboratory testing, and they must be able to take the measures required should emergencies arise among the trial subjects. The institutions must have SOPs for work related to the trial, and take the necessary measures so that the clinical trial is conducted properly and smoothly in compliance with the trial protocol and the SOP. The director of the medical institution performing the trial must cooperate with monitoring or audits by the sponsor or the person conducting the clinical trial and review by the IRB.
- The guidelines also specify provisions related to the investigators' qualifications and experience to conduct the trial properly. The investigator must select the trial subjects in accordance with the objectives of the trial from both ethical and scientific standpoints. The investigator must complete the case report forms as specified in the protocol and sign or seal them.

The subsequent chapters discuss adverse drug reactions and the reporting procedure, the provisions concerning informed consent of subjects, and audit and inspections. Japanese GCP standards specify

Published by Woodhead Publishing Limited, 2012

Clinical research in Japan

Table 2.2 Regulatory requirements for IRB and PMDA

Documents	IRB	PMDA
Application form	Yes (Japanese)	Yes (Japanese)
Protocol with signature pages (copied)	Yes	Yes
Investigator's brochure	Yes	Yes
Principal investigator and/or co-investigator's CV	Yes	No
Patient information sheets	Yes	Yes
Patient consent forms	Yes	Yes
Subject assent (applicable in Australia only)	Not applicable	Not applicable
Patient questionnaires (to be completed by subjects)	No	Yes
Advertisements	No	Yes
Indemnity form	No	No
Insurance certificate	No	Yes
Import permit	Yes	No
Case report form	Yes	Yes
Adverse event report form	Yes	Yes
IRB average timeline in weeks (from initial submission to approval)	4–8 weeks	
RA average timeline in weeks (from initial submission to approval)	30 days (1st protocol for Japanese), 14 days (2nd protocol)	
Sequential or parallel submission/approval	Parallel	
Cost in US$ per IRB application per site (for initial submission)	IRB submission fee is usually free, although some IRBs request a review fee of around $1,500	
Cost in US$ per RA application (for initial submission)	PMDA submission fee is free; PMDA consultation meeting fee is around $50,000 for the first time	

Published by Woodhead Publishing Limited, 2012

44   Clinical Research in Asia: Opportunities and Challenges

that when a prospective subject is asked to participate in a clinical trial, the investigator must appropriately explain the risks and benefits associated with the new drug or devices under trial. The on-site inspections are performed at both the sponsor's facilities and the medical institution(s) performing the trial. Inspections of the sponsor's facilities examine the organisation, structure and management of the GCP-related division; GCP compliance of clinical trials; and confirmation of the items included in the trial results. Inspections in the medical institutions review the outline of the facilities and organisation; the structure and operation of the IRB; GCP compliance of the clinical trial; and items in the case report forms. Table 2.2 summarises the list of documents required by the Japanese IRB and PMDA for review and approval of the clinical trial. It also quantifies the time and cost for both IRB and PMDA.

2.5   Global clinical trials in Japan

With the implementation of the ICH E5 Guideline 'Ethnic Factors in the Acceptability of Foreign Clinical Data', Japan is using bridging strategies to accept and evaluate both Japanese and foreign data on type of drug, targeted disease area, and the global status of clinical development. Over the last decade, Japan has been facing a serious 'drug lag' problem, which translates to several years' delay for new drug approval for drugs from foreign countries. Japan recognises that its drug development regulations need to be more flexible to allow the inclusion of data from global trials involving non-Japanese patients. By making use of such knowledge and experience, sponsors are increasingly incorporating global clinical trials into their drug development strategy from the early stages of development.

The MHFW defines a global clinical trial as a trial designed for a new drug positioned for worldwide development and approval, having multiple countries, regions and medical institutions concurrently participating in a single clinical trial in accordance with a common clinical trial protocol.

Published by Woodhead Publishing Limited, 2012

2.5.1 Basic principles

Japanese regulatory guidelines state that companies undertaking international trials across different geographic regions and populations must account for ethnic differences when gathering and submitting study data for drugs intended for the Japanese market. In addition, any clinical development plan must specifically assess the efficacy and safety of an investigational drug in Japanese subjects. Prior to the conduct of a global clinical trial, the guidelines mandate early clinical pharmacology and single-dose studies involving healthy Japanese volunteers or patients to obtain pharmacodynamic, pharmacokinetic and safety data, and for these results to be compared with results from non-Japanese subjects to confirm that the risks for the Japanese population are equivalent to those for the non-Japanese population. However, if safety among Japanese subjects can be determined from the results of Phase I trials conducted in a foreign country, or if a recommended dose for both Japanese and non-Japanese patients can be judged similar based on data from similar drugs, or if there are other appropriate reasons, a Phase I trial with the Japanese subjects is not necessarily required prior to the global trial.

In addition, PMDA's new drug development guidelines specify that clinical trials can be conducted in compliance with the ICH-GCP in all participating countries and clinical trial sites. All participating countries and clinical trial sites can accept GCP audit data from Japan. For factors such as race, region, patient demographics, etc. that may affect the efficacy and safety of an investigational drug, subgroup analysis based on those relevant factors can be considered. The new guidelines are sensitive to socio-cultural factors and allow some flexibility and procedural waivers through proper documentations without affecting the trial/trial results.

The guidelines emphasise that pharmacokinetics may be different between Japanese and non-Japanese patients, and it is sometimes difficult to conclude whether a recommended dose based on non-Japanese clinical trial results is also appropriate for Japanese patients. Thus, to facilitate drug development and reach regulatory approval in Japan at the same time, it is recommended to include Japanese patients in a dose-finding study to identify any inter-ethnic difference in dose–response relationship early in clinical development, and subsequently design a confirmatory study. Even in the cases of different recommended doses between Japanese and white subjects, if it can be adequately demonstrated that the different doses in different regions yield equivalent efficacy and safety, the results from the subsequent Phase III global trial (a confirmatory trial) in each region can be combined and used as the results of the primary analysis population. It is also noteworthy that in cases when there are similarities in the pharmacokinetics or correlation between pharmacokinetics and pharmacodynamics, and a clear relation with clinical effects can be shown, a dose-finding study based on clinical effect among Japanese subjects is not always necessary. In some areas, including orphan drugs and drugs for life-threatening diseases for which established treatment is not available, it may sometimes be difficult to conduct a domestic dose-finding study. In such cases, other measures should be considered, such as performing Phase III trials under strict monitoring by physicians.

There is some indication in the guidelines that the inclusion of other Asia-Pacific populations in a joint international trial could help address the question of ethnic differences for drug safety and efficacy in Japanese patients, if the equivalency of those other populations to Japanese patients can be scientifically demonstrated. This flexibility offers the possibility that the growing inclusion of other Asian countries could provide valuable data to support new drug applications in Japan. However, the guidelines emphasise that PMDA's long-term goal is the greater participation of Japanese biopharma companies in international trials covering multiple regions and populations, with development schedules that coincide with those in the USA and Europe.

2.6 Emerging outsourcing models in Japan

There are two types of multinational study in Japan. One involves Japan's participation in a global study conducted in the EU and USA. The other is where pharma companies in Japan initiate and manage the multinational study in a number of Asian countries including Japan. This type of study is commonly known as an 'Asian study'.

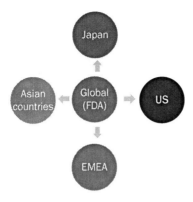

Figure 2.10 Global clinical trials in Japan

As shown in Figure 2.10, for global trials, foreign pharma companies headquartered in the EU and the USA often lead the project plan and the selection of CRO. For Asian studies, on the other hand, Japanese pharma companies primarily lead the decisions. All Asian trials aimed at US Food and Drug Administration (FDA) or European Medicines Agency (EMEA) submission follow international standards along with the stricter local regulatory standards.

As clinical research activities have grown in the last decade, several pharmaceutical CRO partnership models have evolved. While many pharma companies engage global CROs in managing their multinational studies in Japan, a few use a combination of global and local CROs. The sections below will consider a few partnership models prevalent in Japan and discuss the advantages and disadvantages with respect to handling global multinational or local Asian studies.

2.6.1 Model 1: global pharma with global CRO

Many pharma companies prefer to utilise the services of a global CRO which has monitoring operations in Japan to manage their studies globally. Global pharma companies use their local

48   Clinical Research in Asia: Opportunities and Challenges

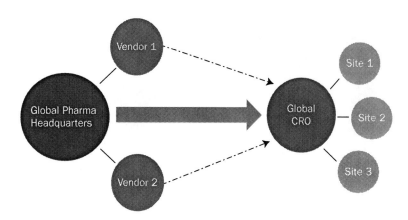

Figure 2.11   Model 1: global pharma with global CRO

pharmaceutical affiliate as the investigational new drug (IND) holder. Safety reports are also filed to PMDA through the IND holder company. Mostly they use the services of the global CRO for monitoring and collecting data from their studies.

The global CRO offers clear-cut advantages of centralised management and more consistent data quality, and also makes it easier to formalise the contracts. However, considering that most global CROs are headquartered in the USA and Europe, it is very difficult for the headquarters of a global CRO to understand the precise situation of a Japanese clinical trial or business. This is essentially because the standard practices may vary due to sociocultural and language barriers. There are several global CROs in the USA and EU but few have the real expanded reach in Japanese cities. Consequently, for pharma companies considering global studies including Japan, the list of global CROs is limited.

2.6.2   Model 2: global pharma with global CRO and its allied local CRO

This partnership model offers the great advantage of managing studies with stricter compliance with Japanese standards as the local CRO has the requisite knowledge and contacts. Communication

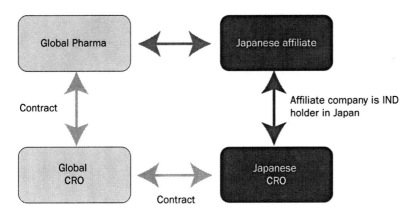

Figure 2.12   Model 2: global pharma with global CRO and its allied local CRO

between investigator sites and the local CRO is much smoother as it is conducted in the local language, resulting in further compliance. Again, however, it is essential to choose the right local partner from among the many local CROs in Japan.

This model is complex to manage due to the multiple players involved, notably the global pharmaceutical company, local affiliate company, global CRO and local CRO. The style of working and standard of procedures and work instructions could vary, possibly resulting in management complications and poor compliance. It could also lead to lower consistency in data quality. To maintain data quality and compliance, this model may require close supervision from pharmaceutical sponsors.

2.6.3 Model 3: global pharma's local affiliate and CRO

This model gives flexibility to the global pharma companies' local affiliates to deal directly with the best service provider at the local level. The local affiliate decides the best CRO and:

- outsources the entire project to a preferred service provider at the local level; or

50 Clinical Research in Asia: Opportunities and Challenges

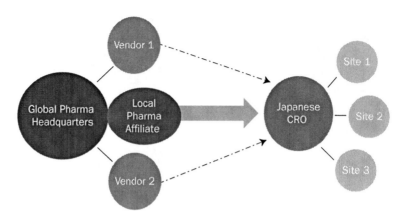

Figure 2.13 Model 3: global pharma's local affiliate and CRO

- outsources by function, such as clinical development, data management and pharmacovigilance, to a functional unit-based service provider.

The local affiliate of the global pharma companies ensures compliance with the global guidelines through the local Japanese CRO. The knowledge and awareness of the local pharma affiliate and the local CRO help manage the local logistical and regulatory challenges smoothly.

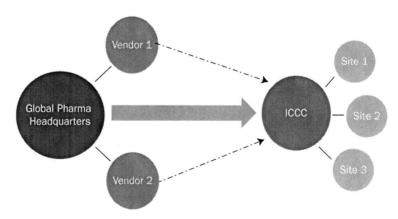

Figure 2.14 Model 4: in-country clinical caretaker

Published by Woodhead Publishing Limited, 2012

2.6.4 Model 4: in-country clinical caretaker

If they wish to conduct clinical trials in Japan, companies without a Japanese subsidiary are required by Article 15 of the Japanese GCP standards to designate a Japan-based third party, known as an in-country clinical caretaker. This body jointly assumes their legal, regulatory and operational obligations.

2.7 Japan's international strategic outlook

Due to the globalisation of the research and development of pharmaceuticals and medical devices, PMDA is determined to harmonise its services with the international community in order to provide people with more effective and safer pharmaceuticals and medical devices. To achieve this, PMDA has set up the following five-pronged international strategies.

2.7.1 Strategy 1: strengthening international collaboration

PMDA plans to review the safety of pharmaceuticals and medical devices in Japan together with the US FDA and the European Commission and EMEA. PMDA proposes to promote continuous bilateral talks based on confidentiality agreements, information sharing, and proactive personnel exchanges with the FDA and EMEA. PMDA regularly invites personnel from these two organisations to its offices, with a view to establishing a system under which detailed information can be gathered and opinions can be exchanged in real time. PMDA will swiftly analyse, evaluate and translate important overseas information and communicate it to the relevant parties.

PMDA has recently promoted collaborative relations with Asian countries, with the primary focus on China and South Korea. If the variance in ethnic factors is small, data from these three countries can be combined and analysed for the quicker delivery of drugs in

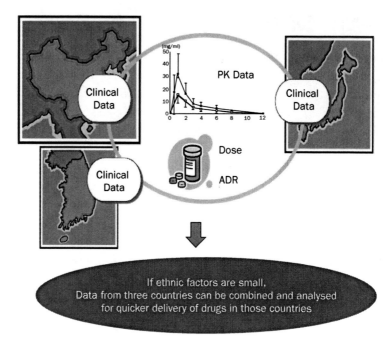

Figure 2.15 Tripartite cooperations to study ethnic factors

these countries. PMDA also plans to strengthen cooperation with foreign countries with respect to inspections and audits conducted to ensure compliance with GLP, GCP, GMP and QMS.

2.7.2 Strategy 2: strengthening international harmonisation

PMDA plans to enhance Japan's contribution to ongoing international harmonisation activities such as the International Conference on Harmonisation of Technical Requirements for Registration of Pharmaceuticals for Human Use, the Global Harmonisation Task Force, Harmonisation By Doing, and the Pharmacopoeia Discussion Group, and maintain and strengthen favourable relations with relevant countries by continuing to send directors and staff members to participate in these harmonisation activities. In addition, PMDA will

Clinical research in Japan **53**

enhance Japan's contribution to and strengthen collaborative relations with the World Health Organization, the OECD and other relevant international organisations by sending directors and staff members to international harmonisation activities led by those organisations.

2.7.3 Strategy 3: promotion of personnel exchange programmes

PMDA has ongoing plans to send its staff members to international meetings and conferences in a variety of specialised fields. The objective is to promote networks globally. To promote relationships with overseas regulatory agencies, PMDA plans to send personnel to the FDA and EMEA and will promote personnel exchanges with other relevant countries and international organisations. To further promote mutual understanding among Japan, China and South Korea in particular, PMDA will promote personnel exchanges with the Chinese State Food and Drug Administration and the Korean Food and Drug Administration, and will build a system under which information on product evaluation and safety measures can be readily exchanged.

2.7.4 Strategy 4: creation of world-class human resources

PMDA will emphasise training and development to develop human resources with an international orientation and good communication skills. The identified directors and staff members will be provided with training on foreign languages such as English.

2.7.5 Strategy 5: international publicity and information sharing

To demonstrate the global orientation of Japan, PMDA plans to improve its website, especially the English version. The website will explain in detail the pharmaceutical regulations, PMDA's services, product review reports, post-marketing safety information, legal notices and other administrative documents.

Published by Woodhead Publishing Limited, 2012

54 Clinical Research in Asia: Opportunities and Challenges

In addition, PMDA will also organise regular lectures and booths/ exhibits at international meetings and conferences, distribute relevant information to media, and grant interviews to the Foreign Correspondents' Club of Japan and overseas media concerning pharmaceutical regulations in Japan.

2.8 Future outlook

Japan is the land of opportunity for pharmaceutical, biotech and medical device companies. In terms of multinational clinical studies, the impact of globalisation is evident among all clinical research stakeholders, whether sponsors, CROs, regulators or those actually running the research facilities in Japan. In the EU and the USA, all clinical development tasks can be outsourced to CROs. In Japan, on the other hand, it is generally difficult for a sponsor to conduct clinical trials if they have no local office or caretaker. This is due to several local cultural barriers. One obstacle in conducting multinational clinical studies has been the English language competency within Japan, as it is generally limited when compared with that of Korea and Taiwan. However, the mindset of the Japanese is moving towards the acceptance of foreign languages and international standards. This is going to boost the clinical research environment in Japan. With more exposure to global trials, the human skills in various functional areas are maturing. The regulatory affairs and pharmacovigilance departments of CROs and pharma companies in Japan are gaining global exposure; as a result they are maturing, with a positive change in attitude towards research and development. Even regulators in Japan are proactively collaborating with established regulatory bodies such as the US FDA and EMEA, to implement international harmonisation and with neighbouring countries to accept clinical trial data from subjects with similar ethnicity.

Published by Woodhead Publishing Limited, 2012

3

Clinical research in India

Abstract: The pharmaceutical industry in India is recognised globally for its successful generics business and its ability to attract a large number of industry-sponsored global clinical trials. This chapter discusses the drug development initiatives of pharmaceutical companies in India and deliberates on the evolution of clinical research in various business segments. It revisits the amount of clinical trials being carried out by pharmaceutical companies in various therapeutic areas. It also discusses the growth of the regulatory environment in India and presents a PESTLE analysis to demonstrate the growing clinical research environment in India.

3.1 Pharmaceutical industry background

The pharmaceutical industry in India is recognised globally for its successful generics business. The pharma industry in India has set new heights in the fields of production, development, manufacturing and research due to its low-cost manufacturing facilities, educated and skilled manpower and cost-effective labour force, among other factors. According to a study by FICCI and Ernst & Young, by 2015 India will represent an $8 billion market for multinational companies to sell expensive drugs, while the domestic pharma market is likely to reach $20 billion. Due to the low cost of R&D, the Indian pharmaceutical off-shoring industry is expected to be worth $2.5 billion by 2012.

Outside the USA, India has the largest number of pharmaceutical manufacturing facilities. India has around 119 US FDA approved

Published by Woodhead Publishing Limited, 2012

and 84 UK MHRA approved manufacturing units. Many of these units are also approved by regulatory bodies from Canada, Australia, Germany and South Africa. These units manufacture and deliver high-quality products globally. As shown in Figure 3.1, in 2008, India received 136 abbreviated new drug approvals (ANDA) from the US FDA, second only to the USA itself.

An ANDA contains data that, when submitted to the FDA's Center for Drug Evaluation and Research, Office of Generic Drugs, provide for the review and ultimate approval of a generic drug product. Generic drug applications are called 'abbreviated' because they are generally not required to include pre-clinical (animal) and clinical (human) data to establish safety and effectiveness. Instead, a generic applicant must scientifically demonstrate that its product is bioequivalent (i.e. performs in the same manner as the innovator drug). Once approved, an applicant may manufacture and market the generic drug product to provide a safe, effective, low-cost alternative to the US public.

As far as drug master filings (DMFs) in USA are concerned, Indian companies are very active. By early 2008, Indian companies had filed 1,155 DMFs, which is significantly higher than China and Japan (Figure 3.2).

A DMF is a submission to the FDA that may be used to provide confidential detailed information about facilities, processes or

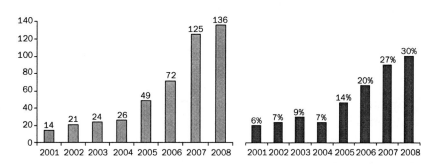

Figure 3.1   India's share of abbreviated new drug approvals granted in the USA (2008)

Source: Media reports

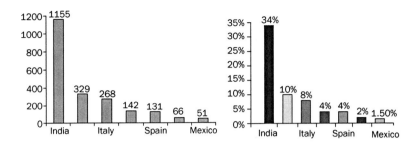

Figure 3.2 Percentage of drug master filings in the USA (2008), by country

Source: Media reports

articles used in the manufacturing, processing, packaging and storing of one or more human drugs. The submission of a DMF is not required by law or FDA regulation. A DMF is submitted solely at the discretion of the holder. The information contained in the DMF may be used to support an investigational new drug (IND) application, a new drug application (NDA), an abbreviated new drug application (ANDA), another DMF, an export application, or amendments and supplements to any of these. A DMF is *not* a substitute for an IND, NDA, ANDA or export application. It is not approved or disapproved. The technical contents of a DMF are reviewed only in connection with the review of an IND, NDA, ANDA or an export application.

Indian pharma companies have expanded their generic base through mergers, acquisitions and several collaborative efforts. Eli Lilly and Jubilant Organosys have formed a 50:50 R&D joint venture to develop molecules in the areas of oncology, diabetes and cardiovascular therapeutic areas. Wyeth has partnered with GVK to establish a dedicated discovery chemistry research site to engage synthetic chemists working exclusively for Wyeth. AstraZeneca in partnership with Torrent intends to brand and market Torrent's 18 generic products in nine emerging markets, where it already has a strong commercial footprint. Table 3.1 summarises these and a few other partnerships in the Indian pharmaceutical industry.

Out of the total global pharma R&D budget of $129 billion, 38 per cent is spent on drug discovery and development. Some 37 per cent of this global drug discovery and development budget is

58 Clinical Research in Asia: Opportunities and Challenges

Table 3.1 Pharma partnerships in India

Pharma company	Partnerships
GSK	Ranbaxy
Eli Lilly	Jubilant, Suven
Zydus	Boringer, Onconova
Dr Reddy's	Rheoscience, Argenta, Clintec
Aurigene	Merck/Serono, Forest Labs, Rheoscience
Merck and Co	Advinus
AstraZeneca	Torrent
Wyeth	GVK
Nicholas	Moruvus, Connexious, Biosynth
Syngene	Innate

Source: Media reports

outsourced. India's share in this global outsourcing business is less than $1 billion, which equals less than 6 per cent of the global outsourcing business by 2010 (Table 3.2). The compound annual growth rate (CAGR) of the outsourcing business to India was more than 30 per cent during 2005–10.

While global outsourcing of clinical trials is on the rise, Indian pharma companies are also becoming innovative and investing heavily in new drug research. The key leaders in the areas of new drug development are Dr Reddy's Laboratories, Ranbaxy, Lupin, Glenmark, Orchid, Piramal Healthcare, Torrent and Wockhardt (Table 3.3).

Table 3.2 Global pharma R&D and outsourcing by 2010

Parameters	$bn	%
Global pharma R&D spend	129	100
Drug discovery and development	49	38
Global drug discovery and development outsourcing	18	37
India's share in drug discovery and development	1	6

Source: Media analysis reports

Published by Woodhead Publishing Limited, 2012

Clinical research in India

Table 3.3 Drug development pipeline of key Indian companies

Company	Research areas	Pre-clinical	Phase I	Phase II	Phase III	Total molecules
Dr Reddy's Laboratories	dyslipidemia, atherosclerosis and associated cardiovascular diseases, diabetes, oncology, metabolic disorders, cardiovascular, metabolic disorders, anti-inflammatory, cancer, viral infections and immuno stimulation, insulin sensitiser for type 2 diabetics	5	3	3	1	12
Glenmark	chronic obstructive pulmonary disease (COPD), asthma, type 2 diabetes, osteoarthritic pain, neuropathic pain, rheumatoid arthritis, multiple sclerosis, inflammatory disorders, anti-platelet, adjunct to PCI/acute coronary syndrome	5	1	1	1	8
Lupin	anti-TB, anti-psoriasis, anti-migraine, diabetes, rheumatoid arthritis	2	0	3	1	6
Orchid	orally active anti-diabetes compound	0	0	1	0	1
Piramal Healthcare	oncology, type 2 diabetes, rheumatoid and psoriasis, dermatology, herpes, non-steroidal anti-inflammatory drug	3	2	4	0	9
Ranbaxy	malaria, urinary incontinence, allergic rhinitis, asthma, dyslipidemia, benign prostatic hyperplasia, anti-bacterial	4	2	1	1	8

Published by Woodhead Publishing Limited, 2012

60 Clinical Research in Asia: Opportunities and Challenges

Table 3.3 Drug development pipeline of key Indian companies (*cont'd*)

Company	Research areas	Pre-clinical	Phase I	Phase II	Phase III	Total molecules
Torrent	heart disease	0	1	0	0	1
Wockhardt	antibiotic, respiratory inspection	0	1	1	0	2

Source: Media reports, company websites/presentations

Between these companies, there are 47 molecules in different stages of development, covering such therapeutic areas as cancer, diabetes, respiratory diseases, cardiovascular diseases, muscular pain and tropical diseases.

3.2 History of clinical research in India

India's proficiency in medical research dates back to 200 BC and 200 AD, when Charaka and Sushruta, masters of their time, had their own methodology for clinical research. Although India was not able to build on its legacy to pursue high-end research in the modern era, the drug development discipline has come a long way since then. Globally, the age-old methodologies have been replaced by harmonised good clinical practice (GCP) and good laboratory practice (GLP), leading to numerous trials being carried out according to these guidelines. Over the last century, the USA, EU and Japan have played a significant role in undertaking well-designed scientific clinical trials, thus helping develop new drugs to eradicate and cure life-threatening diseases.

Within the pharma industry it is well known that the patents of several branded products will expire in developed markets over the coming decade. In the USA, for instance, drug patents worth $61 billion expired during the period 2004–10. As such, many well-established drug manufacturers with reputations in generics are exploring new products and markets in order to expand their commercial base. Before the generic drugs can be exported, however, they must be registered in the specific countries according to the regulations and requirements of each respective country. For

Published by Woodhead Publishing Limited, 2012

example, if a pharmaceutical company wishes to register a molecule in five different regions, it is required to conduct five separate bioanalytical and bioequivalence (BABE) studies of the same molecule to compare it with the innovator product available in each region; only then do the data become acceptable. BABE trials have therefore grown in importance as the means to help achieve this. Due to the generic base of its pharmaceutical industry, India has long been a popular region to conduct BABE studies.

Epidemiological studies are also undertaken globally to assess the factors that affect health and illness, and serve as the foundation and logic of interventions made in the interest of public health and preventive medicine. These are considered a basis of public health research, and are highly regarded in evidence-based medicine for identifying risk factors for disease and determining optimal treatment approaches to clinical practice. The work of communicable and non-communicable disease epidemiologists ranges from outbreak investigation, to study design, data collection and analysis including the development of statistical models to test hypotheses and the writing-up of results for submission to peer-reviewed journals. Epidemiologists draw on a number of other scientific disciplines, such as biology in understanding disease processes, and social science disciplines including sociology and philosophy in order to better understand proximate and distal risk factors.

Besides this, in the last two decades, India has participated in many industry-sponsored and investigator-initiated clinical trials. Indian sites have started making a great contribution to the drug development cycle mostly in late-phase studies (Phase II to Phase IV). It is also worth noting that India has contributed to the generation of trial data for some US FDA approved new drugs produced by multinational pharma companies (Table 3.4).

3.3 Evolution of clinical research in India

India is moving firmly into the front ranks of the rapidly growing Asia-Pacific economy and is witnessing a radical change as a business hub for clinical research. Over the past decade, several players have

62 Clinical Research in Asia: Opportunities and Challenges

Table 3.4 US FDA approved new drugs – data generated from India

Drug company	Molecules/brands researched
Alcon	Vegamox
AstraZeneca	Merenem
Cangene	Hepatitis B vaccine
Eli Lilly	Alimta, Gemcitabine
Galaxo	Lamotrigine
Jannsen	Resperidal
Novartis	Tegaserod
Pfizer	Voriconazole
Roche	Peg-interferon
Santen	Quixin
Wyeth	Influenza A vaccine

Source: Media reports

begun to operate in ancillary business segments of clinical research. Key business segments include:

- drug discovery and chemistry;
- bio-analytical and bioequivalence/Phase I/pre-clinical business;
- clinical research (Phase II/III/IV);
- IT and IT-enabled life science/bioinformatics business;
- central laboratory/central ECG/EKG business;
- clinical research training.

Over the last two decades, India has seen multiple players operating in each business segment. Some of the leading service providers in these segments are highlighted in Figure 3.3.

3.3.1 Drug discovery and chemistry business

India provides contract chemistry and biology services for a large number of US and European pharmaceutical clients. Indian companies

Published by Woodhead Publishing Limited, 2012

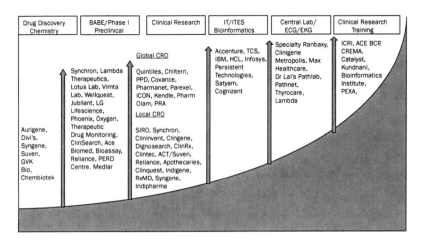

Figure 3.3   Leading service providers in clinical research business

Source: Media reports

have state-of-the-art facilities including instrumentation, analytical capabilities and animal facilities to support all aspects of pre-clinical drug discovery and development. Many have scientific capabilities for chemistry (organic chemistry, medicinal chemistry, combinatorial chemistry and process research), biology (assay development, protein production and purification, and characterisation of biologically-active molecules). In addition, pharmacology capabilities include in-vitro and in-vivo metabolic profiling of lead molecules, pharmacokinetic analysis and animal models of disease. Development capabilities include toxicology and formulation support. These companies offer a unique opportunity to create molecular assets.

3.3.2 Clinical research business

The most attractive business opportunity in clinical research appears to be setting up a CRO that can handle one or more functions for a pharmaceutical sponsor. Today, many global and local CROs have established operations in India to provide clinical monitoring work in Phase II, III and IV studies for the global pharmaceutical industry. India has been witnessing a positive trend, reflected by the growing

64 Clinical Research in Asia: Opportunities and Challenges

numbers of players providing a spectrum of clinical development services at different stages of drug development, such as project management, clinical trial monitoring, medical affairs, regulatory matters, clinical trial supplies, quality assurance, data management and statistical analysis. With the expansion of the clinical research business, several other opportunities have also evolved over the past decade, including pharmacovigilance, medical writing, database programming, medical coding, electronic data capture (EDC) training and support services. Indian service providers are slowly gaining competence in all such support services.

Site management organisation forms another segment of clinical research business which mostly works closely with hospital resources and investigators. Site management organisations help Indian investigators who are equally or even more busy than their counterparts in Europe or USA due to heavy patient loads, to generate high-quality data and improved patient compliance and retention.

3.3.3 BABE/Phase I and pre-clinical business

For the purposes of marketing or export of a drug into a new region, pharma companies register the molecule with the local authorities of that region. This process necessitates the conduct of a bioequivalence trial of the same molecule, comparing it with the innovator drug available in that region, followed by submission of the bioequivalence data to the local authorities for registration. As India is a promising pharmaceutical market, many global and local players are conducting BABE trials in India. Hence, this is another promising business opportunity for many entrepreneurs. Cost-effectiveness and the availability of healthy volunteers combined with the regulatory changes vis-à-vis prescribed guidelines for bioavailability and bioequivalence studies in India are the key attractions. This business needs an initial investment in a bioanalytical, pathological laboratory with a few hospital beds and a small ICU with proper quality control and quality assurance procedures in place, with the provision for a dedicated physician during the conduct of the trial. Figure 3.4 describes the process of BABE trials.

Published by Woodhead Publishing Limited, 2012

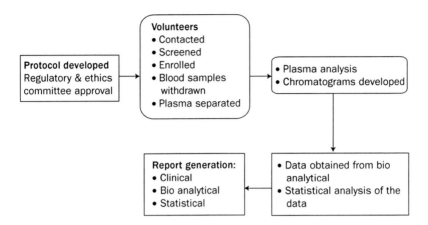

Figure 3.4 Process flow-chart for BABE trials

At industry conferences there is considerable debate concerning the restricted regulations in India with respect to exposing healthy human volunteers to new drugs. As such, molecules developed outside India cannot be used for the conduct of Phase I trials in India. Due to these restrictions, such centres are not common in India. Although the BABE centres and a few hospitals in India are working in the field of Indian Phase I studies, most Phase I studies are presently conducted outside India. Considering the availability of healthy volunteers, the Phase I segment of business could conceivably be a major area for the future. Certainly there appear to be few restrictions in terms of infrastructure as the existing BABE centres and hospital facilities in India could easily be modelled to support Phase I units. Dependent on changes in regulations, global CROs and pharma companies would likely establish their own Phase I units in India.

3.3.4 IT and ITES life science business

Thanks to India's information technology (IT) and IT-enabled services (ITES) experience, there has been massive migration of outsourced data management and statistical analysis business into

66 Clinical Research in Asia: Opportunities and Challenges

India. Large software companies with huge capital bases and critical mass are involved in the biometrics business and hence there are plenty of opportunities in this knowledge-based service sector. This is not surprising when one considers that the cost of data entry operators in India is perhaps one-sixth to one-eighth of their equivalent in Europe and the USA. At present, there are 2–5 times as many people working in data management establishments than in clinical CRO resources in India. Top-level IT companies such as TCS, Cognizant, Accenture, Infosys, Satyam and many others are actively involved in pharmacovigilance, medical writing and data-processing. With the developments in infrastructure, telecommunications, broadband, internet connectivity and web-enabled services in India, another two areas where India sees a lot of growth are EDC and interactive voice recognition systems.

3.3.5 Centralised laboratory/ECG business

The cost of a centralised laboratory with good laboratory certification and national and international accreditation is huge. Given the existing share of clinical research business in India, the projected return on investment is not sufficiently lucrative for India-only studies. However, with the increased globalisation of clinical business and medical tourism, central laboratory services look promising to many service providers. India offers a lot of cost-effectiveness for investment in this area. Many local laboratories have scaled up their facilities and investment to meet the global standards and certifications.

The ECG is an important test when monitoring drug trial participants. Accordingly, it places considerable demands on the time of the cardiology specialist to read, interpret and write reports on the ECGs of study subjects. With the rising charge-out rates of cardiologists in the USA and Europe, only a limited number of global CROs are using this as an opportunity to create centres of excellence in India and hiring young physicians to take up this responsibility under the guidance of the few cardiology specialists. The development in web-based technology for rapid data transfer is a blessing in

Published by Woodhead Publishing Limited, 2012

disguise for these businesses. While the regulators have raised the standards for recording, reading and submitting ECG data, meeting those standards with cost-effectiveness is the challenge in this segment of business.

3.3.6 Clinical research training

Training in clinical research is another important area where there is huge demand and a supply gap for trained professionals in India. Most of the global players started their clinical research work in India with on-the-job training programmes for their initial few staff members before implementing a 'train the trainer' model to localise their training programmes further. More recently, many local universities and global training institutes have recognised the prospects for growth in this industry and started full-time short-term, diploma courses in clinical research management, both classroom-based and/ or online. The setting up of training centres is not particularly difficult as many entrepreneurs/institutions are ready to invest. Furthermore, there is no dearth of candidates interested in pursuing a career in a growing and exciting field such as clinical research. The real challenge for this segment of business is to create good tutors with the operational experience to impart high-quality education to the aspirants and manage them with dignity and respect.

3.3.7 Clinical trials undertaken in India

As of 2011, GCP trials are still predominantly undertaken in Europe and North America, and constitute more than 80 per cent of global clinical trials conducted internationally. However, over last few years, the scenario has begun to change. So-called emerging countries such as India, China and those in Latin America, are increasingly becoming centres of excellence for the conduct of high-quality clinical trials for international pharma companies. Though there is much hype about the growth of clinical research business, less than 2 per cent of global clinical trials are conducted in India.

Published by Woodhead Publishing Limited, 2012

The number of clinical studies initiated in India each year is, on the whole, growing. With recession gripping the global pharmaceutical industry, 2009 was slow in comparison with 2008, but in 2010 the number exceeded 300 for the first time (Figure 3.5). Even though the number of regulatory approvals slowed in early 2011, 112 trials were already listed in the registry by mid-July.

Industry reports suggest that India is host to GCP studies in diverse therapeutic areas. Some 81 per cent of the industry-sponsored trials undertaken in India are in late phases (i.e. Phase II and Phase III) where sponsors can benefit from the country's large pool of potential subjects who are not receiving any other medical treatment. Although India's regulatory authorities permit Phase I trials for molecules developed in India, Phase I trials for molecules developed outside India are not generally permitted. In the event that the regulators identify a molecule developed outside of India that may benefit disease control in India and the public at large, the Drugs Controller General of India (DCGI), the Health Ministry Steering Committee, and the Genetic Engineering Approval Committee together approve the conduct of Phase I trials. As such,

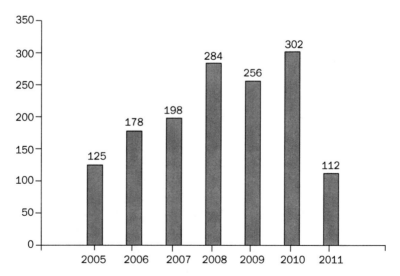

Figure 3.5 Growth of clinical trials in India

Source: www.clinicaltrials.gov (accessed July 2011), *2011 figures up to July

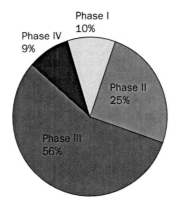

Figure 3.6 Clinical trials in India – by phase
Source: www.clinicaltrials.gov (accessed 20 July 2011)

the volume of industry sponsored Phase I clinical trials in India is relatively low (only 10 per cent of all industry-sponsored trials).

While most of the trials quoted in Table 3.5 are for the global sponsors in Phase II to Phase III, a few could be local registration studies.

Table 3.5 suggests that the pharmaceutical majors like Pfizer, GSK, BMS, Eli Lilly, AstraZeneca etc. have carried out more than

Table 3.5 Pharma companies undertaking trials in India

Pharma company	No. of GCP trials
Pfizer	122
GlaxoSmithKline	73
Eli Lilly and Company	80
Novartis	69
Sanofi-Aventis	60
Bristol-Myers Squibb	55
AstraZeneca	63
Boehringer Ingelheim	41
Roche	23
Bayer	26
Total	612

Source: www.clinicaltrials.gov (accessed 20 July 2011)

70 Clinical Research in Asia: Opportunities and Challenges

50 per cent of the global trials in India. These trials were managed either by themselves or with the support of CROs in diverse therapeutic areas over a decade-long period.

The list in Table 3.5 is not exhaustive and mentions only few players in India. Nonetheless, it clearly shows that over a period of a few years, a number of trials in diverse therapeutic areas have been undertaken by pharma companies and CROs in India. Some key therapeutic areas where trials are undertaken in India are delineated below.

3.3.7.1 Infectious disease

Infectious diseases such as leishmaniasis (Kala-azar), leprosy, tuberculosis, HIV, malaria, etc. are seen in large numbers in India. As such, numerous trials are being conducted in India for hepatitis, HIV, enteric fever, intra-abdominal infection, streptococcus infection and other such serious conditions.

In collaboration with the World Health Organization (WHO) Special Program for Research and Training in Tropical Diseases, OneWorld Health completed a Phase III clinical trial of 667 Kala-azar patients in November 2004 at four centres of excellence in Bihar: the Kala-azar Medical Research Centre, the Kalaazar Research Centre in Muzzafarpur, the Kalaazar Research Centre and the Rajendra Memorial Research Institute in Patna. Several national and international level institutes are also carrying out trials in HIV infection and seronegativity conditions in India.

Important national and international-level institutions collaborating with Indian hospitals/institutions include:

- HIV Prevention Trials Network (HPTN);
- Indian Council of Medical Research (ICMR);
- International AIDS Vaccine Initiative (IAVI);
- International Vaccine Institute (IVI);
- John E. Fogarty International Centre (FIC);
- National Centre for Complementary and Alternative Medicine (NCCAM);
- National Institute of Allergy and Infectious Disease (NIAID);

- National Institute of Child Health and Human Development (NICHD);
- National Institute of Cholera and Enteric Diseases (NICED);
- National Institute of Dental and Craniofacial Research (NIDCR);
- National Institute of Mental Health (NIMH);
- National Institute on Drug Abuse (NIDA);
- Targeted Genetics Corporation (TGC).

3.3.7.2 Oncology

Oncology is the next most promising therapeutic area. India has experienced a large number of trials in diverse disease areas within this field, including breast cancer, renal cell carcinoma, head and neck cancer, non-small cell lung cancer, cervix, and pancreatic cancer. India has an estimated patient pool of 2–2.5 million cancer patients, well-equipped hospitals and well-trained and research-oriented investigators to support these trials in different malignant diseases.

The National Cancer Institute has undertaken several trials with anti-cancer drugs in patients with head and neck cancers and leukaemia. Most of these trials have been part of global multicentric trials, with a few of these sites contributing a significant number of patients to these trials. Eli Lilly's Gemcitabine, GSK's Lapatinib and Pfizer's Droloxifene trials represent examples of this approach. AstraZeneca, Eli Lilly, Pfizer, GSK, and many other companies have carried out several Phase II and III trials in major cancer indications.

3.3.7.3 Central nervous system

Over 20 million Indians suffer from mental illness, such as manic depression, and approximately 9 million suffer from schizophrenia. Because of this large pool of potential patients, many global pharma companies have based their studies in neurology and psychiatry in India. This has particularly been the case for schizophrenia, bipolar disorder, epilepsy, depression, cerebral stroke, episodic migraine and

Published by Woodhead Publishing Limited, 2012

72 Clinical Research in Asia: Opportunities and Challenges

cerebral malaria. There are many centres of excellence in India to handle mental health and neuroscience research. Some of them have contributed significantly to the research and development for new therapies.

3.3.7.4 Cardiology

Due to busy lifestyles, stress, high pollution levels and erratic eating habits, Indians are highly prone to cardiac disease. Indeed, according to WHO estimates, one in every five heart disease cases comes from India. More than 10 per cent of all urban Indians suffer from coronary artery disease. India has several state-of-the-art cardiac centres to provide personalised cardiac disease management programmes.

The Clinicaltrials.gov registry shows that at least 50 trials have been undertaken in India for cardiac disease conditions such as arrhythmias, atrial fibrillation/atrial flutter, coronary artery disease, hypertension and pulmonary hypertension.

3.3.7.5 Endocrinology

From a demographic perspective, the fact that India has a population of over 30 million diabetics, offers an excellent reason for global sponsors to consider conducting large trials in the country. India has been the setting for several trials, including type 2 diabetes, diabetes mellitus/asthma, obesity and diabetic retinopathy, as well as a number of insulin-related investigations.

There are many pharma companies working in the field of endocrinology. Eli Lilly, Novo Nordisk and Takeda are prominent companies carrying out diabetes trials. India has participated in a significant number of industry-sponsored diabetic trials. Company sources suggest that Aventis and Novartis are also carrying out clinical trials in the diabetes segment.

3.3.7.6 Other therapeutic areas

Other therapeutic areas worth mentioning in the context of Indian clinical research include gastroenterology, ophthalmology, and

Published by Woodhead Publishing Limited, 2012

respiratory and metabolism studies. In the gastroenterology segment, Cangene's hepatitis B vaccine, Novartis's Tegaserod and Roche's peg-interferon trials are just some of the notable US FDA trials that have been carried out in India. Alcon, Santen and Allergan have conducted several ophthalmology trials for glaucoma and other eye conditions in India.

3.4 Regulatory environment in India

3.4.1 The Drugs and Cosmetics Act

The key law that governs the pharmaceutical industry in India is the Drugs and Cosmetics Act 1940. The prime objective of the Act is to regulate the import, manufacture, distribution and sale of drugs. The agency that regulates clinical research in India is the Central Drug Standard Control Organization (CDSCO), which functions under the guidance of the DCGI. In 1970, new guidelines for the introduction of new drugs and clinical trials were introduced. The Drugs and Cosmetics Act was then revised in 1988 specifically to incorporate, in Schedule Y of Rule 122, the procedure for the import, manufacture and marketing of new drugs. The Drugs and Cosmetics Act was further amended in 2008 to empower central government to regulate or restrict the manufacture, sale or distribution of drugs that are in the public interest or that are essential to meet the requirement of an emergency arising from epidemics or natural calamities.

3.4.2 Ethical guidelines for biomedical research on human subjects

In 2000, following pressure from the industry and the proactive initiatives of regulators, the ICMR's Central Ethics Committee on Human Research (CECHR) issued its 'Ethical Guidelines for Biomedical Research on Human Subjects'. CECHR was constituted to consider various issues related to the ethical, legal and social dimensions of research involving human subjects. The committee,

Published by Woodhead Publishing Limited, 2012

74 Clinical Research in Asia: Opportunities and Challenges

which first met in September 1996, identified several major areas that needed to be addressed and established expert subcommittees to develop draft guidelines in these areas. The areas included the clinical evaluation of drugs, devices, diagnostics, vaccines and herbal remedies; epidemiological research; human genetics research; transplantation research, including foetal tissue transplantation; and assisted reproductive technologies.

Due to further and rapid developments in science and technology in India, it became necessary to update these guidelines to address the ethical challenges posed by these advances. Necessitated by increasing research in the developing world, the international guidelines released in 2002 by the developed countries, including the revised Council for International Organisations of Medical Sciences guidelines, focused on the observance of ethical norms relevant to the varying cultural environments in these countries for the protection of the research participants. In India, the challenge is to apply universal ethical principles to biomedical research in India's multicultural society, which features a multiplicity of healthcare systems of considerably varying standards. The guidelines were thus revised in 2006 to acknowledge these changes and, in keeping with the national policies and demands of Indian culture, to address ethical issues in specific situations to the extent possible.

Some elements of the international guidelines for biomedical research on human participants with relevance to international collaborative research initiatives (e.g. vaccine trials, herbal products, bio-banking, stem-cell research) have been revised to reflect current ethical requirements and can be applied to research efforts in India from the ethical, legal and social perspective. These guidelines are available on the CDSCO website.

3.4.3 Good clinical practice guidelines

In 2001, CDSCO established a central expert committee in consultation with clinical experts to develop Indian GCP guidelines that would ensure the uniform quality of clinical research throughout the country and that would provide for clinical research that would

Published by Woodhead Publishing Limited, 2012

generate data for the registration of new drugs in India. The Indian GCP guidelines were also to be developed with consideration given to the WHO, ICH, FDA and European GCP guidelines as well as the ICMR's Ethical Guidelines for Biomedical Research on Human Subjects. With the amendment of Schedule Y in 2005, the Drug Technical Advisory Board, the highest technical body under the Drugs and Cosmetics Act, endorsed the adoption of these GCP guidelines for streamlining clinical studies in India.

Guidelines entitled 'Good Clinical Practices for Clinical Research in India' were made mandatory for all stakeholders involved in new drug development and product registration in India. These guidelines are available on the CDSCO website. In 2008, CDSCO issued further industry guidance on the information that should be submitted for biological clinical trials (e.g. vaccines, recombinant products, monoclonal antibodies, blood products) with the goal of simplifying submission requirements. While the submission requirements related to chemistry and pharmaceutical information are detailed more fully in this document, the requirements for the conduct of clinical trials and other requirements remain the same as per Schedule Y of the Drugs and Cosmetic Rules 1945. The new guidance also specifies that the applicant should submit two hard copies and two electronic copies of a submission (i.e. on CD in PDF format). This guidance is also available on the CDSCO website.

3.4.4 Salient features of Indian GCP

India's GCP guidelines are consistent with the ICH's E6 guidelines in both letter and spirit, and the discussions below highlight some of the salient features:

- *Sponsor responsibilities – investigator and institution selection*: The sponsor is responsible for selecting the investigator(s)/institutions after taking into account the appropriateness and availability of the study site and facilities and the necessary qualifications.
- *Contract*: The sponsor should enter into a formal agreement/ contract with the investigator(s)/institution(s) to provide for

Published by Woodhead Publishing Limited, 2012

76 Clinical Research in Asia: Opportunities and Challenges

GCP and protocol compliance, monitoring and auditing visits, record-keeping and other essential elements. The agreement should define the relationship between the investigator and the sponsor in matters such as financial support, fees, honoraria, payments in kind, and other relevant matters. It is the sponsor's responsibility to make arrangements for the secure custody of all study-related documents and materials for a period of three years after the study's completion or the submission of the data to the regulatory authority(ies), whichever is later.

- *Compensation for participants*: In connection with their participation in a research study, subjects may be paid for their inconvenience and time, and should be reimbursed for any study-related expenses. They may also receive free medical services. However, payments should not be so large or the medical services so extensive as to induce prospective subjects to consent to participate in research against their better judgment (inducement). All payments, reimbursement and medical services to be provided to research subjects should be approved by the relevant independent ethics committee.

Indian GCP specifies the following: (1) when a guardian is asked to provide consent on behalf of an incompetent person, no remuneration should be offered except to refund out-of-pocket expenses; (2) when a subject is withdrawn from research for medical reasons related to the study, the subject should receive the benefits associated with full participation; and (3) when a subject withdraws from a study for any other reasons, he/she should be paid in proportion to the degree of participation.

As a prerequisite in study planning, the sponsor is responsible for providing the investigator(s) with an investigator's brochure. In addition, the sponsor is responsible for supplying the investigational products, including comparator(s) and placebo if applicable. The products should be manufactured in accordance with the principles of good manufacturing practices (GMP), and should be packaged in a manner that will protect them from deterioration and that will safeguard blinding procedures (if applicable). The products should include the appropriate investigational labelling.

Published by Woodhead Publishing Limited, 2012

The sponsor should provide adverse drug reaction/adverse experience reporting forms to the participating investigator(s)/institution(s). Further, the sponsor should expedite the reporting of all serious and/or unexpected adverse drug reactions to each of the concerned parties (e.g. the ethics committee and regulatory authorities).

- *Monitoring*: Although a clear and detailed protocol can assure appropriate conduct of the study, the sponsor also should ensure that the studies are adequately monitored. The determination of the extent and the nature of monitoring should be based on considerations such as the study's objective, purpose, design, complexity, blinding, size and endpoints. The sponsor must appoint adequately trained monitors or a CRO to supervise an ongoing study. The monitor should have adequate medical, pharmaceutical and/or scientific qualifications and clinical trial experience. In addition, monitors should be fully aware of all the aspects of both the product under investigation and the clinical trial protocol.

- *Audit*: The sponsor should perform an audit as a part of a quality assurance system. This audit should be independent and separate from routine monitoring or quality control functions.

- *Role of a foreign sponsor*: If the sponsor is a foreign company, organisation or person(s), it must appoint a local representative or CRO to fulfil the appropriate local responsibilities as governed by national regulations. Although the sponsor may transfer any or all of its study-related duties and functions to a CRO, the ultimate responsibility for the quality and the integrity of the study data always resides with the sponsor.

- *Investigator responsibilities – qualifications*: The investigator should be qualified by education, training and experience to assume responsibility for the proper conduct of the study, and should have qualifications prescribed by the Medical Council of India (e.g. have qualifications, such as MD, MS, MBBS, recognised by the Medical Council of India, and be registered with the Medical Council of India). He/she should clearly understand the study-related time and resource demands, and ensure that the site can meet these demands for the duration of the study. A qualified medical practitioner (or a dentist, when

78   Clinical Research in Asia: Opportunities and Challenges

appropriate) who is an investigator or a co-investigator for the study should be responsible for all study-related medical decisions. The investigator must ensure that adequate medical care is provided to a subject for any adverse events, including clinically significant laboratory values related to the study.

- *Communication with ethics committee*: Before initiating a study, the investigator/institution must ensure that the proposed study has been reviewed and accepted in writing by the relevant ethics committee(s). The ethics committee must review the protocol, the written informed consent form, subject recruitment procedures (e.g. advertisements) and any written/verbal information to be provided to the subjects.

  The investigator should promptly report the following to the ethics committee, the monitor and the sponsor:

  - deviations from, or changes in, the protocol to eliminate immediate hazards to the subjects;
  - changes that increase the risk to subject(s) and/or that significantly affect the study's conduct;
  - all adverse drug reactions and adverse events that are serious and/or unexpected;
  - new information that may adversely affect the safety of the subjects or the conduct of the study;
  - for reported deaths, the investigator should supply any additional information (e.g. autopsy reports and terminal medical reports).

- *Investigational product(s)*: The investigator has the primary responsibility for investigational product(s) accountability at the study site(s). The investigator should maintain records of the product's delivery to the study site, the inventory at the site, the product's use by each subject, and the return to the sponsor or the alternative disposal of the unused product(s).

- *Selection and recruitment of study subjects*: The investigator is responsible for ensuring the unbiased selection of an adequate number of suitable subjects according to the protocol. It may be necessary to secure the cooperation of other physicians in order to obtain a sufficient number of subjects.

Published by Woodhead Publishing Limited, 2012

Clinical research in India 79

- *Informed consent of study subjects*: Prior to study initiation, the investigator(s) should obtain the ethics committee's approval for the written informed consent form and all information to be provided to prospective subjects and/or their legal representatives or guardians as well as any impartial witnesses. Before the subject's participation in the study, the written informed consent form should be signed and personally dated by:

  - (i) the subject, or (ii) if the subject is incapable of giving informed consent (e.g. children, patients who are unconscious or are suffering from severe mental illness or disability), by the subject's legal representative or guardian, or (iii) if the subject and his/her legal representative or guardian are unable to read/ write, an impartial witness who should be present during the entire informed consent discussion; and

  - the investigator.

  The information should be provided to the subjects and/or their legal representatives or guardians in a language and at a level of complexity that is understandable to the subject(s) in both written and oral form, whenever possible. Subjects and their legal representatives or guardians should be provided ample opportunity and time to enquire about the details of the study. All questions should be answered to their satisfaction.

- *Ethics committee*: The sponsor and/or investigator should seek the opinion of an independent ethics committee regarding the suitability of the protocol, the methods and documents to be used in subject recruitment and in obtaining the informed consent of study subjects (including the adequacy of the information to be provided to the subjects). Ethics committees are entrusted not only with the initial review of the proposed research protocols before study start-up, but also with the regular monitoring of the ethics of the approved programmes through study completion. The fundamental responsibility of an ethics committee is to provide a competent review of all ethical aspects of clinical study proposals, and to conduct such a review free from any bias and influence that could affect its objectivity.

Published by Woodhead Publishing Limited, 2012

80 Clinical Research in Asia: Opportunities and Challenges

- *Review procedures*: An ethics committee should review each clinical research proposal. Ethics committees should ensure that a scientific evaluation has been completed before ethical review is taken up. Many Indian sites have both a scientific committee and an ethics committee to review proposed clinical protocols. Ethics committees should take up their review only after the scientific committee provides positive feedback on the protocol. For those sites with just a single committee, the committee must undertake the scientific review first, followed by the ethics review (i.e. assuming the scientific review is positive). The ethical review should be done through formal, convened meetings (i.e. not decisions reached after the distribution of proposals). Decisions (e.g. approval, rejection, modifications) must be reached through a broad consensus after the quorum requirements are fulfilled. If one of the committee members has her/his own research proposal under review, then the member should not participate in committee deliberations regarding the project. Negative decisions should always be supported by documented and clearly defined reasons.
- *Ethics committee approval*: India's regulatory framework allows for the concurrent submission of clinical research applications for regulatory and ethics committee approval. Each identified site will have its own institutional ethics committee, and each investigator will submit the essential documents, including the translation of the informed consent form and patient information sheets, to his/her institution's ethics committee. Most institutional ethics committees meet once a month and call for study-related documents to be submitted one week prior to the meeting. The ethics committee's approval letter is issued within one week following the meeting. Although India has a few centralised ethics committees, most investigators prefer to obtain approval from their institution's ethics committee. Exceptions include investigators who work for private clinics that lack their own ethics committees. The proposed Schedule Y1 guidelines would mandate registration of CROs and the strict adherence to standard operating procedures by individuals, institutions or organisations conducting clinical trials in the country. This

Published by Woodhead Publishing Limited, 2012

requirement is viewed by the industry as a positive move and will make India the first country in the world to implement a CRO registration requirement. The proposed guidelines are available on the CDSCO website.

3.5 Clinical trial approval

A clinical trial for a new drug can be initiated only after the licensing authority (the DCGI) has granted its permission and after the ethics committees of the relevant sites have approved the research. To obtain the DCGI's review and approval, the sponsor must seek permission by completing Form 44 and submitting it with the data specified in the Appendices of Schedule Y (amended 2005) of the Drugs and Cosmetics Act 1940, along with an application for the import of a new drug. The DCGI takes 8–12 weeks to review the information and grant regulatory approval for the initiation of a clinical trial in India.

3.5.1 Import permission and processing time

An application for the import of drugs must be submitted concurrently with the regulatory permission letter to the DCGI. The application must be made on Form 12 of the Drugs and Cosmetic Rules 1945 for importing the compounds to be involved in the trial (i.e. investigational product, comparators, placebo, etc.). The application should provide a detailed calculation of the quantity of drugs required for the study, and should specify the country from which these drugs are to be imported. In response, the DCGI issues a test licence (popularly known as a 'T licence') on Form 11 of the Drugs and Cosmetic Rules for the import of drugs. As this application is made concurrently, the test licence is obtained along with the permission for the clinical trial. Companies are therefore not allowed to import the drugs without both DCGI approval and a test licence. The test licence is effective for one year. Through the concurrent submission and approval process outlined above, regulatory

Published by Woodhead Publishing Limited, 2012

82   Clinical Research in Asia: Opportunities and Challenges

permission for the clinical trial, import permission and ethics committee approvals are available within 8–12 weeks of the submission of a completed application.

3.5.2 Export of biological samples – the formalities

Sponsors/sponsor representatives that intend to export human biological specimens (e.g. tissues, blood, etc.) from India for test purposes must apply for a 'no objection certificate' (NOC) by providing the details of the laboratory from which the blood/plasma sample is to be exported, the tests and procedures to be performed with the sample, the quantity of blood/plasma and the number of samples to be collected from each subject, and the number of shipments to be exported. A declaration from the central laboratory shall also be submitted along with the application stating that the blood/plasma samples collected within India will not be misused for genetic purposes or in any other manner. To streamline the approval process for the export of biological specimens for clinical trials, CDSCO has provided the draft templates through which the applicant can submit an application to the DCGI seeking export approval. The template of the no objection certificate is also available in the CDSCO website.

In summary, these efforts undertaken by the DCGI and the Director General of Foreign Trade in collaboration have significantly reduced delays in obtaining permission to export biological samples.

The DCGI has provided clarification on the types of clinical trial amendments that must be submitted to its office for pre-approval as well as those that must be submitted only for notification purposes (i.e. those that do not require pre-approval prior to implementation):

- *Those amendments that do not require notification to or permission of the regulatory authority*: (i) administrative and logistic changes, (ii) minor protocol amendments and additional safety assessments when the institutional ethics committee has already approved these changes.
- *Those amendments that require notification to the regulatory authority but need not wait for approval*: (i) addition of new

Published by Woodhead Publishing Limited, 2012

investigational sites, (ii) a change in the principal investigator with the consent of the previous investigator, (iii) amended investigator's brochure, amended informed consent.

- *Those amendments that require prior approval of the regulatory authority*: (i) additional patients to be recruited (i.e. beyond the number projected in the initial clinical trial application), (ii) major protocol changes with respect to study design, dose and treatment options, (iii) any change in inclusion or exclusion criteria.

In doing this, and in permitting the implementation of larger numbers of changes based on the approval of an ethics committee alone, the DCGI has taken steps to eliminate trial-related delays. Nonetheless, the DCGI's notification does specify that each type of amendment must be approved by the relevant institutional ethics committee before the changes identified in an amendment are implemented.

3.6 Difference between ICH-GCP and Indian GCP

While India's GCP requirements for clinical trials are largely consistent with ICH-GCP standards, some country-specific standards are more stringent – for ethics committees in particular. ICH-GCP standards stipulate five members on an ethics committee, in line with the generally accepted understanding that a quorum requires a minimum of five persons. Indian GCP guidelines also allow the number of persons to be kept fairly small (5–7 members), but there is no specific recommendation for an acceptable maximum number of persons. That said, one should keep in mind that too large a committee will make it difficult to reach a consensus opinion. Indian GCP guidelines also require the chairperson to be otherwise independent from the institution itself, a requirement that initially forced composition changes in many of India's ethics committees.

The member secretary, who generally works for the institution, should conduct the business of the committee. Other members should be a mix of medical/non-medical, scientific and non-scientific

Published by Woodhead Publishing Limited, 2012

84   Clinical Research in Asia: Opportunities and Challenges

persons, including members of the lay public to reflect different viewpoints. A typical composition may be as follows:

- chairperson;
- one or two basic medical scientists (preferably one pharmacologist);
- one or two clinicians from different institutes;
- one legal expert or retired judge;
- one social scientist/representative of a non-governmental voluntary agency;
- one philosopher/ethicist/theologian;
- one lay person from the community;
- member secretary.

As the clinical research industry is still emerging in India, Schedule Y provides a complete template for institutional review board approval letters so that discrepancies in such letters can be avoided. This template can be customised for specific studies and situations.

In addition, Schedule Y provides a format for what is called the 'undertaking by investigator', which each participating investigator completes before the study is initiated. This form is submitted to the regulatory authorities and is as detailed as the FDA 1572 Statement of the Investigator form used in FDA-regulated studies.

The Schedule Y guidelines also provide a checklist of essential documents that must be submitted to the institutional ethics committee for approval.

As far as record-keeping is concerned, Indian GCP guidelines recommend that ethics committees maintain all records securely after the completion/termination of the study for at least five years (i.e. if it is not possible to maintain the same permanently).

3.6.1 Regulatory standards for Phase I and Phase 0 trials

India has special requirements or standards for conducting Phase I first-in-man trials within the country. Most importantly, India does not generally permit Phase I first-in-man studies for new drug

Clinical research in India

substances discovered in other countries, unless the sponsor has Phase I data from other countries to support the safety of such studies in India. However, such trials may be permitted, even in the absence of Phase I data from other countries, if the drug is of special relevance to health problems within India. For new drug substances that have been discovered within the country, Phase I first-in-man clinical trials are allowed in India. In this case, sponsors need to apply for regulatory permission to carry out these trials and, in so doing, must provide the complete results of the pre-clinical and toxicology studies.

To date, Phase 0 or microdosing trials have not been allowed under Indian regulations. There is no doubt that, while India provides a good sample base in terms of its population diversity, gene pool and disease base, it lacks experience in Phase I and Phase 0 trials. Specifically, the DCGI is concerned that India lacks a domestic manufacturer for accelerator mass spectrometry, a technique used in microdosing and Phase 0 trials to obtain information about how a drug candidate is being absorbed, distributed and excreted in humans.

3.7 Regulatory inspections in India

There are no formal data regarding GCP compliance issues in India. The DCGI has recently inspected a few Indian sites, and that it has issued warning letters (e.g. to the site and the CRO/sponsor) for noncompliance with GCP. This initiative is a step forward in ensuring the quality of clinical research in India.

In addition, the ICMR has reviewed the work of independent ethics committees through a survey. The most common findings included a lack of written standard operating procedures for ethics committees, record-keeping issues, and problems regarding the constitution of ethics committees. Based on the survey, regulators have updated existing guidelines and developed new ones, and are pursuing several initiatives through international collaborations with WHO, NIH, FDA, and other bodies to build capacity in bioethics. To improve the situation, the ICMR has published

Published by Woodhead Publishing Limited, 2012

86 Clinical Research in Asia: Opportunities and Challenges

'Guidelines for Preparing Standard Operating Procedures (SOP) for Institutional Ethics Committee or Human Research'. The guidelines are available on the ICMR website.

FDA inspections in India provide some indications of GCP compliance rates. By the end of 2010, the US FDA had conducted 17 inspections of Indian clinical investigators. Nine were found to be in full compliance with GCP and FDA standards (a finding of no action indicated). The remaining eight investigators were cited for minor violations of GCP standards, all of which could be addressed through voluntary actions by the clinical investigators (a finding of voluntary action indicated). The citations included three for failure to follow the investigational plan, seven for inadequate drug accountability, and five for inadequate/inaccurate records.

In addition, the EMEA has conducted nine GCP inspections in India during recent years. While the agency has not released data on its findings, EMEA officials report that findings from GCP compliance inspections of sites located in emerging countries have not triggered any particular concerns.

3.8 Clinical research in India: PESTLE analysis

As an increasing number of clinical research outsourcing activities in India are being initiated by global sponsors (pharmaceutical, biotech and contract research organisations), the country will face many challenges due to barriers created by political, geographical, socio-economic, cultural and environmental factors. The stakeholders of clinical research, including the regulators, investigators and sponsors and/or CROs, will have to play a major role when designing their programme to take into account the India-specific factors.

3.8.1 Political factors

India consists of 28 states and seven union territories with a parliamentary system of democracy. Economic reforms since 1991 have transformed it into one of the fastest-growing economies in the

Published by Woodhead Publishing Limited, 2012

world. India is considered to be a potential superpower, having a rapidly-growing economy and growing political clout. It is a member of the United Nations, Commonwealth of Nations, the South Asian Association for Regional Cooperation, the Non-aligned Movement and many other global forums, as well as one of the BRIC group of countries. A pluralistic, multilingual and multiethnic society, India is considered a hub of clinical research. The political system favours the growth of quality clinical and biotechnological research by providing necessary healthcare infrastructure under the public healthcare system. The healthcare education supplies the quality human resources for the sustenance of clinical research business.

3.8.1.1 Government initiatives for clinical research

While the Indian government has undertaken several initiatives to implement ethical guidelines for the conduct of global clinical research, it has also implemented product patent regulations and data protection norms to attract global business. It has streamlined the regulatory approval, import and export permission process to a single-window approach and reduced approval timelines significantly. The DCGI also reviews the clinical study reports submitted by sponsors/investigators to assess compliance with GCP standards. The DCGI plans to begin regulatory audits as a way to ensure compliance with Schedule Y requirements and GCP standards. The DCGI has inspected a few Indian sites and has issued warning letters (i.e. to the site and CRO/ sponsor) regarding noncompliance with GCP standards. This initiative is another step forward in promoting quality clinical research in India.

The Medical Council of India, the appellate body regulating the country's medical practitioners through various state medical councils, has recently finalised a code of conduct designed to prevent doctors from being influenced by drug manufacturer's gifts and other disguised bribes. The code prohibits doctors from receiving gifts, travel, monetary grants, medical research, endorsements, etc., from companies. The notification on 10 December 2009, amended the Indian Medical Council (Professional Conduct, Etiquette and Ethics), Regulations 2002, which stipulates the guidelines to be followed by medical practitioners in the country.

Published by Woodhead Publishing Limited, 2012

88 Clinical Research in Asia: Opportunities and Challenges

Further, the DCGI has pursued a series of short and long-term goals designed specifically to strengthen clinical trial regulations in India. Various short-term goals of 2008–10 have already been met and include:

- robust review process for clinical trial proposals;
- mandatory registration of clinical trials in a centralised clinical trial registry (*www.ctri.in*);
- expediting the inspection process by identifying and training personnel specifically for clinical trials site inspections (the inspection of clinical trial sites in India will be an ongoing activity, and checklists for the inspection process are being developed);

Some of the short-term goals which are still in the process of review by the Drug Technology Advisory Board and other designated committee are:

- the registration of CROs;
- harmonisation of regulations on toxicity;
- definitions for Phase I consistent with ICH guidelines and support for the development of regulations and infrastructure for early-stage studies (i.e. first-in-man studies, including Phase 0 or micro-dosing).

The DCGI's goals for 2011–12 include the following:

- formulating guidelines for the registration of ethics committees/ institutional review boards;
- the registration of clinical trial sites and investigators;
- GCP training of investigators by an accredited body;
- penalties for the violation of clinical trial regulations;
- conducting micro-dosing studies (i.e. first-in-man or Phase 0).

The DCGI has improved its infrastructure and facilities (after moving to new facilities). Since completing its move, the DCGI has also recruited additional staff to facilitate the approval process. India's drug regulator is also collaborating with the US FDA to

Published by Woodhead Publishing Limited, 2012

Clinical research in India **89**

improve its functioning in several areas, including monitoring drugs for adverse reactions, regulating medical equipment and devices, and increasing its international reach.

3.8.1.2 Government initiatives for biotechnology research

The Indian government, through its Ministry of Science and Technology, has the Department of Biotechnology as the nodal agency for policy, promotion of R&D, international cooperation and manufacturing activities in the biotech segment. Since the mid-1980s, the agency has focused on generating resources, manpower and infrastructure to invest in areas such as genomics, proteomics, transgenics, stem-cell research and product development. Recently, it has devised a very optimistic and rational national biotechnology development strategy recommending several strategies and interventions for human resource development, infrastructure development and manufacturing, promotion of industry and trade, biotechnology parks and incubators, regulatory mechanisms and public communication, and participation in the country's biotechnology revolution. This draft policy directive draws the blueprint for sectoral road maps in different segments of biotechnology, including agriculture, industrial biotechnology, preventive and therapeutic medical biotechnology, regenerative and genomic medicine, diagnostic biotechnology, bio-engineering and nano-biotechnology, bio-informatics and IT-enabled biotechnology, clinical biotechnology and research services, and intellectual property and patent law. Besides the initiatives of private entrepreneurs in the biotech business, major research in India is carried out at government-funded research institutes. Table 3.6 lists research institutes in India. Thanks to the research carried out in these institutions, there have been major achievements in basic biosciences in the last decade or so in India, and the country has expertise in practically all areas of modern science.

3.8.1.3 Public healthcare system

Despite improvements, the healthcare system in India is still considered relatively unadvanced and it is not supported by

Published by Woodhead Publishing Limited, 2012

90 Clinical Research in Asia: Opportunities and Challenges

Table 3.6 Research institutes in India

Institute	URL	Location
Centre for DNA Fingerprinting and Diagnostics	www.cdfd.org.in	Hyderabad
Institute of Bioresources and Sustainable Development	www.ibsd-imphal.nic.in	Manipur
Institute of Life Sciences	www.ilsc.org	Bhubaneswar
National Institute of Immunology	www.nii.res.in	New Delhi
National Centre for Plant Genome Research	www.ncpgr.nic.in	New Delhi
National Brain Research Centre	www.nbrc.ac.in	Gurgaon
National Centre for Cell Sciences	www.nccs.res.in	Pune
Bharat Immunologicals and Biologicals Corporation Ltd.		Bulandshahar
Indian Vaccines Corporation Limited	www.ipcl.co.in/html/ aboutus/joint_ventures.html	Gurgaon
Council of Scientific and Industrial Research	www.csir.res.in	
Center for Human Genetics	www.chg.ecu.edu.au/ index.html	Bangalore
National Chemical Laboratory	www.ncl-india.org	Pune
National Institute of Biologicals		New Delhi
Center for Cellular and Molecular Biology	www.ccmb.res.in	
Central Drug Research Institute	www.cdriindia.org	Lucknow

government-aided social security or universal health insurance. Private medical support is very costly and beyond the financial reach of most people. Thus, the majority of the population still remains largely dependent on government-run subsidised healthcare facilities, even if these facilities are dispersed in diverse geographical locations. The country has 11,613 hospitals, with a total of 540,328 beds. Of these, some 6,281 hospitals, totalling 143,069 beds, are in rural areas, while 3,115 hospitals, totalling 369,351 beds, are in urban

Published by Woodhead Publishing Limited, 2012

areas. Besides the urban and rural hospitals, India is home to 146,036 subcentres, 23,458 primary health centres and 4,276 community health centres (Table 3.7).

Many of the trust or government-run referral hospitals that specialise in certain therapeutic areas are found in major cities and towns. These hospitals have gained popularity because of their subsidised nature, high quality and advanced treatment options. Much like common brand names, some of these hospitals are well known nationally; examples include CMC (Christian Medical College, Vellore), Tata (Tata Memorial Hospital, Mumbai) and AIIMS (All India Institute of Medical Science, Delhi).

Healthcare delivery is also being corporatised, with an increased number of corporate hospitals in multiple locations, mostly concentrated in big cities. Corporate chains of hospitals with state-of-the-art facilities include, among others, Apollo Hospitals, Wockhardt Hospitals, Fortis Healthcare, Max Healthcare, Manipal Health Systems, Care Hospital, Hiranandani Hospital.

3.8.1.4 Government initiatives in healthcare education

Indian healthcare education is much advanced and follows Western standards. Medical, nursing and paramedical personnel in India can learn both allopathic and alternative (ayurvedic, unani, siddha,

Table 3.7 Healthcare infrastructure in India (March 2008)

Type of facility	Number	Beds
Rural hospital	6,281	143,069
Urban hospital	3,115	369,351
Subcentre	146,036	
Primary health centre	23,458	
Community health centre	4,276	
Alternative medicine hospital	3,378	
Alternative medicine dispensary	22,312	

Source: Health Statistics in India, MOHFW/GOI

Published by Woodhead Publishing Limited, 2012

92 Clinical Research in Asia: Opportunities and Challenges

homoeopathic – AYUSH) medicines. The country's educational infrastructure provides opportunities for students to pursue graduate (MBBS/BDS) and postgraduate qualifications (MD) in medical and dental colleges. Those interested in pursuing education in alternative medicine can get admission to AYUSH institutes, nursing courses and paramedical courses. Medical education infrastructures in the country have shown rapid growth during the last 19 years. The country has 300 medical colleges, 290 colleges for BDS courses and 140 colleges that conduct MDS courses; total admissions were 34,595, 23,520 and 2,644 respectively during 2009–10. As of March 2009, there were 2,311 nursing institutes, with aggregate admission capacity of 75,789, and 561 pharmaceutical colleges, with aggregate capacity of 33,635 (Table 3.8).

The number of allopathic doctors possessing medical qualifications recognised under the Indian Medical Council Act 1956 and registered with state medical councils for the years 2008 and 2009 were 736,743 and 757,377 respectively. The number of dental surgeons registered with the central/state dental councils of India up to December 2008 was 93,332. The total number of registered AYUSH doctors in India was 761,673, as at 1 January 2009.

Even though the absolute number of healthcare resources looks great, the average population served by a single allopathic doctor, dental surgeon, AYUSH doctor, nurse and pharmacist is 1,533, 12,438, 1,544, 725 and 1,770 respectively (Figure 3.7).

Table 3.8 Healthcare education infrastructure in India, 2009–10

Institution type	Number	Annual capacity
Medical college	300	34,595
Dental college	290	23,520
Alternative medicine college	492	30,086
Nursing institute	2,311	75,789
Pharmacy institute	561	33,635

Source: Health Statistics in India, MOHFW/GOI

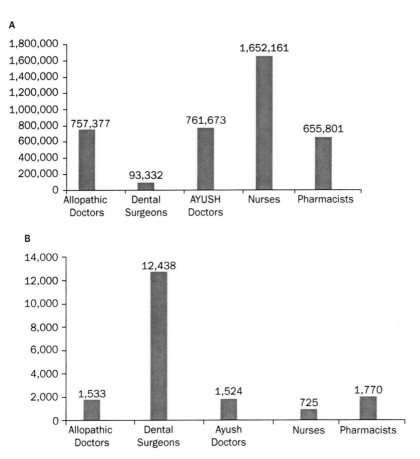

Figure 3.7 Healthcare resources in India: (a) absolute numbers, 2009; (b) average population served by one professional

Source: Medical, Dental, AYUSH, Nursing and Pharmacy Council of India

3.8.2 Economic factors

Over last few decades, the Indian government has invested significantly in health and healthcare research. Over the last two decades, investment in health outlays has increased almost 10-fold, from $3,134 million spent during the eighth five-year plan period to estimated planned outlays of $31,141 million during the 11th five-year plan (Figure 3.8).

During 2006, government expenditure on health as a percentage of total expenditure on health was 25 per cent, while that of private

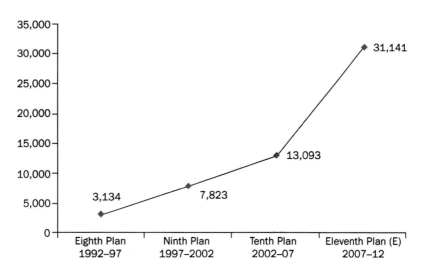

Figure 3.8 Health Investment outlays, 1992–2012

Source: Planning Commission of India

expenditure was 75 per cent. Public spending on health in India has increased from 0.22 per cent of GDP in 1950–51 to 1.05 per cent of GDP during the mid-1980s, stagnating at around 0.9 per cent of gross domestic product (GDP) during later years. India's spending on healthcare is now approximately 4.25 per cent of GDP at market prices (Table 3.9).

3.8.2.1 Tax incentives

The Indian government has waived the service tax of 12.36 per cent for CROs/pharma companies involved in clinical trials or the technical testing and analysis for new drugs, vaccines and herbal remedies. This exemption is being granted to promote clinical trial outsourcing in India. There are no other tax incentives provided to promote clinical research in the country.

3.8.2.2 Price control mechanism

India's generics industry has revolutionised the control of drug prices globally. This price control is achieved by internal competition followed

Clinical research in India 95

Table 3.9 Health expenditure in India

Type of expenditure	2005–06	2006–07	2007–08	2008–09
Public expenditure ($m)	7,655	9,040	10,819	13,040
Private expenditure ($m)	25,556	28,409	31,709	34,976
External flows ($m)	477	498	590	823
Total expenditure ($m)	33,687	37,947	43,118	48,839
GDP ($m)	795,632	921,291.1	1,049,644	1,182,612
Health expenditure as % of GDP	4.23	4.12	4.11	4.13
Public expenditure as % of GDP	0.96	0.98	1.03	1.10

Source: MOHFW/GOI Report

by significant government support. A comparison of drug prices in India and USA for some of the key drugs available in the pharmaceutical market highlights the role of the Indian pharmaceutical industry in controlling the spiralling increase of drug prices (Table 3.10).

3.8.3 Socio-economic-cultural factors

In its 'Belmont Report' of 1979, the US FDA's National Commission for the Protection of Human Subjects of Biomedical and Behavioral

Table 3.10 A comparison of drug prices, USA vs India

Drug	Dosage	US price		Indian price	
Lipitor	10 mg	$2.41	(Rs 113.27)	$0.17	(Rs 7.99)
Omeprazole	20 mg	$3.53	(Rs 165.90)	$0.11	(Rs 5.17)
Plavix	75 mg	$4.25	(Rs 199.75)	$0.17	(Rs 7.99)
Zantac	150 mg	$2.10	(Rs 98.70)	$0.02	(Rs 0.94)
Zocor	20 mg	$4.25	(Rs 199.75)	$0.35	(Rs 16.45)
Hepatitis B vaccine	1 vial	$4.50	(Rs 211.50)	$0.50	(Rs 23.50)
R human insulin	100 IU	$2.50	(Rs 117.50)	$0.75	(Rs 35.25)
Rotavirus vaccine	1 vial	$35.00	(Rs 1,645.00)	$0.50	(Rs 23.50)

Source: Newsweek

Published by Woodhead Publishing Limited, 2012

96 Clinical Research in Asia: Opportunities and Challenges

Research highlighted the ethical principles and guidelines for the protection of human research subjects. In the context of this report, three basic principles (respect for persons, beneficence and justice) are among those generally accepted in the Indian cultural tradition and are particularly relevant to the ethics of research involving human subjects. Yet research involving human subjects remains somewhat contentious, and many fear that the impoverishment, illiteracy and social ills in Indian society may have an impact on the ethical conduct of a clinical trial.

It is a common belief that that impoverished people with less education cannot decide of their free will and may through economic compulsion end up participating in a clinical trial. Numerous observers argue against this belief, however, and point out the danger of generalisations. Indeed, poverty and illiteracy should not be mistaken for a lack of common sense or intelligence, and potential subjects should be capable of making decisions on their own. Potential subjects may not comprehend the complicated statistical design of a clinical trial, but if the investigator engages them through proper coaching and guidance, they will be exposed to adequate information. In this manner they can weigh up the facts and decide whether or not to participate – if they are not convinced, they simply will not participate in the trial. It must be remembered that the rich and literate are no less committed to their life and to their families than the poor and uneducated. Just because they are on the lower social strata, one cannot take their willingness to volunteer for granted; indeed, gaining their participation can be very hard.

Many consider impoverishment to be a compelling factor for potential subjects in India to become involved in clinical trials. But if one examines the existing healthcare system, the majority of the impoverished population already depend on free or subsidised treatment from government-run hospitals and dispensaries as there is no universal healthcare in India. Participating in a clinical trial may thus be seen by the subjects as a means to ease some of their additional economic burdens in terms of medication and treatments. In some studies, the trial design demands additional visits for tests and procedures. In such instances, the sponsor provides compensation towards the conveyance, stay, and loss of wages for the subject and

Published by Woodhead Publishing Limited, 2012

other earning members of the family, as well as incidental expenses. This acts as a motivation and improves subject compliance and retention. Similarly, as few patients from low economic strata have storage infrastructure, if the investigational product is very temperature-sensitive, the sponsors may have to provide pool-refrigerators for patient use, either through a facility attached to investigator's site or through the patients' local physicians. These represent genuine compensation and logistical support for the trial subjects and cannot be construed as an inducement or compulsion for enrolment. At first glance, some of these costs represent additional burdens to the sponsor if the trial is undertaken in India. However, these costs rarely represent a major expense and should be balanced with the rapid recruitment potential in India and the increased subject retention. Poor and illiterate subjects are generally more compliant as they are very sincere and follow protocol tests and procedures as per the instruction and advice of the physician.

To eliminate any concern regarding potential exploitation in developing countries because of illiteracy and poverty, it is in the interest of every pharmaceutical sponsor to maintain high ethical standards for clinical trials. However, where sponsors act with fairness and respect in equal measure, there can be no accusations of exploitation.

3.8.4 Cultural factors

India has diverse cultures across its geographic territory. If one travels from north to south and east to west, various local dialects, sub-dialects, varied festivities and lifestyles will be found. Not surprisingly, communication is achieved through more than one major language. Table 3.11 summarises the languages in India.

Although the official language of the union is Hindi as per the constitution and, barring a few states in southern region, most people understand Hindi, English remains the language used for all official purposes. All higher education in India (i.e. bachelor's, master's and doctoral programmes) is conducted in English. Hence, although culturally India is a Hindi-speaking community, because of

98   Clinical Research in Asia: Opportunities and Challenges

Table 3.11 Languages in India

Northern	Southern	Western	Eastern
Hindi	Tamil	Gujarati	Oriya
Punjabi	Telugu	Marathi	Bengali
Haryani	Malayalam	Konkani	Assamese
Kashmiri	Kanada		Manipuri
Urdu			

the educational system, physicians, nurses, monitors and most literate subjects speak, write and understand English. Even India's judicial and governing institutions, health ministry, regulatory bodies and ethics committees use English as the language for day-to-day communication and management.

Nonetheless, it is a fact that many people are illiterate or able to read, write and speak in their local language only. With this in mind, sponsors and other clinical research stakeholders should make every effort to design information sheets in local languages so they may be understood easily by subjects and their relatives. Proper counselling and thorough guidance from the investigators are also essential in the Indian context. Although mentoring the subjects may demand a lot of time, it is vital for recruitment and retention.

Many other cultural factors have major effects on patient recruitment and retention. Indians celebrate many festivals and cultural programmes and each community has its own set of cultural functions. For example, with poorer, working-class subjects, the harvest season is an important period during which the family members work together to earn their livelihood for the entire year. Patient inflows to hospitals tend to be smaller during festival and harvest seasons, thus leading to slower subject recruitment. Cultural programmes sometimes even compel subjects to miss scheduled follow-up visits should they fall during those days. As such, knowledgeable investigators sometimes change the schedule of visits, window periods and drug dispensing patterns depending on their subjects' cultural factors. Investigators also arrange for the necessary staff, translators, study nurse, and other personnel, who can understand their subjects' cultural differences and languages in a trial context.

Published by Woodhead Publishing Limited, 2012

Another cultural practice to consider is that of the senior male family member (whether the father or the husband) taking charge of the decision-making process. This can manifest as female subjects giving their consent to participate only after consultation with the appropriate male member of their family. With respect to unmarried female subjects, another important socio-cultural issue is that they feel offended if asked to perform pregnancy tests – a common requirement in almost all clinical trial protocols. As such, it is all the more important for the investigator to understand the cultural values of the society and educate both the subject and the leading member of the family to ensure proper compliance.

Another cultural factor in the Indian scenario is that subjects have deep respect for study physicians. Indeed, subjects are very compliant vis-à-vis the instructions and advice of the study physicians. Such cultural values help the study in terms of fast recruitment and better retention. However, this cultural factor also bestows a lot of responsibilities and demands on the physicians to behave appropriately without neglecting patient care and/or abusing their patients' trust.

3.8.5 Technology factors

India has proven competence in IT. Most research in the pharmaceutical arena is driven by IT or IT-enabled service providers. For the collection of data, data transfer and data analysis, EDC is gaining prominence. For online data entry and transfer without data loss, EDC needs robust internet connectivity as well as data security. The success of India's IT industry has helped the country to upgrade quickly and adapt to the changing needs of technology in the clinical research domain. The telecom revolution has enabled several million internet users in India. However, the IT infrastructure and connectivity in most hospital and investigator sites are not fully developed. Although one may find computers and web-connectivity in numerous public and trust hospitals, it is not necessarily for the exclusive use of the investigators. As such, many trials using advanced EDC or remote data capture may ask the sponsor to provide dedicated laptop and/or broadband connectivity with appropriate security

100 Clinical Research in Asia: Opportunities and Challenges

features. Most private hospitals in corporate setups, however, have such technology already in place.

Medical technology for the treatment and care of patients in India is relatively advanced. One will find the most advanced equipment and medical devices in most public and private referral hospitals in India. There may be exceptions (for example, bone-scan facilities may not be available in many small hospitals), but if required, patients can be referred to the nearest city-based centre.

Clinical research also needs support from other technologies, including manufacturing, packaging and labelling technology, laboratory technologies, and cool-chain service technology for the storage and distribution of drugs. Today, India has a significant number of US FDA approved manufacturing facilities providing cost-effective global-standard services, including global central laboratory services providers and reliable cool-chain service providers (Table 3.12).

In India, there are more than 30 strong networks/associations of physicians in different therapeutic areas. These associations are active and meet at frequent intervals at regional and national levels. Most of these associations have a website and publish their research articles in their association journals. Each association has membership

Table 3.12 Technology-driven service providers in India

Manufacturing, packaging and labelling	Central laboratory services	Cool-chain service providers
Jubilant	Specialty Ranbaxy	World Courier
Shasun	Quest	Marken
Divi's	Quintiles	TNT
Bilcare	Pathlab	
Aurigene Advinus	Metropolis	
GVK		
Dr Reddy's Dishman		
Nicholas		
Suven		

Source: Media reports

in the range of 300–500 physicians. As such, all the investigators associated in a clinical trial programme interact to facilitate investigator and subject participation.

3.8.6 Environmental factors

The Indian environment offers many challenges for global clinical research. These include differences in the practices of medical professionals, the availability of alternative medicines, the standard of care and the ease or difficulty in recruitment or retention of trial subjects. Some important environmental factors are highlighted below.

3.8.6.1 Standard of care

Although clinical practice in India is more or less driven by Western education, heavy patient load means that, in normal circumstances, senior physicians tend to dedicate less time and attention to routine patients compared with clinical trial subjects. In larger referral hospitals, routine patients sometimes have to wait a longer period for treatment than their counterpart who is participating in a clinical trial. Although the routine patients are given proper treatment, the clinical trial subjects are given special personalised care by the participating investigator and study staff. This acts as an indirect motivation for subject recruitment and retention.

As most clinical trial protocols are designed using criteria suitable for normal Western populations, it is important to consider ethnic factors for studies in India. Likewise, compared with the Western equivalent, there is a perceptible difference in the stage and severity of disease at presentation in India. This makes it difficult to recruit patients with disease at an early stage or with a mild to moderate severity. For example, most cancer patients in India present at an advanced stage of growth (stage III) and hence do not meet the trial inclusion criteria. Thus, looking solely at the total number of patients with a particular disease does not provide accurate information when determining the recruitment potential.

Published by Woodhead Publishing Limited, 2012

102 Clinical Research in Asia: Opportunities and Challenges

Because of socio-economic factors, many effective evidence-based treatments and practices are not performed in large numbers of Indian patients. For example, the inclusion of a breast cancer patient who had previously failed on Herceptin (trastuzumab) therapy may be more difficult because a large number of patients may not have received this treatment due to cost considerations, even though it may be considered an effective treatment.

Another area of concern in recruitment and retention is the widespread practice of alternative medicines in India. Many subjects may have pursued such treatment but have insufficient documentation of their history and treatment; such patients may not be considered for recruitment in a clinical trial scenario. Furthermore, if the clinical trial procedure, in the subject's opinion, is painful, time-consuming and yields no discernible result, it is conceivable that they may migrate to these less costly alternative methods of treatment.

Another issue of concern is the lack of adequate hospital records and treatment histories for many subjects receiving outpatient treatment. Clearly, without a proper clinical history it is difficult to identify suitable potential subjects for trial. Looking at the current trends, however, many investigators have started creating suitable databases of potential subjects with chronic diseases, and this will facilitate the recruitment process over time.

3.8.6.2 Subject recruitment and retention

Global pharmaceutical and biotech sponsors spend an average of 6 per cent of their clinical trial budgets on advertising and marketing to facilitate subject recruitment. In spite of this level of investment, 86 per cent of these trials fail to meet enrolment expectations. Furthermore, more than 80 per cent of trials worldwide fail to enrol on time. This failure to recruit patients on time leads to a significant loss of time and money. Subject recruitment thus remains one of the main challenges for sponsors internationally. To address this, sponsors are seeking innovative solutions and experimenting with emerging global territories with larger pools of potential clinical trial subjects. To this end, India is an ideal territory for meeting recruitment expectations quickly; indeed, such is India's capacity for

Published by Woodhead Publishing Limited, 2012

fast subject recruitment that it outstrips that of Western countries even without overt advertisement and recruitment campaigns.

Nonetheless, some Indian investigators do not consider subject recruitment to be a barrier and overlook inclusion/exclusion criteria during feasibility studies, resulting in unattainable recruitment targets. In practical terms, they essentially fail to fulfil the recruitment requirement. As such, extra care should be taken to assess the recruitment potential properly during any feasibility studies. Over the years, Indian investigators with experience of participating in global trials have recognised the importance of meeting the sponsors' recruitment needs. In terms of investigator fees, there has been an increase in expectations over the years and some investigators have started demanding fees similar to those investigators in Western countries.

3.8.7 Legal factors

The legal factors that are significantly important for clinical research in India are the evolving regulations and guidelines, patent acts, laws of contract and data protection legislation. These are described below.

3.8.7.1 Guiding regulations and the patent regime

Clinical research in India is strengthened by a well-defined regulatory framework of internationally harmonised standards of good laboratory practice (GLP), good clinical practice (GCP) and current good manufacturing practice (cGMP) in addition to emerging stringent intellectual property rights legislation. The Patents Act 1970 was amended by the Indian government in 2005 in compliance with the Trade Related Intellectual Property Rights (TRIPS) under the World Trade Organization (WTO) mandated product patent regime. As a signatory to TRIPS and the WTO, India has moved from an era of process patents to a product patent regime. This commitment has changed the business environment, increased R&D initiatives by both local and global companies and provided an

Published by Woodhead Publishing Limited, 2012

104 Clinical Research in Asia: Opportunities and Challenges

incentive for increasing foreign investment from global pharma companies.

However, the global intellectual property community is still observing India's progress concerning the new product patent bill as some observers were previously dissatisfied with the implementation of the mailbox facility which was substantially delayed. The majority of the Indian pharmaceutical players are now actively devising methods and processes to ensure the steady and prompt implementation of the new patent bill through an internal scientific advisory committee. While many global critics feel that the process of compulsory licensing in India for future patented drugs will be extremely cumbersome and the lack of ceiling on royalties will lead to endless litigation and delays, some are concerned about the legal and judicial delays of challenging patent protection in India. While a few activists in India foresee the possibility of price hikes due to the new patent bill, both government and industry have assured the public that 95 per cent of the drugs available in India and those on WHO List of Essential Drugs are off-patent drugs and will thus continue to be available at current prices.

Nonetheless, smaller manufacturers remain deeply concerned about the new patent regime because of their small scale of operations and low research spending capability. Smaller players are thus reorienting themselves to contract manufacturers, where they can compete with other low-cost manufacturing destinations such as China. As a result, the Indian pharma industry will continue to grow in the future, but with the emerging industry dynamics driving business consolidation.

3.8.7.2 Contract law

Confidentiality as an ethical principle is an essential part of any research process. This is even more critical for pharmaceutical research as it is such a time-consuming and cost-intensive process. Clinical research is governed by contract between the sponsor and/or its representative and the investigators. The law of the land prevails while executing contracts and agreements. Although the law exists and the agreements are executed, the legal system is bureaucratic

Published by Woodhead Publishing Limited, 2012

Clinical research in India **105**

and time-consuming, and most global sponsors are still uncomfortable sharing key information with Indian sites, service providers and regulators.

3.8.7.3 Data protection

Indian companies are striving hard to ensure the security of data and privacy protection. They are following the stringent security controls specified by their customers through contracts. They are investing huge amounts in purchasing industry-accepted global infrastructure (hardware and software), training staff with domain and operational knowledge, and developing stringent standard operating procedures to ensure data integrity and security. They are increasingly recognising that a single information security breach can tarnish the entire industry's image and the country's reputation as a safe destination for offshoring. Some of the issues addressed by the Information Technology Act 2000 include digital signatures, their legal acceptance and authentication, the attribution, acknowledgment and dispatch of electronic records and digital signatures, the regulations of the certifying authorities, and penalty clauses for any person who accesses, downloads, copies or extracts data without authorised means or permission. The security landscape is also constantly changing due to legislative and regulatory requirements. India is endeavouring to create a world-class security environment in order to meet these global requirements.

3.9 Future outlook

Clinical research in India, though less than two decades old, has made a significant progress in terms of compliance with global standards and the generation of good-quality data. Data quality has been accepted by regulatory authorities and approved by the initial US FDA and EMEA inspections at trial sites. Although India has learned the right way of conducting quality research during the last two decades, its contribution to global clinical research is still meagre. India participates in less than 2 per cent of global trials and

Published by Woodhead Publishing Limited, 2012

contributes 1–2 per cent of global patient recruitment. The contribution of Indian pharma companies to innovation and new product development is miniscule at present, and it may take another 5–10 years before they contribute significantly to the clinical research business, as many of their molecules are at the early stage of development. With the entry of giant IT and ITES companies in the clinical business sector, India may expand more rapidly in late-stage support services such as data management, statistical analysis, pharmacovigilance, EDC call centres and other support services. To flourish in the clinical research business, however, India will depend largely on global projects. Here the growth trend is very promising and it is possible that India could have a 5–10 per cent share in global clinical research business by 2015.

Clinical trials remain a new form of business in India and will continue to grow further. This poses considerable challenges to all stakeholders, including potential service providers. The significant increase in the number of clinical trials in India over the last two decades is a direct result of the improved talent pool in the country. Along with the country's advancement in technology, this talent pool will be a source of national pride, and India's knowledge process outsourcing business will in turn be globally recognised for its sincerity, scientific knowledge base and skill sets. India is rapidly transforming from a pool of inexperienced resources into a pool of quality talents. Only time will tell how these talents will leverage the local expertise and work ethic to acquire the highly-specialised scientific and regulatory skill sets to become global leaders in the CRO industry.

Published by Woodhead Publishing Limited, 2012

4

Clinical research in China

Abstract: China is rapidly modernising to become the world's fifth largest pharmaceutical market and an important hub for local and global clinical trials. This chapter reflects on the revolutionary changes in the pharmaceutical and clinical trial industry in China. It emphasises the growing trends of foreign investments by pharmaceutical companies in China, thus indirectly fuelling the growth of the CRO market. Also considered are China's healthcare delivery system and key parameters that drive the growth of clinical research environments. The chapter goes on to analyse the clinical research environment and accreditation of clinical trial sites, and attempts an environmental analysis to provide a general outlook for this ever-growing market.

4.1 Pharmaceutical market

China is rapidly modernising to become the world's fifth largest pharmaceutical market. Many international biopharma companies have started to invest in China and believe that the healthcare market offers huge long-term commercial potential. China offers biopharmaceutical and other healthcare companies a range of commercial opportunities. Like many other rapidly industrialising nations, a growing proportion of the country's population now lives in cities, with urbanisation having a great impact on society. The changing epidemiological profile of the population has been

Published by Woodhead Publishing Limited, 2012

accompanied by a rise in chronic diseases, particularly cardiovascular and respiratory conditions, and yet there remains a persistence of diseases associated with poverty and social inequality.

China has a well-established leadership in providing other biopharmas with basic intermediaries, active pharmaceutical ingredients and bulk drugs. It is acknowledged as a low-price leader, even compared with other emerging countries such as India. In China, contract research and manufacturing services are thought to be only 20–50 per cent of the same services in the West by volume. China's pharmaceutical market was worth $32 billion in 2009, projected to grow to $40 billion in 2010. It has been suggested that the Chinese pharmaceutical market will expand to $93 billion by 2015, which will account for 9 per cent of the global pharmaceutical market (Figure 4.1).

China has around one-fifth of the world's population, meaning that a wide range of biopharmaceutical applications and approaches will be relevant to Chinese healthcare. Indeed, it is this range of disease profiles that has stimulated the government's efforts to develop its own biopharmaceutical sector and attract back its researchers currently working outside of the country. With such a large population, the demand for new medicines in China will undoubtedly grow. However, purchasing power will be important and therefore no pharmaceutical company can afford to take the country's economic growth for granted. The number of bioventure deals in Asia are increasing significantly. The Chinese contribution

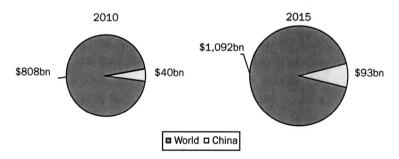

Figure 4.1 Pharmaceutical market size: world vs China – in 2010 and 2015

Source: Media reports

Clinical research in China

to this number is increasing rapidly. Offshore initial public offerings for Chinese companies are picking up. China is especially strong in the areas of antibiotics, vitamins, amino acids and organic acids.

Although nearly all of China's biologics are copies of Western inventions, China has developed more than 30 biotech drugs, with more than 150 in the pipeline. There are more than 200 Chinese biopharma companies, and numerous biogeneric drugs, including epoetin alpha and recombinant human granulocyte colony-stimulating factor, are legally manufactured in China. The growing technical experience of Chinese biotechnologists is demonstrated by the fact that that 20 per cent of international, peer-reviewed papers in life sciences have at least one Chinese national as an author.

4.2 Pharmaceutical investments in China

Over the last decade, as demand for products has grown, there has been a steady influx of European and American bioscience companies forming alliances, opening R&D facilities, planning for sales and marketing operations, and projecting large investments in China (Table 4.1).

In addition to commercial operations, many companies have set up R&D centres in China and these centres are expanding their capabilities and investments year on year. As can be seen from Table 4.1, many companies have invested in multiple locations for R&D, manufacturing, collaborations for pre-clinical research, toxicology and chemistry services. Several of these collaborations are with big Chinese universities involved in research and development activities.

Companies wishing to set up R&D facilities must first be registered with the China's State Drug Administration (SDA) through the relevant provincial drug administrations, otherwise their application will be refused. The requirements for approval are set out in the Notice of the Ministry of Foreign Trade and Economic Cooperation on Issues Relating to the Investment in and Establishment of Research and Development Centers by Foreign Investors, which was issued in April 2000. The minimum capital investment for a 'formal'

Published by Woodhead Publishing Limited, 2012

110 Clinical Research in Asia: Opportunities and Challenges

Table 4.1 Investments by major multinational pharma companies in China

Company	Major locations	Main focus
Pfizer	Dalian, Suzhou and Wuxi	Manufacturing facilities
GlaxoSmithKline	Beijing, Chongqing, Tianjin, Suzhou and Pudong, Shanghai	Manufacturing facilities and joint ventures; global R&D centre in Shanghai opened in 2007
AstraZeneca	Shanghai	Clinical development and manufacturing facilities; R&D centre in Shanghai; collaboration with Wuxi and Bioduro
Merck KgaA	Beijing, Shanghai, Hangzhou, Guangzhou	Manufacturing and possible joint development projects; $225m R&D unit in Beijing
Novartis	Shanghai, Beijing	$1bn investment in R&D in 2009; manufacturing facilities
Roche	Shanghai	R&D facility; collaboration with Bioduro
Sanofi-Aventis	Shenzhen and Beijing, Shanghai	Manufacturing and joint venture importation and distribution; R&D facilities in Shanghai, expanded in 2005, 2008 and 2010
Eli Lilly	Suzhou, Shanghai	R&D centre in Shanghai; collaboration with Wuxi, ShangPharma and CrownBio and local institutions
Wyeth	Wu County Economic Development Zone, Suzhou, Shanghai	Manufacturing facilities and joint ventures
BMS	Minghang (Shanghai)	Joint venture manufacturing facilities
Novo Nordisk	Beijing	R&D facilities
Johnson & Johnson	Suzhou	Collaboration with Wuxi for toxicology and chemistry service in 2010
Abbott Labs	Shanghai	R&D lab
Bayer	Beijing	$130m investment

Source: Company reports

Published by Woodhead Publishing Limited, 2012

R&D centre is $2 million. In contrast, in most Chinese cities the minimum investment for an 'ordinary' R&D wholly foreign-owned enterprise is $200,000.

A 'formal' centre must have a defined specialist area of expertise and undertake specific R&D projects. It must operate from a permanent location and be equipped with appropriate apparatus and equipment to support the chosen research area. Of its full-time management and staff, 80 per cent must hold an undergraduate degree (or equivalent) or higher qualification and must be directly engaged in research.

Beijing and Shanghai have issued their own regulations for the approval of 'formal' R&D centres. The Beijing regulations stipulate higher thresholds for certain aspects of the application. For example, an R&D centre in Beijing must have total assets of at least RMB 5 million (approximately $600,000). Sixty per cent of the Beijing R&D centre's total income must come from technology-related activities.

4.3 China's healthcare system

China's current healthcare system is often considered fragmented, with the quality of service varying in different areas of the country. Although a general overview of the healthcare system can be provided, this is by no means an accurate reflection of the service offered to citizens everywhere in the country. This variability is enhanced by the fact that many of China's provincial governments guard their autonomy with the result that their approach to healthcare can be very different from those in other parts of the country.

The central government has recognised many of the deficiencies in the current healthcare system and is attempting reforms. Although the initial approach was for the government to fund most healthcare services, costs have increasingly been shifted to patients. Unfortunately, this means that many patients are still unable to gain easy access to even a basic level of healthcare.

The Chinese economy expanded 10.30 per cent over 2009, as measured by the year-over-year change in GDP. Unlike the commonly

Published by Woodhead Publishing Limited, 2012

used quarterly GDP growth rate, the annual GDP growth rate takes into account a full year of economic activity, thus avoiding the need to make any type of seasonal adjustment. According to the World Bank, China's GDP is worth $4,909 billion or 7.92 per cent of the world economy. While China's economic growth is indicated by a strong GDP growth of 9–10 per cent, healthcare spending by the government is almost 10 per cent of GDP and continuously increasing year over year (Figure 4.2).

China's political commitment to health system reform was declared at the highest level when President Hu Jintao stated in October 2006 that all Chinese people should have access to affordable essential health services. The Health Care Reform Leading Group was established the same year, composed of 16 ministries and chaired by Vice Premier Li Keqiang of the State Council, with the Ministers of Health and the National Development and Reform Commission (NDRC) as Vice-Chairpersons.

After three years of deliberation, in 2009, the group announced its national health reform blueprint. The plan's main objective is to provide universal coverage of basic healthcare by the end of 2020. Reforms are proposed in five areas: the public health system, the medical care delivery system, the health security system, the pharmaceutical system, and pilot hospital reform. The initial three-year implementation plan for 2009–11 emphasises several

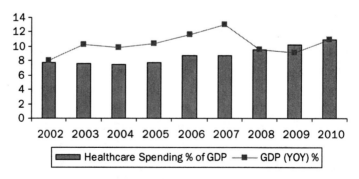

Figure 4.2 Government of China's spending on education, healthcare and social security (% GDP)

Source: Ministry of Finance, Tradingeconomics.com

programmes, including improving the social health security system (urban employees, urban residents, rural Cooperative Medical Scheme, and medical assistance programmes); establishing an essential medicines system; strengthening primary-level healthcare facilities; reducing disparities in public healthcare between regions; and piloting reforms in public hospital financing by reducing the reliance on drug sales for operational costs and salaries. The government has committed to spending 850 billion yuan ($124 billion) on fulfilling the three-year plan (an estimated 0.8 per cent annual increase from 2008 GDP). The central government allocation to implementing health reform in 2009 amounted to 118 billion yuan, including 30.4 billion yuan ($4.4 billion) dedicated to insurance, 24.6 billion yuan ($3.6 billion) for public health and disease control, and 6.5 billion yuan ($2.4 billion) for construction.

Specific targets for 2009 included: (1) building 29,000 township health centres; (2) publishing a revised essential medicines list; and (3) a 15-yuan per capita subsidy for public health. Targets for 2011 included: (1) 90 per cent health insurance coverage for both urban and rural areas; (2) a 120-yuan government subsidy to urban residents' basic medical insurance and the new rural coooperative health insurance; and (3) 2,000 new county hospitals, 3,700 urban community health centres and 11,000 community health stations built or renovated. After one year of implementation, the government has announced a series of achievements, including 94 per cent of the rural population (833 million people) covered by health insurance, 36 per cent of counties adopting the essential medicines list, 32 million people receiving hepatitis B vaccine, 1.49 million women screened for breast cancer, funding for hospital births for 6.27 million women, and formulation of clinical pathways for 112 diseases.

Since 1946, China has been an active member of the World Health Organization (WHO), which has collaborated with the authorities to improve healthcare in a number of areas. A number of Chinese experts have served on WHO committees to address major public health issues. In China, the WHO and the Ministry of Health have prioritised the following areas:

114 Clinical Research in Asia: Opportunities and Challenges

- health promotion and education;
- immunisation;
- malaria and lymphatic filariasis control;
- disease surveillance and control;
- environmental health;
- reproductive health;
- health management and research;
- laboratory services;
- tuberculosis control.

4.3.1 Population factors

If China is to succeed in its aims to improve healthcare for its citizens then it must have a detailed understanding of how its population is increasing and its disease profile changing. This will enable the government to determine where healthcare resources need to be allocated, what problems must be overcome and how demand will grow in the future. These factors are also important for biopharma companies looking at the potential of the Chinese healthcare market. China would appear to offer companies producing the appropriate technologies a potentially large market for the future. This is particularly relevant as they are facing considerable cost-containment pressures elsewhere in the world. Despite the healthcare challenges and economic disparities that are currently a feature of the market, investment in China at this early stage is still expected to be extremely beneficial for biopharma companies in the long term.

4.3.2 Ageing and healthcare

Given its large population, the impact of ageing on medical demand is important for the Chinese government as it reforms the healthcare system. For biopharma companies, these trends are equally important, as they must take account of the changes in population demographics when developing new drugs. As drug development times lie in the 10 to 12-year range, information on diseases of the elderly will need to be factored in to R&D decision-making now.

Published by Woodhead Publishing Limited, 2012

China's population is ageing rapidly, and one in four people living in the country in 2035 will be aged 60 years or older (Figure 4.3). Population ageing leads to a shift towards chronic diseases and disabilities and pressures on the health system to address more complex health conditions that generate higher costs.

In line with the government's policy to accelerate urbanisation, half of the population will be living in urban areas by 2030 (Figure 4.4), placing great pressure on infrastructure.

4.3.3 Political situation

Funding healthcare for the elderly is a problem for most countries. In 2001, a study by the Organization for Economic Cooperation

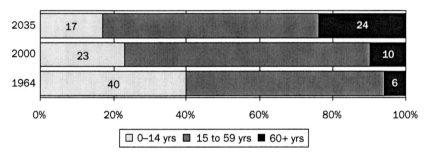

Figure 4.3 Population of China by age group (%), 1964, 2000, 2035

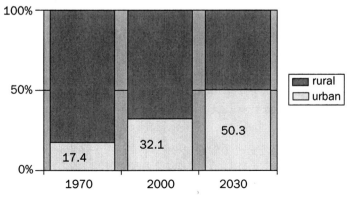

Figure 4.4 China's urban population (%), 1970, 2000, 2030

Published by Woodhead Publishing Limited, 2012

116 Clinical Research in Asia: Opportunities and Challenges

and Development (OECD) revealed that the over-65 age group accounted for 40–50 per cent of healthcare spending and that their per capita healthcare costs were three to five times higher than those under 65. The combination of a growing elderly population and falling birth rates places a great strain on funding for public healthcare in OECD member countries. As the proportion of individuals aged 65 and over is set to double over the next 50 years in OECD countries, further pressure will be placed on healthcare systems.

4.3.4 Disease burden

Global burden-of-disease estimates produced by the WHO indicate that 80 per cent of deaths in China are due to noncommunicable diseases and injuries. Cerebrovascular disease, chronic obstructive pulmonary disease and heart disease account for nearly 50 per cent of all deaths. The rankings based on disability-adjusted life years also highlight the emergence of noncommunicable chronic diseases and injuries as the predominant health conditions. Much of the disability and deaths attributable to chronic diseases, particularly among working-age adults, could be reduced through a reduction in risk factors, including improvements in the quality of air, water and sanitation; reductions in tobacco and alcohol use; improvements in diet and nutrition; and increases in exercise. The WHO projects that disabilities and deaths related to chronic diseases will result in a $550 billion loss in productivity between 2005 and 2015.

The disease burden varies by age group. It is estimated that 70 per cent of deaths among children under five years of age are attributable to maternal, perinatal or nutritional conditions, including sepsis, pneumonia, diarrhoea, measles and tetanus, many of which could be addressed through high-quality healthcare. Among children aged 5–14 years, the number of deaths is a very small part of the total disease burden; however, most of these deaths are attributable to injuries and accidents, including drowning and road accidents. For those aged 5–44 years, injuries and violence account for an even larger share of deaths, at over 50 per cent. Some 69 per cent of

Published by Woodhead Publishing Limited, 2012

Clinical research in China   **117**

disability and 80 per cent of deaths among adults and older people are due to noncommunicable diseases.

Among the remaining infectious diseases, hepatitis B, tuberculosis and lower respiratory infections still account for significant mortality and lost disability-adjusted life years, particularly among children. While infectious diseases attract enormous interest both domestically and internationally, injuries and violence contribute about 11 per cent of total mortality each year, compared with 8.6 per cent attributed to infectious diseases. In 2007, most injury deaths were attributed to suicide (28 per cent), road traffic injuries (25 per cent) and drowning (11 per cent), with the suicide rate for women estimated to be 25 per cent higher than that for men, and traffic injury mortality rates twice as high for males than for females. Mental and neurological disorders are responsible for about 20 per cent of the overall disease burden in China. More than 30 million children and adolescents under 17 years of age have behavioural and emotional problems, of which about 50–70 per cent need mental health services, but remain untreated.

China is one of 22 high-burden countries for tuberculosis, with the prevalence for all forms of the disease estimated at 88 per 100,000 people in 2008. The WHO estimates that each year there are approximately 1 million new cases, of which 500,000 are infectious, smear-positive pulmonary disease. Multidrug-resistant tuberculosis (MDR-TB) and extensively drug-resistant tuberculosis (XDR-TB) are becoming critical public health threats. Based on a national baseline survey on drug-resistant tuberculosis in 2007, 5.7 per cent of new cases (95% CI: 4.6–7.1) and 25.6 per cent of previously treated cases (95% CI: 21.7–30.0); 0.68 per cent (CI: 0.4–1.1) of sputum-smear-positive cases had XDR-TB. It has been estimated that there are approximately 84,000 new MDR-TB cases per year in China. In April 2009, the government hosted a high-level meeting on MDR-TB and XDR-TB, and initiated WHO Resolution WHA 62.15 on Prevention and Control of MDR-TB and XDR-TB, urging all member states to achieve universal access to diagnosis and treatment of MDR-TB and XDR-TB.

Although HIV prevalence in adults is currently low (0.057 per cent), several provinces in central, southern and western areas of the

Published by Woodhead Publishing Limited, 2012

118 Clinical Research in Asia: Opportunities and Challenges

country face serious concentrated epidemics, with the epidemic spilling into the general population in some areas. Yunnan, Sichuan, Guangxi, Xinjiang and Guangdong provinces are the worst affected, with over 33,000 HIV infections reported in 2009. Sexual transmission is now the main mode of transmission. Among those living with HIV reported in 2009, 44.9 per cent of infections were through heterosexual transmission, 10.2 per cent through homosexual transmission, and 27 per cent via injecting drug use.

Emerging disease threats include HIV/AIDS, severe acute respiratory disease syndrome (SARS) and influenza. Emerging infectious diseases, such as SARS, highly pathogenic H5N1 avian influenza (H5N1), and pandemic influenza A (H1N1) are important because of their epidemic potential. In addition to the illness and death they bring, they can cause social instability and considerable financial and economic loss. The SARS outbreak in 2003 affected 5,327 people in mainland China and killed 348. Since 2003, 38 people in China have been reported to have H5N1 and 26 of them have died.

4.4   Healthcare delivery system

Since 2003, dramatic increases in insurance coverage have been accompanied by increased service utilisation, particularly in rural areas. Between 2003 and 2008, national insurance coverage increased from 23.1 per cent to 87.4 per cent, while hospital admission rates nearly doubled to 6.8 per cent.

Changes in health financing have led to other changes in utilisation patterns. Increasing rates of caesarean section, particularly in urban areas, and frequent use of injections and infusions in primary care settings illustrate the unnecessary use of certain treatment measures. Caesarean section rates have increased from 16.3 per cent to 26.8 per cent, with urban rates at 50.9 per cent in 2008. An assessment of 121,471 prescriptions for patients with the diagnosis of a noncommunicable condition in 218 primary care facilities was conducted as part of the National Health Services Survey 2008. In village clinics and township health centres, 66 per cent and

Published by Woodhead Publishing Limited, 2012

Clinical research in China **119**

61 per cent of patients were prescribed antibiotics, respectively. Intramuscular and intravenous injection rates were also very high: 30 per cent and 35 per cent, respectively, of rural prescriptions and 13 per cent and 32 per cent, respectively, of urban prescriptions. These high figures correspond to other smaller-scale studies conducted in China. Such treatment patterns are striking given the prevalence of noncommunicable disease treatment.

While health insurance coverage is increasing, especially in rural areas, many people are underinsured and continue to face high out-of-pocket costs. Households continue to face financial barriers in accessing healthcare, and household health expenditures remain high: in 2008, financial reasons were to blame for some 17.4 per cent of patients failing to receive the hospital treatment for which they had been referred, a decline from 21.8 per cent in 2003. An increase was seen in the percentage of households with catastrophic expenses (5.0 per cent vs. 5.6 per cent), although fewer households became impoverished because of medical care between 2003 and 2008 (6.1 per cent vs. 4.8 per cent respectively). Inpatient medical services frequently require pre-payment. For rural health insurance schemes, reimbursement rates have increased to about 40 per cent of total charges. Benefits are also not portable across localities, which is a major concern for migrant workers.

While major progress has been observed in the expansion of rural insurance schemes and in some indicators of service use and expenditures, gaps remain between the poorest and better-off and, for some indicators, between eastern, central and western China. Survey data from the National Health Services show the need for policies to promote equitable access and risk protection, particularly for the urban and rural poor. The current health reform investments should be monitored closely to determine their impact on trends in service utilisation, health-seeking behaviour, the quality of care, risk protection and, ultimately, health.

As medicine expenditure remains an important component of out-of-pocket expenditure, increasing the availability and affordability of generic essential medicines is an important policy. The government is in the process of outlining reforms to improve access to quality, safe essential medicines, modify the pricing system and strengthen medicine production and distribution systems.

Published by Woodhead Publishing Limited, 2012

4.5 The importance of traditional medicine in modern healthcare

Traditional Chinese medicine has been given a high priority by the government since the outset of healthcare reform and is starting to receive more widestream international recognition and media coverage. Traditional medical practices are well documented, with some of the authoritative medical books being over 2,000 years old. For example, the *Compendium of Materia Medica* compiled by Li Shizhen of the Ming Dynasty details 1,892 types of herbs and 10,000 prescriptions. Traditional medicine is held in high regard and there has been a policy to promote its use and blend its benefits with those of modern Western medicine.

In 1986, the government set up the State Traditional Chinese Medicine Administration, which later changed its name to the State Traditional Chinese Medicine and Pharmaceuticals Administration. A key role of this body has been to formalise education programmes in the field of traditional medicine. There are now a range of education programmes, including night school and correspondence courses, to incorporate its use in modern medicine. A major example of the acceptance of traditional Chinese medical approaches in a more modern context can be found in the field of acupuncture.

In 1991, China organised an international conference on traditional medicine and pharmacology, which was followed by participants signing the Beijing Declaration. There are now a number of international academic-level collaborations in the field of traditional medicine. In Germany, Munich University has set up the Institute on the Theory of Traditional Chinese Medicine, while other foreign universities have expressed an interest in incorporating aspects of traditional medicine into some of their academic courses.

Cooperation is taking place between Chinese academic centres and those in Japan, the USA and Germany. According to government estimates, the study of traditional medicine is the most popular option for those coming to China to pursue courses in the natural sciences. The government estimates that China carries out academic exchanges with more than 100 countries and regions throughout the world.

The overwhelming majority of the Chinese population seek out traditional Chinese medicine to address their health problems. The government promotes the development of a modern traditional Chinese medicine industry, as well as the integration of traditional Chinese medicine into the national healthcare system and the integrated training of healthcare practitioners. In 2008, China's Minister of Health identified several key priorities for traditional Chinese medicine development, including increasing policy support for traditional Chinese medicine; strengthening research on key traditional Chinese medicine issues and building capacity for traditional Chinese medicine research; training prominent traditional Chinese medicine doctors and establishing well-known traditional Chinese medicine hospitals and departments; improving and adapting traditional Chinese medicine services to meet public need; increasing access to and the quality of traditional Chinese medicine services in rural and urban communities; and strengthening international cooperation and communication on traditional Chinese medicine.

However, a number of challenges to the further development of traditional Chinese medicine remain. There is a lack of unified, systematic regulations for assessing the safety and efficacy and ensuring the quality of traditional Chinese medicine products. In addition, there are no national traditional Chinese medicine standards or guidelines for traditional Chinese medicine clinical trials, and evidence-based traditional Chinese medicine product testing and research are still needed. In view of the vast differences in the qualifications of traditional Chinese medicine practitioners, the quality of traditional Chinese medicine education needs to be strengthened, and the management and supervision of traditional Chinese medicine institutions need to be regulated.

According to the WHO, traditional Chinese medicine accounts for between 30 to 50 per cent of total medicinal consumption in China. Furthermore, departments of traditional medicine have been set up in virtually all hospitals, including those offering Western medicine. There are estimated to be more than 500,000 practitioners of traditional medicine in China, and even doctors in rural settings have some basic understanding of acupuncture and medicinal herbs. Thus, traditional medicine represents an important source of primary

Published by Woodhead Publishing Limited, 2012

122   Clinical Research in Asia: Opportunities and Challenges

healthcare for the Chinese population and its impact cannot be ignored.

The international status of traditional medicine has been enhanced by the finding that the Chinese herbal product, *Artemisia annua*, which has been used for over 2,000 years, is highly effective against resistant malaria. There is hope that it may represent a major step forward in tackling the disease, particularly as modern drug development in this area has been considered slow. The WHO is actively supporting clinical studies using Chinese *Artemisia annua* for the benefit of African countries affected by malaria. The WHO has recognised the value of traditional medicine and is actively working with China.

Within Chinese biopharmaceutical industry circles there is hope that many traditional compounds could represent precursors of future drugs. If local companies are able to use traditional medicine to develop innovative new drugs it will boost their chances of competing with foreign companies both nationally and internationally. One of the perceived weaknesses in the current system is that although well documented from a historical perspective, many compounds have not undergone thorough analysis using modern scientific methods. There is also a need to fully characterise potentially beneficial compounds from an intellectual property perspective in order to commercialise their use.

4.6   China's CRO market

The CRO market in China was estimated to be worth approximately $800 million in 2010. That number represents growth of 11 per cent versus the year before, despite the impact of the global recession. During 2004–10, however, the CAGR reached 18 per cent, driven mainly by outsourcing from international firms rather than domestic biopharmas.

Nevertheless, given the Chinese government's drive to improve healthcare for its population, and the support from international healthcare organisations, there is a demand for companies to develop medicines to tackle diseases that affect the poorer sections of society. A limitation for biopharma companies is that, at present, only a

Published by Woodhead Publishing Limited, 2012

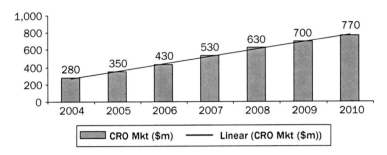

Figure 4.5   China's CRO market
Source: Media reports

proportion of the population can afford modern medicines. However, this section of society is sufficiently large to offer companies a promising consumer base for the future. As with other emerging markets, companies believe that in the long term, the section of society that can afford new medicines and healthcare services will increase. It is estimated that the industry will grow at 21 per cent CAGR from 2010 to 2015, bringing the Chinese CRO market to $2 billion in 2015, comprising 7 per cent of the global CRO market. As CRO expenses in China are only about 30–40 per cent of those in the West, the actual volume of CRO activity in China should be multiplied by a factor of 2.5–3 to compare it with Western countries.

The last decade has seen numerous companies investing in China, particularly because they have seen their rivals do so. In such a competitive world market, late entrants into the Chinese market may be unable to take advantage of the potential opportunities, as rivals will already have gained a head-start. Many global CROs started their Chinese odyssey via the preferred service provider and partnership model, followed by a period of organic growth. However, as the local players have grown and matured, the last decade has seen a number of mergers and acquisitions (Table 4.2). In particular, Charles River, PPD and Parexel's acquisitions have created a new wave in clinical research industry in China.

Other players are very interested in expanding their presence and are exploring alliance or joint-venture options with regional CROs with significant presence in China. ICON Plc has formed an alliance with Tigermed Consulting, a leading Chinese Phase I–IV CRO to

124 Clinical Research in Asia: Opportunities and Challenges

Table 4.2 Mergers and acquisitions in the Chinese CRO industry, 2000–2010

Acquirer	Acquisition	Price	Comments
Czura Thornton (Promoters of Chiltern)	MDS Laboratory	NA	MDS Lab was rechristened as Clearstone Laboratory, and has a significant lab facility in Beijing
Charles River Laboratories	Wu Xi Pharma Tech, Inc	$1.6bn	April 2010
Ricerca Biosciences LLC	MDS Pharma Services (early stage business)	$45.0m	February 2010
Pharmaron Holdings Ltd	Bridge Laboratories	NA	In January 2010, Bridge Lab was a toxicology facility with GLP certifications
PPD, Inc	Bioduro, LLC	$78.5m	In November 2009, Bioduro was a discovery and chemistry CRO
PPD, Inc	Excel PharmaStudies	$21.7m	In October 2009, Excel was a clinical CRO
Parexel International	Apex International	$51.0m	In September 2007, Apex was a Phase II–IV CRO

expand its geographical reach and local expertise. Several other partnerships have been formed among central laboratory and pre-clinical toxicology service providers in China.

As shown in Figure 4.6, a vibrant CRO industry has emerged in China in the last 10 years to attract local entrepreneurs and global players to build and operate CRO business in the country. The majority of these service providers started their operations in Beijing and Shanghai, slowly navigating towards other cities. Most Chinese companies offer services in drug discovery, chemistry and pre-clinical areas that include organic synthesis, medicinal chemistry, biology, pharmacokinetics and toxicology. This shows that the Chinese CRO industry is more developed in discovery and chemistry than late-phase clinical trials. Following the entry of several global CROs, Phase II–IV trials are gaining momentum, although the growth of late-phase industry-sponsored trials is relatively slow due to perceived regulatory barriers in the country.

Published by Woodhead Publishing Limited, 2012

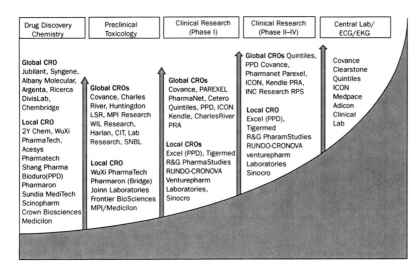

Figure 4.6   Clinical research players in China

4.7   Clinical trials in China

More than 300 trials were conducted in China between 2006 to 2010, with less than 50 per cent of them being industry-sponsored GCP trials. According to the Clinicaltrial.gov registry, only 983 of the 2,299 trials undertaken in China up to July 2011 were industry-sponsored trials, the remaining 58 per cent being local registration trials undertaken by individual investigators and local institutions or hospitals. The trend for industry-sponsored GCP trials in China is increasing constantly. In 2010, a total of 182 were undertaken, and in 2011, China crossed the 200 threshold.

Analysis of the clinical trial registry for industry-sponsored clinical trials in China indicates that GCP studies in diverse therapeutic areas are being conducted. Almost 71 per cent of the industry-sponsored trials undertaken in China are in late phases (i.e. Phase II and Phase III) where sponsors can benefit from the advantages that China can offer with respect to the recruitment of a large number of patients who are not already receiving treatment. Even significant numbers of industry-sponsored Phase IV trials (22 per cent) are undertaken in China.

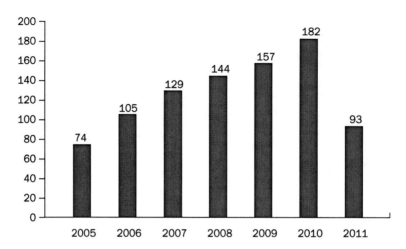

Figure 4.7 Growth of industry-sponsored clinical trials in China

2011 numbers are until July

Source: www.clinicaltrials.gov (accessed 20 July 2011)

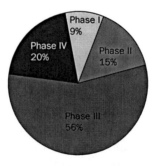

Figure 4.8 Clinical trials in China, by phase

While most of the trials quoted in Table 4.3 are for the global sponsors in Phase II–III, a few could be local registration studies.

Analysis of Table 4.4 and Table 4.5 suggests that pharmaceutical majors like Novartis, GSK, Roche, Pfizer, Bayer, AstraZeneca etc.

Clinical research in China

Table 4.3 Pharma companies undertaking GCP trials in China

Pharma company	No. trials
Novartis	92
GlaxoSmithKline	69
Roche	67
Pfizer	79
Bayer	59
AstraZeneca	68
Sanofi-Aventis	58
Eli Lilly & Company	51
Borhinger Ingelheim	48
Wyeth (now owned by Pfizer)	21
Bristol-Myers Squibb	31
Total	643

Source: *www.clinicaltrials.gov* (accessed July 2011)

Table 4.4 Most active clinical trial sponsors in mainland China

Sponsor	Local		Multinational		Total		Sites/ Protocol	Protocol Local	Sites Local
	Protocol *n*	Sites *n*	Protocol *n*	Sites *n*	Protocol *n*	Sites *n*	*n*	%	%
GlaxoSmithKline	10	77	15	122	25	199	8.0	40.0	38.7
Hoffmann-La Roche	3	25	15	138	18	163	9.1	16.7	15.3
AstraZeneca	9	71	11	91	20	162	8.1	45.0	43.8
Boehringer Ingelheim	9	99	5	26	14	125	8.9	64.3	79.2
Bristol-Myers Squibb	2	13	6	85	8	98	12.3	25.0	13.3
Bayer	6	31	15	56	21	87	4.1	28.6	35.6
Pfizer	4	28	8	48	12	76	6.3	33.3	36.8
Wyeth	4	34	7	39	11	73	6.6	36.4	46.6
Eli Lilly	10	31	10	37	20	68	3.4	50.0	45.6
Novartis	6	35	4	7	10	42	4.2	60.0	83.3
Sanofi-Aventis	12	15	17	17	29	32	1.1	41.4	46.9
Novo Nordisk	8	8	2	17	10	25	2.5	80.0	32.0

Source: Clinical Trial Magnifier 1(8), 2008, *www.clinicaltrialmagnifier.com*

Published by Woodhead Publishing Limited, 2012

128 Clinical Research in Asia: Opportunities and Challenges

Table 4.5 Most common therapeutic areas under clinical trial in mainland China

Therapeutic area	Local		Multinational		Total		Sites/ Protocol n	Protocol Local %	Sites Local %
	Protocol n	Sites n	Protocol n	Sites n	Protocol n	Sites n			
Oncology	13	77	44	233	57	310	5.4	22.8	24.8
CNS	16	104	16	93	32	197	6.2	50.0	52.8
Cardiology	8	43	25	152	33	195	5.9	24.2	22.1
Infectious	20	85	8	87	28	172	6.1	71.4	49.4
Respiratory	4	79	11	71	15	150	10.0	26.7	52.7
Endocrinology	17	38	11	48	28	86	3.1	60.7	44.2
Rheumatology	6	41	7	36	13	77	5.9	46.2	53.2
Kidney/Urology	8	27	2	25	10	52	5.2	80.0	51.9
GI & Hepatology	5	28	4	16	9	44	4.9	55.6	63.6
O&G	4	28	1	1	5	29	5.8	80.0	96.6
Haematology	1	13	1	13	2	26	13.0	50.0	50.0

Source: Clinical Trial Magnifier 1(8), 2008, *www.clinicaltrialmagnifier.com*

have carried out more than 66 per cent of the industry-sponsored trials in China. These trials were managed either by themselves or with the support of CROs in diverse therapeutic areas over a decade-long period.

Table 4.6 shows that oncology, CNS, cardiology, infectious and respiratory trials are undertaken in more than 150 sites in China. This list is not exhaustive and mentions only few sponsors and therapeutic areas. But it clearly shows that over a period of a few years, a number of trials in diverse therapeutic areas have been undertaken by pharma companies and CROs in China.

4.8 Accreditation of clinical trial sites in China

The Chinese SFDA released its guidelines for the accreditation of clinical trial sites in China in February 2004. The Chinese version of the guidelines is available on the SFDA website (*www.sfda.gov.cn*) with English translation provided in the appendix. The guidelines stipulate the following:

Published by Woodhead Publishing Limited, 2012

To accredit a CTC [clinical trial certificate] is to safeguard that all clinical trials-related activities are properly conducted, study results are scientifically reliable, and all rights of study subjects are fully protected. This is also an important measure for quality control. Therefore, all provincial and municipal FDAs and health bureaus must strictly follow the guidelines and be responsible for any accreditation activities taking place in the respective jurisdiction, and, in the meantime, be responsible for the regulation and inspection of clinical trials and the activities of institutional ethics committees (IECs).

As can be noted, the accreditation procedure is strict and substantial. The SFDA has several types of study site accreditation schemes, for conventional medicine, traditional Chinese medicine, Tibetan medicine and Mongolian medicine. Conventional medicine includes the testing of modern drugs, biologics, vaccines and medical devices. Infectious disease and cancer can be tested within each therapeutic area, as well as by conducting Phase I-type trials.

SFDA accreditation is for individual hospitals that can be accredited in more than one therapeutic area. In principle, accreditation is at

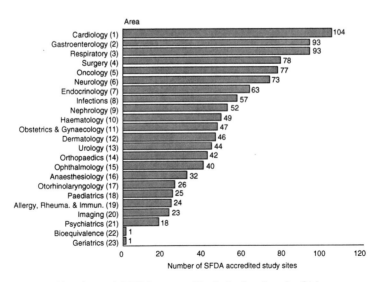

Figure 4.9 Number of SFDA accredited study sites in China

Source: Clinical Trial Magnifier 1(8), 2008, www.clinicaltrialmagnifier.com

130   Clinical Research in Asia: Opportunities and Challenges

study site level, although hospitals must have suitable infrastructure for conducting clinical trials on new medicinal products. In some cases, a hospital is successfully accredited, but only for some of the therapeutic areas in the application. Most medical universities in China have more than one affiliated hospital which makes it possible for one-and-the-same university/institution to have multiple accreditations in the same therapeutic area. This study uses the term 'site accreditation' to describe a single principal investigator accreditation, which is the same as an accreditation of a therapeutic area.

Successfully accredited study sites are posted on the SFDA website. Details in Chinese include the issue date of the accreditation, the accreditation number, city, university, hospital and specialty/therapeutic area. Data on SFDA-accredited study sites were downloaded on 30 July 2008 and translated into English. Information about the specialty or therapeutic areas was not uniformly given, and some re-coding was required to clarify the findings.

4.9   Clinical research in China – environmental analysis

China's admission into the WTO has been seen as a major boost to improved R&D performance. Clinical trial activity in China is on the rise in accordance with international standards and as per WTO requirements. The confidence that this has instilled in the international business community is illustrated by the finding that two-thirds of the US companies surveyed by the American Chamber of Commerce in China believed that the Chinese government would be able to keep the economy under control and that there was a positive outlook for the market.

4.9.1 Political environment

China's 11th Five-Year Plan (2006–2010) forms the basis of the government's current economic and social development efforts. In continuity with the 10th Five-Year Plan, the 11th Plan aims to

Published by Woodhead Publishing Limited, 2012

Clinical research in China

sustain the rapid and steady development of China's 'socialist market economy' while, in addition, aiming to achieve the 'five balances':

- *Balance between urban and rural development*: The gap between urban and rural areas increased during the 1990s for some important economic and health indicators.
- *Balance in regional development*: The government is promoting development in the western regions in an effort to address the regional imbalances that have grown over time.
- *Balance in social and economic development*: The government has made a commitment to focus more on social issues, including poverty, education, medical care and public health, in its overall goal to build a well-rounded, better-off society.
- *Balance between human beings and nature*: Industry, agriculture and humans are competing for scarce resources, including water and air.
- *Balance between domestic and international development*: This balance promotes international cooperation and emphasises the importance of fulfilling international commitments.

The 11th Plan includes two key quantitative targets:

- to achieve an annual GDP growth rate of 7.5 per cent, with the goal of doubling 2000 per capita GDP by 2010; and
- to reduce energy consumption per unit of GDP by 20 per cent, and the total discharge of major pollutants by 10 per cent, by 2010.

The Plan also includes a number of strategic priorities and major tasks, including rebalancing China's pattern of growth; deepening reforms and opening up further to the outside world; constructing a 'new socialist countryside'; promoting more balanced development among the different regions; and increasing capacity for independent innovation.

To enable a larger proportion of the population to take advantage of the opportunities afforded by economic growth, future programmes aim to reduce poverty; develop the education, health, technology,

132 Clinical Research in Asia: Opportunities and Challenges

scientific and cultural fields, among others; and strengthen the social safety net. The Plan is referred to as a 'people's agenda' because it focuses on inclusive social development that will make a measurable difference in people's lives by 2020.

The government is currently preparing its 12th Five-Year Plan; the priorities include the economy and the role of the state in the economy, efficiency, employment, and China's global role.

4.9.2 Economic environment

China has made impressive gains in improving living standards, reducing poverty and maintaining strong economic growth since initiating market reforms in 1979. GDP averaged a real annual growth rate of 10 per cent during the period from 1979 to 2006. During 1979–84, economic growth was driven by the labour shift from agriculture to rural industry. Between 1985 and 1992, growth benefited from improved efficiency in capital allocation stemming from price liberalisation and opening up to foreign trade. Further opening up of the economy to foreign direct investment in the 1990s stimulated technological progress.

China's earlier high health standards have played a pivotal role in the country's economic success. Impressive growth performance has been correlated with reductions in poverty and advancements in social development. Using the standard international poverty line of $1 per day, an estimated 400 million people in China have been lifted out of poverty over the past 30 years. This is primarily a result of the liberalisation of agriculture and other rural industries. At China's official poverty line, the rural population living in absolute poverty with an annual per capita net income below 668 yuan ($87) decreased from 250 million in 1978 (31 per cent of the rural population) to 24 million in 2005 (3 per cent of the rural population). Government estimates of poverty using purchasing power parity (PPP) suggest even greater gains in poverty from 71–77 per cent in 1981 to 13–17 per cent. By any measure, China alone accounts for over 75 per cent of poverty reduction in the developing world over the last 30 years.

Published by Woodhead Publishing Limited, 2012

In March 2009, as a result of the global economic downturn in late 2008, the government put forward an economic stimulus package of 4 trillion yuan ($585 billion) for 2010–11, for 10 key sectors. Of the total, 1.2 trillion yuan is from the central government, and the remainder is to come from local governments, state-owned enterprises and the private sector. Some 63 per cent of the total is dedicated to infrastructure (reconstruction following the 2011 earthquake as well as infrastructure more generally). In addition to the stimulus package, the central government has invested substantial resources in alleviating the impact of the economic crisis in 2009, including investing 293 billion yuan ($43 billion) to improve the social safety net, offering 5 trillion yuan in additional loans, and investing 42 billion yuan ($6.2 billion) to stimulate employment. As a result of the large stimulus package, combined with policies to encourage consumption, China's economy grew by 8.7 per cent in 2009. GDP growth estimates for 2010 are projected at 9.5 per cent, with increases in export activity and declines expected in government-led investments as the crisis eases.

There are around 120,000 retail pharmacies in China and the majority of them are now able to sell Western medicines. Many of these are keen to advertise foreign products as these bring in greater revenue than low-margin products such as traditional medicines. Retail pharmacies are expected to evolve as the economy grows, but is likely that many more will be selling Western products such as over-the-counter medicines in the future.

China will soon announce a plan to invest a massive $1.5 trillion over five years into seven industries. The goal is to transform each sector into a world-class leader in innovative technology. Biotechnology is one of the target industries. Unlike most of the strategies presently in place for creating innovation, the plan does not call for huge government subsidies, but relies instead on creating incentives for bank lending, corporate investment and help from local governments. It is thought that China will cut the income tax rate in half – to 7.5 per cent – for investors in these industries.

The NDRC has ordered price reductions on 174 drugs from 60 companies. Since 2000, it has been the policy to allow pharmas

134   Clinical Research in Asia: Opportunities and Challenges

to set their own prices where the drugs are innovative, patented formulations. Now, it seems the NDRC will be in control of all pricing. The price cuts, which average 17 per cent, will come into effect from December 2012.

4.9.3 Regulatory environment

The Chinese governmental structure is complex, with the highest level of state legislative power being the National People's Congress (NPC). The NPC is elected for a period of five years with real power in the NPC being exercised by the Standing Committee, which has around 150 members and represents the main legislative body. There are a series of permanent special committees, including the Educational, Science, Culture and Public Health Committees. The President appoints Members of the State Council and it is these officials who have much of the responsibility for the development and implementation of government policies.

With regard to healthcare responsibilities, the Ministry of Health, the SDA and Ministry of Labour and Social Security all play a role. The Ministry of Health handles the main healthcare-related functions:

- drafting of health laws, regulations and policies;
- developing regional healthcare plans;
- coordination and overseeing implementation of health plans;
- producing and implementing plans for rural and maternal health;
- developing health education programmes, especially regarding preventive medicine;
- monitoring of infectious diseases;
- drawing up and implementing standards for medical institutions;
- supervising the country's blood collection and storage service;
- organising and supervising health programmes with external bodies such as the WHO;
- promotion of traditional Chinese medicine.

Published by Woodhead Publishing Limited, 2012

The Ministry of Labour and Social Security is mainly responsible for medical insurance issues, while the SDA is involved in the regulation of medical devices and biopharmaceutical products and the registration of foreign companies operating in China.

4.9.4 Overview of regulation in China

China's Drug Administration Law is the umbrella legislation for regulations regarding the administration and registration not only of drugs (new chemical/biological drugs as well as natural drugs and traditional Chinese medicine) but also the supervision and administration of medical devices.

4.9.5 Evolution of GCP

China has attempted to streamline its regulation and align the country with international standards of practice; as a result, the country's legal system governing pharmaceutical research, production and marketing has been substantially modified in recent years. To take one example, China's Ministry of Health first issued GCP guidance in 1998. The following year saw the establishment of the State Drug Administration (now SFDA), with the SFDA's GCP guidance formally published in 1999. The latest version of GCP was issued in 2003 after the new Drug Administration Law came into effect in 2001, and the new Drug Registration Procedure came into effect in 2002.

New drug regulations were introduced in 2002, and in mid-2003 more changes were brought in by the SFDA. While some changes were intended to shorten approval timelines, many introduced obstacles into the approvals process. The changes were designed to reduce evaluation timelines to 120 working days, and from October 2007, just 90 working days. China has also adjusted its multicentre clinical trial policy since December 2002.

Since 19 February 2004, SFDA regulation authorises only GCP-certified sites to conduct clinical trials. At present, 80 per cent of

Published by Woodhead Publishing Limited, 2012

136   Clinical Research in Asia: Opportunities and Challenges

medical resources are located in big cities, and 30 per cent of these resources are focused in large hospitals. As a result, treatment of patients with major maladies is concentrated in major hospitals. In 2005, China's population reached 1.3 billion people. With the largest population in the world, China has a uniquely abundant pool of potential study subjects, meaning that manufacturers can recruit subjects relatively quickly.

4.9.5.1 Article 30

Any drug clinical trial, including bioequivalence study, shall be approved by the SFDA, and shall be in compliance with GCP guidance. The relevant drug regulatory department shall supervise and inspect approved clinical trials.

4.9.5.2 Article 31

Clinical trials shall be conducted for new drug registration applications. As for generic drug registration applications and supplementary applications, clinical trials shall be conducted in accordance with the requirements in the Annex of the Provisions. Article 31 covers bioequivalence studies and the four stages of the clinical trial process (i.e. Phases I–IV):

- *Phase I – initial clinical pharmacology and safety evaluation studies in humans*: These studies are designed to observe tolerability of humans to and pharmacokinetics of a new drug, in order to provide a basis for establishing the administration regimen.
- *Bioequivalence study*: A bioequivalence study refers to a human study, which applies bioavailability study methods with pharmacokinetic parameters as indicators to compare active ingredient absorption rate and extent of the preparations in the same or different dosage forms of a drug in terms of statistical differences under the same experimental condition.
- *Phase II – preliminary evaluation of therapeutic effectiveness of a drug*: The purposes are to preliminarily evaluate the therapeutic

Published by Woodhead Publishing Limited, 2012

effectiveness and safety of the drug for particular indication(s) in patients, and provide evidence for the design of Phase III clinical trials and settlement of administrative dose regimen. According to specific trial objectives, this phase of trial may be designed in various forms, including the randomised blind controlled clinical trial.

- *Phase III – confirmation of therapeutic effectiveness of a drug*: The purposes are to further verify drug therapeutic effectiveness and safety on eligible patients with target indication(s), to evaluate overall benefit–risk relationships of the drug, and ultimately to provide sufficient evidence for the review of drug registration application. The study, in general, shall be a randomised blind controlled trial with an adequate sample size.
- *Phase IV – new drug post-marketing study*: The purposes are to assess therapeutic effectiveness and adverse reactions when a drug is widely used, to evaluate overall benefit–risk relationships of the drug when used among the general population or specific groups, and to adjust the administration dose, etc.

4.9.5.3 Article 32

The sample size of a drug clinical trial shall conform to the objectives of the clinical trial and fulfil statistical requirements, and shall be no smaller than the minimum number of subjects required by the Annex of the Provisions. Where there are circumstances, regarding rare or special diseases, etc., which request clinical sample size reduction or clinical trial exemption, a request shall be made with the clinical trial application, and reviewed and approved by the SFDA.

4.9.5.4 Article 33

As for vaccines prepared during bacterial or viral strain screening or other special drugs, if confirmed without any suitable animal model and laboratory measurement in terms of curative effectiveness, clinical trials may be applied for to the SFDA, subject to ensuring the safety of trial subjects.

Published by Woodhead Publishing Limited, 2012

4.9.5.5 Article 34

When a drug clinical trial is approved, the applicant shall select institutions for the clinical trial from those certified for conducting drug clinical trials.

4.9.5.6 Article 35

Drugs used for clinical trials shall be manufactured in facilities in compliance with the good manufacturing practice (GMP) for pharmaceutical products. The manufacturing process shall strictly meet the requirements of the GMP. The applicant shall be responsible for the quality of the drugs used for clinical trials.

4.9.5.7 Article 36

The applicant may conduct the testing for clinical trial drugs by itself, or entrust a drug testing institute specified in the Provisions to conduct such testing, according to its proposed specifications. Vaccines, blood products and other biological products specified by the SFDA shall be tested by drug testing institutes designated by the SFDA.

A drug can be used for a clinical trial only after tested as qualified. Drug regulatory departments may conduct sampling and testing on drugs used for clinical trials.

4.9.5.8 Article 37

Prior to conducting a clinical trial, the applicant shall report to the SFDA for record. The applicant shall also copy the following information to the drug regulatory department of the seat of the clinical trial institution and that of the province, autonomous region or municipality directly under the central government to receive the application: a confirmed clinical trial protocol, the name of the principal investigator at the institution in charge of the clinical trial, a list of participating institutions and names of investigators wherefrom, an ethic committee approval letter, and a template of the informed consent form, etc.

4.9.5.9 Article 38

Where the applicant finds a clinical trial institution violating relevant regulations or failing to implement the clinical trial protocol, it shall urge the institution to make corrections. If the circumstances are serious, the applicant may demand suspension or termination of the clinical trial, and shall report the matter to the SFDA and the drug regulatory departments of the relevant provinces, autonomous regions or municipalities directly under the central government.

4.9.5.10 Article 39

After completion of a clinical trial, the applicant shall submit a clinical trial final report, a statistical analysis report and its database to the SFDA.

4.9.5.11 Article 40

A clinical trial shall be conducted within three years after approval. If overdue, the original approval documents shall be invalid. If the clinical trial is still needed, the application shall be reapplied for.

4.9.5.12 Article 41

If any serious adverse event occurs during the clinical trial, the investigators shall report to the drug regulatory departments of the relevant provinces, autonomous regions or municipalities directly under the central government and the SFDA and notify the applicant within 24 hours, and report to the ethic committee in time.

4.9.6 Monitoring adverse drug reactions

China has established a network for reporting and monitoring adverse drug reactions (ADRs). In 1998, China officially joined the WHO Collaborating Center for International Drug Monitoring. In 2004, the state promulgated the Measures on Administration of

140 Clinical Research in Asia: Opportunities and Challenges

Reporting and Monitoring of Adverse Drug Reactions, thereby formally adopting a system of reporting and monitoring ADRs. By the end of 2002, ADR monitoring institutions at the provincial level and over 200 centres and stations below the provincial level had been set up for this purpose in 31 provinces, autonomous regions and municipalities directly under the central government. By then, a nationwide information network for monitoring ADRs had emerged, making it possible for electronic reporting and online real-time reporting. Since 2000, China has made visible progress in ADR reporting. In 2007, some 400 cases of ADR per 1 million people were reported, a ratio approaching that of the developed countries. This demonstrates the considerable improvement in China's monitoring and early-warning capability regarding ADRs. Drug administration departments promptly collect, evaluate and publish information about ADRs. By the end of June 2008, they had issued 13 bulletins in this respect, involving 44 types of drug.

4.9.6.1 Article 42

In any of the following circumstances during a clinical trial, the SFDA may order the applicant to modify the protocol, suspend or terminate the clinical trial:

- the ethics committee fails to perform its duty;
- the safety of the subjects cannot be adequately ensured;
- a serious adverse event is not reported within the specified timeline;
- there is evidence to prove that the drug used for the clinical trial is not effective;
- a quality problem occurs with the drug used for the clinical trial;
- there is a fraud in the clinical trial; or
- there is any other case violating the GCP guidelines.

4.9.6.2 Article 43

Where there is any unexpected large-scale adverse reaction or serious adverse event, or there is evidence to prove any serious quality problem with the drug used for a clinical trial, the SFDA or the drug regulatory department of the province, autonomous region or municipality directly under the central government may take emergency control measures and order the clinical trial to be suspended or terminated. The applicant and clinical trial institution must stop the clinical trial immediately.

4.9.6.3 Article 44

An overseas applicant intending to conduct an international multicentre clinical trial in China shall submit an application to the SFDA in accordance with the Provisions, and fulfil the following requirements:

- The drugs used for clinical trials shall be already approved or in Phase II or III clinical trial overseas. The SFDA does not accept any overseas applicant's international multicentre clinical trial application for any preventive vaccine not yet registered overseas.
- Before approving the conduct of an international multicentre clinical trial, the SFDA may first require the applicant to conduct a Phase I clinical trial in China.
- If any serious adverse reactions are observed when conducting an international multicentre clinical trial in China, or there are unexpected adverse reactions associated with the drug in any other country, the applicant shall, in accordance with relevant regulations, report to the SFDA in time.
- The applicant shall submit a complete clinical trial report to the SFDA after the completion of the clinical trial.
- The data obtained from an international multicentre clinical trial for drug registration application in China shall conform to the clinical trial requirements in the Provisions. All the study materials of the international multicentre clinical trial shall be submitted.

4.9.7 Application and approval of new drugs

4.9.7.1 Article 45

The SFDA may implement special review and approval in cases of the following applications:

142 Clinical Research in Asia: Opportunities and Challenges

- active ingredients extracted from plants, animals and minerals, etc. and their preparations not yet marketed in China, and newly discovered Chinese crude drugs and their preparations;
- chemical drug substances and their preparations and biological products not yet approved for marketing in China or abroad;
- new drugs for the treatment of diseases such as AIDS, malignant tumours and rare diseases, etc. with significant clinical advantage; and
- new drugs for the treatment of diseases for which effective therapeutic methods are not available.

For drugs specified in the previous clause, applicants may apply for special review and approval in the process of drug registration. The SFDA's Centre for Drug Evaluation shall organise expert meetings to determine whether or not to conduct special review and approval for the drugs. Specified measures for special review and approval shall be formulated separately.

4.9.7.2 Article 46

Where a new drug is co-developed by several institutions, the registration can be applied for by one of the institutions, and its duplicate application shall not be made by the others. If a joint application for registration is needed, the institutions shall co-sign as the applicant of the new drug. Each approved new drug, including its different strengths, shall be produced by only one institution.

4.9.7.3 Article 47

Registration applications to change the dosage form of a marketed drug without changing the administration route shall employ new techniques to improve drug quality and safety, and the changed dosage form shall have significant clinical advantage compared with the previous dosage form.

Registration applications to change the dosage form without changing the route of administration or to claim any new indication shall be submitted by certified manufacturers, with exceptions for

Published by Woodhead Publishing Limited, 2012

Clinical research in China

special dosage forms such as targeting delivery, sustained release and controlled-release preparations, etc.

4.9.7.4 Article 48

In the process of the review and approval of a new drug, the registration classification and technical requirements thereof shall not be changed, even though the preparations of the same active ingredients are approved for marketing abroad. In the process of the review and approval of a new drug, the registration classification and technical requirements thereof shall not be changed, even though the preparations of the same active ingredients applied for by domestic manufacturers are approved for marketing in China.

4.9.7.5 Article 49

The dossier for drug registration application shall be submitted in its completed form only. After the drug registration application is accepted, the applicant shall add no other technical materials, with the exception of applications of special review and approval, new findings regarding drug safety, or supplementary materials as required. Should an applicant deem it necessary to supplement the application with new technical material, the submitted application shall be withdrawn. If there is no dossier for a similar product submitted by another applicant currently under review, the applicant may reapply in line with the relevant requirements in the Provisions.

4.9.8 Clinical trials for new drugs

4.9.8.1 Article 50

After completing the pre-clinical study, the applicant shall complete the Application Form for Drug Registration, and report authentically relevant materials to the drug regulatory department of the province, autonomous region or municipality directly under the central government where the applicant is located.

Published by Woodhead Publishing Limited, 2012

144 Clinical Research in Asia: Opportunities and Challenges

4.9.8.2 Article 51

Drug regulatory departments of provinces, autonomous regions or municipalities directly under the central government shall conduct the preliminary review of the application dossiers and issue a acceptance notice of drug registration application if requirements are met, or a non-acceptance notice in which reasons shall be given if requirements are not met.

4.9.8.3 Article 52

Drug regulatory departments of provinces, autonomous regions or municipalities directly under the central government shall organise onsite inspections of the drug research and development conditions and raw data, conduct a preliminary review of the submitted dossiers, and provide review opinions within five days from the date the application is accepted. Where the drug for which the registration is applied is a biological product, samples from three production batches thereof shall also be collected for testing, and a notice for the testing for registration shall be issued to the drug testing institute.

4.9.8.4 Article 53

Drug regulatory departments of provinces, autonomous regions or municipalities directly under the central government shall deliver the review opinions, inspection reports and the application dossiers to the SFDA's Centre for Drug Evaluation within the specified timeline, and serve notice to the applicants.

4.9.8.5 Article 54

The drug testing institute that receives a notice for the testing for registration shall test the samples according to the drug specifications submitted by the applicant, verify the submitted drug specifications, and submit a certificate of analysis for drug registration to the SFDA's Centre for Drug Evaluation within the specified timeline, and copy to the applicant.

Published by Woodhead Publishing Limited, 2012

4.9.8.6 Article 55

After receiving submitted dossiers, the SFDA's Centre for Drug Evaluation shall organise pharmaceutical, medical and other technical personnel to conduct the technical review of the submitted dossiers within the specified timeline, and when necessary may request, with reasons, applicants to provide supplementary materials. After completing technical reviews, the Centre for Drug Evaluation shall give technical review opinions and report together with relevant documents to the SFDA.

The SFDA shall make review and approval decisions based on the technical review opinions. Where the regulations are conformed to, a Drug Clinical Trial Approval shall be issued; where the regulations are not conformed to, a Disapproval Notice shall be issued with reasons provided.

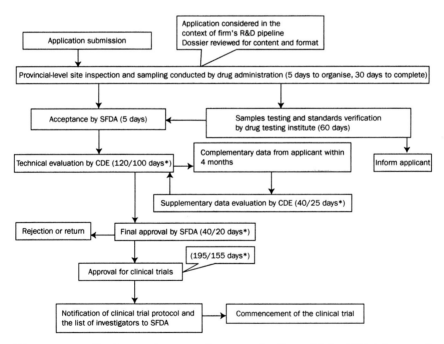

Figure 4.10 Review and approval process for Drug Clinical Trial Approval

Note: Days before forward slash refer to timeline for ordinary approval; days following the slash represent the timeline for fast-track approval. All figures refer to working days.

146 Clinical Research in Asia: Opportunities and Challenges

4.9.8.7 Article 150

The time for technical review shall be kept in accordance with the following provisions:

- *New drug application for clinical trial*: 90 days; any drug permitted to enter the special review and approval procedures: 80 days.
- *New drug application for production*: 150 days; any drug permitted to enter the special review and approval procedures: 120 days.
- *Application for changing the dosage form of a marketed drug or for a generic drug*: 160 days.
- *Supplementary application subject to technical review*: 40 days.

The time for the technical review of an import drug registration application shall be kept in accordance with the previous clause. Table 4.6 compares the investigational new drug review process of the US FDA and Chinese SFDA.

Table 4.6 Comparison of investigational new drug review process between the US FDA and Chinese SFDA

FDA	SFDA
Pre-IND meetings	No pre-CTA meeting – CTA filed at manufacturer's risk
Submit IND to FDA	
FDA review time (30 days)	SFDA coordinated review (165/125 days*)
CMC requirement correlated with the stage of drug development; no sample testing by FDA during IND review process	Comprehensive CMC data, cGMP inspection, and conformance lot testing required at early stage of drug development
Start clinical trial or put on hold	Clinical trial approved, or rejection similar to market approval dossier
Total review time: 30 days	Total review time: 165/125 days

*Note: The revised version of the drug registration regulation has been in effect since 1 October 2007; the 'Special Review Procedure' was released on 7 January 2009 (*www.sfda.gov.cn*)
CMC, chemistry manufacturing & control; cGMP, current good manufacturing practices

Published by Woodhead Publishing Limited, 2012

4.10 Future outlook

China's large and growing population suggests that there will be a rising demand for modern medicines and this has led to many pharma companies investing in China. However, the size and structure of the future Chinese pharmaceutical market will depend on the purchasing power of people in different areas of the country and the government's efforts to reform healthcare. At present, the Chinese market is fragmented with only certain sections of the population able to afford modern healthcare. The biopharmaceutical industry has a clear interest in the country's economy improving as greater affluence will increase the demand for their products. It is widely predicted that the Chinese biopharmaceutical market is set to grow, but it is unclear as to what course this will take, as widening access to healthcare across the country represents a huge challenge to the government.

Provision of healthcare is expensive and requires ongoing investment. Governments around the world have become concerned at how much they must spend as their populations grow and demand for the latest healthcare services and medicines increases. In this regard China is no exception. Furthermore, the rising elderly population and falling birth rate are placing a great strain on funding for public healthcare. As the elderly population grows, the number of potential workers whose tax contributions can help support the care of their fellow citizens will decline.

China's enormous population has presented the government with unique challenges in the field of healthcare. Any increased investment in healthcare must be accompanied by a strategy that effectively targets the various healthcare requirements of different regions in the country and their local communities. Unfortunately for China, although many countries around the world have examined different approaches to widening access to healthcare, no country faces such a large medical demand. Therefore, although the country may look at other examples of healthcare systems around the world for guidance, China's healthcare system will need to evolve in its own way.

Published by Woodhead Publishing Limited, 2012

148 Clinical Research in Asia: Opportunities and Challenges

Biopharma companies will need to be aware of how healthcare policies affect their operations in the country and relate their market strategies to these developments. Assumptions that work in other markets may not necessarily apply in China and companies must be careful not to get caught out by political events and social developments. The Chinese biopharmaceutical market has considerable potential, but it is still emerging and there is no clear indication as to which type of companies will best succeed. There is no doubt that China will prove to be a prosperous market, but as with other emerging markets, a cautious approach to expansion will be the key. Many biopharma companies have found it useful to set out a range of outcomes in their predictions so that they can survive even the most hostile scenario.

On an optimistic note, many companies have operated in similarly evolving conditions in other global markets and have become well accustomed to incorporating local social, political and economic factors into their market strategies.

Published by Woodhead Publishing Limited, 2012

5

Clinical research in South Korea

Abstract: South Korea has grown significantly as a destination for industry-sponsored clinical trials since 2005. This chapter focuses on the CRO market in South Korea. It then analyses the clinical trial environment and the evolution of good clinical practices in South Korea. It goes on to describe the clinical trial process and key market players undertaking clinical research in South Korea. Finally, it provides an environmental analysis and outlook for future of the South Korean pharmaceutical industry.

5.1 Pharmaceutical industry overview

Demographically, South Korea has a fairly large population, which is over double the size of Australia or Taiwan. Economically, South Korea's economy was quite badly affected by the global recession, but it started growing from 2010 onwards. In 2009, South Korea spent $66.2 billion on healthcare, and this is expected to increase to $114.4 billion in 2016. The South Korean pharmaceutical market was valued at around $9 billion in 2008 and $9.6 billion in 2009, representing a compound annual growth rate (CAGR) of 7 per cent for the period spanning 2005–09. In comparison, the Chinese and Japanese markets grew with CAGRs of 20.1 per cent and 2.3 per cent respectively, over the same period. Cardiovascular sales proved the most lucrative for the South Korea pharmaceuticals market in 2009, generating total revenues of $1.8 billion, equivalent to

Published by Woodhead Publishing Limited, 2012

150   Clinical Research in Asia: Opportunities and Challenges

18.8 per cent of the market's overall value. In comparison, alimentary/metabolism sales generated revenues of $1.3 billion in 2009, equating to 13.9 per cent of the market's aggregate revenues. Table 5.1 shows the revenue of the top 10 Korean companies and top 10 global pharma companies in South Korea.

The recent failure of multinational companies to protect their drug patents illustrates how patent protection is somewhat limited in South Korea. Novartis has been engaged in legal action over the pricing of Glivec in South Korea. Since 2008, due to the patent expiration of market-leading products such as Lipitor, Plavix and Cozaar, domestic drug companies in South Korea have been focusing their attention on generic formulations, while the multinationals prepare to launch select patented and in-licensed products in the near to medium term. The growth in generic business has fuelled the emergence of a number of Korean companies, including SK Chemicals and Chon Kun Dang. Even the Japanese generics manufacturer Nichi-iko announced in October 2010 that it plans to

Table 5.1   Top 10 local and foreign companies in South Korea

Company	Revenues 2004 ($m)	Revenues 2003 ($m)	% Δ (Y/Y)	Company	Revenues 2004 ($m)	Revenues 2003 ($m)	% Δ (Y/Y)
Dong-A	541.2	492.5	9.9	Pfizer	257.7	244.5	5.4
Yuhan	340.4	306.6	11.0	Han Dok	241.5	222.8	8.4
Han Mi	317.0	243.5	30.1	GSK	228.7	222.3	2.9
Choong Wae	303.2	282.4	7.4	Bayer	208.2	170.1	22.4
Dae Woong	281.5	248.4	13.3	MSD	173.9	172.5	0.8
Jeil	221.1	188.6	17.2	Sanofi-Aventis	162.0	115.6	40.1
LG Life Sciences	213.6	179.0	19.3	Novartis	145.4	117.6	23.6
Il Dong	197.3	171.6	15.0	Janssen	137.6	138.7	–0.8
Kwang Dong	187.3	134.2	39.6	Abbott	107.5	102.7	4.7
Chong Kun Dang	186.2	162.0	14.9	Lilly	105.9	84.7	25.0

Source: media reports

Published by Woodhead Publishing Limited, 2012

buy a large stake in Aprogen, a South Korean generic pharmaceutical company. Besides their strong generic background, companies such as LG Life Sciences, Dong-A, SK, Green Cross and Bukwang are active in drug development programmes. Table 5.2 summarises their initiatives and the progress of their drug development programmes.

The South Korean government has supported a lot of development in the areas of biologics and biotechnology R&D. South Korea's biologics sector is witnessing rapid growth and many domestic companies have been expanding their operations. RNL Bio has announced plans to build a stem-cell R&D and manufacturing plant in Shanghai, and intends to build a new influenza vaccine factory in Eumseong, North Chungcheong Province. Furthermore, 2010 has also seen the completion of several significant competitive strategies in the biologics and biosimilars sector. CrystalGenomics has merged with the pharmaceutical distributor BexPharm, Seoul Pharma has signed an alliance agreement for biosimilars with the Japanese drug developer consultancy GDDRI. GlaxoSmithKline has also entered into a strategic alliance with Dong-A, and SK Chemicals has signed a memorandum of understanding with US-based Xcellerex to develop vaccines.

Table 5.2 South Korean companies' investigational new drugs and new drug applications

Product	Indication	Company	Stage of development
Factive	Quinolone antibiotic	LG Life Sciences	Marketed
SR-hGH	Growth deficiency	LG Life Sciences	Phase III
Clevudine	Hepatitis B	Bukwang	Phase III
LB80380	Hepatitis B	LG Life Sciences	Phase II
DA-8159	Erectile dysfunction	Dong-A	Phase II
YKP 509	Epilepsy	SK	Phase II
YKP 10A	Depression	SK	Phase II
Osteoporosis treatment	Bone formation	Green Cross	Phase I

Source: Media reports

152 Clinical Research in Asia: Opportunities and Challenges

5.1.1 New drugs marketed in South Korea

The last decade has seen a handful of new drugs receive regulatory approval in South Korea, including new chemical entities, herbal drugs and bio-drugs (Table 5.3). These drugs are for various indications such as cancers, arthritis, gastritis, duodenal ulcer, diabetic foot ulcers. A few of these drugs are antibiotic and are for cartilage repair.

Over-the counter (OTC) medicines represent another growing segment in South Korea due to the trend for self-medication. Switching from prescription to OTC drugs is likely to trigger the introduction of newer pharmaceuticals in product portfolios.

Every South Korean citizen is entitled to free healthcare through universal insurance coverage, but in many cases they end up paying for a lot of drugs out of their own pockets as their insurance premiums are not high enough. Health expenditure is modest if expressed as a percentage of GDP. However, health expenditure is expected to rise considerably over the forecast period, both in total and per capita terms. South Korea has advanced hospitals, but its rate of beds per thousand population is fairly low.

Table 5.3 New drugs being marketed in South Korea

	Product	Indication	Date of approval
NCE drugs	Sunfla	Stomach cancer	1999
	Millican	Liver cancer	2001
	Q-Roxin	Quinolone antibiotic	2001
	Factive	Quinolone antibiotic	2002 (Korea) 2003 (US)
	Camtobell	Ovarian cancer	2003
	Maxmarvil	Osteoporosis	2004
	Revanex	Duodenal ulcer	2005
Bio drugs	Chondron	Cartilage repair	2001
	EGF	Diabetic foot ulcer	2001
Herbal medicine	Joins	Arthritis	2001
	Stillen	Acute/chronic gastritis	2002

Source: Media reports

Published by Woodhead Publishing Limited, 2012

5.2 CRO market in South Korea

The South Korean CRO market is driven by pre-clinical and clinical CROs, bioequivalence studies and clinical laboratory business. The total CRO market size of South Korea including pre-clinical, bioequivalence and clinical laboratory and clinical business is estimated to be approximately $100 million. Within these segments, clinical CRO market size is estimated to be $50 million. South Korea's clinical CRO domain hosts full-service CROs, monitoring-only CROs and electronic data capture CROs. Some are local Korean CROs, but a few global CROs, including Japanese CROs, also have their operations in South Korea.

The local CRO segment in South Korea has grown very rapidly, especially in the last five years due to the increased number of global trials. Moreover, Japanese, US and European pharmaceutical and biotech companies have shown great interest in conducting clinical trials in South Korea, as it is one of the most recommendable countries in Southeast Asia due to its supportive environment for clinical trials, market size (ranked 12th in the world), high and rapid enrolment rates, well-equipped facilities, quality data and experienced investigators. The Korean CRO Association has operated since 2000 and its members include Korean CROs, Japanese and global CROs. The Korean CROs are all clinical CROs, providing mainly monitoring, study development, and data management and statistical analysis services.

Although pipeline developments for South Korean pharma companies are not public knowledge, in fact only a few companies who are into fully-fledged R&D are researching new chemical entities. LG Life Sciences is one of the few South Korean companies active in drug development. Figure 5.1 describes some of the products in its development pipeline.

5.2.1 Government initiatives

Due to government initiatives, the investigational new drug (IND) approval timeline has been accelerated, adding to the supportive

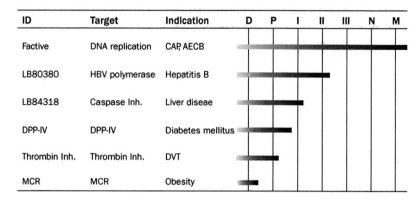

Figure 5.1 New chemical entities in the LG Life Sciences pipeline
Source: Media reports

environment. The government has also declared its intention to eradicate unnecessary laws related to the conduct of global clinical studies. Since 2004, the government has also designated 15 sites nationwide as 'local clinical trial centres'. The South Korean government is to provide these with up to $1 million annually for five years to build infrastructure.

5.3 Clinical trial environment

In South Korea, there is no specialised site management company. This means that CROs generally have to take care of all activities related to site management, including institutional review board (IRB) submission and training clinical research coordinators (CRCs). Clinical research associates (CRAs) need to translate and explain in Korean written English communication such as urgent questions and data queries to or from the clinical trial site. Once they have accrued a year or two of experience, most CRCs seek to become CRAs. Hundreds of CRAs have been recruited by global pharma companies and CROs in recent times as there is plenty of opportunity and the unstable working conditions (both contractual and environmental) associated with CRC positions – some of which come without dedicated workspace or insurance – offer little incentive to stay. In short, site facilities for clinical trials in South Korea can be described as good, but the working environment for staff is less than ideal: the position of CRA in Korea is attractive but considered one of the toughest medical jobs for clinical trial staff.

The trend of moving to global companies is also applicable to the local CROs. Each year almost 5–10 per cent of CRAs leave local CROs and go abroad just to study English. After learning English, they usually choose to pursue their careers with global CROs or pharma companies in the belief that a global company can provide them with sound training, good management and a stable working environment, thus giving them the opportunity for personal development while at the same time maintaining a good work–life balance.

Against this background, local CROs have been competing with global CROs to conduct clinical studies in Korea. Local CROs are at a disadvantage here, however, as the clinical study environment is broadening to become more global in reach (consider, for example, the change in Japan's regulatory environment to encourage Asian studies). Local CROs need to be comparable with global CROs, not only in cost and personnel capability, but also in the standard of their structure and systems, and their quality as measured by certain key criteria. For local CROs to survive, they must provide global-quality service to Korean companies that may have not used global CRO services.

5.4 Evolution of GCP in South Korea

Guidance for GCP in South Korea dates back to 28 December 1987, although it has only been enforced since 1 October 1995. To meet the demand for global harmonisation, Korean GCP guidance was further revised in accordance with ICH-GCP in 2000. In 2002, the Korean FDA introduced the systems for IND application. Prior to this, the Korean FDA required the safety and efficacy data of the investigational product in order to approve the clinical trial application. Drug trials then were generally small, with only 30–90 patients. Along with the implementation of new systems for IND in December 2002, Korean GCP guidance was brought in line with the

156 Clinical Research in Asia: Opportunities and Challenges

ICH-GCP E6 guidelines. The Korean FDA implemented a good review practice (GRP) by early 2007 which has improved the efficiency and effectiveness of reviewing the drug products, and improved the transparency and reliability of the review process. Because of the short history of clinical trials in South Korea, the regulators tend to benchmark US FDA regulations and cases.

With the adoption of ICH-GCP, the Korean GCP guidelines complied with the key features of the ICH-GCP vis-à-vis the protection of subjects' rights, IRB composition, serious adverse event (SAE) reporting procedures, record access and monitoring. In addition, Korean GCP guidance includes additional features such as making heads of hospitals responsible for the contract with and supervision of the investigator and IRB. Korean GCP guidance specifies that only Korean FDA accredited hospitals can conduct clinical trials and that a study pharmacist should be designated for each site (Table 5.4).

5.4.1 IND review process

The IND application is submitted in prescribed formats for each phase. The Korean FDA aims to respond to the IND application in 30 working days. Invariably, it requests supplementary materials. It is thus safe to assume that the IND application will take 90–120 working days from the date it was initially filed. There is no need to have Korean partners when filing INDs as only Korean entities can make

Table 5.4 ICH-GCP vs Korean GCP

Common features	Additional features of Korean GCP
Protection of subject's rights	Head of hospital has responsibility for contract with and
Composition of institutional review board	supervision of investigator and institutional review board
Reporting of serious adverse events	Only Korean FDA-accredited hospitals can conduct clinical trials
Record access and monitoring	Designated pharmacist for each study site

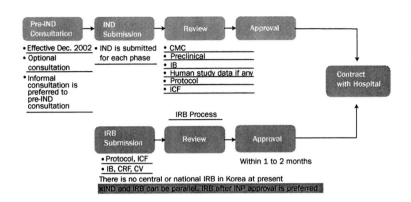

Figure 5.2 The IND review process in South Korea

the IND application. An authorised person from a locally registered pharmaceutical company (sponsor) with a permanent address in Korea can make the IND application. In the case of an investigator-initiated trial, the principal investigator can also make the IND application. The applicant shall be responsible for the product and all information supplied in the clinical trial import licence/clinical trial exemption (CTIL/CTX) application. The applicant shall also be responsible for updating any information relevant to the product or application. There is no fee for the processing of IND applications in South Korea. The review process is illustrated in Figure 5.2.

Table 5.5 presents the material required by the Korean FDA for filing the IND application.

5.4.2 IRB review process

There is no centralised or national IRB in South Korea. Each medical centre runs its own IRB, which generally meets once a month. The protocol, investigator's brochure and case report form (CRF) are generally required. The IRB submission is independent of the IND application. The IRB submission package must include the following documents:

158 Clinical Research in Asia: Opportunities and Challenges

Table 5.5 Documents required for IND submission

Document	Description
Protocol	The protocol must be fully translated into Korean
Investigator's brochure	Its summary must be translated into Korean
Specification and analysis method	Submitted in Korean using the Korean FDA template, with the original version attached; GMP certificate and QC lab contact to be provided
Introductory statement and general investigational plan	Its summary must be translated into Korean
Chemistry, manufacturing and control (CMC) information/ biological characteristics	Detailed information, including flow-chart where possible, to be submitted in Korean using the Korean FDA template, with the original version attached
Pharmacology (efficacy, general pharmacological effects)	Its summary must be translated into Korean
Pharmacokinetics and pharmacodynamics (ADME)	Its summary must be translated into Korean
Toxicology information	Its summary must be translated into Korean
Results of clinical trials	Phase I–III data to be submitted
References	Literature, published materials etc

ADME, absorption distribution metabolism and excretion

- trial protocol(s)/amendment(s);
- case record forms;
- written informed consent form(s) (ICFs);
- patient information sheet;
- investigator's brochure;
- available safety information;
- investigational product (IP) label translated into Korean;
- information about payments and compensation for subjects;
- investigator's current curriculum vitae and/or other documentation;
- standard operating procedures (SOPs) and any other documents that the IRB/IEC may need to fulfil its responsibilities.

Published by Woodhead Publishing Limited, 2012

The IRB shall review a proposed clinical trial within the period defined in the SOP and document its views (identifying the trial and list of documents reviewed). The IRB can approve the trial or seek modifications prior to its approval/favourable opinion. The IRB has every right to disapprove or terminate/suspend the trial.

5.4.3 Study start-up timeline

Translation of essential documents takes a lot of time during the study start-up process. For Korean FDA and IRB submission, full translation is required for the protocol and protocol synopsis, investigator's brochure and brochure summary, the ICF, patient information sheet and IP label into Korean. This usually takes four weeks. In addition to the translation, site selection, arranging insurance, preparing the ethics committee submission package, getting investigator contracts etc. takes a lot of time. Study start-up timelines are summarised in Table 5.6.

5.4.4 Import, storage and labelling requirements of the investigational product

The IND is the import permit for investigational products. It takes about one day for the investigational product to clear customs. There are a number of companies with IP storage space that meets the

Table 5.6 Study start-up timeline in South Korea

Activity	Estimated timeline
Pre-regulatory activities (e.g. translations, insurance, ethics committee submissions)	6–8 weeks
Ethics committee approval process	4–8 weeks
Regulatory authority approval process	4–12 weeks
Post-regulatory activities	4 weeks
Estimated total	32 weeks

Published by Woodhead Publishing Limited, 2012

160 Clinical Research in Asia: Opportunities and Challenges

requirements of good storage practice. These are generally drug importers or wholesalers. They will deliver the investigational product to study sites upon request. The charge is reasonable. Although drug labelling in the local language is not mandatory, labelling in Korean is recommended. Certified vendors can prepare Korean labels to use while packaging.

5.4.5 Insurance

There is no specific insurance requirement for studies conducted in South Korea. Trial-related injuries must be indemnified under a global insurance cover or a local cover or both. Both global and local insurance players have started providing clinical trial insurance.

5.4.6 Safety reporting

Unexpected fatal or life-threatening ADRs occurring in clinical investigations must be reported quickly. The Korean FDA should be notified (e.g. by telephone, fax transmission or in writing) as soon as possible, but no later than seven calendar days after the sponsor first becomes aware of the ADR; as complete a report as possible must then be filed within eight additional calendar days. Serious unexpected ADRs that are not fatal or life-threatening must be filed as soon as possible but no later than 15 calendar days after the sponsor first becomes aware that the case meets the minimum criteria for expedited reporting. The CIOMS-I form is a widely accepted standard for expedited adverse event reporting. However, no matter what the form or format used, it is important to include, when available, certain basic information/data elements with any expedited report.

The sponsor shall submit to the regulatory authority(ies) all safety updates and periodic reports, as detailed in the applicable regulatory requirement(s). Every submission must also include a cover letter and expedited safety report(s) from the same clinical trial protocol. Reports submitted electronically must have the expedited safety report(s) attached to the e-mail as a PDF file; local and foreign expedited safety reports should be split into two separate PDF files.

Published by Woodhead Publishing Limited, 2012

Clinical research in South Korea

For expedited safety reports sent in printed copy, an acknowledgment of receipt shall be made upon submission; for expedited safety reports sent by e-mail, an acknowledgment of receipt will be sent by e-mail.

5.4.7 Recruitment modalities

South Korean investigators are well trained and conversant in English. They are well networked and it is common practice to recruit one investigator and use his/her network of investigators to recruit more investigators for the trial. Indeed, the referral system works well in South Korea: each investigator has his/her own pool of patients, and clinical trial participants are recruited from the pool rather than by referral.

5.4.8 Interim report submission

The Korean FDA specifies that in cases of trials lasting for more than six months, an interim report shall be submitted at six-monthly intervals. The interim report shall include the number of patients treated, number of SAEs reported, number of discontinued patients post-randomisation with reasons, progress of trial and any findings obtained up to the time of the report.

5.4.9 Discontinuation/termination of trial

The licence holder shall inform the Korean FDA of any decision to discontinue the trial to which the licence relates and shall state the reason for the decision. The licence holder should return the CTIL/CTX as soon as possible. On termination of the trial, the CTIL or CTX licence holder shall submit to the Korean FDA an end-of-study summary report pertaining to the sites conducting the trial within three months from the last patient out/last patient last visit. In cases of a multicentre trial where the study is completed at different times at each site, an end-of-study summary report should be submitted within three months of site closure.

Published by Woodhead Publishing Limited, 2012

162 Clinical Research in Asia: Opportunities and Challenges

5.4.10 Final study report

The Korean FDA shall be informed on the trial findings within one year after the completion of the trial or within one year from frozen file or data lock date for international multicentre studies. The Korean FDA shall be informed of any possible delay in submission of the report particularly where the delay is unavoidable, as in multicentre studies.

5.4.11 Drug accountability/disposal report

A product accountability/disposal report shall be submitted to Korean FDA after site closure. This report should include the original or copy of the CTIL/CTX, statement of the quantity of drug(s)/study medication(s) received, the balance of the study medication(s), letters for additional quantity and disposal-related information. In the case of disposal and/or return of used/unused drug supplies, confirmation/approval from sponsor and appropriate local regulatory authorities must be verified. In the case of return, the drug must be returned to the sponsor's regional depot within South Korea or to the depot in the country of origin.

5.5 Clinical trials in South Korea

During 2008 to 2010, South Korea participated in more than 200 industry-sponsored GCP trials every year (Figure 5.3). In 2010, the flow of new trials grew more than 20 per cent versus 2009. By mid-July, 2011, there were 2,620 trials listed in the clinical trials registry for South Korea, out of which 1,042 trials were active and recruiting. Of the 2,620 trials undertaken in South Korea, 1,501 trials are industry-sponsored trials and 1,091 trials are sponsored by individual investigators, local institutions or hospitals, universities or other organisations.

Further analysis of the industry-sponsored clinical trials suggests that numerous GCP studies in diverse therapeutic areas are being

Published by Woodhead Publishing Limited, 2012

Clinical research in South Korea

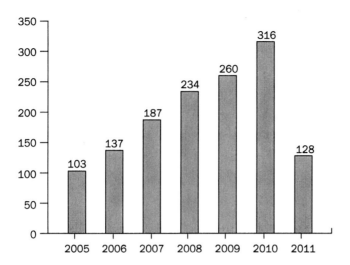

Figure 5.3 Growth of industry-sponsored clinical trials in South Korea

Source: www.clinicaltrials.gov (accessed July 2011); 2011 figures are from January to mid-July

conducted in South Korea. Some 47 per cent of these trials are in Phase III, 24 per cent in Phase II and 18 per cent in Phase IV (Figure 5.4). A small number of Phase I trials (11 per cent) are also undertaken in South Korea.

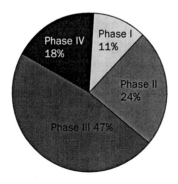

Figure 5.4 Industry-sponsored clinical trials in South Korea, by phase

Source: www.clinicaltrials.gov (accessed February 2011)

Published by Woodhead Publishing Limited, 2012

164 Clinical Research in Asia: Opportunities and Challenges

While most of the trials quoted in Table 5.7 are from global sponsors, there are a significant number of trials undertaken by institutes of national repute.

Table 5.8 lists the institution/hospital sponsored trials in South Korea. Certain institutes, such as Seoul National University Hospital, Samsung Medical Centre, Asan Medical Centre, the Catholic University, Yonsei University and the Cardiovascular Research Foundation are conducting a particularly large number of trials.

Table 5.7 Industry-sponsored trials in South Korea

Industry sponsor	No. of trials
Pfizer	157
GlaxoSmithKline	148
AstraZeneca	94
Sanofi-Aventis	90
Novartis	86
Eli Lilly and Company	82
Bayer	76
Boehringer Ingelheim Pharmaceuticals	76
Bristol-Myers Squibb	74
Hoffmann-La Roche	45
Astellas Pharma Inc	41
Korea Otsuka Pharmaceutical Co., Ltd.	30
Merck	30
Bukwang Pharmaceutical	23
Dong-A Pharmaceutical Co., Ltd.	22
Chong Kun Dang Pharmaceutical	20
Novo Nordisk	19
Boryung Pharmaceutical	14
Hanmi Pharmaceutical	13
LG Life Sciences	10
Total	1,150

Source: *www.clinicaltrials.gov* (accessed July 2011)

Published by Woodhead Publishing Limited, 2012

Clinical research in South Korea 165

Table 5.8 Institution/hospital sponsored trials in South Korea, July 2011

Medical centre	No. of trials
Seoul National University Hospital	251
Samsung Medical Centre	208
Yonsei University	165
Asan Medical Centre	137
National Cancer Centre, Korea	77
Korea University	61
Cardiovascular Research Foundation, Korea	40
Inje University	40
The Catholic University of Korea	39
Severance Hospital	29
Gachon University Gil Medical Centre	27
Hallym University Medical Centre	27
Chonnam National University Hospital	23

Source: *www.clinicaltrials.gov* (accessed on July 2011)

5.6 Accreditation of medical centres

Medical centres must pass Korean FDA inspection to participate in Phase II and III clinical trials. Approximately 142 centres have been accredited by Korean FDA for the conduct of clinical trials. Only a handful of medical centres have the facility and government permits for Phase I.

A non-exhaustive list of accredited medical centres is as follows:

- Seoul University Hospital;
- National Cancer Centre;
- Kwandong University;
- East-West Neo Medical Centre;
- Keimyung University;
- Asan Medical Centre;

Published by Woodhead Publishing Limited, 2012

166   Clinical Research in Asia: Opportunities and Challenges

- Yonsei University Health System;
- Seoul St. Mary's Hospital, The Catholic University of Korea;
- Seoul National University Bundang Hospital;
- Gangnam Severance Hospital, Yonsei University College of Medicine;
- Yongdong Severance Hospital;
- Korean Institute of Tuberculosis;
- Hanyang University Medical Centre;
- Haeundae Paik Hospital, INJE University School of Medicine;
- Wonju Christian Hospital;
- Sanggye-Paik Hospital;
- Gyunghee University Medical Centre;
- Hanyang University Guri Hospital;
- Korea University Guro Hospital;
- Chonbuk National University Hospital;
- Chungnam National University Hospital;
- Kyungpook National University Hospital;
- St. Paul's Hospital.

An analysis of the trials registered between 2005 and 2008 suggests that sites are spread across cities, though Seoul has the highest number of study sites (Table 5.9). Although figures are not yet available, smaller cities are now contributing in a big way and more and more new sites are being opened in smaller cities.

5.6.1 Therapeutic focus

Due to advancement in medical infrastructure and availability of patient population, pharmaceutical sponsors involve South Korea in global clinical trials. As can be seen from Table 5.10, the most common therapeutic areas are oncology, cardiology, central nervous system, endocrinology, infectious disease and respiratory trials.

Published by Woodhead Publishing Limited, 2012

Clinical research in South Korea

Table 5.9 Number of industry-sponsored study sites in South Korea by city (trials registered 2005–08)

	Total sites n	Total sites (A) %	Population n	Sites/ million population n	Part of Korean population (B) %	Ratio A/B %	Multi-national sites n	Local sites n	Local %
Seoul Metro	770	53.4	23,800,000	32.4	48.5	1.2	579	191	24.8
Suwon	95	7.2	1,105,953	85.9	2.3	3.2	76	19	20.0
Busan	77	5.8	3,719,989	20.7	7.6	0.8	58	24	81.2
Daegu	69	5.2	2,595,202	26.6	5.8	1.0	45	24	84.8
Incheon	51	8.9	2,716,702	18.8	5.5	0.7	40	11	21.6
Gwangju	42	8.2	1,440,012	29.2	2.9	1.1	80	12	23.6
Seongnam	86	2.7	1,028,007	85.2	2.1	1.8	27	9	25.0
Daejeon	82	2.4	1,490,888	21.5	8.0	0.8	1.8	14	43.8
Coyang	19	1.4	1,078,088	17.7	2.2	0.7	18	1	5.8
Jeonju	18	1.4	645,106	27.9	1.8	1.0	8	10	55.6
Buchaon	17	1.8	850,788	20.0	1.7	0.7	12	5	29.4
Cheongju	10	0.8	687,646	15.7	1.8	0.6	7	8	80.0
Chuncheon	10	0.8	260,468	38.4	0.5	1.4	8	2	20.0
Wonju	10	0.8	291,129	84.8	0.6	1.8	7	8	80.0
Cheonan	7	0.5	434,088	14.5	1.0	0.5	8	4	57.1
Anyang	6	0.5	609.884	9.8	1.2	0.4	4	2	88.8
Curi	5	0.4	211,720	28.6	0.4	0.9	8	2	40.0
Uijeongbu	5	0.4	417,915	12.0	0.9	0.4	8	2	40.0
Ulsan	4	0.8	1,108,279	8.9	2.8	0.1	2	2	50.0
Jinju	4	0.8	848,850	11.6	0.7	0.4	2	2	50.0
Hwaseong	4	0.8	248,068	16.5	0.5	0.6	8	1	25.0
Iksan	2	0.2	335,787	6.0	0.7	0.2	0	2	100.0
Ansan	2	0.2	717,789	2.8	1.5	0.1	1	1	50.0
Unknown/ Other	28	1.7	NA	NA	0.0	NA	20	8	18.0
Total	1,818	100.0	46,121,755	28.6	94.0		969	849	26.5

Source: Clinical Trial Magnifier 1(10), 2008 *www.clinicaltrialmagnifier.com*

Table 5.10 Therapeutic areas of industry-sponsored trials in South Korea

Therapeutic area	Total sites n	Multinational sites n	Local sites n	Local sites %
Oncology	808	232	26	8.4
Cardiology	222	152	70	81.5
CNS	162	188	29	17.9
Endocrinology	187	94	48	81.4
Infectious	121	78	48	89.7
Respiratory	112	87	25	22.8
Kidney/Urology	98	44	49	52.7
Rheumatology	59	42	17	28.8
CI & Heoatology	27	25	2	7.4
Orthopaedics	25	6	19	76.0
Haematology	12	8	9	75.0
Anaesthesiology & ICU	11	9	2	18.2
Dermatology	8	7	1	12.5
ENT	6	6	0	0.0
O&C	5	2	3	60.0
Allergy	3	0	3	100.0
Ophthalmology	3	2	1	83.3
Other	3	1	2	66.7
Imaging	1	1	0	0.0
Total	1,818	969	849	100.0

Source: www.clinicaltrialmagnifier.com, Vol. 1(10), October 2008

5.7 Environmental analysis

The healthcare environment in South Korea is ideal for global clinical trials thanks to the supporting infrastructure, good-quality investigators, high investigator and subject compliance, supporting regulatory mechanisms, and regional cooperation and data acceptance. Nevertheless, there are a few legal, cultural and language barriers and a shortage of skilled clinical research professionals which can act as potential challenges for clinical trials.

Published by Woodhead Publishing Limited, 2012

5.7.1 Hospital infrastructure

Before they can conduct clinical trials, sites require approval from the Korean FDA. As of early 2011, 142 sites are eligible to conduct clinical trials. These sites are all teaching hospitals, large and self-contained with modern medical equipment and laboratories. Most clinical trial hospitals have more than 1,000 beds. The largest hospital has over 2,600 beds. These hospitals can run clinical trials themselves, and do not need site management organisations. Clinical trial sites in South Korea may be the best equipped in Asia, if not in the world. Patients with common conditions such as light injury, infection or pregnancy attend private hospitals or clinics, making it hard to recruit for trials for such conditions in South Korea. The Korean FDA has recently relaxed its requirement that only teaching hospitals can qualify as clinical trial sites. Now specialty hospitals and general hospitals can participate in clinical trials if approved by the Korean FDA. Such hospitals may need the help of site management organisations. Furthermore, some incentives may have to be offered to encourage participation in clinical trials.

5.7.2 Other infrastructure

South Korea is one of the most connected countries in the world in terms of internet, mobile, and high-speed road and rail transportation. Some sponsors need clinical trial sites to be equipped with ADSL connection. This is unlikely to be a problem in South Korea as the country is a world leader in terms of internet connection and electronic industry. More than 95 per cent of South Korean households have high-speed internet access, and all hospitals are connected via fibre-optic cable.

5.7.3 Quality investigator

Most physicians in South Korea have trained in the USA for 2–4 years after their medical education in Korea. The standards of care and the clinical practices in South Korea are equivalent or similar to

US medical practices. In addition, South Korean physicians have a good command of English. Even investigators with no US experience are familiar with clinical trials and US medical practices, due probably to peer influence. Korean investigators are actively engaged in medical research, rarely leave their academic position until retirement, and are motivated to participate in global clinical trials. They respond quickly to the feasibility requests of multinational clinical trials and are generally enthusiastic. They are all familiar with clinical trial procedures and well versed with GCP. Because Korean investigators are on an academic payroll, monetary reward is not a motivation. This may act as a stumbling block for some investigators in terms of the attention they are prepared to dedicate to trials.

5.7.4 Regional cooperation and data acceptance between Japan, China, South Korea and Taiwan

Were a multinational sponsor looking to register drugs in China, it would prefer to conduct studies in Asian populations on account of the possible genetic and racial similarities. The sponsors could opt to file the IND application in South Korea first, and then file the IND application in China once it has the Korean IND approval. This could facilitate the IND approval process in China as the authorities there recognise the genetic similarities between the two countries' subject pools and are prepared to include South Korean data in certain regional trials. Similarly, the Japanese authorities now accept data from South Korea as well as Taiwan. Such regional cooperation helps the clinical trial environment to grow more quickly in East Asia.

5.7.5 Compliance

It is well known that compliance improves with education level. Korea has a high literacy rate (98 per cent) and a high college education rate (84 per cent). The data show a high compliance rate (mean of 91 per cent, with 70–100 per cent from 16 studies) and a low drop-out rate (mean of 11 per cent, with 0–30 per cent from

Clinical research in South Korea

21 studies). These data are from Phase II–IV, and health food studies for which LSK Global performed the data analysis (see Table 5.11). South Korean data from pivotal global studies are not available, although their compliance rate may even be better.

Table 5.11 Drop-out and compliance rates of trials in South Korea

Sponsor	Phase	Indication	No. subjects	Drop-out rate	Compliance rate
D	IIb	Hypertension	195	0.123	0.90
M	IV	Gastric ulcer	132	0.076	0.90
D	III	Gastric ulcer	266	0.026	0.94
D	II	Atopy	73	0.150	0.95
M	IV	Asthma	53	0.083	0.92
D	Health food	Exercise performance	117	0.300	0.93
M	IV	Immunosuppressant	282	0.050	NA
M	IIT	Acne vulgaris	768	0.220	0.70
D	II	Arthritis	159	0.180	NA
M	IIT	Hyperparathyroidism	156	0.190	NA
D	III	Erectile dysfunction	167	0.020	NA
M	IV	Schizophrenia	292	0.284	0.90
D	III	Gastric ulcer	373	0.057	0.95
M	IV	Hepatitis B	104	0.290	0.92
D	III	Combined vaccine	101	0.030	1.00
D	II	Functional dyspepsia	184	0.038	0.93
D	III	Menopausal disorder	132	0.050	0.9
D	III	Hyperlipidaemia	91	0.077	NA
D	IIT	Gastric cancer	855	0.000	0.9
D	IIT	Gastric cancer	521	0.023	0.9
D	II	Thrombus	124	0.020	NA
D: domestic; M: Korean branch of multinational; IIT: investigator initiated trial			Min–Max	0.000–0.300	0.700–1.000
			Median/ mean	0.076/ 0.109	0.920/0.909
			Standard deviation	0.098	0.064

Source: Young, J. L., *Clinical Trials in Korea: Why Korea*, Seoul: LSK Global Pharma Services

Published by Woodhead Publishing Limited, 2012

172 Clinical Research in Asia: Opportunities and Challenges

5.7.6 Language barrier

In spite of all the developments in South Korea, most of the global clinical trials are initiated from USA or Europe. As such, the English language is an integral part of global research. Most essential documents are in English and most sponsors and regulators in the USA and Europe prefer data in English. Even communications with sites and investigators across global project management teams are conducted in English. To facilitate the regulatory submissions, many documents are required to be translated into Korean. Translation services are available in South Korea, though qualified service providers/translators can help with one-off translations.

Most sponsors/CROs face the challenge of communications in South Korea. Luckily, many investigators can speak and write good English. CRAs, though not fluent in English, with training, can read and write with no difficulty. South Korean project managers/ investigators may feel uncomfortable while participating in conference calls with multiple participants. SOPs, CRFs, and monitoring reports are all in English. Multinational sponsors and auditors from abroad come to audit the sites and they sometimes find the language barrier makes it challenging to monitor facts.

5.7.7 Shortage of skilled professionals

Most South Korean CRAs are registered nurses or pharmacists. There is a serious shortage of clinical trial professionals, particularly experienced CRAs and monitors. Multinational pharmaceutical company and global CRO branches in South Korea have raised CRA pay levels and expectations have increased significantly. This leads to high attrition rates of about 20–25 per cent in South Korea. The number of IND trials in South Korea is expected to quadruple in the next four to five years. With the increased number of studies due to the branching out of more global CROs and the establishment of small local players, the gap between supply and demand for skilled professionals will persist for a while.

Published by Woodhead Publishing Limited, 2012

5.7.8 Cultural barriers

South Korea has only a short history of rigorous pivotal new drug trials and its professionals are not yet attuned to the global way of doing things. The language barrier can sometimes limit proactive decisions by the project manager or CRA. Furthermore, team members may lack common understanding with respect to SOPs or processes. Extra care must therefore be taken to ensure clinical trial staff follow SOPs, and that they understand and conduct themselves like their counterparts in USA or Europe.

5.8 Future outlook

Rigorous multinational pivotal trials are new to South Korea, and the Korean FDA constantly updates regulations and guidelines in its effort to improve the clinical trial environment. There are still problems. For example, the pre-clinical data required for oncology drugs are the same as for non-oncology drugs. This has to change. Another example is the informed consent form for pharmacogenetic tests. Study samples can be shipped to central labs outside South Korea, but participants have the legal right to see their results. Sponsors oppose this provision. This may also have to be relaxed. Korean FDA reviewers are regularly rotated, and IND reviewers can change in the middle of an IND review, causing delays and frustration for IND applicants.

Despite these problems, the Korean FDA tries hard to be timely and as accommodating as possible. Korean investigators are trained in GCP, and can recruit patients in a timely manner. Clinical trial sites are all equipped to meet complicated diagnostic and treatment requirements. The IND timeline is competitive, and other regulatory requirements such as SAE reporting are compatible with ICH guidelines. Trials in South Korea are not low-cost but are cost-effective and of the highest quality and hence worth investigating.

6

Clinical research in Taiwan

Abstract: Taiwan is the world's fifteenth most densely inhabited nation and home to a growing biotech industry. The CRO market in Taiwan is driven by pre-clinical and clinical CROs, bioequivalence studies and clinical laboratory business. This chapter describes the evolution of GCP, the clinical trial processes and key pharmaceutical players undertaking clinical research in Taiwan. Finally, it provides an environmental analysis, highlighting opportunities and challenges for the CRO industry.

6.1 Pharmaceutical industry overview

Taiwan is the world's fifteenth most densely inhabited nation, with a population density of 635 people per square kilometre. In 2009, the estimated population of Taiwan was over 23 million. According to governmental statistics, 98 per cent of Taiwan's population comprises of Han Chinese, while 2 per cent are aboriginal Taiwanese. Demographically, Taiwan has a fairly large population, which is over double that of Singapore. The development of Taiwan relies upon its transformation to an economy driven by technology and services. Taiwan's economy has become progressively more allied with China. Taiwan firms had invested significantly in China via Hong Kong and other third-party jurisdictions. It is expected to nurture these associations further through dialogue under the Economic Cooperation Framework Agreement.

Published by Woodhead Publishing Limited, 2012

176 Clinical Research in Asia: Opportunities and Challenges

The Taiwan pharmaceutical industry can be distinguished into manufacturers of Chinese medicines and manufacturers of Western ones. Both segments have distinctive resources with respect to bulk material, manufacturing technology and marketing channels. Taiwan has more than 200 registered Chinese medicine manufacturers, some of which have been certified as following the guidelines of good manufacturing practice (GMP). Over 90 per cent of these firms are small or medium-sized ventures with capitalisation of less than $2 million. There are also around 280 Western medicine manufacturers in Taiwan. Of this number, 31 focus on producing bulk pharmaceutical chemicals. The total production volume of Western medicine now exceeds $1.5 billion. Hong Kong and Japan remain the major export markets for the Taiwanese pharmaceutical industry, although many firms have of late started to export to other markets due to the recent recession in Asia. Multinational companies control 70 per cent of the Taiwan market, with 30 per cent served by local generic producers. A joint investment plan by the Taiwan Pharmaceutical Industry Association in conjunction with the Taipei World Trade Centre overseas office has fuelled pharmaceutical development in Latin America. Major local pharmaceutical firms, such as Standard, Yung Shin and Shin yuan, have constructed US FDA compliant plants in Latin American countries such as Guatemala.

In tandem with Taiwan's transformation into a contemporary and recognised pharmaceutical industry, the government has upgraded the certification standards for drug manufacturing and processing. In addition to the increasingly accepted GMP standard, the good clinical practice (GCP) and good laboratory practice (GLP) standards are also evolving. To cope with the technology lag vis-à-vis their Western counterparts, most Taiwanese pharmaceutical firms focus on the manufacture of generic drugs following the expiry of the related patents, with many offering analogous product lines as a consequence. As the most obvious corollary of this situation, no completely new drugs have been registered in the country to date. However, a few local pharma companies, such as Gwo Chyang Pharmaceutical and Maywufa, and a few co-developers, are conducting clinical trials that may lead to the first registered new

Published by Woodhead Publishing Limited, 2012

drugs developed in Taiwan. Many of these new drugs have their origins in Chinese herbal medicines. As governmental bodies around the world, including the UN World Health Organization, establish institutes and regulations focusing on alternative treatments, the once neglected domain of Chinese medicines may very well be able to boost the position of the pharmaceutical industry in Taiwan as the island's firms have an advantage over their Western counterparts. R&D in Chinese herbal medicine is already picking up rapidly. Large firms such as Taiwan Sugar and Standard Chemical are entering the line, a trend that may spark strategic alliances and help generate financing for R&D. With the help of the China External Trade Development Council, industry associations are taking an active role in encouraging such cooperation. They have, for instance, made an initial proposal to invest over NT$4 billion ($0.12 billion) over a five-year period to develop and commercialise Chinese herbal medicines. This ambitious proposal will target a variety of medicines for development, as well as fund the construction of warehousing facilities and three GMP certified plants around the island. The plan also includes creating joint ventures among domestic firms, establishing logistics centres, constructing databases, and conducting clinical tests. Regardless of whether this particular plan is ultimately implemented, industry analysts are certain that the sector will see more cooperative ventures in the near future.

6.2 Biotech industry in Taiwan

The Development Centre for Biotechnology (DCB) in Taipei was established in 1984 to foster the development of the biotechnology industry in Taiwan. The Ministry of Economic Affairs (MOEA) funds DCB, an autonomous, non-profit research organisation that links academic-based research with private firms. The DCB's Bio-Fronts programme identifies, evaluates and funds start-up biotechnology companies in Taiwan. In 2001, the pre-clinical toxicology programme at DCB expanded its infrastructure and began to function as a CRO for GLP toxicology work. In the last

Published by Woodhead Publishing Limited, 2012

178 Clinical Research in Asia: Opportunities and Challenges

10 years, CROs have grown in Taiwan, and large international CROs have entered the market. The cost of doing pre-clinical and clinical development work is substantially lower in Taiwan than in the USA or Europe. To improve the flow of business with foreign and local companies, the MOEA set up the Biotechnology and Pharmaceutical Industries Programme Office to coordinate business, regulatory and legal processes in order to facilitate business locally and globally. Taiwan also has several biotechnology parks, including the Taipei City Neihu Technology Park and the Taipei County Wu-Ku Industrial District.

The Taiwan-America Biotechnology Association (TABA) bridges the biotechnology gap between Taiwan and the USA. A group of biotechnology professionals who work in southern California and have ties to Taiwan started TABA in 2000. TABA initially focused on knowledge exchange, but eventually extended into business deals. TABA hosted several bio-forums in the USA and Taiwan to unite researchers, executives and investors, and also to publicise its mission to help the fusion of scientific breakthroughs and business exchanges between the USA and Taiwan. US companies benefit from TABA's bio-forums as they can learn about the efficient infrastructure of Taiwan's economical CROs and medical device manufacturing firms and how to launch their products in the Asia-Pacific market. Meanwhile in Taiwan, local biotech firm TaiGen Biotechnology (Taipei) has a few compounds in pre-clinical development for tissue ischaemia, transplant rejection, solid tumours and SARS. The company is also involved in clinical trials for obesity, insomnia, atherosclerosis and diabetes. Its scientists are using constitutively activated receptor technology licensed from Arena Pharmaceutical (San Diego) to discover new drugs and it has become a significant discovery-based biotechnology company in Asia.

6.3 Healthcare system in Taiwan

Taiwan has a world-class hospital care system and 40 per cent of its doctors work at the top 15 hospitals in Taiwan. A total of 126 hospitals in Taiwan can conduct clinical trials. Most of these

Published by Woodhead Publishing Limited, 2012

Clinical research in Taiwan

179

hospitals are multi-specialty hospitals with world-class infrastructure and several hundred beds. These hospitals invest heavily in research and training, and undertake exchange programmes with Western countries. Table 6.1 provides a non-exhaustive list of key hospitals in Taiwan that offer multi-specialty services. As the table shows, the top medical centres in Taiwan are concentrated in the major cities of Taipei, Taichung City, Tainan and Kachsiung City.

Table 6.1 Hospital infrastructure in Taiwan

Hospital	Location	Number of specialties	Comments
Cathay General Hospital	Taipei	37	Young Investigator Award for participation in clinical trials in multiple therapeutic areas
Chang-Gung Memorial Hospital	Taipei	54	Strong research team that has published many papers
China Medical University Hospital	Taichung City	62	Oncology department has tie with US centre
Chi Mei Hospital	Tainan	49	Investigators with research experience and publications
Kaohsiung Medical University Chung-Ho Memorial Hospital	Kaohsiung	53	Emphasis on continuing education and training
Kaohsiung Veterans General Hospital Veterans Affairs Commission, Exec. Yuan	Kaohsiung City	43	Passed ISO 9001 certification; published many research papers
Mackay Memorial Hospital	Taipei	52	Focus on family care
National Taiwan University Hospital	Taipei	52	Published 808 papers in SCI journals in 2004; cancer treatment and clinical trials are areas of focus
Nonprofit Proprietary Chang-Gung Memorial Hospital	Kaohsiung	35	Extensive international exchange programme for physicians including USA and China

Published by Woodhead Publishing Limited, 2012

180 Clinical Research in Asia: Opportunities and Challenges

Table 6.1 Hospital infrastructure in Taiwan (*cont'd*)

Hospital	Location	Number of specialties	Comments
Taichung Veterans General Hospital	Taichung City	52	Programme for international experience for personnel
Taipei Medical University Municipal Wang Fang Hospital	Taipei City	48	Experience with large diabetes education programme
Taipei Veterans General Hospital	Taipei	61	Has research centres of excellence
Buddhist Tzu Chi General Hospital	Huahen City	54	Received medical centre classification in 2002; ISO 9001 certification in 2001
Changhua Christian Hospital	Tao-Yuan Country	51	Hospitals in four locations; 14 research units on-site
Shin Kong Wu Ho-Su Memorial	Taipei City	54	Between 2002 and 2004, 149 staff (including 86 physicians) went to study abroad and it hosted 318 foreign medical specialists
Tri-Service General Hospital	Taipei	83	Teaching hospital of the National Defense Medical Center; Class A teaching hospital; best hospital in quality English environment

Source: 'Hospital Care in Taiwan', Department of Health, Taiwan, January 2006

6.4 CRO market in Taiwan

The CRO market in Taiwan is driven by pre-clinical and clinical CROs, bioequivalence studies and clinical laboratory business. In the clinical CRO domain, there are full-service CROs, monitoring-only CROs and EDC services CROs. Some of them are local CROs while others are offshoots of large global CROs. The CRO segment in Taiwan has evolved and is further evolving due to the increased number of global trials in the recent past. Moreover, Japanese, US and European pharmaceutical and biotech companies have shown great interest in conducting clinical trials in Taiwan, it being one of the most

Published by Woodhead Publishing Limited, 2012

recommendable countries in Southeast Asia due to its supportive environment for clinical trials, market size, rapid and successful enrolment rates, excellent infrastructure, quality data and experienced investigators. Pipeline developments for Taiwanese pharma companies are not in the public domain; that said, only a few Taiwanese pharma companies are into full-fledged R&D and have new chemical entities in their research pipelines. The tax enticement strategy for the biotech and drug development industry has proven to be a strong impetus for the cultivation of the biotech and CRO industry in Taiwan. Taiwan has implemented the requirement for bridging study evaluation as a part of new drug registration since 2000, thus prompting many global/ regional pharma companies to include Taiwan in the earlier phases of their clinical trial development plans. Many global/regional CROs actively operate in Taiwan, currently offering full services for all phases of clinical trials, data management, regulatory affairs in IND and new drug applications, feasibility studies, and pre-clinical development and studies. Taiwan's largest CRO, Apex has been acquired by Parexel. CMIC and EPS, two large regional CROs, have offices in Taiwan. The global CROs with a presence in Taiwan are Parexel, Omnicare, PPDi, Quintiles, Pharmanet, Covance, INC Research and PRA International. Other operators include PPC, Stat Plus, Farmosa, Genovate and VCRO. There are also a couple of CROs mainly for bioequivalence, pharmacokinetic, toxicology and pharmacology studies, such as Mithra, MDS Pharma etc.

CROs in Taiwan acquire some of their projects from the headquarters of multinational pharma companies as multinational trials, while some are contracted by local/regional biotech and pharma companies to conduct different levels of clinical trials in Taiwan. All the trials conducted are all fully compliant with the most current GCP standards and are inspected by regulatory authorities including the local FDA and Department of Health (DOH).

6.5 Evolution of GCP in Taiwan

Prior to 1993, there was no registration requirement for local clinical trials in Taiwan. Only a handful of marketing trials for listing purpose

182   Clinical Research in Asia: Opportunities and Challenges

in different medical centres were conducted. Even until 1996, only a few Phase IIIb and mostly Phase IV trials were conducted. Taiwan's GCP guidelines were officially announced first in 1996 and revised in 2002 according to the ICH-E6 guidance. In 1999 and 2000, the DOH in Taiwan announced the guidance for clinical trials of drugs in a variety of medical subspecialties, such as anti-infectious drugs, anti-cancer drugs, cardiovascular drugs, endocrine drugs and radioactive drugs in 1999, and herbal extracts in 2000. In 2001 and 2002, the DOH further published guidance for clinical trials of drugs in special populations, such as geriatrics, paediatrics, populations with impaired hepatic function or impaired renal function; guidance for bridging studies, including ethnic factors in the acceptability of foreign clinical data; and also guidance for the content and format of clinical trial reports.

Since 1995, under the tutelage of DOH, The Foundation of Medical Professionals Alliance in Taiwan has cooperated with medical centres and professional medical alliances to hold a string of education courses for clinical trials. The courses have incorporated clinical trials in heart and vascular diseases, oncology, infectious diseases, endocrine and metabolic diseases, gastroenterology, clinical trial inspection, neurology, anti-inflammatory and analgesics, statistics in clinical trials, GCP issues, the assessment of drug safety, respiratory diseases, protection of research subjects, ethics regulations and responsibilities, GCP inspection and ethnic factors, developing new therapies from alternative sources, clinical trials for radiological agents, pharmacokinetics, case studies and bridging studies in oncology, anti-infective and cardiovascular trials, and safety evaluation for biological products, etc. These training courses were well received with phenomenal response by physicians, pharmacists, nurses and other participants. Since then, thousands of medical and paramedical professionals have partaken in these courses. To assure the quality and credibility of clinical trials, the DOH performed its first GCP inspection in 2002 where 37 trials were inspected.

6.5.1 IND review process

As per the regular IND application process, after making the e-application, the dossier is submitted to the Taiwan FDA, who grant

Published by Woodhead Publishing Limited, 2012

a case number after the prescribed fee is paid. The Centre for Drug Evaluation usually takes 20 days (~4 weeks) to evaluate the application and preparation of the technical report which is thereafter submitted to the DOH. In case of queries/insufficient data, the query letter is forwarded to the sponsor, who is expected to reply as soon as possible. Upon receipt of reply, an additional 20 days (~4 weeks) are required for the review process, after which the technical report is forwarded to the FDA, which usually takes another 20 days (~4 weeks) to issue the IND approval letter. If necessary, the Centre for Drug Evaluation (CDE) also arranges face-to-face meetings or provides a teleconference with the sponsor for the IND issues.

The Taiwan FDA adopts most of the recommendations and directly issues the administrative decision. A few cases, however, may require further discussion by the Drug Advisory Committee (e.g. safety issues or major deficiency), and the timeline to obtain the official letter will depend on the date of committee meeting.

The FDA can grant fast-track approval in one month (~6 weeks) if regulatory approval is available from at least one key jurisdiction, such as the USA, Germany, Japan, France, Canada, Australia, Switzerland or Belgium. To meet the requirements for a fast-track review, the sponsor is required to provide the FDA with the so-called Guarantee Letter.

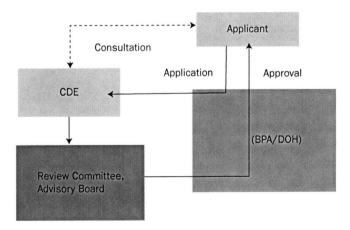

Figure 6.1 IND review process in Taiwan

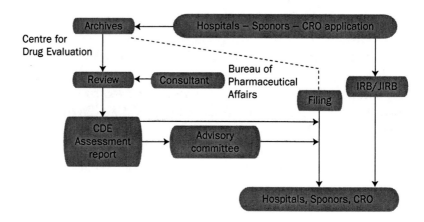

Figure 6.2 IND review process

The CDE requires the following documents for filing IND submission:

- application for import certificate;
- pharmaceutical company licence;
- IND letter or IRB approval letter from other participating countries (if available);
- IRB approval letter;
- clinical trial application form;
- protocol with principal investigator's signature;
- informed consent form with principal investigator's signature (Chinese version);
- case report form (draft version is acceptable);
- SAE reporting form;
- investigators' CV;
- insurance certificate or indemnity letter;
- investigator's brochure or product characteristics information;
- certificate of analysis and stability data registration;
- fee for registration trial;
- Chinese/English synopsis;
- Questionnaire (if completed by patient, the questionnaire must be in Chinese and be validated);
- amendment history.

6.5.2 Bridging study evaluation

To fulfil the spirit of ICH-E5, reduce repetitions of clinical trials and integrate ethnic concerns into global drug development programmes, the DOH announced bridging study guidelines on 12 December 2000. If ethnic concerns are considered during the early stage of drug development, there may be no need to conduct bridging studies in Taiwan.

The bridging data package and summary of self-evaluation are submitted to the DOH's Bureau of Pharmaceutical Affairs (BPA) which is assisted by the Centre for Drug Evaluation (CDE), a non-profit organisation. After internal review with the sponsor and consultants, the BPA's Drugs Advisory Committee decides whether or not the bridging study is required.

6.5.3 Consultations: online application

Pharmaceutical industry sponsors are encouraged to enter into dialogue with CDE throughout the R&D process. To this end, the CDE provides free scientific advice according to the specific needs of each individual sponsor. The sponsor may apply for the consultation via the internet or by phone. After receiving the necessary information,

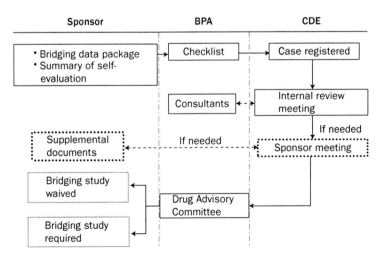

Figure 6.3 Bridging study – current evaluation process

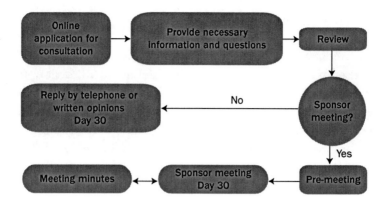

Figure 6.4 Online application consultation process flow

the CDE provides the response by writing (e-mail, fax or letters), telephone communication or face-to-face meetings within one month. Consultations regarding pre-IND issues are recommended in order to provide pre-clinical information and clinical trial synopsis prior to the IND meetings.

6.5.4 Institutional review board approval process

A joint institutional review board (IRB) was established in Taiwan in March 1997 with the aim of enhancing the country's competitiveness in attracting multicentre trials, including Phase IIIa global trials. The missions of the joint IRB are:

- to improve the safety of study subjects in human clinical trials;
- to shorten the time required to obtain the permission for clinical trials;
- to avoid repetition of trial application and the variability of application formats;
- to encourage pre-marketing clinical trials in Taiwan;
- to further Taiwan's competitiveness and international reputation in IRB-related issues;
- to establish the communication network in regional IRB-related issues;

Clinical research in Taiwan 187

- to review multicentre clinical trials, Phase I–III studies of new drugs, and cases undertaken by medical institutions without a clinical trials regulation committee.

Taiwan instituted the joint IRB to provide a single entity for ethics review. Joint IRB decisions are accepted widely by Taiwanese hospitals although individual IRBs can request an independent review. Joint IRB response takes at least 25 working days. Submission to the DOH and the joint IRB can be undertaken simultaneously.

Documents required for IRB submission include:

- trial protocol(s)/amendment(s);
- case record forms;
- written informed consent form(s);
- patient information sheet;
- investigator's brochure;
- available safety information;
- IP label translated into Chinese;
- information about payments and compensation for subjects;
- investigator's current curriculum vitae and/or other documentation;
- SOPs and any other documents that the IRB/IEC may need to fulfil its responsibilities.

The IRB shall review a proposed clinical trial within the period described in the standard operating procedure (SOP) and document its views (identifying the trial, list of documents reviewed). The IRB can approve the trial or seek modifications prior to its approval/favourable opinion. The IRB has every right to disapprove the trial or terminate/suspend the trial.

6.5.5 Regulatory approval process

Trial protocols are submitted to the BPA, assisted by the CDE. DOH protocol review typically takes typically 30 days. Fast-track approvals are available for IND applications that have already been approved in the USA. Total clinical review time including IRB approval takes 2–4 months. The regulatory and IRB approval process in Taiwan has become increasingly efficient and responsive and the process of the same is summarised in Figure 6.5.

6.5.6 Study start-up timeline

The translation of essential documents takes a sizeable amount of time during the study start-up process. For DOH and IRB submission, full translation into Taiwanese is required for the protocol and protocol synopsis, investigator's brochure and brochure summary, informed consent forms, patient information sheets and investigational product label. This usually takes four weeks. In addition to the translation, site selection, arranging insurance, preparing the ethics committee submission package and getting investigator contracts etc. takes a lot of time. The study start-up timelines are summarised below. As shown below, the activities prior to submission for regulatory and IRB approval take one month, and it takes a further 3.5 months to obtain all regulatory approvals. Hence, the total start-up timeline in Taiwan is 4.5 months.

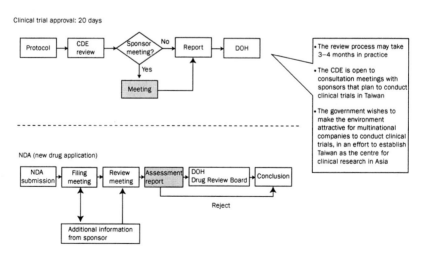

Figure 6.5 Regulatory approval process in Taiwan

Source: Center for Drug Evaluation, Taiwan

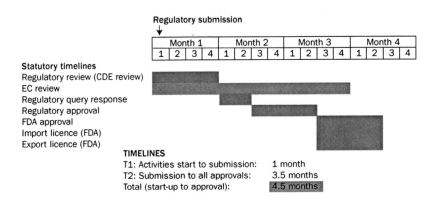

Figure 6.6 Study start-up timelines in Taiwan

6.5.7 Safety reporting

Every suspected unexpected serious adverse reaction (SUSAR) during clinical trials should be reported to the DOH for their judgment on the approval of drugs. The purpose of submitting these reports is to make regulators, investigators, and other appropriate people aware of important new information on serious reactions. Therefore, according to the Application Guideline for Clinical Trials, the sponsor must expeditiously report each unexpected serious adverse drug reaction to the DOH approving the clinical trial regardless of whether or not it happened in Taiwan. The SUSAR reporting timeframes detailed in Article 106 of the Guidance of Good Clinical Practice, published by the DOH are listed below.

6.5.7.1 Fatal or life-threatening SUSARs

The DOH or the National ADR Reporting Centre should be notified by the sponsor as soon as possible, but no later than seven calendar days after the investigator first becomes aware of the SUSAR. A complete report should follow after no more than eight additional calendar days. This report must include an assessment of the importance and implication of the findings and/or previous experience on the same or similar medical products.

6.5.7.2 All other SUSARs

The DOH or the National ADR Reporting Centre should be notified by the sponsor in a complete report as soon as possible but no later than 15 calendar days after the investigator first becomes aware of the SUSAR. To expedite SUSAR reporting, it is necessary to complete the clinical trial reporting form. All SUSAR reports should be sent to the National ADR Reporting Centre by facsimile, postal mail, or electronically.

6.5.8 Recruitment modalities

Taiwanese investigators are well trained, and are conversant in English. They are well networked and it is common for one committed investigator to persuade other investigators to participate in clinical trials. Indeed, the referral system works well in Taiwan. It is an effective practice to recruit one investigator and use his/her network of investigators to add more investigators. Each investigator has his/her own pool of patients, and clinical trial participants are recruited from the pool rather than by referral.

6.6 Clinical trials in Taiwan

Taiwan has participated in more than 150 industry-sponsored trials every year during 2008 to 2010. There are 2,275 trials already listed in the clinical trials registry in Taiwan, out of which 706 trials are active and recruiting. Of the 2,275 trials undertaken in Taiwan, only 980 trials are industry-sponsored trials and 1,285 trials are sponsored by individual investigators, local institutions or hospitals, universities and other organisations.

Further analysis of industry-sponsored clinical trials suggests that GCP studies in diverse therapeutic areas are being conducted in Taiwan. Some 61 per cent of the trials undertaken in Taiwan are in Phase III, 24 per cent trials in Phase II and 11 per cent trials are in Phase IV. A small number of Phase I trials (4 per cent) are also undertaken in Taiwan.

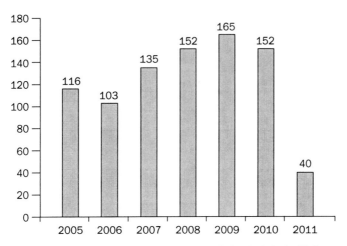

Figure 6.7 Growth of industry-sponsored clinical trials in Taiwan

Source: www.clinicaltrials.gov (accessed July 2011); 2011 figures are from January to mid-July

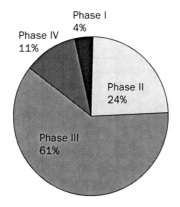

Figure 6.8 Industry-sponsored clinical trials in Taiwan – by phase

Source: www.clinicaltrials.gov (accessed July 2011)

While most of the trials quoted in Table 6.2 are being undertaken by global sponsors, a significant number of trials are being undertaken by institutes of national repute.

National Taiwan University Hospitals and the National Science Council undertake a large number of trials. Some of the other important hospitals and research centres undertaking a large number of local trials are listed in Table 6.3.

192   Clinical Research in Asia: Opportunities and Challenges

Table 6.2 Industry-sponsored trials undertaken in Taiwan

Industry sponsor	No. of trials
Pfizer	106
GlaxoSmithKline	87
Eli Lilly and Company	75
Sanofi-Aventis	60
Hoffmann-La Roche	59
Boehringer Ingelheim Pharmaceuticals	58
Bristol-Myers Squibb	55
AstraZeneca	49
Novartis Pharmaceuticals	47
Bayer	45
Merck	33
Novartis	32
Astellas Pharma Inc	27
Novo Nordisk	23

Source: *www.clinicaltrials.gov* (accessed July 2011)

6.6.1 General clinical research centres

To create an environment conducive to the research and development of new drugs in Taiwan, the DOH has supported a number of medical centres in Taiwan to establish centres for clinical trials, known as general clinical research centres (GCRCs). These establishments will also reinforce the development of clinical trial infrastructure and the conduct of early-phase clinical trials. A non-exhaustive list of GCRCs is as follows:

- Chang Gung Memorial Hospital Linkou Branch;
- Buddhist Tzu Chi General Hospital;
- Koo Foundation Sun Yat-Sen Cancer Centre;
- Taichung Veterans General Hospital;
- Mackay Memorial Hospital;

Published by Woodhead Publishing Limited, 2012

Clinical research in Taiwan

Table 6.3 Hospitals/institutions undertaking clinical trials in Taiwan

Hospital/institution	No. of trials
National Taiwan University Hospital	725
National Science Council	142
China Medical University Hospital	96
Taipei Medical University WanFang Hospital	95
Chang Gung Memorial Hospital	93
National Health Research Institutes	78
Far Eastern Memorial Hospital	73
Taipei Veterans General Hospital	72
Mackay Memorial Hospital	42
National Cheng-Kung University Hospital	41
Kaohsiung Medical University Chung-Ho Memorial Hospital	40
Department of Health	31
Kaohsiung Veterans General Hospital	24
Changhua Christian Hospital	16
Chi Mei Medical Hospital	16

Source: *www.clinicaltrials.gov* (accessed July 2011)

- Changhua Christian Hospital;
- Jianan Mental Hospital;
- Yuli Hospital;
- Bali Psychiatric Centre;
- Taipei Medical University Hospital;
- Chung Shan Medical University Hospital;
- China Medical University Hospital;
- Chung-Ho Memorial Hospital, Kaohsiung Medical University;
- Chi Mei Medical Centre.

These centres provide services for the implementation and follow-up of clinical trials, including randomisation of study subjects, storage and dispensing of investigational drugs, monitoring of pharmacokinetic parameters, biostatistical consultation, key-in of research data, and

Published by Woodhead Publishing Limited, 2012

194 Clinical Research in Asia: Opportunities and Challenges

analysis of research data. A clinical trial regulatory committee is established to manage and audit the performance of clinical trials in each GCRC.

6.6.2 Environmental analysis

The healthcare environment in Taiwan is well suited to global clinical trials due to the supporting infrastructure, good-quality investigators, high compliance by the investigators and study participants, supporting regulatory mechanisms, and regional cooperation and acceptance of data. Challenges for the clinical trial environment include significant legal, cultural and language barriers and a shortage of skilled professionals.

6.6.3 Infrastructure and facilities

Taiwan has very large hospitals, self-contained with modern medical equipment and laboratories. Most clinical trial hospitals have multi-specialty facilities with several hundred beds. These hospitals can run multiple clinical trials. Taiwan is one of the most connected countries in Asia in terms of internet and mobile communication and high-speed road and rail transportation. All hospitals in Taiwan have good internet connection and have capacity for EDC trials.

6.6.4 Quality investigators

The standards of care and clinical practice in Taiwan are equivalent or similar to US medical practice. In addition, investigators have a good command of English. Even investigators with no direct US experience are likely to be familiar with clinical trials and US medical practice due probably to peer influence. Taiwanese investigators are actively engaged in medical research, rarely leave their academic position until retirement, and are motivated to participate in global clinical trials. They respond quickly to the feasibility requests of

Published by Woodhead Publishing Limited, 2012

multinational clinical trials and are generally enthusiastic. They are all familiar with clinical trial procedures and well versed with GCP. Because Taiwanese investigators are on an academic payroll, monetary reward is not a motivation; this may act as a stumbling block in terms of some investigators not taking trials as seriously as their academic work.

6.6.5 Regional cooperation and data acceptance between Japan, China, South Korea and Taiwan

Due to possible genetic similarities, multinational sponsors that want to register drugs in Japan and China prefer to conduct studies in Asian populations including South Korea and Taiwan. The Chinese government appreciates this and sometimes suggests including Taiwan. On 21 December 2010, Taiwan and China signed the Cross-Strait Medical and Healthcare Cooperation Agreement. In this agreement, Taiwan and China agreed to cooperate on several areas including clinical trials.

6.6.6 Language barriers

In Taiwan, English is widely spoken as a second language. Although record-keeping has switched primarily to English, 80 per cent of the population speaks Mandarin or Taiwanese (Min Nan). To complicate matters, while Taiwanese is the most widely spoken language, Mandarin is the official written language. However, most global clinical trials are initiated from the USA or Europe and hence the English language has become an integral part of global research. Most essential documents are in English and most sponsors and the regulators in the USA and Europe prefer data in English. Even communications across globally distributed sites, project management teams and investigators are conducted in English. To facilitate the regulatory submissions, many documents are required to be translated into Mandarin. Translation services are available in Taiwan through qualified service providers/translators. Most sponsors/CRO face the

Published by Woodhead Publishing Limited, 2012

196 Clinical Research in Asia: Opportunities and Challenges

challenge of communications in Taiwan. Luckily, many investigators can speak and write good English. Clinical research associates (CRAs), though not fluent in English, can with training read and write with no difficulty. SOPs, CRFs and monitoring reports are all in English. When multinational sponsors and auditors from abroad come to audit the sites, they sometimes find the language barrier makes it challenging to monitor facts.

6.6.7 Shortage of skilled professionals

A significant number of CRAs are academically trained, with nursing and pharmacy as their academic background. There is a huge demand for experienced clinical trial professionals, particularly CRAs and monitors. With the increased number of studies being undertaken, the branching out of more global CROs, and the establishment of small local players, the gap between the supply and demand for skilled professionals is likely to endure.

6.6.8 Cultural barriers

Taiwan has a short history of rigorous pivotal new drug trials and professionals are not tuned to the global way of doing things. Communication media and language challenges sometimes prevent proactive action from the project manager or CRA. Sometimes, a lack of understanding of SOPs or processes is observed across team members. As such, extra care must be taken to ensure clinical trial staff follow SOPs, and that they understand and interpret information in a similar way to their counterparts in USA or Europe.

6.7 Future outlook

The clinical research industry in Taiwan will go a long way and the country may well become an important hub for clinical research. In addition to improved infrastructure and the willingness to become a

Published by Woodhead Publishing Limited, 2012

global player, the Cross-Strait Medical and Healthcare Cooperation Agreement between China and Taiwan will play a major role in strengthening the Taiwanese pharmaceutical and CRO industry. Because of this agreement, both countries have agreed to share data and cooperate on their systems and regulations relating to clinical trials, to have common management teams, to have common objectives regarding the protection of subjects' rights and interests, and to help improve the approval mechanisms for clinical trial plans and trial results. Cooperation in R&D for clinical trials and pharmaceuticals will be actively strengthened with a view towards reducing repetitive trials through the preferential methods of pilot and special projects.

7

Clinical research in Singapore

Abstract: The pharmaceutical industry in Singapore is growing at a fast pace. The industry is heavily supported by the Singapore government as a part of its policy to encourage the pharmaceutical, biotechnology and healthcare industries in Singapore. This chapter describes the pharmaceutical investments in Singapore and the evolving healthcare system and infrastructure to support quality research. It goes on to discuss the CRO market and key pharmaceutical players undertaking clinical research in Singapore. Finally, it provides an environmental analysis highlighting public–private partnerships and the operational challenges of doing clinical trials in Singapore.

7.1 Overview of the pharmaceutical industry in Singapore

Singapore is a small country, with a geographical area of 697.1 km². In 2003 it had a population of 4.2 million, of which 3.44 million were resident. Its ethnic composition is 76.5 per cent Chinese, 13.8 per cent Malay, 8.1 per cent Indian, 1.6 per cent other. The pharmaceutical industry in Singapore is a growing at a fast pace. The industry is heavily supported by the Singapore government as a part of its policy to encourage the pharmaceutical, biotechnology and healthcare industries in Singapore. In the mid-1990s, the Singapore government designated a 50-hectare site at Tuas, the industrial hub of the country, as a pharmaceutical and biotechnology zone, known as the Pharma Zone. The particular focus of the zone is to encourage the growth of new pharmaceutical and biotechnology manufacturing companies.

Published by Woodhead Publishing Limited, 2012

200 Clinical Research in Asia: Opportunities and Challenges

It has proven successful thus far, with an established cluster of leading foreign companies with multi-million dollar manufacturing facilities in Jurong Island and Tuas. The Singapore government's approach has been to adopt a proactive policy and plan to integrate pharmaceuticals with drug discovery, healthcare and clinical testing.

With the rapid establishment of new discoveries and robust growth, the biomedical sciences sector is targeted to be the fourth pillar of manufacturing in Singapore. The nation aims to develop the biomedical sciences to achieve the same level of success as the other three industry pillars, namely electronics, chemicals and engineering. Furthermore, it is hoped that Singapore will soon host a large number of world-class biomedical science companies and become the region's hub for drug discovery and development, clinical research and healthcare delivery. The companies present so far include GlaxoSmithKline, Merck & Co., Schering-Plough, Aventis, Genset, Oculex, Baxter and Becton Dickinson. This is in line with Singapore's aim to be a knowledge-based economy that places a premium on technology, innovation, capabilities and talent.

The pharmaceutical industry in Singapore has achieved a significant growth. According to the Singapore Economic Development Board report, the biomedical sciences industry in Singapore is targeted to reach S$20.7 billion ($14.3 billion) by 2010, from S$11.3 billion in 2003. Governmental agencies such as the Economic Development Board Biomedical Sciences Group and Biomedical Research Council and the Agency for Science, Technology and Research (A*STAR) are working in close partnership with other agencies to adopt an integrated approach with synergistic initiatives in R&D, education and industry development.

7.2 Pharmaceutical investments in Singapore

Due to the strong legal and political system and central location in Asia, Singapore's international business environment has attracted many European and US bioscience companies to open up R&D facilities, sales and marketing operations and regional headquarters. Table 7.1 details some recent investments from the pharmaceutical and healthcare industries in Singapore.

Published by Woodhead Publishing Limited, 2012

Clinical research in Singapore

Table 7.1 Investments by multinational companies in Singapore

Year	Company	Main focus
2009	GlaxoSmithKline	Celebrated its 50th anniversary in Singapore and opened a S$600 million biologics plant. This facility produces bulk polysaccharides and conjugates. Published plans to set up an Academic Centre of Excellence for Discovery Research and announced a S$30 million endowment fund to support graduate studies and research in green manufacturing and public health policy.
2009	Icon Central Laboratories	The global CRO expanded its central laboratory – a 836 square-metre facility to serve as a regional hub for test samples from the Asia-Pacific region and expand offerings in the region to include increased esoteric testing as well as flow cytometry, molecular diagnostics and biomarkers.
2009	Quintiles	Opened its expanded Asia-Pacific headquarters in Singapore. The new 7,340 square-metre facility houses regional and clinical functional groups, as well as one of the region's most advanced central laboratory facilities. The expanded lab facility also provides a range of globally harmonised lab services with plans in the pipeline to expand these capabilities, with the addition of an assay development lab and an anatomic pathology lab.
2010	Emergent BioSolutions Inc	A US-based developer and manufacturer of vaccines and antibody therapies launched its Singapore operations.
2010	GlaxoSmithKline	Announced the start of four new academic collaborations between its global drug discovery network and Singapore-based scientists for longer-term alliances on early-stage research projects of interest to GSK and the researchers.
2010	Roche	Announced investment of $134 million for a translational medical research hub in Singapore.
2011	Abbott	Announced grand opening of its formulation R&D centre, which will accelerate the development of therapeutics to bring innovative medicines to patients faster.

Published by Woodhead Publishing Limited, 2012

202 Clinical Research in Asia: Opportunities and Challenges

Table 7.1 Investments by multinational companies in Singapore (*cont'd*)

Year	Company	Main focus
2011	Pfizer	Announced a $100 million investment into the expansion of its Singapore nutrition plant, helping it continue to set the standard for the manufacture of high-quality, safe and environmentally sustainable nutritional products for infants and children. This expansion, which brings the total investment in the plant to $372 million, makes it one of the largest nutritional plants worldwide.
2011	World Courier	The global leader in investigational drug and trial-related transport, storage and distribution, will expand its GMP-compliant clinical trial supply chain services network to 13 strategic and emerging markets, including a new 12,500 square-metre regional distribution facility in Singapore.

Source: Company and media reports

Singapore has established a core base of 20 leading CROs and pharma companies (e.g. Quintiles, Covance, Kendle, PPD, Pharmanet, Parexel and Chiltern) that manage regional clinical trials from the city-state. These international CROs offer a wide range of services, ranging from Phase I to pharmacovigilance studies, while some are setting up innovative biomarker discovery and validation services. As these companies seek to harness the growing base of clinical research carried out in Asia, they are expanding their operations in Singapore, where they can better leverage the region's growth opportunities.

Besides the above, a large number of companies have invested in R&D, manufacturing, collaborations for pre-clinical research, toxicology and chemistry services, central laboratories and logistics hubs in Singapore. By 2009, global biomedical sciences companies had located strategic functions in Singapore that included regional headquarters (e.g. Medtronic, Quintiles, Takeda), first-in-Asia and global manufacturing facilities (e.g. GlaxoSmithKline, Illumina, Lonza, Medtronic, ResMed, Roche) and R&D bases in Asia (e.g. Abbott, 3M, Merck, Roche, Inviragen, FORMA).

Published by Woodhead Publishing Limited, 2012

7.3 Governing authority and regulatory structure

Prior to Singapore attaining independence in 1965, medical services in Singapore were controlled by a Director of Medical Services, supported by a Chief Health Officer and a Chief Medical Officer. While the health services of the urban area of Singapore were under the direction of the Municipal Health Officer and Municipal Commission, the Medical Department was in charge of hospital organisation, the port and the rural health division. After 1965, the former City (Municipal) Health Department was merged with the government Medical Department to form the Ministry of Health (MOH). The MOH was tasked with improving public health, hospital services, primary health services, dental services and support services. It was a period of consolidation following the post-war rehabilitation and expansion of medical services.

The pharmaceutical industry is governed by the National Pharmaceutical Administration (NPA) set up under the MOH. The NPA is charged with, inter alia, planning and developing national drug policies, pharmaceutical programmes and services, administering and enforcing legislations governing the control of Western and Chinese medicinal products, controlling cosmetic products, inspecting pharmaceutical factories, wholesale and retail premises, issuing advertisement permits for medicinal products, planning for emergency pharmaceutical supplies, and establishing international relationships on pharmaceutical matters.

Under the NPA, there are a number of divisions or units which have been assigned specific administrative tasks.

7.3.1 Drug Administration Division

NPA's Drug Administration Division is responsible for registering and licensing Western medicines, and controlling the import of medicinal products into Singapore. The Drug Administration Division also processes applications for new product licences, amending and renewing existing product licences; approving the

204 Clinical Research in Asia: Opportunities and Challenges

import of unregistered medicinal products and issuing permits (on a per consignment basis) for the import of medicinal products to be re-exported (within six months upon approval). More particularly, the Medicines Act (Cap 176) provides that the responsible authority is the Director of Medical Services. The Act further adds that the responsible authority is the Director of Primary Production where the functions to be performed relate exclusively to veterinary medicinal products and animals.

7.3.2 Chinese Proprietary Medicine Unit

NPA has set up a Chinese Proprietary Medicine Unit to administer regulatory control over Chinese proprietary medicine. This is to warrant that Chinese proprietary medicines sold in Singapore are safe, of good quality and labelled appropriately. The unit facilitates the prompt withdrawal of Chinese proprietary medicines from the market when necessary. While Chinese proprietary medicine dealers need not register individual products, they are obliged to provide information on the Chinese proprietary medicine which they intend to import or manufacture, and they are only allowed to deal in approved products.

7.3.3 Good Manufacturing Practices and Licensing Unit

This unit was formed within the NPA to inspect and license pharmaceutical manufacturers and cosmetic products, as well as importers/wholesale dealers in accordance with current international standards in good medicine and distribution practice respectively.

7.3.4 Cosmetic Control Unit

This unit was set up to administer regulatory control of cosmetic products, in particular, to ensure that cosmetic products are safe to

Published by Woodhead Publishing Limited, 2012

Clinical research in Singapore

use, to prohibit the use of certain toxic substances as ingredients in cosmetic products, as well as to ensure that cosmetic products are properly labelled.

7.3.5 Adverse Drug Reaction Monitoring Unit

This unit was set up at the NPA to collate adverse drug reaction reports on a nationwide basis for analysis and investigation, and to collaborate with other national centres, with an ultimate view to help decrease drug-induced reactions locally and internationally. As new knowledge about a drug's safety profile is discovered, the NPA assesses the risk and decides on the most appropriate way to manage new risk or new perspectives on a previously known risk.

7.4 Healthcare system in Singapore

The healthcare system in Singapore comprises of public and private healthcare, complemented by rising standards of living, housing, education, medical services, safe water supply and sanitation, and preventive medicine. Over the years, the MOH has been continuously fine-tuning its systems to ensure that good and affordable basic medical services are available to all Singaporeans. In 2005, Singapore spent about S$7.6 billion or 3.8 per cent of GDP on healthcare. Out of this, the government expended S$1.8 billion or 0.9 per cent of GDP on health services. The unique healthcare model in Singapore has won international praise and recognition. In April 2000, public healthcare institutes were divided into two integrated healthcare delivery networks comprising of hospitals (tertiary and regional), national specialist centres and polyclinics.

Healthcare in Singapore begins with building a healthy population through a preventive medicine programme and the promotion of a healthy lifestyle. Good, affordable basic healthcare is available to Singaporeans through subsidised medical services at public hospitals and clinics. The hospitals and healthcare systems will never withhold

206 Clinical Research in Asia: Opportunities and Challenges

help to a Singaporean because of financial limitations. The healthcare philosophy promotes individual responsibility towards healthy living and medical expenses. Medisave, Medishield, ElderShield and Medifund schemes exist to help Singaporeans 'co-pay' their medical expenses.

7.4.1 Primary healthcare

Primary healthcare includes preventive healthcare and health education. Private practitioners provide 80 per cent of primary healthcare services while government polyclinics provide the remaining 20 per cent. However, public hospitals provide 80 per cent of the more costly hospital care, with the remaining 20 per cent provided by private hospital care. The island network of 18 outpatient polyclinics and about 2,000 private medical practitioner clinics provides the primary healthcare services. Each polyclinic is an affordable subsidised one-stop health centre, providing outpatient medical care, follow-up of patients discharged from hospitals, immunisation, health screening and education, investigative facilities and pharmacy services. The needy elderly receive further help through the Primary Care Partnership Scheme. The scheme is most helpful for those who cannot travel to polyclinics. The seven public hospitals comprise five general hospitals, a hospital for women and children, and a psychiatric hospital. The general hospitals provide inpatient and specialist outpatient services, and a 24-hour emergency department. Seventy-five per cent of public hospital beds are heavily subsidised. There are also national specialty centres for cancer, cardiac, eye, skin, neuroscience and dental care.

7.4.2 Intermediate and long-term care

There is a comprehensive range of residential and community-based healthcare services catering to the long-term care needs of Singaporeans. The services available include community hospitals, chronic sick hospitals, nursing homes, sheltered homes for the

Published by Woodhead Publishing Limited, 2012

ex-mentally ill, inpatient hospice institutions, home medical, home nursing and home hospice care services, day rehabilitation centres, dementia day-care centres, psychiatric day-care centres and psychiatric rehabilitation homes.

7.4.3 Health research

The MOH focuses on scientific and health research with the aim of driving the translation of basic research to advance human healthcare, and to increase the translational and clinical research capabilities of public hospitals, research institutions and medical researchers. The National Medical Research Council (NMRC) was established by the MOH to engender the growth of research talent, to support high-quality scientific and clinical research, and to improve medical care and human health in Singapore. The NMRC supports the development of core manpower and research capabilities and funds research programmes and projects carried out by restructured hospitals, national disease centres and public tertiary educational institutions. The NMRC also awards health research fellowships for the development of health research manpower. The Health Services Research Competitive Research Grant is a new MOH research grant established in 2009. This grant aims to promote the conduct of health services research and enable the translation of health services research findings into policy and practice.

7.5 Clinical research in Singapore

Like many other Asian countries, there is an increasing interest in conducting clinical trials in Singapore. This is primarily because of (i) the ease of access to treatment-naive patients; (ii) the ability to generate Asian data to address ethnic diversity; (iii) early exposure of key Asian opinion leaders to new therapies; (iv) the potential for shortening the investigational drug development time; and (iv) the capacity to reduce research costs in Asia (due to the lower cost of medical care in Asia). Singapore is an attractive site for clinical trials due to its excellent infrastructure. This includes the establishment of

Published by Woodhead Publishing Limited, 2012

208 Clinical Research in Asia: Opportunities and Challenges

GCP standards, training activities, new CROs and site monitoring organisations in hospitals and institutions, and changes in regulatory guidelines. Hence, many multinational pharma companies have set up their regional Asia-Pacific headquarters in Singapore.

7.6 CRO market

The estimated size of the CRO market in Singapore was approximately $137 million in 2010. Table 7.2 details the CRO market size by phase and in total for Singapore from 2009 to 2010. While total market size is projected to increase, the Phase I and II portions are increasing faster than Phase III, while Phase IV is declining.

Additionally, based on the number of CTCs issued by the Singapore Health Science Authority, which are reflective of the total number of trials started each year, the CAGR of Phase I and II trials combined from 2000 to 2009 was 6.5 per cent, while that of Phase III and IV combined was 5.4 per cent.

While the Asia-Pacific CRO market leans towards Phase III and Phase IV trials as a whole, a combination of factors have resulted in Singapore having greater increases in Phases I and II. Two major drivers are the strategic governmental focus on early-phase trials and investments made by major pharma companies, including:

- Lilly Centre for Clinical Pharmacology, National University of Singapore;
- Pfizer Clinical Research Unit, Singapore General Hospital;

Table 7.2 CRO market size in Singapore, 2009–10

Year	Phase I ($m)	Phase II ($m)	Phase III ($m)	Phase IV ($m)	Total market size ($m)
2009	20.3	33.8	47.3	27.0	128.4
2010	22.3	36.6	48.4	25.3	132.6

Source: Frost and Sullivan

Published by Woodhead Publishing Limited, 2012

Clinical research in Singapore

- Changi General Hospital Clinical Trials Research Unit;
- National University Hospital Clinical Trials Unit.

Early-phase studies require small subject numbers and can be completed over a shorter period in a single site. The availability of dedicated resources and infrastructure providing the full spectrum of scientific and technological expertise has facilitated the growth of early-phase business. Singapore's Biomedical Sciences initiative has also been key in enabling multinational companies to set up dedicated Phase I centres in Singapore and to conduct their drug development programme. Thanks also to the country's advanced infrastructure (especially necessary for the early phases) and stringent GCP guidelines (which establish credibility in quality control), Singapore has become an attractive location for early-stage clinical outsourcing.

7.6.1 Focus on specialised therapeutics

To create a strategic advantage in the CRO market space, the Singapore government is promoting growth in specific therapeutic areas. Considering that oncology is estimated to have constituted 40 per cent of all pharmaceutical R&D projects in 2010, focusing on certain therapeutic areas will prove beneficial to both CROs and trial locations. The government has committed $1.1 billion to translational and applied research, which includes expanding the base of clinician scientists and clinical research publications, as well as the focus on biomarker research. It has also committed $90 million to translational and applied research programmes that centre on diseases in key therapeutic areas, such as oncology, ophthalmology and metabolic disorders, all of which are of significant interest to pharmaceutical drug developers.

Additionally, multiple multinational pharma companies have set up R&D facilities in Singapore over the past three years, making Singapore all the more attractive for early-phase outsourcing. Meanwhile, Pfizer, Merck and Eli Lilly will be combining their resources to form the Asian Cancer Research Group, in order to accelerate research in lung and gastric cancers in Asia. Singapore

Published by Woodhead Publishing Limited, 2012

also has strong intellectual property protection, which brings reassurance to the many pharma companies investing in drug development there. The intellectual property and copyright laws hold up to standards set by the WTO's Trade-Related Aspects of Intellectual Property Rights (TRIPS) Agreement, along with those from the Paris and Berne conventions. Figure 7.1 provides a breakdown of clinical trials by their therapeutic area in 2009 in Singapore. As per the figure, oncology (34 per cent) remains the most popular therapeutic area, followed by clinical pharmacology (19 per cent), cardiology (6 per cent), gastroenterology (5 per cent) and endocrinology (5 per cent).

The CRO market across Asia is on the rise and each country must focus on its own strengths in order to maximise its share of this growing market. As a small country, Singapore must especially capitalise on its strengths as a specialised location, both in trial types and therapeutic areas, in order to keep attracting interest in an increasingly competitive marketplace.

However, the combination of governmental backing and multinational investments bode well for Singapore's position within the CRO market. The last decade has seen numerous companies investing in Singapore (Figure 7.2), while several other players have set up central laboratory and pre-clinical toxicology centres in Singapore.

As we can see from Figure 7.2, in the short span of the last 10 years, Singapore has emerged as a vibrant location for attracting local entrepreneurs and global players to build and operate CRO business

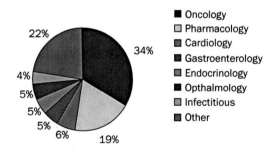

Figure 7.1 Clinical trials in Singapore by therapeutic area

Source: Health Sciences Authority website

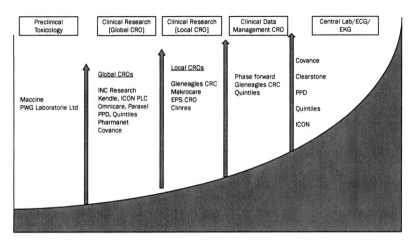

Figure 7.2 Clinical research players in Singapore

in the country. Most companies offer services in drug discovery, chemistry and pre-clinical areas that include organic synthesis, medicinal chemistry, biology, pharmacokinetics and toxicology. Hence the CRO industry Singapore is more developed in pre-clinical early-phase trials. However, with the entry of several global CROs, Phase II, III and IV trials are gaining momentum. But the growth of these late-phase industry-sponsored trials is relatively slow.

7.7 Clinical trials in Singapore

Singapore is participating in approximately 80–100 industry-sponsored trials every year. Even with the global slowdown in 2009, the flow of new trials to Singapore has been maintained, although the trend is not increasing significantly. In 2011 there were 842 trials already listed in the registry, out of which 236 trials were active and recruiting. Of the 842 studies undertaken in Singapore, only 573 trials are industry-sponsored trials and 245 trials are sponsored by individual investigators, local institutions or hospitals, universities and other organisations.

Further analysis of publicly available industry reports suggests that several GCP studies in diverse therapeutic areas are being conducted

212   Clinical Research in Asia: Opportunities and Challenges

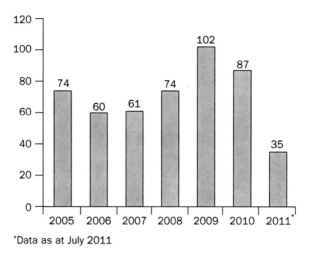

Figure 7.3   Growth of clinical trials in Singapore

Source: www.clinicaltrials.gov (accessed 20 July 2011)

in Singapore. Eighty per cent of the trials undertaken in Singapore are in late phases (i.e. Phase II–IV). Even significant numbers of trials in Phase I (20 per cent) are undertaken in Singapore.

Table 7.3 describes the number of industry-sponsored trials in being undertaken in Singapore. While most of the trials quoted are being undertaken by global sponsors, there are a significant number being undertaken by institutes of national repute. Such institutes include (but are not limited to) Singapore General Hospital,

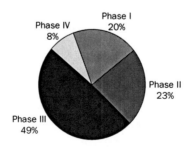

Figure 7.4   Clinical trials in Singapore, by phase

Source: www.clinicaltrials.gov (accessed July 2011)

Published by Woodhead Publishing Limited, 2012

Clinical research in Singapore

Table 7.3 Industry-sponsored trials in Singapore, 2011

Industry sponsor	No. of trials
Pfizer	124
Novartis	62
GlaxoSmithKline	44
Bristol-Myers Squibb	42
Bayer	37
Sanofi-Aventis	32
Hoffmann-La Roche	20
Eli Lilly & Co.	19
AstraZeneca	17
Merck	13
Novo Nordisk	12
Abbott	11
UCB, Inc.	10
Boehringer Ingelheim Pharmaceuticals	9
Genentech	9
Johnson and Johnson	8
Actelion	7
Allergan	6
Total	482

Source: www.clinicaltrials.gov (accessed July 2011)

National Medical Research Council, Singapore National Eye Centre, National Cancer Centre and National University Hospital, Singapore (Table 7.4).

7.7.1 Clinical trial approval

Before initiating any clinical trials on medicinal products in Singapore, the clinical investigator must obtain both ethical and

Published by Woodhead Publishing Limited, 2012

214 Clinical Research in Asia: Opportunities and Challenges

Table 7.4 Hospital/institution initiated trials in Singapore

Hospital/Institution	No. of trials
National University Hospital, Singapore	121
Singapore General Hospital	37
Singapore National Eye Centre	36
National Cancer Institute	23
National Cancer Centre, Singapore	21
National Medical Research Council, Singapore	21
National University, Singapore	15
Tan Tock Seng Hospital	13
Changi General Hospital	10
National Healthcare Group, Singapore	10
Singapore Eye Research Institute	10
Total	317

Source: *www.clinicaltrials.gov* (accessed July 2011)

regulatory approval. In Singapore, the document granting regulatory approval is known as the Clinical Trial Certificate (CTC). In 1978, the Medical Clinical Research Committee (MCRC) was set up to advise on the licensing of clinical drug trials. The members of this committee are appointed by the Minister under the Medicines Act 1975, Chapter 176 and the Medicines (Clinical Trial) Regulations 1978. This legislation was designed to ensure that clinical trials conducted in Singapore are properly controlled and also to safeguard the wellbeing of the participants involved. The MCRC is responsible for the evaluation of the safety and efficacy of all drugs where an application for a CTC has been filed by the principal investigator.

The MCRC deliberates and reviews:

- new applications for CTCs;
- amendments to clinical trial protocols and informed consent documents;
- serious adverse event reports;
- requests for CTC extension.

Published by Woodhead Publishing Limited, 2012

The drug company sponsoring the clinical trial assists the principal investigator to put up the application for the CTC through the hospital's ethics committee to the MCRC. The application details the protocol of the trial and includes pre-trial toxicological studies in animals, the patient consent form and the letter of indemnity to indemnify the principal investigator and the hospital/institution. After the MCRC has approved the trial, the CTC is issued and sent to the principal investigator with a copy to the CEO of the hospital. The CTC is valid for two years. If the trial is not completed at the end of two years, the CTC extension through a new application is required. A report is submitted by the principal investigator to the MCRC at the end of the trial. Any adverse reaction must be reported to the MCRC. Due to changes in regulatory environment and regulations, the time required for application and approval of CTCs has been reduced from 3–6 months to about two months.

The study start-up timeline in Singapore is as follows:

- Pre-regulatory activities (translations, insurance, ethics committee submissions): 6–8 weeks
- ethics committee approval process: 4–8 weeks
- CTC approval process: 8–10 weeks

7.7.2 Application for CTC

With effect from January 2006, parallel submissions can be made to both the Health Science Authority and to the respective institutional review board/domain-specific review board. The regulatory approval would be issued independently of the ethics approval. The applicants should initiate the study only when both regulatory and ethics approvals have been obtained. Applications for CTC are to be made by the sponsor, which should be a locally registered company. Only one application is required for multicentre clinical trials of the same drug using the same trial protocol to be conducted at two or more local institutions. Electronic applications for CTC can be made online. The application form and supporting trial documents can be submitted online without the need to submit multiple sets of the

216 Clinical Research in Asia: Opportunities and Challenges

Table 7.5 Number of CTCs issued

Phase	2000	2001	2002	2003	2004	2005	2006	2007	2008	2009
I	21	19	20	24	31	44	48	47	54	54
II	44	50	52	19	49	50	35	45	61	61
III	63	68	97	91	88	90	116	135	140	108
IV	29	28	26	26	32	17	18	26	31	39
Total	157	165	195	160	200	201	217	253	286	262

Source: Health Sciences Authority website

hard copies. An electronic authentication system is utilised for all users (principal investigators and sponsors), meaning that no physical signatures are needed to transact application services.

The number of CTCs issued by the Health Science Authority from 2000 to 2009 is summarised in Table 7.5.

7.7.3 Import of clinical trial material

Import of clinical trial test materials (CTMs) into Singapore requires the approval of the Health Sciences Authority. Approval is requested using the CTM form available from the Clinical Trials Branch of the Health Products Regulation Group, Health Sciences Authority. The sponsor submits the completed form together with the CTC application to the Health Sciences Authority. The CTM form is protocol-specific, and one must be submitted for each CTC application. The trial title, protocol number, principal investigator(s), trial institution(s) and local sponsor are to be stated in Section A. Section A is to be signed by the person (local sponsor applicant) responsible for the import. The name, strength and estimated total quantity of the CTM to be imported for the whole trial are to be stated in Section B.

From a business perspective, apart from licensing issues where pharmaceutical products are to be imported into Singapore, an import permit has to be obtained from the Controller of Imports and Exports before the products can be imported into Singapore. The regulatory body in this area is primarily the Trade Development Board. However, before an import permit can even be obtained,

Published by Woodhead Publishing Limited, 2012

a business entity seeking to import and sell pharmaceutical products on a wholesale basis must first be duly registered under the applicable Singapore laws to do business as a Singapore incorporated company, a Singapore branch of a foreign company or a firm/sole proprietorship. The relevant acts of parliament are the Companies Act and the Business Registration Act.

7.8 Evolution of GCP in Singapore

Prior to the publication of Singapore's GCP guidelines, investigators conducting clinical trials in Singapore complied with the Medicines (Clinical Trials) Regulations 1978 and the Declaration of Helsinki. In accordance with the recommendations of the committee appointed by the Chairman of the APEC Coordinating Centre and respecting the universal acceptance of the principles of GCP, it was proposed that the ICH-GCP guidelines will be followed for the conduct of clinical trials in Singapore.

With the increase in clinical research activities in Singapore and the need to accord appropriate protection to ensure the safety and wellbeing of trial subjects, the Health Product Regulations Group reviewed and updated the Medicines (Clinical Trials) Regulations in April 1998 and implemented the Singapore Guidelines for Good Clinical Practice (SGGCP) on 1 August 1998. The SGGCP, which were adapted from the ICH Harmonised Tripartite Guideline E6: Note for Guidance on Good Clinical Practice were then revised in October 1999. In tandem with the growing importance of developing GCP when conducting clinical trials, Singapore has established a coordinating APEC Centre for GCP, which provides a platform for the APEC countries to come together to address GCP needs and also a common framework for medicines to be evaluated for safety, quality and efficacy.

7.8.1 Salient features of the SGGCP

The SGGCP ensures that clinical trials are conducted to internationally acceptable ethical and scientific standards. The launch of the SGGCP

218 Clinical Research in Asia: Opportunities and Challenges

together with the amendments to the Medicines (Clinical Trials) Regulations has contributed to the further enhancement of the existing ethical and scientific standards of clinical investigations in Singapore. All clinical trials, unless exempted under the Medicines (Clinical Trials) Regulations, are required to be approved by the Ministry of Health and comply with the SGGCP. CTCs are exclusively supplied by the MCRC. Concurrently, investigators are required to submit their trial protocol to the institution's ethics committee, which upon review of the submission makes its recommendation to the MCRC. The composition and function of the MCRC are laid down by the committee. The work-flow plan when a sponsor applies for a CTC is also defined by the committee.

In Singapore, clinical trial applications are reviewed by two committees: the MCRC and the hospital ethics committee.

7.8.2 Medical Clinical Research Committee

The MCRC is an advisory committee with a three-year term appointed by the Ministry for Health to oversee the conduct of clinical trials in Singapore. It is an independent body constituted of medical members, whose responsibility is to ensure the protection of the rights, safety and wellbeing of human subjects involved in a trial, as well as reviewing, approving and providing continuing review of trial protocol and amendments of the methods and materials to be used in obtaining and documenting the informed consent of trial subjects.

The MCRC reviews applications for all clinical trials. The sponsor makes the clinical trial application to the MCRC after the investigator has applied to the hospital ethics committee for permission to conduct the trial at that particular institution. Having reviewed the proposed clinical trial, the MCRC grants approval for it to be conducted at the institution site within the constraints set forth by the MCRC or ethics committee, the institution, GCP, and the applicable regulatory requirements.

Published by Woodhead Publishing Limited, 2012

Clinical research in Singapore

No clinical trial on medicinal products, unless exempted under the Medicines (Clinical Trials) Regulations, may take place in Singapore without a CTC from the Ministry of Health. The MCRC will review a proposed clinical trial within 30 working days, discounting waiting time for further information from the sponsor(s) and/or investigator(s) and within 90 days if external review of toxicology data is necessary.

7.8.2.1 Composition, functions and operations

The composition of the MCRC should include:

- a clinician involved in clinical research as its chairperson;
- a qualified and experienced pharmacist (working in drug registration) as secretary;
- five clinicians (approved by the Ministry of Health) as members;
- guest members where necessary;
- a lay person to look into the social and ethical aspects of the trials in cases where trial applications are forwarded by doctors not in institutional practice, and where protocols are not reviewed by the ethics committee of the hospital.

The MCRC will meet regularly and make decisions only when there is a quorum. The MCRC review takes into account the medical and scientific basis of the application, as well as the ethical aspects of the trial and also ensures that the ethics committees in hospitals, sponsors and investigators comply with the Singapore Medicines Regulations pertaining to clinical trials with regards to the conduct of clinical trials.

7.8.3 Hospital ethics committee

Hospital ethics committees have a two-year term of office and are set up in hospitals by their medical board. The ethics committee

220 Clinical Research in Asia: Opportunities and Challenges

considers applications for clinical trials to be conducted in the particular institution and submits its recommendations to the MCRC. The ethics committee will review a proposed clinical trial within 30 working days, discounting waiting time for further information from the sponsor(s) and/or investigator(s).

7.8.3.1 Composition, functions and operations

The ethics committee will consist of a reasonable number of members, who collectively have the qualifications and experience to review and evaluate the science, medical aspects and ethics of the proposed trial.

The ethics committee will include at least five members, including:

- at least one member whose primary area of interest is in a non-scientific area;
- at least one member who is independent of the institution/trial site;
- guest members, who may be invited when deemed necessary.

Only those ethics committee members who are independent of the investigator and the sponsor of the trial will vote/provide opinion on a trial-related matter. The ethics committee secretariat will maintain a list of ethics committee members and their qualifications.

7.8.3.2 Role of hospital ethics committee

Hospital ethics committees need to be conversant with the changes to the Medicines Act and the Singapore GCP guidelines. Apart from the initial vetting to ensure the feasibility, safety, potential efficacy of the drug, scrutinising the trial protocol, checking the consent form and letter of indemnity for the principal investigator and hospital, hospital ethics committees also monitor all trials under their purview. Just like the principal investigator, hospitals' ethics committees are directly accountable to the hospital to ensure that trials are properly conducted in accordance with legislation and GCP guidelines.

Published by Woodhead Publishing Limited, 2012

All manner of clinical trials (drug and non-drug), with and without certification by MCRC are under the purview of the hospital ethics committee.

7.8.3.3 Responsibilities of ethics committee

The responsibilities of ethics committee are as follows:

- The ethics committee will safeguard the rights, safety and wellbeing of all trial subjects and ensure that the clinical research data are credible.
- The ethics committee will review the CV of the investigator of the proposed trial to gauge his competence.
- The ethics committee will conduct continuing review of each ongoing trial at regular intervals.
- When a non-therapeutic trial is carried out, the ethics committee will ensure that the proposed protocol addresses relevant ethical concerns and meets regulatory requirements for such trials.
- The ethics committee will review the amount and method of payment to subjects to assure that neither presents problems of coercion or undue influence on the trial subjects.

7.8.3.4 Terms and reference of the ethics committee

The terms and reference of the ethics committee are as follows:

- to review the investigator's request to conduct a clinical trial (review medical, scientific and ethical basis of trial);
- to evaluate safety of ongoing trial based on reports from sponsors and investigators;
- to ensure ongoing trials are carried out in accordance with Singapore GCP guidelines;
- to report change of protocol or termination of trial to the MCRC;
- to ensure the MCRC has issued the CTC before allowing the trial to commence.

Published by Woodhead Publishing Limited, 2012

222 Clinical Research in Asia: Opportunities and Challenges

The following documents shall be submitted to the ethics committee:

- trial protocols;
- consent forms;
- subject recruitment procedures;
- written information to be provided to subjects;
- investigator's brochure;
- available safety information;
- information about payment and compensation available to subjects;
- investigator's CV.

7.8.4 Other salient features of the SGGCP

While the broad elements of the SGGCP are derived from the ICH-GCP guidelines, a few points are specific to the SGGCP. Although the SGGCP do not demand any documentary evidence such as financial disclosures or debarment, the document clearly delineates that the investigator, his team or the study subject should not have any direct or indirect financial interest in the trial. With regards to the medical care of trial subjects in case of an emergency, the SGGCP delineate that any doctor or dentist may, in the absence of the investigator or his assistants, undertake the patient management should this be necessary.

On investigational product labels, SGGCP require the inclusion of the words: 'This product shall only be used under strict medical surveillance' or 'This product shall be used under strict dental surveillance', as the case may be, or the words 'For clinical trial use only'.

With regards to the informed consent of trial subjects, SGGCP require that in the case of emergency situations, when the subject's prior consent is not possible, the consent of the subject's legally acceptable representative, if present, should be requested. When the subject's prior consent is not possible, and the subject's legally acceptable representative is not available, enrolment of the subject

Published by Woodhead Publishing Limited, 2012

should require measures described in the protocol and/or elsewhere, with documented approval by the MCRC and ethics committee, to protect the rights, safety and wellbeing of the subject and to ensure compliance with applicable regulatory requirements. The latter includes written certification from the principal investigator and two specialists who are not involved in the trial that:

- the person is facing a life-threatening situation necessitating intervention;
- the person is unable to give his consent as a result of his medical condition;
- it is not feasible to request consent from that person or to contact his legal representative within the crucial period in which treatment must be administered;
- neither that person or his legal representative nor any members of that person's family has informed the principal investigator of his objection to that person being used as a subject in the clinical trial.

The SGGCP mandates access to the ethics committee by any research subjects who may be unhappy about their participation in the research project. With regards to the archiving of records and reports, the SGGCP require that essential documents should be retained until at least two years after the last approval of a marketing application and until there are no pending or contemplated marketing applications, or at least two years have elapsed since the formal discontinuation of clinical development of the investigational product or six years after the completion of the clinical trial. ICH-GCP does not define a six-year retention period after the completion of the clinical trial.

These documents should be retained for a longer period, however, if required by the applicable regulatory requirements or by an agreement with the sponsor. It is the responsibility of the sponsor to inform the investigator/institution as to when these documents no longer need to be retained. It is acceptable for the documents to be archived by electronic means, microfilm or other suitable archiving technology.

Published by Woodhead Publishing Limited, 2012

224 Clinical Research in Asia: Opportunities and Challenges

SGGCP require that where there is a change of principal investigator during a clinical trial, the current principal investigator must inform the sponsor, ethics committee and MCRC and furnish them with the particulars of the new principal investigator. The new principal investigator must be issued with a new CTC before conducting any trials.

With regards to the coding of investigational products, SGGCP delineate that in blinded trials, the coding system for the investigational product(s) should include a mechanism that permits rapid identification of the product(s) in case of a medical emergency, but does not permit undetectable breaches in the blinding. The key to the code/cipher shall be made known to the ethics committee, the MCRC and the Ministry of Health and be readily accessible to any doctor (or dentist) in an emergency.

7.9 Role of clinical trial resource centre

The majority of national hospitals in Singapore have their own clinical trial resource centre (CTRC) similar to the Clinical Trial and Epidemiological Research Unit of the MOH, which functions as the resource centre for the MOH. The CTRC has a manager or clinical trials coordinator who maintains a database of all clinical trials in the hospital. The CTRC helps the ethics committee to monitor the progress of the trial, adverse effects, status of trial, sends reminders and monitors reports to the MCRC. It also helps to coordinate site audits, arranges for storage of case report forms and archives all relevant trial material. The CTRC provides training for company-sponsored clinical trial nurses or other personnel involved in clinical trials. It helps to coordinate clinical trials and GCP workshops for the principal investigator and their trial nurse and other personnel. It also explores common problems like the sourcing of companies to provide insurance to indemnify the principal investigator and hospitals. The CTRC can be a self-managed business unit in the hospital or it could be a joint venture of the hospital and one or more drug companies. A levy can be imposed on drug companies utilising the facilities of the CTRC.

Published by Woodhead Publishing Limited, 2012

7.10 Environmental analysis

Singapore has established a strong track record as a global manufacturing site in Asia. Today, leading pharmaceutical, biotechnology and medical technology companies have invested in more than 50 commercial-scale facilities, and continue to partner with Singapore in enhancing manufacturing excellence in areas such sustainable manufacturing, process development and upgrading suppliers' capabilities to address niche requirements. Singapore presents key advantages for companies that seek to improve R&D productivity and develop innovative medical devices for Asia. Biomedical sciences companies can tap into the multidisciplinary capabilities offered by Singapore's integrated research network in basic and translational research. Today, 4,300 researchers carry out biomedical sciences R&D in more than 50 companies and 30 public sector institutes, with more than S$1 billion dedicated to R&D annually.

As companies seek to expand their footprint in Asia to tap into the region's fast-growing healthcare markets, Singapore has emerged as a key beach-head for both global companies and Asian enterprises. Leading companies, including eight of the top 10 pharmaceutical and all of the top 10 medical technology companies, have established their regional headquarters in Singapore to drive their business expansion and innovation in Asia.

7.10.1 Political and economic environment

Since 2000, when Singapore launched its biomedical sciences initiative, the Singapore Economic Development Board has worked closely with other public sector agencies, such as A*STAR, the MOH, and the country's universities, to build up scientific and clinical excellence, which is essential in fuelling the growth of Singapore's biomedical sciences sector.

Singapore's vision is to be the Biopolis of Asia, a leading international biomedical sciences cluster advancing human health by achieving excellence across the entire value chain.

Published by Woodhead Publishing Limited, 2012

226 Clinical Research in Asia: Opportunities and Challenges

Singapore has committed S$1.55 billion to drive translational and clinical research. Initiatives include training schemes to expand its base of clinician scientists and clinical research publications. Today, companies can tap into the multidisciplinary capabilities of Singapore's integrated network of 30 research institutes, academic medical centres, medical institutes and hospitals to increase their knowledge of Asian disease biology and improve R&D decision making.

Singapore has also launched five S$25 million translational and clinical research (TCR) flagship programmes to bring scientists and clinicians together to work on key diseases. The five TCR flagship programmes awarded in 2007–08 are as follows:

- Singapore Gastric Cancer Consortium (cancer);
- translational research innovations in ocular surgery (eye diseases);
- vulnerability, disease progression and treatment in schizophrenia and related psychoses (neuroscience);
- developmental pathways to metabolic diseases (cardiovascular/metabolic diseases);
- scientific exploration, translational research, operational evaluation of disease prevention and preventive measures through new treatment strategies against dengue (infectious diseases).

7.10.2 Public–private partnership

Amidst the trend towards increased medical technology (medtech) innovation in Asia to harness the region's opportunities, 30 medtech companies now carry out R&D that includes value engineering and product development for regional and global markets in Singapore. They include 3M, Becton Dickinson, Hill-Rom, Siemens, Thermo Fisher, Welch Allyn, AB Sciex as well as local start-ups such as Amaranth Medical, HealthSTATS and Veredus Laboratories. Singapore is committed to partner companies in developing new solutions that can address unmet healthcare needs in Asia's fast-growing markets.

Published by Woodhead Publishing Limited, 2012

Singapore-Stanford Biodesign Program is designed to meet the medtech industry's need for Asian medical device innovators who are familiar with the medtech innovation process and Asia's healthcare needs. A*STAR's collaboration with the Center for Integration of Medicine and Innovative Technology in Boston, USA will enable engineers, clinicians and scientists in Singapore to work with clinicians in Boston to develop engineering solutions that have clinical and market relevance.

A*STAR's Biomedical Engineering Programme currently oversees eight research projects which involve collaborations between A*STAR's research engineers and clinicians/researchers at local hospitals and universities. These projects seek to develop and provide cost-effective, innovative and clinically effective solutions for healthcare systems.

Singapore has built up a strong scientific foundation with seven research institutes and five research consortia in key fields that include clinical sciences, genomics, bioengineering, molecular/cell biology, medical biology, bioimaging and immunology. Prominent international research institutes including the Liggins Institute and American Association for Cancer Research are working with these research institutes in Singapore.

Singapore has also made significant progress in translational and clinical research. It has built key infrastructure such as investigational medicine units dedicated for early-phase trials in public hospitals, as well as the Singapore Clinical Research Institute, which focuses on supporting later-stage trials. In line with Singapore's focus on expanding and strengthening its capabilities in translational and clinical research, the development of a national-level, clinical research organisation fills an important gap in the development of human capital and infrastructure as part of the second phase of Singapore's Biomedical Sciences Initiative.

Through National Research Foundation funding, the Singapore Clinical Research Institute has been established as a one-stop entity that provides the necessary expertise, support, scientific leadership and scientific collaborations for the conduct of both investigator-initiated and commercially-sponsored clinical research studies in Singapore. The Singapore Clinical Research Institute evolved from

Published by Woodhead Publishing Limited, 2012

228 Clinical Research in Asia: Opportunities and Challenges

the Clinical Trials and Epidemiology Research Unit, which was an NMRC funded unit to help support clinical research in Singapore. Singapore offers excellent intellectual property protection, sophisticated infrastructure and a skilled manpower base to drive process development and support the commercial-scale production of the industry's most innovative products.

In addition, the city-state offers a stable political and civic environment to ensure long-term returns for global manufacturers' capital-intensive investments. The government has set aside a 360-hectare stretch of prepared and specifically-zoned land, called Tuas Biomedical Park (TBP), for pharmaceutical and biologics manufacturing. Equipped with established infrastructure such as roads, drainage systems, power, water supply and telecommunication lines, TBP presents a plug-and-play environment that enables leading biomedical sciences companies to set up manufacturing facilities with minimal lead time. These companies can also benefit from third-party utilities and services such as steam, natural gas, chilled water and waste treatment. TBP is currently home to leading pharmaceutical, biotechnology and medical technology companies such as Abbott, Alcon, CIBA Vision, GlaxoSmithKline Biologicals, Lonza, Merck Sharp and Dohme, Novartis, Pfizer and Roche. These companies have collectively invested over S$6 billion to set up manufacturing facilities in TBP.

The government is committed to working with the industry to upgrade employees' skills, train new workers and promote best practices. The recent launch of the National University of Singapore Academy of GxP Excellence (NUSAGE) is a case in point. NUSAGE, a collaboration between the Singapore government, the National University of Singapore, and industry partners, is one of the first industry-wide training initiatives in the region and complements company-specific training centres in Singapore.

Singapore hosts cosmopolitan research teams in both public sector research institutes and corporate R&D labs. The Novartis Institute for Tropical Diseases, for example, houses more than 100 researchers from 18 nationalities. Singapore's MerLion Pharmaceuticals made it

Published by Woodhead Publishing Limited, 2012

Clinical research in Singapore

to FierceBiotech's 2007 industry listing of biotechnology companies to watch worldwide. It is the first Asian company on the annual roll of top emerging companies since the inaugural awards in 2003. In December 2007, the company received the Best Company in an Emerging Market award at the annual Scrip awards in London. Companies can leverage Singapore's pro-business environment to commence operations with short lead time. It takes 15 minutes to register a business online, 4–8 weeks to receive approval for clinical trials, and 24–36 months for a manufacturing facility to be operational.

7.10.3 Socio-cultural environment

Singapore is cosmopolitan, uses English, and is strategically located at the heart of Asia and well connected with key regional markets. Beyond geography and socio-cultural characteristics, Singapore provides diverse partnership opportunities with its public sector research institutes, base of leading pharmaceutical and biotechnology companies, clinical-research units in hospitals and international research organisations. Singapore has established world-class scientific and clinical excellence that enables pre-clinical development and early-phase clinical testing of novel drug candidates to be carried out in a single location.

Research published by Wiley-Blackwell in 2007 puts Singapore is among the world's most prolific research locations, with 1.41 papers per 1,000 people. Singapore's population comprises three key Asian ethnic groups – Chinese (75 per cent), Malay (14 per cent) and Indian (9 per cent). This presents an ideal base for companies and scientists to develop innovative solutions and therapies for the regional and global markets.

English, the language of science, is the medium of instruction in schools, and most Singaporeans are bilingual in English and their respective Asian mother-tongue (Mandarin, Malay or respective Indian language). Singapore thus presents an ideal location to forge and drive strategic scientific collaborations in Asia.

Published by Woodhead Publishing Limited, 2012

230 Clinical Research in Asia: Opportunities and Challenges

7.10.4 Regulatory and legal environment

The Medicines Act and the regulations promulgated thereunder govern pharmaceuticals in Singapore. These regulations control all aspects of dealings in medicines and related products. To help the authorities ensure the safety, efficacy and quality of medicinal products, the act provides for the licensing of their manufacture, wholesale and import. It also deals with issues relating to the advertisement of medicinal products and Chinese proprietary medicines. The summary of health authorities, acts and guidelines are mentioned in Table 7.6. Import and wholesaling of pharmaceutical products are governed by the Medicines Act. There are four types of licence: product, import, wholesale dealer's and manufacturer's licences. Apart from these licences, the Drug Administration Department also issues a Certificate for Importers of Medicinal

Table 7.6 Summary of health authorities, acts and guidelines in Singapore

Authority name	Description
Health Science Authority	A multidisciplinary agency administering the national regulatory frameworks for pharmaceuticals, complementary medicines, medical devices and other health products
Medicines Act 1975	Regulation of clinical trials
The Medicines (Clinical Trials) (Amendment) Regulations 1998	In addition to the Medicines Act, the conduct of clinical trials in Singapore is also regulated by The Medicines (Clinical Trials) (Amendment) Regulations 1998
The Singapore Guidelines for GCP	Information on the conduct of clinical trials in Singapore as per SGGCP; can be obtained from the Health Products Regulation Group
Clinical Trial Certificate	Document granting regulatory approval to conduct a clinical trial
SingHealth	Represents the eastern cluster of public healthcare institutions in Singapore; as a site facilitator, SingHealth Clinical Trials can act as liaison between the industry (biopharma companies) and member institutions

Published by Woodhead Publishing Limited, 2012

Products. This is required as Singapore, like many importing countries, requires proof of registration of medicinal products in the country of origin before sales are permitted.

As a corollary to the Medicines Act, the Misuse of Drugs Regulations provide for the possession, supply, import, manufacture and record-keeping of controlled drugs to regulate the legitimate use of controlled drugs by professionals. The Sale of Drugs Act (Cap 282) ensures that consumers are supplied with the quantity and quality of drugs demanded by them, explicitly or implicitly. The Poisons Act (Cap 234) and the Poisons Rules regulate the importation, possession, manufacture, compounding, storage and sale of potent medicinal substances and toxic chemical substances, so as to prevent accidents arising from their use or misuse. These legislations will come into play only if the pharmaceutical product is also a poison.

On the international front, Singapore has acceded to the Pharmaceutical Inspection Cooperation Scheme (PICS). This is an international accreditation and liaison unit, membership of which enhances the status of Singapore as a regional pharmaceutical and life sciences hub. The PICS also facilitates the process of mutual recognition on GMP inspection by PICS countries and enables global acceptance of the quality of pharmaceutical products manufactured and exported from Singapore. Singapore is also a party to the 1971 United Nations Convention on Psychotropic Substances, and to the 1961 United Nations Single Convention on Narcotic Drugs.

NUSAGE was set up in 2008 to promote good practices in health product safety or vigilance as well as GMP and GCP. A collaboration between key industry leaders, leading government agencies and the National University of Singapore, NUSAGE is one of the first industry-wide training initiatives in the region and complements company-specific training centres in Singapore. NUSAGE also provides basic training for people who are interested in joining the industry.

In addition, an ethical code of practice was drawn up to guide doctors and drug companies on how they should deal with each other. For instance, doctors are discouraged from accepting money from pharma companies to conduct research or clinical trials if it

232 Clinical Research in Asia: Opportunities and Challenges

also means being required to buy the company's products. This code does not, however, have the force of law. In addition, a new accreditation scheme for laboratory testing was recently established in the country by the Singapore Accreditation Council, in partnership with the College of American Pathologists, which will enhance the capability and credibility of testing services provided by local laboratories.

7.11 Clinical trial challenges

With its modern healthcare system and advanced infrastructure, Singapore has been a key hub for clinical research. Nonetheless, it does pose operational challenges for doing clinical trials. Some of the challenges are listed below.

7.11.1 Competition for experienced investigators

As a small country, Singapore offers a limited pool of experienced and seasoned investigators. This means there is intense competition within the pharmaceutical industry for experienced and qualified clinical investigators. As a technologically advanced country, investigators prefer cutting-edge clinical trial opportunities over traditional trial designs. To attract investigators to perform clinical trials, multinational pharma companies and CROs must evolve appropriate negotiation mechanisms.

7.11.2 Competition for patient database

With a limited number of hospitals and relatively small database of potential patients, there is much competition for patient recruitment. In addition, patients already have a wide variety of treatment choices, reducing their inclination to consider clinical trial participation. This eventually leads to higher drop-outs and

Published by Woodhead Publishing Limited, 2012

withdrawals. Stakeholders need to be mindful about the ethical conduct of clinical research.

7.11.3 Advanced healthcare and medical practice

A large pool of patients already has access to sophisticated ultra-modern technology in interventional and non-interventional medicine without major financial implications. This potentially limits clinical trial participation.

7.11.4 Cosmopolitan society

Singapore's population is racially and ethnically diverse. Many citizens are still not open to 'experimental' medicine and hence relatively fewer subjects and hospital sites consent to participate in clinical trials.

7.11.5 Financial stability and social security

Singapore's government makes hospital care affordable through schemes like Medisave, the national medical savings account system. Through such schemes, Singaporeans receive treatment in the event of any medical contingency, without personally having to worry about the financial consequences. Competitive health insurance policies combined with Singaporeans' willingness to top up their basic coverage for additional protection also help to mitigate any such worries.

As a social security savings plan, Singapore's Central Provident Fund comprehensively covers needs in retirement, healthcare, home ownership, family protection and asset enhancement. This flexible and accessible security system provides reassurance to the residents of Singapore when it comes to the management of medical contingencies without affecting their day-to-day life.

Published by Woodhead Publishing Limited, 2012

234 Clinical Research in Asia: Opportunities and Challenges

7.11.6 Widespread awareness

The high education and literacy levels of Singaporeans give them an edge over equivalent Asian populations. This scenario increases the awareness about drugs and diseases. With increased awareness about healthcare, many rich and educated do not agree to participate in clinical trials.

7.11.7 Cultural outlook

In spite of their highly cosmopolitan outlook, the 'conformist' side of Singaporeans is still inclined to traditional medicine, which often includes alternative treatment methodologies such as Chinese medicine, which is practised very widely in Singapore.

7.11.8 Ethnic limitations

Malay Singaporeans are not open to trial-based treatment methodologies and associated interventions due to deep-rooted religious beliefs. People from various cultural or ethnic backgrounds hold values and beliefs that may differ from principles associated with Western medicine. Many people have cultural beliefs that Western medicine cannot address their health concerns. Different ethnic and cultural views of health and disease (e.g. fatalism, family decisions about treatment, use of 'traditional healers', prayer, herbal medicines, or use of complementary/alternative health practices) may make clinical trials a less attractive treatment option. For prevention trials, many may feel that the risk of a potential disease and its consequences may be less important than meeting daily needs.

7.11.9 Traditional medicine practices

Alternative treatments, including 'ancestral herbal remedies', remain very popular in Singapore. A considerable number of people may opt for them in addition to modern medicine.

Published by Woodhead Publishing Limited, 2012

7.11.10 *Higher cost of medical practice and technology*

The state-of-the-art medical infrastructure in Singapore comes at a high price – higher than that in other Asian countries and in many situations in line with Western countries. When combined with the high labour costs, this represents a cost disadvantage for trial sponsors compared with other Asian countries. It also increases the financial risk due to the disparity between the investment and rewards.

7.11.11 *The widening gap of demand-supply for quality resources*

There are insufficient quality resources to meet the huge demand of seasoned investigators. Multinational pharma companies and CROs find it a significant challenge to recruit and retain experienced medical staff, project managers and monitors who have knowledge, experience and multilingual skills.

7.12 Future outlook

Although growth in clinical research has slowed down, the Asia-Pacific region remains one of the highest growth regions and therefore remains a high priority for global pharma companies. This means the market access driver of trial placement is becoming even stronger for Asia – combined with the already strong cost efficiency and patient recruitment drivers. Based on all of these factors, the rapid growth in clinical trials in Asia is sure to continue. With access to patients with disease patterns similar to the rest of the world, and access to half of the world's population, along with improved regulatory timelines, growth in the Asia-Pacific region is not likely to decline any further. Being a central hub with an excellent socio-economic environment, Singapore will facilitate the growth of the region.

There is a great potential for pharmaceutical R&D in Singapore. The country needs more skilled resources and more trained investigators so as to attract more pharma companies to invest in

Singapore. The Economic Development Board is doing a great job to attract investment in the areas of healthcare, life sciences and biomedical science. Companies will come to conduct multicentre trials with Singapore as their headquarters, not only for Phase III and IV but even Phase I and II trials. Though Singapore has world-class infrastructure, there is a need to practise and improve GCP to international standards. There is a need to develop expertise and facilities for pre-trial animal drug testing and Phase I and II trials and establish systems for trial audits in order to maintain high standards so as to produce credible results. With an international reputation for the conduct of clinical trials, Singapore will be the centre of attention for giant pharmaceuticals and will capture the global market.

8

Clinical research in Thailand

Abstract: Thailand is a newly industrialised country with an emerging economy and a growing pharmaceutical market. This chapter discusses the pharmaceutical market, clinical research environment and the healthcare system in Thailand. It goes on to describe the process of undertaking clinical trials in Thailand and analyses the historical facts about the trials undertaken in the country.

8.1 Pharmaceutical industry in Thailand

Thailand is dependent on imported pharmaceuticals and raw materials to manufacture pharmaceuticals locally to meet domestic demand. Because of this dependency on imported pharmaceuticals, the country is vulnerable to changes in the international trade environment. By mandating its Board of Investment to develop the pharmaceutical industry, the Thai government aims to address this vulnerability. As part of its programme of modernisation, it is hoped that Thailand will introduce and enforce legislation to facilitate the growth of the pharmaceutical industry, for example, by reinforcing intellectual property rights. The increasing demand for pharmaceuticals is caused by, among other factors, the increasing number of expatriates, health tourists visiting Thailand and changing lifestyles among the Thai population. According to the Pharmaceutical Research and Manufacturers Association, 10.3 per cent of the population was aged over 60 years in 2005, a figure it estimates will

Published by Woodhead Publishing Limited, 2012

238 Clinical Research in Asia: Opportunities and Challenges

increase to 13.8 per cent by 2015. Such an ageing population will increase the demand for pharmaceuticals and medicines. The Thai government has attempted to improve standards of public healthcare, considerably increasing the demand for pharmaceuticals. Given this government-backed increased demand for pharmaceuticals, prospects for the industry appear favourable.

In Thailand, drug manufacturers are categorised into three groups:

- multinational corporations which manufacture active ingredients and pharmaceutical formulations;
- Thai-owned companies, which focus primarily on producing pharmaceutical formulations and, to a lesser extent, manufacturing active ingredients; and
- the Government Pharmaceutical Organisation (GPO), which primarily prepares pharmaceutical formulations for the public sector health service.

In 2006, IMS Health Quarterly ranked the top 10 pharmaceutical manufacturers in Thailand as follows:

1. Pfizer International Corp.
2. Sanofi-Aventis
3. GlaxoSmithKline
4. AstraZeneca
5. Novartis Corp.
6. Siam Pharm.
7. Roche Corp.
8. Merck & Co.
9. GPO
10. Berlin Pharm. Ind.

The GPO is noteworthy as it holds a near-monopoly over pharmaceutical supply to the public sector. This position was established in 2006 when public hospitals were legally obliged to purchase 80 per cent of their drugs from the GPO. Not only focusing on serving domestic demand under the Thai government's healthcare scheme, the GPO is exporting its products to neighbouring countries in Asia and Africa.

Published by Woodhead Publishing Limited, 2012

8.2 The pharmaceutical regulatory environment

There are two main bodies of law applicable to drugs in Thailand. The first, the law of patents, relates to the intellectual property protection of new drugs, while the second body of law, principally codified in the Drug Act 1967 (BE 2510) and subsequent amendments, sets out a regulatory regime for the supervision of drug production, importation, sale and marketing of drugs in Thailand. The regulation of pharmaceutical products in Thailand began in 1909 with basic laws prohibiting the adulteration of drug products and narcotic substances. Key laws include the Drug Act of BE 2546 (1967) as amended in 1987, and the New Drug Act 2003. It is not presently possible to extend the 20-year term of a patent because of time lost due to regulatory hurdles and procedures that must be adhered to before a drug can released to the market. The sale of drugs and medicines in Thailand is supervised by the Thai FDA, under the auspices of the Ministry of Public Health. Part of the FDA's mandate is to supervise drugs in accordance with the regime under the Drug Act. The licensing of the manufacture, importation and sale of drugs is required by law and applications for permission and licences are granted in accordance with the various rules and supplementary ministerial regulations promulgated to govern the FDA approval process. New drugs are registered and approved before being sold on the open market. In fact, the drug registration process has been declared necessary to ensure efficacy, safety and effectiveness for the drugs sold in Thailand. A drug developer who has successfully patented a drug in Thailand must obtain approval from the FDA before the drug can enter the Thai market. Approval must also be obtained for generic versions of drugs as proof of bioequivalence. The Trade Secrets Act also will come into play when implementing regulations that deal specifically with the confidential clinical safety data submitted to the FDA during the regulatory approval process. The issue of data exclusivity arises in the context of how generics try to prove bioequivalence – do they prove it with their own clinical safety data or do they simply refer to the data submitted by an R&D based company?

The Medical Device Act of BE 2531 (1988) was the first legislation to specifically address issues related to medical devices (prior to

Published by Woodhead Publishing Limited, 2012

240 Clinical Research in Asia: Opportunities and Challenges

enactment of this legislation, medical device issues were referred to provisions of the Drug Act). Medical devices are categorised by potential patient risk and parallel European Union and US systems (i.e. Thai categories II and III versus classes II and III). Additionally, the requirements for general GMP standards for drugs and medical devices have been in place since 1984. The Thai FDA has also established its stance on future trends related to medical product regulations and is aligning itself internationally through APEC's Life Science Innovation Forum and regionally with ASEAN's Harmonisation on Healthcare Products, which includes both drug and medical device product working groups.

8.3 Pharmaceutical market

IMS Health valued the Thai pharmaceutical market at $2.9 billion in 2009 (this being the most recent figure available at the time of writing). The pharmaceutical market in Thailand is expected to display the same upward future trends as neighbouring countries. According to IMS Health, in 2009, the pharmaceutical market grew by 5.6 per cent versus the previous year. The Thai government continues to step up total healthcare spend in an effort to support universal healthcare. The public healthcare system accounts for two-thirds of total healthcare spend and almost 4 per cent of total GDP. Thailand has widespread access to healthcare, as roughly 90 per cent of the total population is covered under the Universal Health Scheme. While this covers nearly 47.5 million patients, those who can afford treatment in private facilities do so and the use of private facilities is on the increase. The Thai generic sector is on the rise and the locally manufactured products dominate the pharmaceutical market. The domestic pharmaceutical industry is primarily a formulating industry with little R&D, and neighbouring countries such as Singapore offer stronger incentives and better protection of intellectual property. Ninety-five per cent of the ingredients used in locally manufactured drugs are imported from low-cost countries such as India and China. Thailand's pharmaceutical market is made up of locally produced domestic drugs (generic products, which account for 46 per cent of the

Published by Woodhead Publishing Limited, 2012

drugs on the market), locally produced international brands (about 32 per cent of the market), and imports (22 per cent of the market). The main drugs produced domestically are analgesics and penicillin.

8.3.1 Demography

Thailand is an independent country in the heart of Southeast Asia. The largest city is Bangkok, the capital, which is also the country's centre of political, commercial, industrial and cultural activities. It is the world's 50th largest country in terms of total area and, with a population of 67 million, the 21st most populous country.

Thailand is a newly industrialised country with an emerging economy. Exports account for more than two-thirds of the country's GDP, making it heavily export-dependent. According to the CIA World Fact Book, in 2010, Thailand's economy expanded 7.6 per cent, its fastest since 1995, as exports rebounded from their depressed 2009 level. CIA World Fact Book estimates that Thailand has a GDP of $586.9 billion based on purchasing power parity in 2010. This classifies Thailand as the second largest economy in Southeast Asia after Indonesia. Despite this, Thailand ranks midway in the wealth spread in Southeast Asia as it is the fourth richest nation by GDP per capita, after Singapore, Brunei and Malaysia.

About 75 per cent of the population is ethnically Thai, 14 per cent is of Chinese origin, and 3 per cent is ethnically Malay, the remaining 8 per cent being made up of, among others, Khmer, Lao, Vietnamese and Indians. The official language is Thai, with various dialects spoken in rural regions. Other languages spoken include Chinese and Malay. English is a mandatory subject in state schools, and is widely spoken and understood, particularly in Bangkok and other major cities.

In terms of health, life expectancy is 70.51 years and 75.27 years for females and males, respectively; the infant mortality rate is 18.23 per 1,000 live births. Two thirds of the Thai population will die before the age of 70. More than 30,000 people infected with HIV die annually. More than 11 million Thais are addicted to tobacco-smoking, up to half of which may die from tobacco-related diseases.

Published by Woodhead Publishing Limited, 2012

Thailand's well organised school system has resulted in a high level of adult literacy of 90.5 per cent and 94.9 per cent for females and males, respectively. The country's primary religion is Buddhism, which is practised by around 95 per cent of all Thais.

8.4 Clinical research in Thailand

Thailand is one of several countries that meet the needs of the international drug development community for conducting cost-effective and expeditious clinical trials. Furthermore, Thailand has several advantages over its competitors. First, Thailand's large population centres can provide a patient base that will facilitate the rapid enrolment of clinical trials. Second, the lower costs of operation in Thailand (relative to other countries) translate into significant savings for trials conducted in the country. Third, Thailand has a large English-speaking population which facilitates trials. Very importantly, the country also has a well-developed university and medical training network which feeds the manpower needs of the industry. Finally, the government is very supportive of companies that are keen to set up in Thailand or work with companies based in Thailand. To date, Thailand's medical centres have served as sites for clinical trials conducted by global biotech/pharma companies, world health organisations and international CROs. As of December 2007, Thailand ranked seventh in Asia in terms of the number of trials conducted.

8.5 CRO market in Thailand

The CRO market in Thailand is driven by pre-clinical and clinical CROs, bioequivalence studies and clinical laboratory business. In the clinical CRO domain, there are full-service CROs, monitoring-only CROs and EDC service CROs. Some of them are local CROs while others are offshoots of large global CROs. Although information about exactly what Thai pharma companies are developing is not in the public domain, only a few companies are into full-fledged R&D and have new chemical entities in their research pipelines.

8.5.1 Major CROs operating in Thailand

The key global operators include PPDi, Quintiles, Pharmanet, Kendle, INC Research, Omnicare and Novotech. Local CROs include Asia Global Research, IATEC CRO, Gleneagles CRC, NanoAsia Company Ltd and CMIC. There are also a few CROs that focus on bioequivalence, pharmacokinetics, toxicology and pharmacology.

8.5.2 Clinical trial conduct in Thailand

The advantages of conducting clinical research in Thailand are similar to those of other countries within the region, and include: ease of subject recruitment, fewer competing clinical trials than in the West; highly educated and trained personnel pool; potential to generate sound clinical data and access to low-cost infrastructure and labour pools.

Clinical trials in Thailand are conducted under the auspices of the Thai Ministry of Public Health and the Thai Food and Drug Administration. Thai regulatory standards are well established and requirements are similar to those of other regional governments (e.g. South Korea, Singapore and Taiwan) in detail and application. Thailand's National Policy on Clinical Studies states that:

> Thailand is dedicated to supporting and promoting the conduct of clinical studies in compliance with the Good Clinical Practice Standard so as to ultimately advocate Thailand to be a world-class centre of excellence in clinical trials.

To achieve this goal Thailand requires all clinical investigators and sponsors to conduct clinical research under ICH-GCP E6.

Published by Woodhead Publishing Limited, 2012

244   Clinical Research in Asia: Opportunities and Challenges

In order for a clinical trial to be conducted in Thailand, it must be approved by the clinical trial site's independent ethics committee and the Thai FDA. Clinical trial approval by the Thai FDA and specific ethics committee cannot be run in parallel. To conduct a clinical trial at a single investigational site or institution, protocol approval from the institution's ethics committee must be secured. If multi-institutional sites are to be utilised by the clinical trial sponsor, then the protocol must be approved by the Thai Ministry of Public Health (MOPH) ethics committee and any site-specific ethics committees that require protocol approval as per each entity's ethics committee requirements.

Once the sponsor's protocol is approved by the appropriate ethics committee(s), the sponsor must then submit the ethics committee approval letter to the Thai FDA to secure an import permit for the drug, biologic or medical device being considered. Thai FDA states that the import permit approval process will take no more than four weeks; however, as ethics committee approval must be secured prior to submission to the Thai FDA, this could delay the approval process for the clinical trial significantly. On average, approval for clinical trials should take from 12 to 16 weeks.

The advantages of conducting clinical trials in Thailand begin with the regulatory environment, which is supportive of the industry needs for performing international clinical trials. The regulatory body in Thailand is the FDA. The Thai FDA is officially organised into two main groups. First, the Health Product Control Division group consists of the Bureau of Cosmetic and Hazardous Substances Control, and five other divisions, namely Drug Control, Food Control, Medical Devices Control, Narcotics Control and Import and Export Inspection. Second, the Support Division group consists of three divisions, namely Public and Consumer Affairs, Rural and Local Consumer Health Products Protection Promotion, Technical and Planning, and the Office of the Secretary. In addition, six internal units have been established to perform specific tasks, namely the Information Technology Centre, Food and Drug Legal Group, Public Sector Development Group, Internal Audit Group, Complementary Health Product Group, and Community Health Product Quality Improvement Coordinating Centre.

Published by Woodhead Publishing Limited, 2012

Local ethics committees adhere to ICH-GCP and comply with local regulatory requirements in terms of composition and function of the ethics committee. International standards are in place to control the ethical execution of research projects. The system is set up to facilitate rapid study approval and start-up time, often in 8–12 weeks depending on the compound or the molecule.

8.5.3 Patient recruitment/willingness to participate in clinical trials

Thailand's population has access to healthcare resources through a complex network. Table 8.1 shows the proportion of people with health insurance coverage in municipal areas under various schemes.

The proportion of insured persons with private health insurance in 2004 was 4.4 per cent of the total population, with some of them covered by more than one programme. However, patients still shoulder a large portion of treatment expenses. Access to clinical trials is therefore an alternative for Thai patients. Patient recruitment in Thailand is relatively easy and quick because of the high level of respect and trust that patients have for physicians. Due to good doctor–patient relationships, informed consent is typically received in a positive manner among Thai patients. Important facts about medical procedures or treatments in clinical trials conducted in Thailand are publicised by the Thai government, and public awareness of healthcare interventions is high.

Table 8.1 Health insurance coverage

Coverage	Percentage
No insurance	7.7
Civil servants and state enterprise officials	14.1
Universal coverage healthcare	56.3
Social security	19.8
Private health insurance	1.6

Source: Report on Health and Welfare Surveys, National Statistical Office.

Published by Woodhead Publishing Limited, 2012

8.6 Hospital systems in Thailand

The Thai healthcare system is divided between the public and private sectors. The total number of beds in the public hospital system is around 90,000 and more than twice the number in the private hospital system (40,000 beds). Most of the public hospitals in Thailand come under the jurisdiction of the MOPH. There are 95 general hospitals at the provincial level, 725 community hospitals at the district level and 9,765 health centres at the sub-district level. At the national and regional levels there are 33 hospitals under the MOPH primarily categorised as special hospitals, including the National Cancer Institute, mental health hospitals, neurological institutes and children's hospitals. There are also approximately 75 general hospitals under other ministries such as the Ministry of Defence, the Bureau of University Affairs, the Police Department, the Bangkok Metropolitan Administration, and others. If one includes the over 300 private hospitals, access to study participants is therefore broad.

A non-exhaustive list of key hospitals in Thailand which offer multispecialty services is as follows:

- Bangkok General Hospital, Bangkok;
- Bangkok Nursing Home Hospital, Bangkok;
- Bumrungrad Hospital, Bangkok;
- Nonthavej Hospital, Bangkok;
- Phuket Adventist Hospital, Phuket;
- Research and Development Institute;
- Samitivej Hospital, Bangkok;
- Sikarin Hospital, Bangkok;
- Piyavate Hospital, Bangkok;
- Phyathai Hospital, Bangkok;
- St. Carlos Hospital, Bangkok;
- St. Louise Hospital, Bangkok;
- Thai Nakarin Hospital, Bangkok;
- Thonburi Hospital, Bangkok;
- Vichaiyut Hospital, Bangkok.

8.6.1 Compliance with 21 CFR Part 11

A large and increasing number of data management centres in Thailand are in compliance with 21 CFR Part 11 with respect to their systems and SOPs. Quality system documentation is rigorously performed and routinely assessed. A number of sites have also implemented electronic case report forms (CRFs). Data management centres in Thailand follow 21 CFR Part 11, which declares that the computer systems used in a regulated data management environment must be validated depending upon the user's requirement in a specific working environment. The aim of the validation is to maintain the accuracy, reliability, availability and authenticity of the required records and signatures.

8.6.2 Economic advantages

Trial sponsors can realise significant financial benefits by conducting their clinical trials in Thailand. The shortened timeline due to quicker subject recruitment by qualified investigators is a factor contributing to cost savings. Lower salaries of clinical site and laboratory personnel all help reduce the per-subject costs. Domestic travel costs for monitoring sites are lower because of the concentration of sites in major cities and comparatively less costly fares and tariffs. Support services such as printing, translation and local courier fees are also less expensive.

8.6.3 Qualified site staff

The Thai medical profession is one of the most advanced in the region. Successive governments have invested heavily in the education of Thai doctors, ensuring that they receive training that rivals that offered elsewhere in the region. Many doctors undertake specialist training abroad at leading medical centres in the USA and Europe. As such, these doctors also speak and write fluently in English. The number of medical graduate students in academic years 2000–06 is shown in Table 8.2.

248 Clinical Research in Asia: Opportunities and Challenges

Table 8.2 Numbers of medical graduate students

Sector	Number of graduate students							Total
	2000	2001	2002	2003	2004	2005	2006	
Public	1,222	1,272	1,504	1,422	1,462	1,422	1,426	12,932
Private	40	66	79	56	91	92	73	622
Total	1,262	1,338	1,583	1,478	1,553	1,514	1,499	13,554

The Thai government has made major investments in infrastructure and equipment in the healthcare sector and Thai hospitals are recognised as having high management standards. Hospital Accreditation is an accreditation programme of the Thai government that aims to raise hospital standards to international levels. Health management groups further ensure that service standards are comparable to regional hospitals. These measures help Thai hospitals attain high levels of medical expertise and service quality, thus making them a natural choice for local and foreign patients who are seeking good-quality medical treatment.

8.6.4 Therapeutic areas

As Thailand becomes more industrialised, the contribution of biotechnology research to the country's national development is becoming well recognised. Biotechnology research in Thailand focuses on the integration of knowledge from multiple disciplines within the growing life sciences industry. Research opportunities in Thailand are found in many therapeutic areas such as central nervous system, respiratory, cardiovascular, endocrinology, dermatology, oncology and infectious diseases (the latter including HIV and hepatitis). Furthermore, Thailand offers a unique opportunity for researchers focusing on tropical diseases such as dengue, malaria, SARS, diarrhoea, avian flu and Japanese encephalitis.

8.6.5 Monitoring sites in Asia

Monitoring sites in Asia is easy as the majority of investigator sites are located in medical schools, and general and special hospitals at

Published by Woodhead Publishing Limited, 2012

Clinical research in Thailand

the provincial, regional and national levels. In most medical schools and research centres, there are institutional review boards (IRBs) that support the organisation's activities in this area. A growing clinical development sector is providing many opportunities for sites to participate in clinical trials. Thailand has a large subject population and a pool of experienced investigators. Furthermore, due to the relatively fewer trials that are currently being conducted here compared with North America and Europe, there is substantial room for growth in the number of monitoring sites. The availability of site facilities and subject population as well as well-trained and motivated investigators and support staff all help contribute to the establishment of successful monitoring sites that can provide high-quality and timely clinical data. These same qualities make Thailand an attractive location for the rapid establishment of monitoring sites.

8.6.6 Biomedical research – ethical issues in Thailand

Presently, the regulation of biomedical research in Thailand is governed through civil and criminal laws as well as directives from the Medical Council of Thailand. Biomedical research conducted on humans must be evaluated and approved by the ethics committees of relevant institutions such as the medical schools in universities. The limitation of this approach is that although the physicians and nurses involved in such research must adhere to the guidelines and regulations set out by the ethics committee, other individuals involved in the same research, such as pharmacists, medical technologists and scientists are largely unaffected. In addition, the social science aspect of biomedical research is another important consideration because of the potential effect of such research on a subject's psychosocial status. The ethics committee therefore has many considerations when dealing with human drug testing and clinical trials. The Forum for Ethical Review Committees in Thailand (FERCIT) has thus been created to achieve the following objectives:

- ensure the safety of subjects involved in clinical trials;
- look after the welfare of subjects involved in biomedical research in Thailand;

Published by Woodhead Publishing Limited, 2012

250 Clinical Research in Asia: Opportunities and Challenges

- exchange knowledge and share experience;
- cooperate with international biomedical research partners and ethical forums.

FERCIT is under the purview of the Forum for Ethical Review Committees in the Asian and Western Pacific Region (FERCAP). FERCAP aims to raise the awareness, enhance the understanding and improve the ethical review of biomedical research in the region. FERCAP is part of the Strategic Initiative for Developing Capacity in Ethical Review (SIDCER) which is a network of independently established regional forums created to develop global capacity in ethical review and good research practices. The SIDCER steering committee is composed of representatives of the regional forums and representatives of invited partner organisations. Besides FERCAP, other regional forums include the Forum for Ethics Committees in the Confederation of Independent States, the Latin American Forum of Ethics Committees in Health Research, and the Forum for Institutional Review Boards/Ethics Review Boards in Canada and the United States, as well as the Pan-African Bioethics Initiative standards as stipulated by organisations such as FERCAP/SIDCER and the Office for Human Research Protections (OHRP). Furthermore, physicians and scientists who are accredited by the OHRP must have their accreditation renewed by the organisation every three years.

Currently, the Thai FDA plays a key role in controlling the importation of new drugs for clinical trials. The FDA is also involved with numerous international collaborations and initiatives which help to ensure product safety. When a pharmaceutical company wishes to conduct a clinical trial in a medical school in Thailand, it must send a proposal to the ethics committee of the medical school for its consideration. After the ethics committee has positively evaluated the proposal, it will forward the proposal and certificate of approval (COA) to the FDA to approve the importation of study drugs. The FDA has already certified the ethics committees of eight medical schools, namely, Chulalongkorn University, Siriraj Hospital, Ramathibodi Hospital, the Faculty of Tropical Medicine at Mahidol University, Phramongkutklao Hospital, Chiang Mai University, Khon Kaen University and Songkla University. These institutes can

Published by Woodhead Publishing Limited, 2012

now apply for the importation of new drugs for the purpose of conducting clinical trials in Thailand.

The Joint Research Ethics Committees (JREC) is a private organisation that was established in 2006 with support from the Thailand Center of Excellence for Life Sciences. This organisation aims to be the focal point for multicentre clinical trials and works to protect the rights of clinical trial volunteers. The JREC will follow the basic ethical principles for human subject research set out in the Belmont Report Historical Archive of the OHRP, namely, respect for persons, beneficence and justice. Ethics in biomedical research development in Thailand is moving in the right direction. In the short term, the various developments as outlined above will culminate in the adoption of international standards for clinical trial activities in Thailand. Furthermore, the industry as a whole (including the relevant agencies) will come to better understand the responsibilities and roles of various players involved in the process from the ethics committee to the physician, nurse, medical technologist, scientist, down to the volunteer in the clinical trial. The advantages of the JREC are given below.

8.6.7 Reduction in steps and resource loss

Multicentre researches were previously submitted for consideration by the ethics committees of the individual institute. Each institute has different processes, procedures and standards, thus making the process more resource-intensive and time-consuming. JREC will be able to improve efficiency and make the review and approval processes more cost-effective.

8.6.8 World-class research standards

JREC is constituted from the independent ethics committees of a number of institutes. Together, these selected persons have greater power to ensure that research projects are in line with international standards. Because of the constitution, design and standardised

252 Clinical Research in Asia: Opportunities and Challenges

processes, JREC can attract a large number of global multicentre trials research to Thailand.

8.6.9 Motivation for sponsors

Submission of research through JREC requires less time and cost, making this stage of the process more competitive versus other countries.

8.6.10 Opportunities for Thai researchers

JREC has a greater focus on multicentre clinical research. Its members therefore have greater knowledge of international research. This will be beneficial for Thai researchers in terms of bringing their standard operating procedures up to internationally recognised standards so that they are better able to collaborate in a variety of research.

8.6.11 Opportunities for patients

JREC has more potential to attract international research in new drugs. Patients participating in JREC approved projects will be able to participate in new research projects and have more options for treatment as well as the potential opportunity to try new drugs.

8.7 Conducting clinical trials in Thailand

Thailand has quickly become the country to watch in the pharmaceutical field since the MOPH began the compulsory licensing of key patented drugs. The attempts of the MOPH to intervene in the pharmaceutical market have attracted considerable attention from governments, stakeholders and various interest groups and experts

Published by Woodhead Publishing Limited, 2012

around the world. While the pharmaceutical regulatory system in Thailand operates independently of the intellectual property system, interactions between the two systems are crucial to the existence of the pharmaceutical industry and directly affect the development of the healthcare system in Thailand.

The Thai pharmaceutical regulatory system is based on the Drug Act BE 2510 (1967) together with its four amendments, ministerial regulations and ministerial notifications. The fundamental basis of Thai drug regulation is that all activities in relation to the trading of pharmaceutical products must be licensed/approved by the competent authorities.

In the last decade, Thailand started to see a large number of clinical trials of new drugs being carried out at hospitals, medical centres and research institutes nationwide. From a regulatory standpoint, it is surprising that the process of approving clinical trials has not yet been centralised. While drug regulation is centred at the Thai FDA, the FDA does not directly monitor clinical trials of drugs in humans. The FDA's role in this area is at most an indirect one, through its authority to control the import of drugs into the country for research purposes. Government agencies that play a central role in regard of clinical trials include the MOPH's Ethical Review Committee for Research in Human Subjects (ERC) and the Department of Medical Services.

Prior to launching a clinical trial in Thailand, a drug developer/sponsor must obtain approval from an ethics committee overseeing human research projects undertaken in an implementing institution. Approval must also be obtained from the ERC and from the ethics committee of the research institute or university that will conduct the trial. A protocol for the conduct of the clinical trial must be established and approved at the outset before approval can be obtained. The proposed protocol is sent to the MOPH's Department of Medical Services for review and consultation. Once a drug developer/sponsor receives approval from an ethics committee to conduct a study in humans, the developer/sponsor may proceed to request a licence from the FDA to import drugs into Thailand for research purposes.

Published by Woodhead Publishing Limited, 2012

8.7.1 Marketing approval for new drugs and generics

Before launching any drugs in Thailand, companies must obtain a licence to produce, sell or import pharmaceuticals into the country, as well as register their products for actual sale. The Thai FDA is the main agency in charge of drug approval and regulation. Generally, the procedure for seeking marketing approval for drugs will depend on whether the applicant is the drug originator or a generic producer. Drug originators face the most onerous task as each element of drug safety, efficacy and effectiveness must be demonstrated to the satisfaction of the Drug Control Division of the FDA.

Generic producers, on the other hand, receive more lenient treatment before the FDA. Such practice is partially due to the government's healthcare policy, which seeks to improve access to medicines and make affordable drugs available to all patients who need them. This policy seemed to have translated itself into an almost pro-generic policy before the Thai FDA. As in many countries, an abbreviated form of approval is available in Thailand for generic drugs. The generic applicant needs only to submit bioequivalence data as opposed to conducting rigorous trials and tests to prove the safety and efficacy of the chemical entity or biological molecule. Currently, the Thai FDA does not require the generic applicant to reproduce clinical trials or pre-clinical tests.

Other than the leniency shown with regard to the approval of generics, the MOPH has also taken various efforts towards making affordable drugs available for all. The most recent and perhaps most controversial attempt was the MOPH's decisions to issue licences for six key drugs that are still under patent in Thailand.

8.7.2 Compulsory licensing

During December 2006 to January 2007, the MOPH, acting under a post-coup military-appointed administration, decided to issue the first set of compulsory licences on three patented drugs. The Health Minister at the time, Dr Mongkol na Songkla, took a strong view against expensive patented drugs and believed that compulsory licensing was the solution to improving access to medicines for Thai patients. The three drugs that were subject to compulsory licences were Merck's antiretroviral efavirenz (Stocrin®), Abbott Laboratories' antiretroviral lopinavir/ritonavir (Kaletra®) and Sanofi-Aventis's heart disease drug clopidogrel (Plavix®). The legitimacy of these compulsory licences was debated extensively both at home and abroad. As a policy matter, it was widely questioned whether the actions of the MOPH would benefit Thai patients and help to improve the healthcare system and access to medicines in the long run.

From the legal perspective, the validity of the compulsory licences issued by the MOPH remains questionable. A careful reading of Section 51 of the Thai Patent Act and its reference to the procedures for the issuance of compulsory licences under Section 50 would seem to suggest that the MOPH has not taken the appropriate steps required by law in seeking to impose compulsory licences on the patented drugs. This view is not, however, the prevalent view among Thai government authorities at present.

Despite the question as to the legitimacy of the first three compulsory licences issued by the MOPH, and the efforts of the industry to work with the Ministry to improve Thai patients' access to medicines and resolve compulsory licensing issues through collaboration and dialogue, the MOPH has insisted upon implementing the compulsory licences to import generic products into Thailand through the state-owned GPO. In early 2008, Dr Mongkol na Songkla signed a further announcement of compulsory licences on three cancer drugs just before the end of his term as Health Minister. The new compulsory licences include the breast cancer drug letrozole produced by Novartis, the breast and lung cancer drug docetaxel made by Sanofi-Aventis, and the lung cancer drug erlotinib produced by Roche.

In view of the newly elected government, it is yet to be seen whether the compulsory licence policy will be continued or whether the new administration will adopt a less drastic measure to solve the problem of access to medicines.

Published by Woodhead Publishing Limited, 2012

256 Clinical Research in Asia: Opportunities and Challenges

8.7.3 Clinical trial approval process and timelines

Clinical trials in Thailand require sequential approval from the independent ethics committee and the Thai FDA. The approval process cannot be run in parallel. To conduct a clinical trial at a single investigational site or institution, a protocol approval by the institution's ethics committee must be secured. If multi-institutional sites are to be utilised by the clinical trial sponsor, then the protocol must be approved both by the MOPH ethics committee and any site-specific ethics committees that require protocol approval as per each entity's ethics committee requirements. The proposed protocol is sent to the Department of Medical Services within the MOPH for review and consultation. Should a clinical trial involve an AIDS vaccine, the protocol must first of all be submitted to the MOPH's Department of Communicable Diseases Control and reviewed and approved by the MOPH's National Sub-Committee of HIV Vaccine before it can be submitted to the ERC(s). After the ethics committee has positively evaluated the proposal, it will forward the proposal and COA to the FDA for approval of importation of study drugs. As discussed previously, the FDA has already certified the ethics committees of several medical schools.

Once the sponsor's protocol has been positively evaluated by the appropriate ethics committee(s), the sponsor must then submit the ethics committee's approval letter to the Thai FDA to secure an import permit for the drug, biologic or medical device being considered. According to the Thai FDA, the import permit approval process will take no more than four weeks; however, as ethics committee approval must be secured prior to Thai FDA submission, this may delay the approval process significantly. On average, approval for clinical trials should take from 12 to 16 weeks. While drug regulation is centred at the Thai FDA, the FDA does not directly monitor clinical trials of drugs in humans. The FDA's role in this area is at most an indirect one, through its authority to control the import of drugs into the country for research purposes.

Local ethics committees adhere to ICH-GCP and comply with local regulatory requirements in terms of composition and function of the ethics committee. International standards are in place to

Published by Woodhead Publishing Limited, 2012

Clinical research in Thailand **257**

control the ethical execution of research projects. The system is set up to facilitate rapid study approval and start-up time, often in 8–12 weeks depending on the compound or molecule.

In January 2009, the Thai FDA issued a list of 10 ethics committees who can apply for the FDA import licence. Most of the major (public) institutions in Thailand are on the list, which also includes the MOPH ethics committee. None of the ethics committees listed is a private entity. As many public universities (medical schools) and research institutions are now being restructured, some of the Thai FDA-approved ethics committees may no longer be considered government bodies (in the strict sense) or may not remain so in the near future.

8.7.4 Study start-up timeline

Once the authorisation for conducting a clinical trial is granted, the involved parties can proceed with relevant start-up activities like translations, appointment of investigator and other ancillary agreements, processing of clinical trial insurance etc. Translations of English informed consent forms (ICF) are usually completed in approximately four weeks. In addition to translations into Thai, translations may be required into other languages, such as Chinese, Malay and/or Vietnamese, depending upon the territory where the site is located. Finalising the hospital contracts at most sites takes an average of 8–12 weeks.

Documents required for IRB submission include:

- trial protocol(s)/amendment(s);
- case record forms;
- written informed consent form(s);
- patient information sheet;
- translations (the protocol synopsis, ICFs, research proposal and the conflict of interest form are also required in Thai in addition to their generic English versions);
- investigator's brochure;
- available safety information;

Published by Woodhead Publishing Limited, 2012

- investigational product label translated into Thai;
- information about payments and compensation for subjects;
- clinical trial insurance;
- clinical research agreement;
- investigator's current curriculum vitae and/or other documentation;
- special requirements, such as any other documents that the ethics committee may need to fulfil its responsibilities.

The ethics committee will review the proposed clinical trial and document its views (identifying the trial and list of documents reviewed) within the period specified in the SOP. The IRB can approve the trial or seek modifications prior to its approval/favourable opinion. The IRB has every right to disapprove the trial or terminate/suspend the trial.

The MOPH ethics committee and/or independent ethics committee analyse and review (i) new applications for COAs; (ii) amendments to clinical trial protocols and ICFs; and (iii) serious adverse event reports. The drug company sponsoring the clinical trial or their authorised representative(s) assist the principal investigator to drive the application for the COA through the hospital's ethics committee to the MOPH ERC. The proposal application details the protocol of the trial and includes pre-trial toxicological studies in animals, the ICF and the

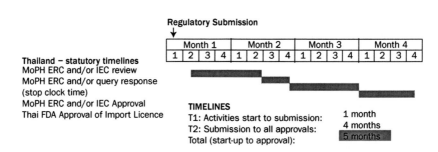

▶ JREC/ERC Approval and FDA approval – run sequentially
▶ JREC and/or IEC would review & revert with queries or additional information
▶ Stop Clock Time: Time taken by sponsor to respond regulatory query
▶ ECs review period differ from site to site, in average 4 to 8 weeks; which may extend upto 12 weeks in some situations
▶ The import licence is granted by FDA within 20 days (~4 weeks) of receiving the JREC/IEC Approval

Figure 8.1 Study start-up timelines

letter of indemnity to indemnify the principal investigator and the hospital/institution. The COA and import licence remain valid for two years. If the trial is not completed at the end of two years, an extension through a new application is required. At the end of the trial, the principal investigator submits a report to the MOPH ERC.

8.7.5 Import, storage and labelling requirements of investigational product

The import permit for investigational products is granted by the Thai FDA usually within four weeks after the favourable opinion from the MOPH ERC and/or independent ethics committee is submitted. It takes about one day for the investigational product to clear customs. Various companies – generally drug importers or wholesalers – meet the requirements of good storage practice and offer storage space for investigational products. For a reasonable charge, they will deliver the investigational product to study sites upon request. Although drug labelling in the local language is not mandatory, a Thai label is recommended. There are certified vendors who can prepare Thai labels for application while packaging.

8.7.6 Insurance

There is no specific insurance requirement for studies conducted in Thailand. Trial-related injuries must be indemnified under a global insurance cover or a local cover or both. Both global and local insurance players have started providing clinical trial insurance.

8.7.7 Suspected unexpected serious adverse reaction reports for investigational drugs under pre-marketing clinical trials

Any suspected unexpected serious adverse reaction (SUSAR) during a clinical trial must be reported to the MOPH as it will consider this in its judgment regarding the approval of the drug. The purpose of

Published by Woodhead Publishing Limited, 2012

260 Clinical Research in Asia: Opportunities and Challenges

submitting these reports is to make regulators, investigators and other appropriate people aware of new important information on serious reactions. Therefore, according to the Application Guideline for Clinical Trials, the sponsor must expeditiously make the MOPH aware of any SUSAR regardless of whether or not it happens in Thailand.

8.7.8 Recruitment modalities

Thai investigators are well trained, and are conversant in English. They have a good working network and in general, one committed investigator persuades other investigators into participating in clinical trials. Thus, the referral system works well in Thailand. It is an effective practice to recruit one investigator and use his/her network of investigators to recruit more investigators. Each investigator has his/her own pool of patients, and clinical trial participants are recruited from the pool rather than by referral.

8.7.9 Interim report submission

The MOPH specifies that in cases of trials lasting for more than six months, an interim report shall be submitted at six-monthly intervals. The interim report shall include number of patients treated, number of serious adverse events reported, number of discontinued patients post-randomisation with reasons, progress of trial and any findings obtained up to the time of the report.

8.7.10 Discontinuation/termination of trial

The licence holder shall inform the MOPH ethics committee of any decision to discontinue the trial to which the licence related and shall state the reason for the decision. The licence holder should return the COA as soon as possible. On termination of trial, the licence holder shall submit to the MOPH an end-of-study summary report

Published by Woodhead Publishing Limited, 2012

pertaining to the sites conducting the trial within three months from the last patient out/last patient last visit. In cases of multicentre trials where the study is completed at a different timeframe at each site, an end-of-study summary report should be submitted within three months from site closure.

8.7.11 Final study report

The MOPH ethics committee shall be informed on the trial findings within one year after the completion of the trial or within one year from frozen file or data lock date for international multicentre studies. The authority shall be informed of any possible delay in submission of the report, particularly where the delay is unavoidable, as in multicentre studies.

8.7.12 Drug accountability/disposal report

A product accountability/disposal report shall be submitted to the MOPH ethics committee after site closure. This report should include original or copy of the COA and quantity received for each product, balance of the study medication(s), letters for additional quantity and disposal-related information in detail. In the case of disposal and/or return of the used/unused drug supplies, confirmation/approval from sponsor and appropriate local regulatory authorities, must be verified.

8.8 Clinical trials in Thailand

Since 2008, more than 70 new industry-sponsored trials have been undertaken in Thailand every year. As at July 2011, there were 964 trials already listed in the clinicaltrials.gov registry, out of which 317 trials were active and recruiting. Of the 964 trials undertaken in Thailand, only 548 trials are industry-sponsored trials and 351 trials are sponsored by individual investigators, local institutions or hospitals, universities and other organisations.

Published by Woodhead Publishing Limited, 2012

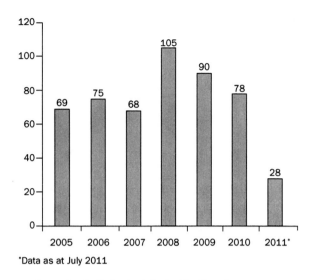

Figure 8.2 Growth of clinical trials in Thailand

Source: www.clinicaltrials.gov (accessed July 2011)

Further analysis suggests that GCP studies in diverse therapeutic areas are being conducted in Thailand. Almost 62 per cent of the trials undertaken in Thailand are in Phase III, 21 per cent trials in Phase II and 14 per cent trials are in Phase IV. A small number of Phase I trials (3 per cent) are also undertaken in Thailand, which clearly demonstrates the country is not ready to compete for Phase I studies. Most of the abovementioned trials have global sponsors (see Table 8.3).

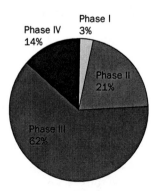

Figure 8.3 Industry-sponsored clinical trials in Thailand by phase

Source: www.clinicaltrials.gov (accessed July 2011)

Table 8.3 Trials undertaken in Thailand by major players

Industry sponsor	No. of trials
GlaxoSmithKline	79
Novartis	69
Hoffmann-La Roche	53
Sanofi-Aventis	40
Pfizer	40
AstraZeneca	39
Bayer	35
Bristol-Myers Squibb	31
Boehringer Ingelheim	24
Merck	12
Eli Lilly	12
Johnson & Johnson	9
Astellas	9
Abbott	9
Genentech	8
Gilead Sciences	6
H. Lundbeck A/S	5

Source: www.clinicaltrials.gov (accessed August 2011)

8.9 Environmental analysis

The healthcare environment in Thailand is very encouraging for global clinical trials due to supporting infrastructure, good-quality investigators, high compliance by investigators and study participants, regulatory mechanisms and regional cooperation and acceptance of data. However, there are significant legal, cultural and language barriers and a shortage of skilled professionals that act as challenges for the clinical trial environment.

The standards of care and the clinical practices in Thailand are equivalent or similar to US medical practices. In addition, investigators

264 Clinical Research in Asia: Opportunities and Challenges

command good English. Even those investigators with no US experience are familiar with clinical trials and US medical practices, due probably to peer influence. Thai investigators are actively engaged in medical research, rarely leave their academic position until retirement, and are motivated to participate in global clinical trials. They respond quickly to the feasibility requests of the multinational clinical trials and are generally enthusiastic. They are all familiar with clinical trial procedures and well versed with GCP. Because Thai investigators are on an academic payroll, monetary reward is not a motivation. This may act as a stumbling block for some investigators in terms of the attention they are prepared to dedicate to trials.

8.9.1 Shortage of skilled professionals

A significant number of CRAs are academically trained, and have nursing or pharmacy as their academic background. There is a huge demand for experienced clinical trial professionals, particularly CRAs and monitors. With the increased number of studies, branching out by global CROs and the establishment of small local players, the gap in demand and supply for skilled professionals is likely to endure.

8.9.2 Cultural barrier

Thailand has only a short history of rigorous pivotal new drug trials and its professionals are not yet attuned to the global way of doing things. The language barrier can sometimes limit proactive decisions by the project manager or CRA. Furthermore, team members may lack common understanding with respect to SOPs or processes. Extra care must therefore be taken to ensure clinical trial staff follow SOPs, and that they understand and conduct themselves like their counterparts in USA or Europe.

Published by Woodhead Publishing Limited, 2012

8.10 Future outlook

8.10.1 Personal data protection

One of the concerns regarding informed consent is the use of participants' personal data. According to the ICH-GCP and the Declaration of Helsinki, the requirements for an informed consent agreement include voluntary confirmation from the participant to contribute and complete information on all aspects of the trial that are relevant to the participant's decision to participate. In Thailand, no personal data protection legislation has yet been implemented. However, a Personal Data Protection Bill is under consideration and is designed to protect the personal data of individuals and private sector entities and prevent the misuse of such data. This bill will deeply affect the understanding of personal data in Thailand as it would provide guidelines on the meaning and use of such data. Section 35 of the 2007 Constitution of Thailand provides the current determination of what type of protection a subject is granted. Its brief reference to data privacy and data protection states that 'it is prohibited to spread or publicise news or images by any means to the general public, which violates or infringes a person's rights ... including disclosure of personal information without the owner's consent, except in the public interest'. In other words, consent is mandatory if an investigator intends to disclose certain personal information, for example in a publication. However, the legislation has yet to define clearly what falls within the scope of personal data.

8.10.2 Pro-generic policies

Thailand's endeavour to become a regional medical hub is being held back by pro-generic policies and burdensome regulatory approval processes. For instance, the government's liberal granting of compulsory licences in 2007 combined with burdensome regulatory approval processes deter pharmaceutical developers from establishing a presence in Thailand.

Published by Woodhead Publishing Limited, 2012

8.10.3 Drug registration process

Before considering filing a drug application with the Thai FDA, pharma companies have to apply for a licence to produce, sell and/or import pharmaceuticals in the country. However, Thailand does not yet have any active pharmaceutical ingredient (API) production facilities, and thus few licences to produce have been granted to date. The Thai FDA is organising training to ensure that these manufacturing companies follow the ICH-GMP guidelines to facilitate development of API production sites in the near term. Pharmaceutical companies have to register their products for actual sales and submit an application for marketing approval. Usually, the procedure for applying for marketing approval for drugs will depend on whether the applicant is the drug originator or a generic producer, with requirements varying accordingly.

8.10.4 New drug registration process

A full marketing approval application must be compiled to accompany samples of the new drug. All the required documents such as the relevant application form, the proposed labels and leaflets, the human and animal pharmacological study data and animal toxicology studies, the data generated from the safety and efficacy studies including clinical trial results dossiers and the full chemical (or biological) details of the new drug have to be submitted to the Drug Control Division of the Thai FDA. Drug originators have to prove the safety, efficacy and effectiveness of the drug in order to get approval from the Drug Control Division of the Thai FDA. In Thailand, the process by which the Thai FDA reviews a new drug application takes up to two years. Very often, the reasons cited for these lengthy approval times include a lack of staff competent to review the applications, as well as the increasing list of documents required for submitting not only new drug applications, but clinical studies as well. However, in a desire to harmonise with the most efficient regulatory practices worldwide and thus accelerate the approval process, ASEAN countries have implemented the ASEAN

Common Technical Requirements and Dossier on Quality, Safety and Efficacy, which provide guidelines on analytical and process validation, stability studies and bioavailability/bioequivalence. Thailand was an early proponent.

8.10.5 Generic process approval

Generic producers receive more lenient treatment before the Thai FDA. The timeframe for obtaining marketing approval for generic drugs is usually shorter – six months to one year only. The generic applicant has only to submit bioequivalence data as opposed to conducting rigorous trials and tests to prove the safety and efficacy of the chemical entity or biological molecule. Reproductions of clinical trials or pre-clinical tests are not required. This practice is partially due to the government's healthcare policy, which seeks to improve access to medicines and make drugs affordable and thus available for everyone – a practice that many would term pro-generic.

8.10.6 A level playing field

If Thailand hopes to attract pharmaceutical developers, there must be a shift in the government's preference for generics to one in favour of innovators (or at least a levelling of the playing field). The establishment of a stronger regime of personal data protection and a more streamlined regulatory approval process are important first steps in the right direction. These measures would help to draw more drug developers to Thailand, thereby facilitating the country's desired reputation as a medical hub.

9

Clinical research in Malaysia

Abstract: Malaysia is a small country with a diverse ethnic composition. The potential of the domestic pharmaceutical industry has been recognised by the Malaysian government, which views it as a strategic industry. This chapter gives a brief overview of the pharmaceutical industry and the market in Malaysia. It further discusses the healthcare system and the prevailing pharmaceutical regulations in the country. It goes on to describe clinical trials undertaken and registered in Malaysia and outlines the challenges and opportunities of doing clinical trials in the country.

9.1 Pharmaceutical industry overview

Malaysia, a small country with a population of approximately 28.5 million, is a diverse and cosmopolitan nation with an ethnic composition of Malay (53.3 per cent), Chinese (26.0 per cent), indigenous (11.8 per cent), Indian (7.7 per cent) and others (1.2 per cent). The healthcare industry and pharmaceutical market in Malaysia, heavily supported by the government, has emerged at a fast pace in the last two decades. The government's keenness to encourage the local production of drugs, particularly in the fields of biotechnology and the manufacture of off-patent drugs, combined with encouraging policies including tax exemptions for biotechnology companies have contributed to the growth of the healthcare industry in this region. Malaysia's biotech initiative has attracted many

Published by Woodhead Publishing Limited, 2012

270 Clinical Research in Asia: Opportunities and Challenges

multinational pharmaceutical giants to invest in the country in manufacturing plants and research projects in recent times. In Malaysia, local manufacturers almost exclusively produce generics and other off-patent medicaments, both traditional and over-the-counter (OTC) products, but medicines imported from multinational manufacturers still command the lion's share of the market. Emerging challenges for healthcare comprise demographic changes including rising costs, pecuniary constraints, mounting disease burden, and the changing social, technological, economic and political environment. Driven by the changing demographics, with a growing middle class, as well as rising expectations, the domestic industry is projected to grow at a compound annual growth rate of 10 per cent. The pharmaceutical authority's aim is to create a pro-business environment and stimulate the economy in line with the Government Transformation Programme.

The indigenous pharmaceutical industry includes manufacturers engaged in the process of drug production from research, development and licensing. The potential of the domestic pharmaceutical industry has been recognised by the Malaysian government as a strategic industry worthy of further attention and endorsement. Products manufactured by the Malaysian pharmaceutical industry can be broadly categorised as prescription products, OTC products, traditional medicines, and health/food supplements. Prescription medicines comprise patented and generic drugs, the sale and transaction of which are confined to doctors and pharmacists. OTC, traditional medicines and health/food supplements may be sold by non-professional outlets and to members of the public. The Malaysian pharmaceutical industry has the capability to produce almost all dosage forms, including sterile preparations, time-release medications and powders for reconstitution.

9.2 Pharmaceutical market

Over the decade to 2010, the Malaysian pharmaceutical market grew at between 8–10 per cent annually. However, the market still relies, to a significant extent, on imports. Another significant

Published by Woodhead Publishing Limited, 2012

development in the industry is the growth in pharmaceutical exports. The increasing awareness by local manufacturers of the export potential of Malaysian pharmaceuticals resulted in an average growth of over 10 per cent over the decade to 2010. With a range of services encompassing clinical research, medical tourism and generic pharmaceuticals manufacturing, the Malaysian pharmaceutical and medical device industry aspires to contribute $10.4 billion to gross national income (GNI) by 2020. Frost & Sullivan estimates that by 2013, the Malaysian pharma industry will be valued at about $1.8 billion, growing at an annual rate of 10.5 per cent.

Some notable multinational health and pharma companies and their affiliates have manufacturing and research development units in Malaysia. GlaxoSmithKline, for example, has been operating in the country for over five decades, while Pfizer started its Malaysia operations more than four decades ago as a branch of a Singapore registered company; today, the company employs more than 400 staff in Malaysia. Procter & Gamble works closely with the Education Ministry to help disabled children in Malaysia. Other big pharma companies with a significant presence in Malaysia include Merck, Sharp & Dohme, Eli Lilly, Johnson & Johnson, Bayer AG and Abbott Malaysia.

9.3 Pharmaceutical regulation

In Malaysia, medicines are regulated under the Poisons Act 1952, the Dangerous Drugs Act 1988 and the Sale of Drugs Act 1952. Medicine advertisements require prior approval by the Medicines Advertisement Board. Malaysia is a member of the World Trade Organization (WTO) and has acceded to the Trade Related Aspects of Intellectual Property Rights (TRIPS) agreement. Patents are registered and copyrights are protected. Currently, there are roughly 250 pharma companies with GMP certification, registered with the Drug Control Authority (DCA) of the Ministry of Health (MOH). Although over three-quarters of these are local manufacturers, about one-quarter are engaged in the production of modern medicines in various formulations including ophthalmic and nasal preparations.

Published by Woodhead Publishing Limited, 2012

The intellectual property laws of the country meet international standards and provide sufficient protection to both local and overseas investors. Malaysia has also agreed to the Patent Cooperation Treaty, which aids patent registration and provides intellectual property protection to foreign inventions. The manufacture and marketing of pharmaceutical products in Malaysia are as heavily regulated as in most developed countries.

Registration of pharmaceutical products and licensing of pharmaceutical manufacturers were initiated by the MOH in 1985 with the enforcement of the Control of Drugs and Cosmetics Regulations 1984 to ensure products marketed in the country are safe, efficacious and of quality. All medicines marketed in Malaysia are required to be registered by the DCA. All manufacturers, importers and wholesalers are required to be licensed by the DCA. The registration of prescription and OTC medicines requires proof of efficacy, quality and safety, and is subject to stringent screening and testing as well as regular and random post-marketing surveillance and testing. All manufacturers in Malaysia are subject to regular and random inspection by DCA inspectors. The upgrading of manufacturing facilities by local pharmaceutical industries in accordance with GMP requirements has undergone a huge transformation. With licensing and GMP inspection systems well in place, the Pharmaceutical Inspection Cooperation Scheme accepted Malaysia as its 26th member in January 2002. A stringent regulatory surveillance system that complies with international standards has resulted in Malaysian pharmaceuticals being widely accepted and recognised for their quality. Currently, pharmaceutical product manufacturers export their products to about 70 countries worldwide. Since 1999, the DCA has required bioequivalence studies for generic pharmaceuticals. These studies are performed at clinical research centres and aim to prove that the effectiveness of a generic product is equivalent to the innovator drug. Initially, most bioequivalence studies are conducted overseas due to the limited number of local bioequivalence centres that meet the required standard. In line with international practice, the MOH enforced the Malaysian Guidelines for the Conduct of Bioavailability and Bioequivalence Studies in 2004, which was further amended in the ASEAN Consultative

Committee on Standards and Quality – Pharmaceutical Product Working Group (ACCSQ – PPWG) in 2007 and 2008 to include regional cooperation and to further discuss the technical guidelines on BABE studies. Therefore, all bioequivalence research centres must strengthen their clinical and laboratory infrastructure to comply with these requirements. The need for more bioequivalence study centres in the country is crucial as there is a great demand for generic pharmaceutical products in line with the World Health Organization (WHO) recommendations to increase affordability and accessibility.

9.4 Healthcare systems in Malaysia

Healthcare in Malaysia is split across the private and public sectors. Doctors are required to undergo a two-year internship and perform two years of service with public hospitals throughout the nation, ensuring adequate coverage of medical needs for the general population. Foreign doctors are encouraged to apply for employment in Malaysia, especially if they are qualified to a higher level. Malaysian society places importance on the expansion and development of healthcare, putting a significant portion of the government's social sector development budget into public healthcare. Because of the country's growing and ageing population, the government recognises the need to improve in many areas including the refurbishment of existing hospitals, building and equipping new hospitals, expanding the number of polyclinics, improving training, and expanding the take-up of telemedicine. Over the last few years the government has increased its efforts to overhaul the systems and attract more foreign investment.

The Malaysian government continues to encourage foreign medical talent, particularly specialists, to practise in Malaysia. Due to this longstanding cosmopolitan attitude and favourable foreign policy, Malaysia has witnessed a significant influx of trained medical personnel as well as, to a notable extent, the urbanisation of medical services. As a result of this urbanisation, public hospitals in non-urban regions have a paucity of advanced diagnostic and imaging facilities.

Published by Woodhead Publishing Limited, 2012

9.5 Clinical trial environment

In the past few years, Malaysia has succeeded in creating an environment ideal for the growth of clinical trials and the establishment of a CRO industry. The CRO industry has thus been identified as one of the national key economic areas in the government's Economic Transformation Programme. The single information and referral system for government hospitals comprising of a network of 20 clinical research centres (CRCs) across Malaysia provides an opportunity to develop new trial sites. This, combined with Malaysia's diverse ethnicity, subject registries and conducive regulatory environment, helps the country stand out as an ideal location for global pharmaceutical firms and CROs in the drug development business. Malaysia has several international and local CROs operating on its shores and the number is growing. The country has 138 secondary and tertiary MOH hospitals that service over 15 million patients in various therapeutic areas. This has generated about 175 active investigators – a mere fraction of the approximately 2,800 specialists at MOH facilities (or 5,000 specialists, if one combines both the public and private sectors). The government aims to galvanise these forces and transform the clinical trials industry from about 100 trials in 2009 to a target of 1,000 in 2020. This transformation is expected to result in a contribution of over $130 million to GNI , as well as over 1,000 trial opportunities. One of the strategic initiatives undertaken has been the corporatisation of these CRCs and their direct engagement in business development activities. The facilitation and promotion of investigator-initiated trials and other clinical research activities can be continued by CRCs at the same pace without affecting their relations with the conglomerates. Clinical trial registration and ethics reviews can be fast-tracked in MOH hospitals where CRC units are based.

The Malaysian government's endowment initiative to provide corpus towards the establishment of CRC hubs to become centres of excellence illustrates its commitment to develop clinical research in the regions. Healthcare services, research and training, are just some of the areas on which these centres of excellence focus. The programme is expected to be self-funding from 2014 onwards.

A fraction of the institutional fees paid by sponsors is used to fund the operational expenses of Clinical Research Malaysia (CRM). CRM is a corporatised but non-profit entity. In addition to the operational expenses, a fraction of the fee is also used for training as necessary. The government retains its responsibility to release directives and augment and influence clinical research in Malaysia. The government also assumes responsibility for the development of policies and adaptation of technical changes therein for the promotion of contract research in private and government healthcare facilities including universities. The establishment of CRM as a corporate entity with the CRC, MOH and Malaysian government as collaborators was ventured following discussions with CROs and R&D based pharmaceutical players.

To further augment the growth of clinical research in Malaysia, a more robust strategic approach would be warranted in the coming years. Some of these approaches could include involvement of more private and academic medical institutes as trial sites, augmentation of the investigator and patient database, and development of units for early phase, analytical, bioavailability and bioequivalence studies.

9.6 Regulatory environment in Malaysia

Clinical trials in Malaysia are essentially governed by the following guidelines:

- Malaysian Guidelines for GCP (updated 2004);
- Guidelines for Application of CTIL and CTX in Malaysia (updated);
- Guidelines for GCP Inspection (October 2010).

These guidelines should be read together in accordance with the legal requirements of the Control of Drugs and Cosmetics Regulations 1984, The Poison Regulations (Psychotropic Substances) 1989 and Sale of Drugs Act 1952 where controlled substances are involved.

Published by Woodhead Publishing Limited, 2012

276 Clinical Research in Asia: Opportunities and Challenges

As per Malaysian Guidelines for GCP, the regulatory authorities are bodies with the power to regulate, review clinical data and conduct inspection, while the DCA is the authority established for the purpose of regulating the Control of Drugs and Cosmetics Regulations 1984. The DCA is also the main authority to regulate the production, import and sale of pharmaceuticals in Malaysia. Established under the Control of Drugs and Cosmetic Regulations 1984, the DCA's main task is to ensure the quality, safety and efficacy of pharmaceutical and related products that are marketed and sold in Malaysia. The primary tasks of the DCA are: (a) registration of pharmaceutical products, (b) licensing of importers, manufacturers and wholesalers; and (c) monitoring the quality of registered products and adverse drug reactions.

The DCA is constituted as follows:

- chairman – the Director General of Health;
- alternate chairman – the Director of Pharmaceutical Services;
- the Director of the National Pharmaceutical Control Bureau;
- seven members appointed by the Minister of Health;
- one consultant physician from the public sector;
- one pharmacist from the public sector;
- three persons from any local university with expertise in pharmaceutical sciences;
- two fully registered medical practitioners.

The DCA's mission is to ensure the safe use of regulated products that are themselves safe and efficacious. The DCA also ensures the conduct of well-designed, ethical and well-monitored clinical research with complete and accurate information following GCP standards.

9.7 Evolution of Malaysian GCP

The first edition of the Malaysian Guidelines for GCP was published in October 1999. The guidelines provide a unified GCP standard with the objective of assisting local investigators to conduct clinical trials in accordance with international standards and to facilitate

Clinical research in Malaysia 277

mutual acceptance of clinical data by regulatory authorities. In line with the greater demand for clinical trials in Malaysia and increased awareness about the GCP among clinicians, the second edition of the guidelines was published in 2004. This second edition synchronised the elements of the ICH-GCP (CPMP/ICH/135/95) and also included the local regulatory requirements for the manufacture of investigational medicinal products, a prerequisite of approved GCP training.

9.7.1 Clinical trial permission

The DCA has listed certain products that require a clinical trial import licence (CTIL) and clinical trial exemption (CTX). The principal investigator or sponsor is required to apply for the CTIL/CTX from the DCA, prior to importation/manufacturing the product locally. Products that require a CTIL/CTX include placebos that are not registered with the DCA and that are intended for clinical trial purposes, and any product with a marketing authorisation when amassed in a way different from the approved form, or when used for an unapproved indication or when used to gain further information about an approved use. In addition to these, an exemption is also required for an unregistered product manufactured locally for the purpose of the clinical trial.

The CTIL/CTX can be requested by the principal investigator or by the authorised person from the locally registered pharmaceutical company. The holder of a CTIL/CTX for a particular product need not necessarily conduct the clinical trial on its own but could be a local CRO or a representative office or agency of the pharmaceutical company who facilitate the import of investigational products for clinical trial purposes. The accuracy of all information in the application and the supporting documents will remain the responsibility of the applicant, who in turn will also be responsible for any applicable updates relevant to the product or application. When the applicant is not the manufacturer, it is acceptable to submit confidential information to the DCA through the applicant in a sealed envelope marked as confidential. Any misleading information supplied in the application will be considered as a felony under the purview of the Drugs and Cosmetics Regulations 1984.

Published by Woodhead Publishing Limited, 2012

278 Clinical Research in Asia: Opportunities and Challenges

The applicant is required to submit the CTIL/CTX application at the Office of Senior Principal Assistant Director. The documents required by the DCA in a fresh CTIL/CTX application are listed below:

- a completed application form for a CTIL (Borang BPFK 442) or CTX (Borang BPFK 443) – application forms can be downloaded from the DCA website and should be signed by the applicant;
- two copies of the application submission form (Borang BPFK 001);
- two copies of the submission checklist (Borang BPFK 002);
- processing fee – every application for CTIL and CTIL renewal must be accompanied with the non-refundable processing fee (presently RM 500 per product; foreign currencies are not acceptable), whereas the application for CTX is free of charge;
- a copy of the company registration certificate;
- letter of authorisation/agreement in cases where the sponsor or principal investigator is using a CRO to conduct the clinical trial or the applicant is not the sponsor or product owner;
- approval letter from the ethics committee of the institution(s) where the clinical trial is to be conducted – although it is permissible to submit parallel applications to the DCA and the independent ethics committee, no CTIL/CTX will be issued prior to independent ethics committee approval, hence the ethics committee approval letter should be submitted to the DCA as soon as available (note also that the ethics committee of the institution(s) must be registered with the DCA);
- current copy of GMP certificate or statement from the manufacturer and re-packer – the former must be issued by an authority recognised by the DCA, the latter can be issued by the quality assurance department where the product is manufactured;
- manufacturing licence (for local products);
- certificate of GMP for comparator product – if GMP certificate is not available, one of the following documents can be submitted: approval letter from the regulatory authority *or* annual registration document of drug establishment *or* package insert for repacked product *or* certificate of GMP (or statement of GMP from re-packer);

Clinical research in Malaysia

- study protocol and amendments signed by principal investigator;
- informed consent form (initial version only);
- pharmaceutical data, including certificate of analysis of the recent, representative batch of the product, and sample label(s) for the imported products;
- investigator brochure, which should include product particulars, and sufficient data and supporting documentation to establish safety, efficacy and quality.

All applications for CTIL/CTX must be accompanied with the product particulars and data necessary for product evaluation. The product particulars and data shall be presented in A4 format with supporting documentation in the form of annexes. A contents page must be provided with the application and detail the contents of the annexes. Everything must be labelled in an orderly manner. Every document page should be well annotated and numbered sequentially with separate series for each annex. Drawings, tables, graphs etc. must be appropriately captioned and referenced. The application form must be written in Bahasa Melayu or English. All other data, supporting documents, labels and package inserts can be in Bahasa Melayu or English. In cases where supporting documents are not originally in Bahasa Melayu or English, a copy of the document in its original language, accompanied by authenticated translation in Bahasa Melayu or English shall be submitted. An incomplete application will be rejected by the DCA within one week of the submission date.

The DCA reserves the right to terminate the licence if the licensee does not comply with regulatory requirements as specified in the Control of Drugs and Cosmetics Regulation 1984, Malaysian GCP Guidelines and CTIL/CTX Guidelines. The DCA will inform the applicant about their decision in writing. Applications for additional quantities of study medication(s), additional trial site(s), additional new products, additional manufacturers/re-packers, additional ports of entry, changes of applicant, extensions of the product's shelf life and new protocols are considered as applications of variation. Every application of variation requires a new application form (Borang 442) along with copies of CTILs pertaining to the products. More

Published by Woodhead Publishing Limited, 2012

280 Clinical Research in Asia: Opportunities and Challenges

details about the supplementary documents to be included for the application of variation can be obtained from the official Gazette for the Application for CTIL and CTX Edition 5.

At the end of each study, the licence holder is required to submit to the DCA a copy of the endorsed CTIL/CTX (including Borang A) and/or evidence of delivery to the approved investigator(s)/trial centre(s) on importation and supply of each consignment of the product. The DCA requires that the product should be supplied only to the investigator(s) at the trial centre(s) named in the application for the CTIL/CTX for the purpose and use stated in the application. No change in investigator, trial centre or trial protocol is allowed to be made without notification to the DCA. The licence holder is also required to ensure that adequate precautions are taken for all study medication(s), such as secure storage, access to which is limited to prevent theft or illegal distribution.

9.7.2 Regulatory, ethics committee approval and start-up timeline

Submission to the DCA and ethics committee is undertaken in parallel. The regulatory authority reviews and usually responds with queries or additional information within two weeks of the application being filed. After the response has been filed, it then takes up to another two weeks for regulatory approval (or further queries if the response is not satisfactory) to be issued. The regulatory authority approval letter is issued as the import licence for the import of investigational products in Malaysia. The export licence is not currently required in order to export samples from Malaysia. In the case of normal pharmaceutical products, the usual timeline for the National Pharmaceutical Control Bureau to grant a CTIL to international sponsors or CTX to local Malaysian sponsors is 30 days (maximum six weeks) excluding the time taken by the sponsor to respond to queries ('stop clock time'). If the queries are posted (usually by e-mail) to the sponsor between two weeks of application, CTIL/CTX is granted within four weeks after receipt of satisfactory answers to queries from the sponsor. The total review clock time does not usually exceed six weeks. In the case of

Published by Woodhead Publishing Limited, 2012

biological/biotech products, the approval timeline can be extended up to 45 days. For regulatory submissions, documents must be in English. The regulatory authority will issue the approval letter only after the submission of the ethics committee approval letter. The name of the site is specified on the approval letter issued by the regulatory authority. Documents required for submission are the complete application form, submission checklist, processing fee, company registration certificate, applicant licence, GCP certificate for each investigator, letter of authorisation, ethics committee approval letter, GMP certificate, protocol and protocol amendments, patient information and informed consent form, pharmaceutical data, investigator's brochure and published clinical data.

For the sites under the purview of MOH, submissions will be made to the medical research ethics committee (MREC). For other sites, e.g. university hospitals, submissions will be made to the respective university ethics committees. Ethics committee review and approval timelines differ from site to site, averaging four to eight weeks; this may extend up to 12 weeks in some situations. The MREC ethics committee takes on an average six to eight weeks to grant approval. Approvals from the university-based ethics committees take from four to eight weeks. Institutes of national repute, such as the National Heart Institute, take from three to six weeks to grant ethics committee approval. ICFs are translated into Malay and/or Chinese as per ethics committee requirements and the translation process is usually completed in two weeks. Hospital contracts at most sites demand a minimum of three months. The inclusion of a contract template is not usually required at the time of ethics committee submission.

9.7.3 Safety reporting

The sponsor/licence holder must inform any Malaysian investigator(s) and through them, the independent ethics committee, of any significant safety issues arising from the analysis of overseas reports or safety-related action taken by another country's regulatory agency within 48 hours of becoming aware of this information.

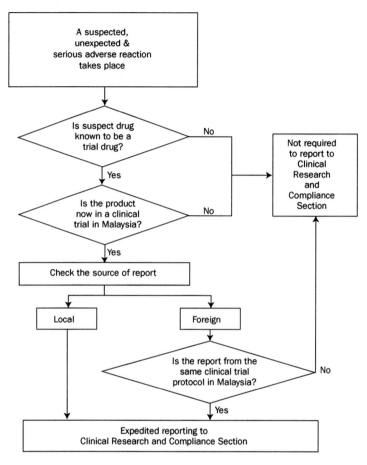

Figure 9.1 Safety reporting process for drugs in clinical trial in Malaysia

The sponsor/licence holder is also required to provide promptly the clinical details of any individual overseas adverse drug reaction reports if requested by the DCA. The CIOMS-I form is a widely accepted standard for expedited adverse reaction reporting. Key data elements for expedited safety reports in clinical trials are described in the appendices of the GCP guidelines.

Expedited safety reports should be submitted to the Clinical Research and Compliance Section as hard copy or via e-mail. It is preferable to supply a cover letter for the submission of each expedited safety report. A single cover letter may be standardised to include multiple expedited safety reports, if from the same clinical trial protocol. If the reports are submitted electronically, the report should be a PDF file. Reports should be separated into separate PDF files according to local and foreign reports. Where hard-copy reports are provided, an acknowledgment of receipt shall be made upon submission; for expedited safety reports sent by e-mail, an acknowledgment of receipt will be sent by e-mail.

9.7.4 Interim report

In cases of trials lasting for more than six months, the DCA requires an interim report to be submitted at six-monthly intervals. This should include the number of patients treated, number of serious adverse events reported, number of discontinued patients post-randomisation and the reason of discontinuation, progress of the trial and any findings obtained up to the time of the report. More details on the format of the interim report can be found in the guidelines.

9.7.5 Discontinuation/termination of trial

The licence holder is required to inform the DCA of any decision to discontinue the trial to which the licence related along with the reasons for the decision. Under such instances the licence holder should return the CTIL/CTX document as soon as possible. The CTIL/CTX licence holder is required to submit to the DCA an end-of-study summary report pertaining to the sites conducting the trial within three months from the last patient out/last patient last visit. In cases of multicentre trials when the study is completed at different timeframes at each site, an end-of-study summary report should be submitted within three months from site closure. The template provided in the guidelines should be used for the end-of-study summary report.

Published by Woodhead Publishing Limited, 2012

9.7.6 Final study report

The DCA should be informed of the trial findings within one year after the completion of the whole trial or within one year from the frozen file or data lock date for international multicentre studies. The DCA is also required to be informed of any possible delay in submission of the report, particularly where the delay is unavoidable, as in multicentre studies. The relevant appendix in the guidelines provides the structure of the final study report.

9.7.7 Drug accountability and disposal

The applicant is required to submit a product accountability/disposal report to the DCA within three months of site closure. The report should include the original or copy of the CTIL/CTX, Borang A for the relevant site, date(s) and quantity received for each product, balance of the study medication(s) and the letter for additional quantity. With regards to disposal, it is necessary to provide confirmation of appropriate local drug disposal, and/or return the used/unused drug supplies to the country of origin or regional depot. For local disposal, all investigative products should be documented and disposed of by the authorised bodies. An inspection/auditing of clinical trial site may be conducted by the regulatory authority, the aim of which is to evaluate the acceptability of clinical data submitted to the DCA, and to ensure compliance with legislation, GCP principles and the Declaration of Helsinki. The authorised officer of the regulatory authority may contact the principal investigator or sponsor regarding the date of inspection when required.

9.8 CRO market in Malaysia

The Malaysian government has played a big role in providing initiatives to the pharmaceutical industry, including the provision of grants and financing schemes to support R&D initiatives. To develop the country's biotechnology sector, the government of Malaysia has

Published by Woodhead Publishing Limited, 2012

established the Penang Science Park at Bukit Minyak. The new science park's first tenant is a pre-clinical CRO, named Progenix and is part-funded by a UK venture capital fund. India's Veeda Clinical Research has also set up a Phase I unit in Malaysia, joining the growing list of CROs attracted to the country. The new 28-bed unit, which is located at Ampang Hospital in Kuala Lumpur, will provide support for early-stage clinical development projects. Veeda has set up this facility in collaboration with a team from the Malaysian Ministry of Health. To strengthen the clinical infrastructure in the country, the Malaysian government has courted the contract research sector. This has resulted in companies such as Kendle, Novotech, Quintiles, Parexel, MDS Pharma Services (now INC Research), PPC and Siro Clinpharm setting up a variety of early and late-stage clinical research capabilities in the country. In addition to the growing number of global CROs, the Malaysian government has established accredited medical centres commonly known as clinical research centres (CRCs) since 2000. These are the clinical research arm of the MOH and conduct clinical trials, clinical epidemiology and economic research, and manage complex medical databases. Under the purview of the National Institutes of Health, the CRCs promote, support and conduct quality and ethical research to improve patient outcome. The CRCs also conduct training and professional development courses and assist in problems faced by clinicians in the conduct of their clinical research.

Since the first CRC was established in Kuala Lumpur, the CRC network has gradually expanded into 22 CRCs nationwide (Table 9.1).

Table 9.1 Accredited CRCs in Malaysia

Clinical research centre	Year established
Kuala Lumpur Hospital, Wilayah Persekutuan Kuala Lumpur	2000
Raja Perempuan Bainun Hospital, Perak	2001
Penang Hospital, Penang	2003
Sarawak General Hospital, Sarawak	2003
Tengku Ampuan Afzan Hospital, Pahang	2004

Published by Woodhead Publishing Limited, 2012

286 Clinical Research in Asia: Opportunities and Challenges

Table 9.1 Accredited CRCs in Malaysia (*cont'd*)

Clinical research centre	Year established
Sultanah Bahiyah Hospital, Kedah	2006
Selayang Hospital, Selangor	2006
Tuanku Ja'afar Hospital, Negeri Sembilan	2006
Melaka Hospital, Melaka	2006
Sultanah Aminah Hospital, Johor	2006
Sultanah Nur Zahirah Hospital, Terengganu	2006
Raja Perempuan Zainab II Hospital, Kelantan	2006
Queen Elizabeth Hospital, Sabah	2006
Tuanku Fauziah Hospital, Perlis	2007
Ampang Hospital, Kuala Lumpur	2007
Serdang Hospital, Selangor	2008
Tengku Ampuan Rahimah Hospital, Selangor	2008
Sungai Buloh Hospital, Selangor	2010
Putrajaya Hospital, Wilayah Persekutuan Putrajaya	2010
Sibu Hospital, Sarawak	2010
Likas Hospital, Sabah	2011
Taiping Hospital, Perak	2011

9.9 Clinical trials in Malaysia

Since 2008, Malaysia has been participating in approximately 60 new industry-sponsored trials every year. There are 414 trials already listed in the registry, out of which 113 trials are active and recruiting. Of the 414 trials undertaken in Malaysia, 364 trials are industry-sponsored trials and 48 trials are sponsored by individual investigators, local institutions or hospitals, universities and other organisations.

Further analysis of the industry-sponsored clinical trials suggests that several GCP studies in diverse therapeutic areas are being conducted in Malaysia. Almost 72 per cent of the trials being undertaken in Malaysia are in Phase III, 15 per cent trials are in Phase II and 11 per cent trials are in Phase IV. A small number of Phase I trials (2 per cent) are also being undertaken in Malaysia. Most of these trials are sponsored by big pharmaceutical players as listed in Table 9.2.

Published by Woodhead Publishing Limited, 2012

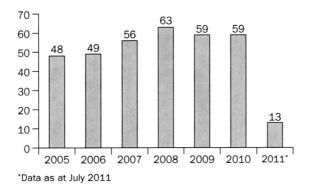

*Data as at July 2011

Figure 9.2 Growth of clinical trials in Malaysia
Source: www.clinicaltrials.gov (accessed July 2011)

Table 9.2 Trials undertaken in Malaysia by major players

Industry sponsor	No. of trials
Pfizer	40
Sanofi-Aventis	39
Novo Nordisk	28
AstraZeneca	27
Boehringer Ingelheim	27
GlaxoSmithKline	20
Bristol-Myers Squibb	17
Hoffmann-La Roche	16
Bayer	15
Eli Lilly	15
Johnson & Johnson	12
Novartis	10
Abbott	7
Astellas	7
H. Lundbeck A/S	7
Actelion	4
Amgen	4
ALTANA	3

Source: www.clinicaltrials.gov (accessed July 2011)

Published by Woodhead Publishing Limited, 2012

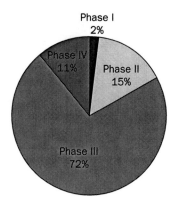

Figure 9.3 Industry-sponsored clinical trials in Malaysia – by phase
Source: www.clinicaltrials.gov (accessed July 2011)

9.10 Registration of clinical trials

Registration of clinical trials as an international standard is endorsed by both the International Committee of Medical Journal Editors and the WHO. This is to ensure transparency and to increase public trust and confidence in the conduct of medical research as well as inform physicians and prospective volunteers about ongoing/future research in which they may wish to enrol. The National Medical Research Register (NMRR) is a registry that encompasses all research activities that involve MOH personnel or that are conducted in MOH facilities or funded by MOH research grants. Registration of all such medical researchers has been mandatory since 1 January 2008.

All clinical trials that apply for CTIL/CTX must be registered with the NMRR. The directive requiring this was issued by the Director of Pharmaceutical Services under Regulation 29 of the Control of Drugs and Cosmetics Regulations 1984 (Amendment) 2006. Failure by the sponsor/applicant/investigator to register his/her clinical research with NMRR may result in delay/non-issuance of CTIL/CTX.

Registration schemes enable MOH management to document the level of research activity in the MOH and also to track the progress of any research it has approved and/or financially supported. At the moment, data captured through NMRR do not reflect the real number of clinical trials conducted in Malaysia because not all clinical trials that require CTIL/CTX are conducted in MOH facilities. This directive will facilitate the monitoring of clinical trial activity and will also give a better reflection of the number of clinical trials conducted in Malaysia.

9.10.1 Value proposition and challenges

Malaysia offers a significant value proposition for the conduct of quality clinical trials. Regulatory approval and study start-up timelines are very competitive and the regulatory environment in Malaysia is ideal for clinical trials. Thanks to government support and initiatives, the enforcement of compliance with GCP through certification of study staff is an added dimension in the area of quality clinical research in Malaysia. The CRCs act as 'one-stop centres' and electronic databases help sponsors to access quality sites with skilled resources that produce good-quality data. As with many Asian countries, the large pool of experienced English-speaking investigators, the diverse culture with multi-ethnic population and competitive costs will be attractive to many global pharmaceutical and biotech sponsor companies thinking of conducting clinical trials in Malaysia (Figure 9.4).

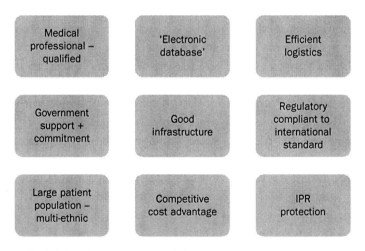

Figure 9.4 Malaysia value proposition

9.11 Challenges and future outlook

In most emerging and developing economies, new businesses suffer a lack of skilled resources. The supply and demand gap is wide, and can lead to huge staff attrition at the sponsor, CRO and site level. As a result of such attrition, clinical trials can have problems adhering to timelines, there are delays in recruitment, and sponsors and CROs put in more time and resources in retraining staff and reorganising the trials.

Even with GCP certification, and the training and retraining by sponsors and CROs, there is a high level of hand-holding at clinical trial sites in Malaysia. In terms of query resolution, completion of case report forms and submission of essential documents, excessively long response times are a common complaint. But it is reassuring to note that with time, there have been significant improvements in the overall clinical research environment, even with the understanding that the standard of care can be quite divergent and there remains a lack of quality human resources such as researchers and support staff.

The Ninth Malaysia Plan notes that a multipronged approach is required to develop Malaysia into a regional hub for clinical trials. Some of the issues that we can explore include the need to introduce new legislation and review existing legislation, to facilitate the approval process, management of finances and protection of intellectual property rights. There is much to be done with regards to the use of information and communications technology to increase efficiency in conducting clinical trials, and to create a database of the clinical investigators and research undertaken in the country.

Malaysia's multi-ethnic population of 26 million is, in itself, an attraction. The National Ethics Board to be established under the Ninth Malaysia Plan should also monitor compliance with ethical standards of biomedical and clinical research with regard to safeguarding the dignity, safety and wellbeing of patients. The establishment of Singapore's Health Sciences Authority – a multidisciplinary body to regulate healthcare products, and among other things, coordinate approvals for clinical trials, as well as conduct continuous reviews of clinical trials and monitor adverse events – is also to be welcomed.

Published by Woodhead Publishing Limited, 2012

Efforts are being made to build innovation capability for local industry, such as developing local CROs into internationally competitive players and to create R&D capabilities in biopharmaceutical, biotech and traditional Chinese medicine. There remains a need for specific human resource development strategies to create a pool of experienced healthcare professionals who are trained and committed as clinical investigators and site coordinators. There is also the need to strategise the marketing of Malaysia as a regional hub for clinical trials, in line with other government campaigns to promote Malaysia as a clinical trial destination.

10

Clinical research in Hong Kong

Abstract: Even though the pharmaceutical market of Hong Kong is relatively small, it is still an attractive market due to its location bordering the world's fastest-growing economy, China. This chapter gives a brief overview of the pharmaceutical industry and healthcare system in Hong Kong. It discusses the evolution of GCP and regulatory and ethics framework in the country. It goes on to list the number of trials undertaken in various therapeutic areas and gives an environmental analysis and future outlook for the industry.

10.1 Background and history

Hong Kong is essentially a city state with a correspondingly small population of 7.03 million, growing at an annual rate of 0.9 per cent. In 2009, it had a birth rate of 11.7 per 1,000 population and a fertility rate of 1,032 children per 1,000 women; infant mortality was 1.5 per 1,000 births. As of 2009, life-expectancy in Hong Kong was 79.16 years for males and 84.79 years for females, making it one of the highest life-expectancies in the world. The percentage of the population aged over 65 is way above the Asia-Pacific average. About 95 per cent of the people of Hong Kong are of Chinese descent, the majority being Taishanese, Chiu Chow, other Cantonese people, and Hakka. Hong Kong's Han majority originate mainly from the Guangzhou and Taishan regions in Guangdong province. The remaining 5 per cent of the population is composed of non-ethnic

Published by Woodhead Publishing Limited, 2012

294 Clinical Research in Asia: Opportunities and Challenges

Chinese. There are South Asians, Indians, Pakistanis, Nepalese and also Vietnamese. There are also Europeans (mostly British), Americans, Canadians, Japanese, Koreans, Indonesians and Philippinos working in the city's commercial and financial sector. Hong Kong has two official languages, namely Chinese (Cantonese) and English. The English language is used in higher education and in many important sectors of society. Hospital records are all in English.

Hong Kong's population is highly literate (adult literacy rate: 98.7 per cent and 95.4 per cent for males and females, respectively) and highly trained. Fifty per cent of the working population is employed by international companies. Hong Kong is one of the world's most open and dynamic economies. In 2010, Hong Kong's real economic growth rate rose to 6.8 per cent as it recovered from the global financial turmoil. Inflation rose gradually to 2.4 per cent in 2010 from 0.5 per cent in 2009. The government introduced several rounds of measures to forestall the risk of a housing market bubble arising from the low interest rates and increased liquidity in the global financial system. Its deepwater harbour is a unique natural resource and local notable industries include textiles, clothing, electronics, plastics, toys, watches and clocks. Hong Kong's economic strengths include a sound banking system, virtually no public debt, a strong legal system, ample foreign exchange reserves, and an able and rigorously enforced anti-corruption regime, enabling it to respond quickly to changing circumstances. The government promotes measures designed to improve its attractiveness as a commercial and trading centre and is continually refining its financial architecture. Hong Kong's exports of goods and services rebounded strongly in 2010, by 17.3 per cent and 15.0 per cent respectively in real terms, fuelled by the quicker than expected recovery of the global economy and a massive Chinese fiscal and monetary stimulus programme. Its GDP (PPP) for 2010 is estimated to have reached $326 billion ($45,736 per capita), which translates to a nominal GDP of $225 billion ($31,590 per capita). The unemployment rate in 2010 dropped to 4.3 per cent, the lowest since the fourth quarter of 2008. The Hong Kong government predicted GDP growth of 4–5 per cent in 2011.

Published by Woodhead Publishing Limited, 2012

10.2 Pharmaceutical industry in Hong Kong

Even though the pharmaceutical market of Hong Kong is relatively small, it is still an attractive market. It is geographically well located, bordering the world's fastest-growing economy, China, as well as having close proximity to many emerging economies. Economically, Hong Kong is heavily influenced by events in mainland China. The healthcare system is of an extremely high standard, and is indeed better than most in the Asia-Pacific region. The population is well looked after by the health services, and therefore has a high life-expectancy and low infant mortality rate. There are laws for intellectual property protection, GXPs, but piracy is common in the country and the authorities find it hard to prosecute. In early 2009, a number of incidents concerning pharmaceutical products in Hong Kong raised public concerns on drug safety. A major regulatory review published in January 2010 identified certain areas of the regulatory environment as ripe for improvement, specifically: GMP; pre-market control of drugs; regulations for importers/exporters, wholesalers and retailers; pharmacovigilance and public awareness; and increasing penalties for manufacturers/vendors who disobey the law.

Although biologics and biosimilars do not form a large part of the Hong Kong pharmaceutical market, there has been an increase in joint-venture activities in recent months. Hong Kong's largest domestic company, CK Life Sciences, is growing rapidly through a policy of aggressive acquisitions. CK also claims to operate the most sophisticated R&D facility in Hong Kong. On top of this, the Hong Kong government has offered research funding for treatments for infectious diseases. However, the branded generics market is still the largest market sector in Hong Kong, and it is dominated by local manufacturers that have been operating in the market for many years. Overall, demand for OTC products is expected to grow gradually in a market that has matured and lacks impetus for dynamism. The presence of traditional Chinese medicines also slows the growth of the OTC market. Growth of the pharmaceutical market in Hong Kong is expected to be steady over the medium term. The market should reach HK$10.56 billion ($1.35 billion) in consumer price value by 2014, up from HK$7.19 billion in 2009.

Published by Woodhead Publishing Limited, 2012

10.3 Healthcare system in Hong Kong

Hong Kong has an outstanding healthcare system as indicated by one of the lowest infant mortality rates and the longest life-expectancy in the world. Public hospitals provide 90 per cent of the medical care in Hong Kong; all public hospital records are computerised and stored in a central computer. There are 13 private hospitals and more than 50 public hospitals in Hong Kong. The special administrative region (SAR) boasts one of the widest ranges of healthcare services in the world, and some of its private hospitals are globally considered to be among the very best of their type. There are two medical schools in the SAR, one based at the Chinese University of Hong Kong and the other at Hong Kong University. Both have strong links with public sector hospitals. With respect to postgraduate education, many Hong Kong doctors have traditionally looked overseas for further training, and many have taken British Royal College exams such as the MRCP(UK) and the MRCS(UK). However, Hong Kong has been developing its own postgraduate medical institutions, in particular the Hong Kong Academy of Medicine, and this is gradually assuming responsibility for all postgraduate medical training in the SAR. There are also strong public health systems in Hong Kong, and the Centre for Health Protection, founded after the SARS outbreak of 2003, is particularly worthy of mention.

Hong Kong has a rather simple system of financing and delivering healthcare. Outpatient care, mostly primary healthcare, is provided predominantly by private general practitioners, who provide over 70 per cent of all outpatient consultations. Public general outpatient clinics provide approximately 15 per cent of all outpatient consultations at a subsidised rate mostly to those with low income and patients with chronic conditions. The remaining 15 per cent of outpatient visits are provided by private practitioners of alternative medicine, of which traditional Chinese medicine practitioners constitute the largest group. Expenditure on outpatient services constitutes around 50 per cent of total healthcare expenditure. Roughly 75 per cent of outpatient expenditure is financed by out-of-pocket payments, with the remaining financed by employers or insurance.

Published by Woodhead Publishing Limited, 2012

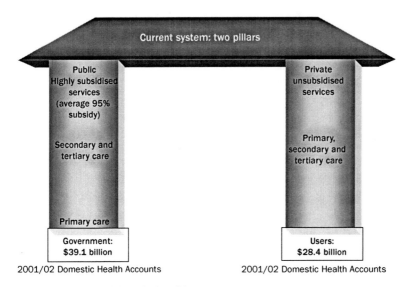

Figure 10.1 Hong Kong's healthcare system

The bulk of specialist and inpatient care, mostly secondary and tertiary care, is financed and delivered through the public sector. The Hospital Authority owns and manages 41 public healthcare institutions, and provides over 90 per cent of all hospital beds in Hong Kong. Institutions under the Hospital Authority provide a comprehensive range of services at a heavily subsidised rate. The Hospital Authority receives over 90 per cent of its income from the government. Presently, private hospitals deliver roughly 6 per cent of total inpatient care.

All Hong Kong residents are eligible to receive care from public hospitals and clinics at a heavily subsidised rate. Patients in public hospitals pay a fixed per diem fee which is far lower than the actual average cost of a patient day in an acute public hospital. The per diem fee is all-inclusive with the exception of a shortlist of privately purchased medical items (PPMI) and drugs not included in the Hospital Authority's Drug Formulary, for which patients have to pay the full cost separately. The system, whereby the bulk of hospital services is funded by the government and delivered by public hospitals, and the bulk of general outpatient care is funded and delivered privately, has not changed much since the 1950s. This arrangement has been criticised as too compartmentalised, resulting in poor coordination and workload imbalance between the public and private sectors as well as between primary and secondary/tertiary care sectors, and not sustainable in the long run. Within the public hospital system, all healthcare providers are compensated on a fixed salary basis. Funding from the government to the Hospital Authority has been mostly historically and facility based, recently moving towards becoming more population based. Money does not follow patients. There is insufficient financial incentive for public healthcare providers to be responsive to patients' needs. Disincentives within the system are extensive, for example, units that serve patients well will attract more patients, who will not bring in more resources. Despite these disincentives, quality of care in public hospitals generally improved after the establishment of the Hospital Authority, although spending also went up considerably. Waiting time for some non-urgent conditions, however, has worsened significantly in recent years.

Hong Kong has no compulsory health insurance or medical savings contributions. Public hospital services are financed almost entirely through the government, despite the fact that tax rates in Hong Kong are among the lowest in the world, and the percentage of taxpayers is also low by industrialised countries' standards. Private hospital services are financed through direct payment or private health

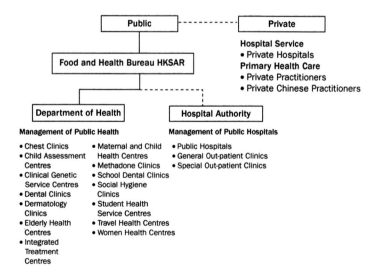

Figure 10.2 Overall structure of the healthcare system in Hong Kong

insurance. Hong Kong's Food and Health Bureau is responsible for forming policies and allocating resources for the running of Hong Kong's health services. It also ensures these policies are carried out effectively to protect and promote public health, provide lifelong holistic healthcare to every citizen of Hong Kong, and ensure that no one is denied adequate medical treatment due to lack of means.

Hong Kong departed from a UK-style National Health Service in 1990 with the creation of the Hong Kong Hospital Authority. The Hong Kong Hospital Authority, in conjunction with the Department of Health, oversees the management of all public healthcare facilities in the city. As one would expect, many foreign ex-pats living in the city, and even Hong Kong nationals, turn to insurance to help them cope with the high costs associated with quality medical treatment. In this regard, people usually have two options: local or international health insurance. While these options may at first glance seem remarkably similar, they are in fact extremely different.

A local Hong Kong insurance plan will adjust premiums in line with the prevailing medical costs in the city; any individuals who make claims on their policy will also see their premiums increase accordingly. In addition to this, local health insurance plans will not work outside of Hong Kong. International health insurance plans are more versatile in their nature, and while they are not specifically designed with the Hong Kong market in mind, they will typically afford a policyholder higher levels of coverage than are usually associated with a local health insurance policy. International health insurance plans are community rated; this means that premiums are not calculated on an individual basis but rather on the rate of global medical inflation. International health insurance plans are globally portable, so even if the policyholder relocates away from Hong Kong, their coverage will travel with them.

10.4 Clinical trials in Hong Kong

Hong Kong is an outstanding modern international metropolis in Asia. For decades it has been well known for its unrivalled location, state-of-the-art infrastructure, high-calibre workforce, transparent legal system and free flow of information, as well as its international

300 Clinical Research in Asia: Opportunities and Challenges

lifestyle. Besides being an Asian business and logistics centre, Hong Kong has also emerged as an Asian hub for clinical research. Hong Kong's history of clinical research can be traced back to the foundation of the Hong Kong College of Medicine in 1887. Adoption of the ICH-GCP guidelines in 1996 facilitated international collaboration, which stimulated an upsurge of clinical research activities in Hong Kong. The number of certificates for clinical trial issued by the Hong Kong Department of Health increased sharply from around 20 per year before the mid-1990s to 139 in 2002.

Hong Kong's outstanding conditions have been attracting a continuous inflow of industrial sponsorship of Phase I–IV clinical trials. Most of the major research-based healthcare and medical product companies, including the top 20 global pharma companies, have already run clinical trials in Hong Kong.

The CRO market in Hong Kong is driven by pre-clinical and clinical CROs, bioequivalence studies and clinical laboratory business. In the clinical CRO domain, there are full-service CROs, monitoring-only CROs and EDC service CROs. Some of them are local CROs while others are offshoots of large global CROs. Although information about exactly what Hong Kong pharma companies are developing is not in the public domain, only a few companies are into full-fledged R&D and have new chemical entities in their research pipelines. The key global CROs operating in Hong Kong include Quintiles, PPD, Pharmanet, Kendle, INC Research, Omnicare, and Novotech; local CROs include Asia Global Research, IATEC CRO, Gleneagles CRC, NanoAsia Company Ltd and CMIC. There are also a couple of CROs that concentrate on bioequivalence and ADME, toxicology and pharmacology.

Hong Kong has an excellent infrastructure in terms of transportation, workforce and legal framework. The university and medical training network comprise a public healthcare system with 41 public hospitals managed by the Hospital Authority, which contributes to one of the lowest infant mortality rates in the world and an average life-expectancy of 80 years – one of the highest in the world. Centralised electronic patient records are accessible on an intranet system linking all hospitals and clinics under the Hospital Authority. Accredited central laboratory facilities capable of

Published by Woodhead Publishing Limited, 2012

supporting multinational clinical trials are also available. Hong Kong is a prime logistical hub which is less than five hours' flight from most Asian countries and links to some 130 destinations worldwide by over 3,600 flights per week.

Hong Kong is an affluent multicultural city-state with English used in higher education and in many important sectors of society; as such the CRO industry is not hard-pressed to find English-speaking talent, investigators and support staff to perform global clinical trials. Hong Kong has decades of experience in clinical research as illustrated by the large quantity of quality scientific publications in clinical research and its vast experience of conducting Phase I–IV clinical trials in a wide range of therapeutic areas. Hong Kong has demonstrated extensive collaboration with multinational and local trial sponsors with full compliance with the ICH-GCP guidelines and other international standards. Overseas regulatory agencies, including the US FDA and Japan Ministry of Health, Labour and Welfare have performed satisfactory regulatory inspections in Hong Kong, thus underlining the SAR's credibility as a location for clinical trials. Hong Kong is officially accredited by the State FDA in Beijing, meaning that data from drug trials in Hong Kong may be used in filing new drug applications in China, within accredited therapeutic areas.

10.5 The regulatory environment

The regulatory framework for testing new drugs in Hong Kong is quite straightforward. The whole approval process takes two months for a normal trial. The first requirement is ethics committee approval, which is followed by approval for trial conduct and an import licence for the test drug. These regulations apply only to drug trials and not to device or cell therapy trials, which are unregulated; such clinical trials require only ethics committee approval.

Under Regulation 36B of the Pharmacy and Poisons Regulations, a Certificate for Clinical Trial/Medicinal Test is required for the purpose of conducting a clinical trial on human beings or a medicinal test on animals. Applications for such a certificate should be made

302 Clinical Research in Asia: Opportunities and Challenges

to the Pharmaceuticals Registration Section of the Department of Health. The application should contain the following documents:

- a completed application form and a completed clinical trial checklist;
- the application fee (currently $1,420);
- a copy of the proposed protocol for the clinical trial or medicinal test;
- information on the new drug (e.g. its pharmaceutical data, pharmacological action, toxicology, studies on humans if any, package insert, etc.);
- copies of pre-clinical studies (if not submitted, justification must be supplied);
- a sample of the product or substance;
- a letter from the principal investigator confirming his involvement in the clinical trial or medicinal test;
- curriculum vitae of the principal investigator;
- documentary evidence that the clinical trial has been approved by the ethics committee of the institution in which it is to be conducted (this may be submitted when available at a later date);
- patient information and patient consent form, in both English and Chinese, or in Chinese only;
- evidence that the trial medication is manufactured in accordance with GMP (e.g. copy of manufacturer's GMP certificate);
- a sample certificate of analysis of the drug.

Applications for studies for which a CTC was issued previously but has expired/will soon expire must include a copy of the previous CTC and clinical trial progress report(s). If the progress report is not available or if the trial has not been started, justification must be provided. Applications for studies which are subject to approval from the State FDA must include the drug clinical trial approval document issued by the State FDA (this may be submitted when available at a later date) and a copy of the protocol submitted to the State FDA.

Published by Woodhead Publishing Limited, 2012

Clinical research in Hong Kong **303**

10.5.1 Ethics committees

The 50 public hospitals in Hong Kong are organised into six clusters (Table 10.1). The ethics committees operate according to international standards such as the Declaration of Helsinki and ICH-GCP, and also according to unified operational guidelines. Most ethics committees/institutional review boards (IRBs) schedule meetings every two weeks.

10.5.2 Regulatory and ethics committee approval

The regulatory authority usually takes 30 days (~6 weeks) to evaluate the application. In the case of queries/insufficient data, a query letter is faxed to the sponsor. Upon receipt of reply, the review process will take an additional 30 days. One application is made per site and the CTC is issued only after the ethics committee approval letter is submitted to the authorities. The prescribed application fee is to be paid at the time of application. Once the CTC is ready for collection, the applicant is informed and must pay the CTC fee at the time of collection. The CTIL is valid for three years according to Regulation 12(5) of the Control of Drugs and Cosmetic Regulations 1984.

10.5.3 Import and export permission

It is necessary to apply for import and export licences, as applicable. Import and export licences can be issued within one day if the CTC, antibiotic permit or wholesale poison licence is available. Evidence of importation and delivery of the product to the investigator(s) is tracked and documented on the reverse of the original licence (CTIL/CTX).

Under the import and export ordinance, Chapter 60 of the Laws of Hong Kong, all imports and exports of pharmaceutical products and medicines must be covered by import and export licences issued by the Trade and Industry Department. This includes any substance

Published by Woodhead Publishing Limited, 2012

304 Clinical Research in Asia: Opportunities and Challenges

Table 10.1 Ethics committees in Hong Kong

Hong Kong Island	Kowloon	New Territories
HK West Cluster REC	*Kowloon Central and East Cluster REC*	*NT East Cluster REC*
Grantham Hospital	HK Red Cross Blood Transfusion Service	Alice Ho Miu Ling Nethersole Hospital
MacLehose Medical Rehabilitation Centre	Hong Kong Buddhist Hospital	Bradbury Hospice
Queen Mary Hospital	Hong Kong Eye Hospital	Cheshire Home, Shatin
The Duchess of Kent Children's Hospital at Sandy	Kowloon Hospital	North District Hospital
Tsan Yuk Hospital	Queen Elizabeth Hospital	Prince of Wales Hospital
Tung Wah Group Hospitals-Fung Yiu King Hospital	Rehabaid Centre	Shatin Hospital
Tung Wah Hospital	Haven of Hope Hospital	Tai Po Hospital
	Tseung Kwan O Hospital	
	United Christian Hospital	
HK East Cluster REC	*Kowloon West Cluster REC*	*NT West Cluster REC*
Cheshire Home,Chung Hom Kok	Caritas Medical Centre	Castle Peak Hospital
Pamela Youde Nethersole Eastern Hospital	Kwai Chung Hospital	Pok Oi Hospital
Ruttonjee Hospital	Kwong Wah Hospital	Siu Lam Hospital
St. John Hospital	Our Lady of Maryknoll Hospital	Tuen Mun Hospital
Tang Shiu Kin Hospital	Princess Margaret Hospital	
Tung Wah Eastern Hospital	Tung Wah Group Hospitals-Wong Tai Sin Hospital	
Wong Chuk Hang Hospital	Yan Chai Hospital	

Published by Woodhead Publishing Limited, 2012

or mixture of substances manufactured, sold, supplied or offered for sale or supply for use in:

- the diagnosis, treatment, mitigation, alleviation or prevention of disease or any symptom thereof;
- the diagnosis, treatment, mitigation, alleviation of any abnormal physical or physiological state or any symptom thereof;
- altering, modifying, correcting or restoring any organic function, in human beings or in animals.

The relevant licence application forms are Import License Form 3 [TRA 187] and Export License Form 6 [TRA 394]. Except for the pharmaceuticals mentioned below, the import licence application for pharmaceutical products and medicines must be completed in quadruplicate; the export licence application must be completed in triplicate. In both cases, the application should be lodged with the Pharmaceuticals Registration and Import/Export Control Section of the Department of Health. A numbered receipt is then issued to the applicant. After one working day, applicants must present this receipt in order to collect the processed applications from the Pharmaceuticals Registration and Import/Export Control Section. In the case of an import licence application, the applicant will be given the original copy and duplicate of the licence. The original copy enables the licensee to take delivery of the goods from the carrier (shipping company, airline or the transport company).

10.5.4 Study start-up timeline

Once the authorisation for conducting a clinical trial is granted, the involved parties can proceed with relevant start-up activities such as translations, finalisation of investigator and other ancillary agreements, processing of clinical trial insurance etc. Translations of English informed consent form (ICFs) are usually completed in approximately four weeks; ICFs must also be translated into Cantonese. Finalising the hospital contracts at most sites takes an average of 8–12 weeks.

Published by Woodhead Publishing Limited, 2012

306   Clinical Research in Asia: Opportunities and Challenges

The documents required for IRB submission in Hong Kong are as follows:

- trial protocol(s)/amendment(s);
- case record forms;
- written ICFs;
- patient information sheets;
- translated documents (e.g. the protocol synopsis, informed consent forms, research proposal);
- investigator's brochure;
- available safety information;
- investigational product label translated into Cantonese;
- information about payments and compensation for subjects;
- clinical trial insurance;
- clinical research agreement;
- investigator's curriculum vitae and/or other documentation;
- special requirements, such as any other documents that the ethics committee may need to fulfil its responsibilities.

The ethics committee shall review the proposed clinical trial within a period described in its SOP and document its views (identifying the trial and list of documents reviewed). The IRB can approve the trial or seek modifications prior to its approval/favourable opinion. The IRB has every right to disapprove the trial or terminate/suspend the trial (Figure 10.3).

10.5.5 Clinical trial insurance

There is no specific insurance requirement for studies conducted in Hong Kong. Trial-related injuries must be indemnified under a global insurance cover or a local cover or both. Both global and local insurance players now provide clinical trial insurance.

Published by Woodhead Publishing Limited, 2012

Clinical research in Hong Kong 307

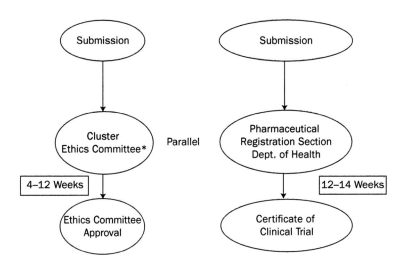

The jurisdiction of the cluster ethics committee extends to its respective cluster of hospitals/institutions.

Figure 10.3 Flow chart for ethics committee and regulatory submissions

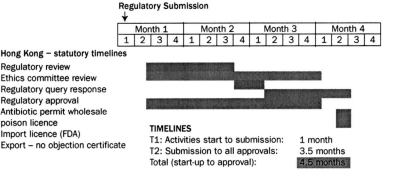

Comments
- Regulatory and ethics approval run in parallel
- Regulatory authority review and get back with queries or additional information usually within six weeks of filing the application
- The ethics committee review period differs from site to site, on average 4–8 weeks; this may extend up to 12 weeks in some situations
- Stop clock time: time taken by sponsor to respond regulatory query
- Regulatory approval/requery (if response is not satisfactory) is issued within additional 6 weeks of filing the response
- As per the Import & Export Section, Dept. of Health, these licences must be applied for where applicable
- The import and export licence can be issued within one day if the CTC, antibiotic permit or wholesale poison licence is available

Figure 10.4 Study start-up timelines in Hong Kong

Published by Woodhead Publishing Limited, 2012

308 Clinical Research in Asia: Opportunities and Challenges

10.5.6 Safety reporting

The Department of Health, Pharmaceuticals Registration Section has laid down the requirements relating to local drug-related safety reports, progress reports and final study reports in clinical trials. All certificate holders responsible for clinical trials/medicinal tests are required to report all local drug-related safety reports, i.e. reports on adverse drug reactions (ADRs). Adverse drug reactions that are both serious and unexpected must be reported as soon as possible. The prescribed Council for International Organisations of Medical Sciences forms are to be used for reporting. Fatal or life-threatening unexpected ADRs should be reported as soon as possible but no later than seven calendar days after first knowledge by the sponsor that a case qualifies, followed by as complete a report as possible within eight additional calendar days. This report must include an assessment of the importance and implication of the findings, including relevant previous experience with the same or similar medicinal products. Other serious unexpected ADRs that are not fatal or life-threatening should be reported as soon as possible but no later than 15 calendar days after first knowledge by the sponsor that the case meets the minimum criteria for expedited reporting. Non-serious adverse reactions and serious adverse reactions that are expected should be reported in a brief summary at the conclusion of the trial. The terms 'serious adverse drug reaction' and 'adverse event' are defined as per ICH-GCP guidelines. Medical and scientific judgment should be exercised in deciding whether expedited reporting is appropriate in other situations, such as serious medical events that may not be immediately life-threatening or result in death or hospitalisation, but may jeopardise the patient or may require intervention to prevent death or hospitalisation.

10.5.7 Recruitment modalities

Hong Kong investigators are well trained, and are conversant in English. They have good working networks and in general, one committed investigator persuades other investigators into participating in clinical trials. Thus, the referral system works well

Published by Woodhead Publishing Limited, 2012

in Hong Kong. It is an effective practice to recruit one investigator and use his/her network of investigators to recruit more investigators. Each investigator has his/her own pool of patients, and clinical trial participants are recruited from the pool rather than by referral.

10.5.8 Progress report submission

Progress reports must be submitted to regulatory authorities and IRBs on a yearly basis in addition to a final study report at the end of the study. The prescribed forms may be used for reporting. The licence holder shall inform the ethics committee of any decision to discontinue the trial to which the licence related and shall state the reason for the decision. The licence holder should return the CTC as soon as possible. On termination of the trial, the licence holder shall submit to the ethics committee an end-of-study summary report pertaining to the sites conducting the trial.

10.6 Clinical trials in Hong Kong

Hong Kong is participating in approximately 100 new industry-sponsored trials every year. With the global slowdown in 2009, the flow of new trials to Hong Kong declined to 67 trials in 2010. There are 1,027 trials already listed in the registry for Hong Kong, out of which 380 trials are active and recruiting. Of the 1,027 studies undertaken in Hong Kong, only 593 trials are industry-sponsored trials and 398 trials are sponsored by individual investigators, local institutions or hospitals, universities and other organisations.

Further analysis of publicly available industry reports suggests that several GCP studies in diverse therapeutic areas are being conducted in Hong Kong. Almost 94 per cent of the trials undertaken in Hong Kong are in late phases (i.e. Phase II–IV) with a small number of trials in Phase I (6 per cent) also undertaken in Hong Kong. While a large number of these trials are sponsored by the big pharma companies (see Table 10.2), a significant number of trials are undertaken by institutes of national repute, including the Chinese University of Hong Kong (191 trials), the University of Hong Kong

310 Clinical Research in Asia: Opportunities and Challenges

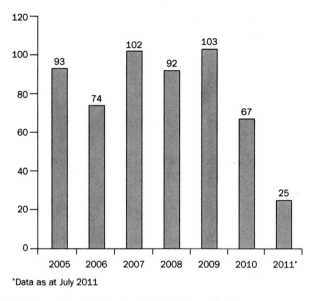

Figure 10.5 Growth of clinical trials in Hong Kong

Source: *www.clinicaltrials.gov* (accessed February 2011)

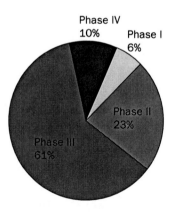

Figure 10.6 Trials in Hong Kong, by phase

Source: *www.clinicaltrials.gov* (accessed July 2011)

Table 10.2 Trials undertaken in Hong Kong by major players

Industry sponsor	No. of trials
Pfizer	80
GlaxoSmithKline	72
Hoffmann-La Roche	52
Novartis	43
Sanofi-Aventis	40
AstraZeneca	28
Bayer	27
Bristol-Myers Squibb	25
Boehringer Ingelheim	21
Novo Nordisk	14
Eli Lilly	13
Merck	12
UCB	10
Amgen	10
Johnson & Johnson	9
Genentech	8
Abbott	7
Total	471

Source: *www.clinicaltrials.gov* (accessed August 2011)

(112 trials), Hospital Authority Hong Kong (55 trials), Hong Kong Polytechnic University (29 trials) and the National Cancer Institute (23 trials).

10.7 Environmental analysis

The healthcare environment in Hong Kong is ideal for global clinical trials due to its supporting infrastructure, good-quality investigators, higher compliance by investigators and study participants, regulatory mechanisms and regional cooperation and acceptance of data. There

Published by Woodhead Publishing Limited, 2012

312 Clinical Research in Asia: Opportunities and Challenges

are, however, significant legal, cultural and language barriers and a shortage of skilled professionals that act as challenges for the clinical trial environment.

The standards of care and the clinical practices in Hong Kong are equivalent or similar to US medical practices. In addition, investigators command good English. Even those investigators with no US experience are familiar with clinical trials and US medical practices, due probably to peer influence. The investigators are actively engaged in medical research and are motivated to participate in global clinical trials. They respond quickly to the feasibility requests of multinational clinical trials and are generally enthusiastic. They are all familiar with clinical trial procedures and well versed with GCP.

10.7.1 Regional cooperation and data acceptance

Due to genetic and racial similarities, China includes Hong Kong in pivotal regional trials. Multinational sponsors who want to register drugs in China should bear this in mind.

10.7.2 Shortage of skilled professionals

A significant number of CRAs are academically trained with a background in nursing and pharmacy, hence there is a huge demand for experienced clinical trial professionals, particularly CRAs and monitors. With the increasing number of studies, branching out by global CROs and the establishment of small local players, the gap between supply and demand for skilled professionals is likely to endure.

10.7.3 Cultural barrier

Hong Kong has only a short history of rigorous pivotal new drug trials and its professionals are not yet attuned to the global way of doing things. The language barrier can sometimes limit proactive

Published by Woodhead Publishing Limited, 2012

decisions by the project manager or CRA. Furthermore, team members may lack common understanding with respect to SOPs or processes. Extra care must therefore be taken to ensure clinical trial staff follow SOPs, and that they understand and conduct themselves like their counterparts in USA or Europe.

10.8 Future outlook

Rigorous multinational pivotal trials are new to Hong Kong and the regulatory bodies constantly endeavour to invigorate the clinical trial environment. Despite problems, the environment for conducting trials in Hong Kong is conducive due to various factors. Investigators are GCP trained, and can recruit patients in a timely manner. Clinical trial sites are all equipped to meet complicated diagnostic and treatment requirements. The timeline for investigational new drugs is competitive, and other regulatory requirements, such as serious adverse event reporting, are compatible with ICH guidelines. Trials in Hong Kong are cost-effective and of the highest quality, and hence the future is bright.

11

Clinical research in the Philippines, Indonesia and Vietnam

Abstract: This chapter discusses the clinical research environments in Philippines, Indonesia and Vietnam. These three countries are catching up with the other Asian countries in terms of their clinical trial infrastructure and know-how to be among the attractive nations for clinical research. This chapter briefly discusses the healthcare system, the disease burden, regulatory environment, evolution of clinical trial regulations and summarises the number of trials in these countries.

11.1 Clinical research in the Philippines

11.1.1 Background and history

The Philippines is one of the world's most populous countries and boasts a population of more than 90 million, growing at an annual rate of 2.1 per cent. Its population is relatively young: of the 92 million Filipinos, about 37 million (34 per cent) are aged 18 years old or younger. Average life-expectancy is 66.6 years for males, and 71.8 years for females. In Philippines, crude birth rate is about 2.4 per cent while crude death rate is 0.5 per cent.

Published by Woodhead Publishing Limited, 2012

316   Clinical Research in Asia: Opportunities and Challenges

The leading causes of morbidity in the Philippines are communicable diseases. From 1995 to 2000, these included diarrhoea, bronchitis, pneumonia, influenza, tuberculosis, malaria, chicken pox and measles (Table 11.1). Leading non-communicable causes of morbidity are hypertension and heart disease. Unlike the 10 leading causes of morbidity, deaths are mainly due to non-communicable diseases. Diseases of the heart and the vascular system are the two most common causes of death (Table 11.2).

11.1.2 Regulatory environment

The Philippine Council for Health Research and Development (PCHRD) is the primary focal point for health research activities in the Philippines. The PCHRD is an agency of the Department of Science and Technology and is responsible for coordinating and monitoring research activities in the country. The PCHRD formed the National Ethics Committee (NEC) in 1984 in an effort to ensure that all health R&D proposals conform to ethical standards. The PCHRD has also promoted the establishment of institutional ethics review committees (IERCs) within institutions that conduct

Table 11.1   Causes of morbidity in the Philippines

Cause	Number	Rate per 100,000 population
1. Diarrhoea	866,411	1,134.8
2. Bronchitis	700,105	917.0
3. Pneumonia	632,930	829.0
4. Influenza	502,718	658.5
5. Hypertension	279,992	366.7
6. TB respiratory	126,489	165.7
7. Diseases of the heart	52,957	69.4
8. Malaria	50,869	66.6
9. Chicken pox	35,306	46.2
10. Measles	23,287	30.5

Published by Woodhead Publishing Limited, 2012

Clinical research in the Philippines, Indonesia and Vietnam   317

Table 11.2 Causes of mortality in the Philippines

Cause	Number	Rate per 100,000 population
1. Diseases of the heart	60,417	79.1
2. Diseases of the vascular system	48,271	63.2
3. Malignant neoplasm	36,414	47.7
4. Pneumonia	32,637	42.7
5. Accidents	32,355	42.4
6. Tuberculosis, all forms	27,557	36.1
7. Chronic obstructive pulmonary disease and allied conditions	15,904	20.8
8. Certain conditions originating in the perinatal period	15,098	19.8
9. Diabetes mellitus	10,747	14.1
10. Nephritis, nephrotic syndrome and nephrosis	7,963	10.4

Source: Philippines Health Statistics (2000)

biomedical and behavioural research. The PCHRD and the Department of Health (DOH) of the Philippines jointly established the Philippine National Health Research System (PNHRS) in 2003. The PNHRS launched a working group on ethics, which evolved into the Philippine Health Research Ethics Board (PHREB). The board was formally constituted in early 2006 as a national policymaking body on health research ethics. The PNHRS envisions creating regional ethics boards that will function similarly to the PHREB and will be supervised by the PHREB.

The DOH is the principal health agency in the Philippines. It is responsible for ensuring universal access to basic public health services through the provision of quality healthcare and the regulation of providers of health goods and services.

An earlier national guidelines document has been replaced by the 2006 National Ethical Guidelines for Health Research, issued by the PNHRS and PHREB. Ethical clearance of a research protocol is to be based on: (1) science; (2) the nature and gravity of the risk to human subjects; (3) the adequacy of safeguards and protection against risk; (4) the magnitude of potential benefits vis-à-vis harm to individuals or

Published by Woodhead Publishing Limited, 2012

318 Clinical Research in Asia: Opportunities and Challenges

community; (5) the validity of the study participants' informed consent; (6) the ecological impact; and (7) clarification of potential conflicts of interest. The guidelines discuss requirements for ethics committee approval and obtaining informed consent from research participants as well as requirements for subject groups that require special consideration. There are also specific guidelines regarding clinical trials, herbal medicine, complementary and alternative medicine, epidemiological research, social and behavioural research, research involving traumatised populations, HIV/AIDS, assisted reproductive technology, genetic research, and international collaboration.

There are a number of regulations pertaining to clinical trials, including rules on the registration of clinical trials, including approval and conduct, and lot or batch release certification of vaccines and biologic products (Administrative Order No. 47) and the Food, Drugs and Devices, and Cosmetic Act 1987 (Republic Act No. 3720).

11.1.3 Ethics committee approval

The guidelines indicate that the following documents must be submitted when seeking IERC approval:

- the application;
- the research protocol;
- written information for participants about the study and the nature of their participation;
- written informed consent documents;
- safety information;
- description of recruitment procedures;
- statement about ethical considerations for the study in question;
- investigators' qualifications;
- information about funding sources and other potential conflicts of interest;
- information about compensation for participants.

The National Ethical Guidelines publication encourages research institutions to establish IERCs, and instructs IERCs to use as

Published by Woodhead Publishing Limited, 2012

reference both those guidelines and the World Health Organization's Operational Guidelines for Ethics Committees that Review Biomedical Research. IERCs apparently formulate their own standard operating procedures. According to PCHRD, researchers at institutions without their own IERCs should seek review from the NEC or from other institutions. Both private and government researchers at institutions without IERCs have asked the NEC, the National Institute of Health, the University of the Philippines and other institutions to review their proposals.

11.1.4 Clinical trials in the Philippines

The Philippines is participating in approximately 70 new industry-sponsored trials every year. Even with global slowdown in 2009, the flow of new trials to Philippines has been maintained although the trend is not increasing significantly. There were 481 trials already listed in the registry, out of which 109 trials are active and recruiting. Of the 481 studies undertaken in the Philippines, 457 trials are industry-sponsored trials and only 16 trials are sponsored by individual investigators, local institutions or hospitals, universities or other organisations.

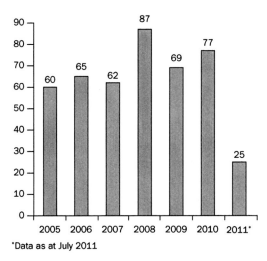

Figure 11.1 Growth of clinical trials in the Philippines

Source: www.clinicaltrials.gov (accessed August 2011)

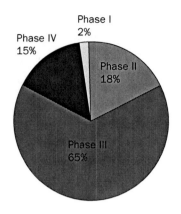

Figure 11.2 Trials in the Philippines, by phase

Source: www.clinicaltrials.gov (accessed February 2011)

Further analysis of publicly available industry reports suggests that GCP studies in diverse therapeutic areas are being conducted in the Philippines. Almost 65 per cent of the trials undertaken in the Philippines are in Phase III, 18 per cent trials in Phase II and 15 per cent trials are in Phase IV. A small number of Phase I trials (2 per cent) are also undertaken in the Philippines, which clearly demonstrates the country is not ready to compete for Phase I studies.

As can be seen from Table 11.3, more than 80 per cent of the GCP trials in the Philippines are undertaken by the top 15 pharma companies.

11.1.5 Challenges and future outlook

There are currently no formal national enforcement mechanisms in place for the National Guidelines for Biomedical/Behavioural Research. Compliance is promoted primarily through 'moral force'. Individual IRECs may have their own enforcement mechanisms in place.

Clinical research in the Philippines, Indonesia and Vietnam   **321**

Table 11.3 Trials undertaken in the Philippines by major players

Industry sponsor	No. of trials
GlaxoSmithKline	87
AstraZeneca	46
Pfizer	44
Sanofi-Aventis	39
Boehringer Ingelheim	33
Bristol-Myers Squibb	31
Novartis	24
Bayer	20
Hoffmann-La Roche	16
Eli Lilly	15
Novartis	12
Merck	10
Astellas	9
Genentech	8
Allergan	7
Total	401

Source: *www.clinicaltrials.gov* (accessed August 2011)

11.2 Clinical research in Indonesia

11.2.1 Background and history

Indonesia is an archipelago of more than 17,000 islands. Its population currently exceeds 220 million, with annual per capita income of $2,271. There are 69 medical schools, 53 of which have been accredited by the Philippine Accrediting Association of Schools, Colleges and Universities under the Commission on Higher Education. Currently, about 10 medical schools are actively involved clinical research. In 2008, there were almost 57,000 GPs and around 15,000

Published by Woodhead Publishing Limited, 2012

322 Clinical Research in Asia: Opportunities and Challenges

Table 11.4 Major causes of death in Indonesia, 2007

No.	Disease	%
1	Stroke	15.4
2	Tuberculosis	7.5
3	Hypertension	6.8
4	Trauma	6.5
5	Perinatal disorders	6.0
6	Diabetes mellitus	5.7
7	Malignancy	5.7
8	Liver diseases	5.1
9	Ischaemic heart disease	5.1
10	Lower resp. tract infections	4.6

Source: Ministry of Health, Indonesia (2007)

specialists in Indonesia. Today the implementation of simultaneous global clinical trials is very important to accelerate new drug development. Clinical research in Indonesia and other Asian countries is associated with potential benefits such as lower trial cost, more relaxed regulations, a wide variety of diseases and good availability of research subjects. Table 11.4 lists the major causes of death in Indonesia.

11.2.2 The regulatory environment

Health research in Indonesia is governed by Article 69 of the Indonesian Health Act No. 23/1992. Research and development in the healthcare sector is covered under regulation No. 39/1995 of the Indonesian Health Act. With increased awareness about global clinical research, Indonesia implemented GCP guidelines in 2001.

All pre-marketing clinical trials (i.e. Phases I–III) are required to adhere to the GCP standard. All trials must secure approval from the regulatory authority prior to their implementation. The sponsor should submit an application (using form UK-1) along with the following documents:

Published by Woodhead Publishing Limited, 2012

- research protocol and written information for the research subjects;
- approvals from the ethics committee and scientific committee;
- investigator's brochure;
- amount of drug needed for the trial.

If approved by the regulatory authority, both the letter of approval and licence for drug importation will be sent to the investigator within 10 working days. The same policy applies for studies on new indications (pivotal studies) and bioanalytical/bioequivalence studies for drugs that are already on the market.

In the case of post-marketing trials (Phase IV studies), the sponsor should send a notification to the regulatory authority prior to their implementation. If there is no response from the authority within 10 working days, the trial may be started, but the GCP should be followed. In Indonesia, post-marketing surveillance is not classified as clinical trial. Post-marketing trials for educational purposes (medical students, residents, etc.) must all follow the Declaration of Helsinki, but not necessarily the GCP standard.

The regulatory authority requires that research protocols be reviewed not only by the ethics committee but also by the scientific committee. If an in institution does not have a scientific committee, then the scientific aspect should be reviewed by the ethics committee.

11.2.3 Evolution of GCP

Prior to 2000, clinical trials in Indonesia were mostly limited to small-scale marketing trials. Quality control was an issue as there were no guidelines to control the quality of these trials and informed consents were often neglected. In addition, most institutions had no ethics committee, and most investigators had no idea what GCP was. In 2000, the Clinical Trial Working Group (CTWG) was established with a mission to improve the quality of clinical trials in Indonesia. The CTWG consisted of people from academia, industries, clinical labs, and the regulatory authority. In 2001, Indonesia

324 Clinical Research in Asia: Opportunities and Challenges

adopted the ICH-GCP and the regulatory authority issued some regulations related to the implementation of GCP. Since 2001, the CTWG has carried out training in GCP and research methodology in various medical faculties and research centres. Other organisations are now also providing GCP training. Today, approximately 200 clinical researchers throughout the country hold the GCP certificate, which can usually be obtained after attending a two-day course and passing an examination. GCP courses are often provided by sponsors prior to the commencement of a clinical trial.

11.2.4 Ethics committee

The first ethics committee in the country was established in 1982. Today, ethics committees exist in the majority of schools and hospitals conducting clinical research (34 ethics committees nationwide in 2009). The Minister of Health established the National Committee on Ethics of Health Research and tasked it with improving the capability of these ethics committees, rolling out the National Guidelines on Ethics in Health Research in 2003.

11.2.5 Clinical trials in Indonesia

Indonesia is undertaking approximately 10–15 new sponsored trials every year. With global slowdown in 2009, the flow of new trials to Indonesia in 2010 has reduced significantly. There were 162 trials already listed in the registry, out of which 40 trials are active and recruiting. Of the 162 studies undertaken in Indonesia, 117 trials are industry-sponsored trials and 34 trials are sponsored by individual investigators, local institutions or hospitals, universities or other organisations. As can be seen from Table 11.5, 104 of the 162 trials are being undertaken by top 15 pharma companies in Indonesia.

Further analysis of publicly available industry reports suggests that GCP studies in diverse therapeutic areas are being conducted in Indonesia. Almost 68 per cent of the trials undertaken in Indonesia

Published by Woodhead Publishing Limited, 2012

Clinical research in the Philippines, Indonesia and Vietnam 325

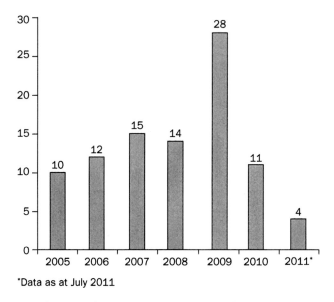

*Data as at July 2011

Figure 11.3 Growth of clinical trials in Indonesia

Source: www.clinicaltrials.gov (accessed July 2011)

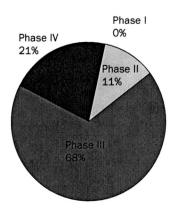

Figure 11.4 Trials in Indonesia, by phase

Source: www.clinicaltrials.gov (accessed July 2011)

326 Clinical Research in Asia: Opportunities and Challenges

Table 11.5 Trials undertaken in Indonesia by major players

Industry sponsor	No. of trials
Bayer	23
AstraZeneca	18
Sanofi-Aventis	10
Bristol-Myers Squibb	9
Pfizer	8
Johnson & Johnson	7
Hoffmann-La Roche	6
Astellas	5
Novo Nordisk	5
Dexa Medica Group	3
Innogene Kalbiotech	3
Boehringer Ingelheim Pharmaceuticals	2
GlaxoSmithKline	2
H. Lundbeck A/S	2
PT Otsuka Indonesia	2

Source: www.clinicaltrials.gov (accessed July 2011)

are in Phase III, 11 per cent in Phase II and 21 per cent trials in Phase IV. These figures clearly demonstrate that the country is not ready to compete for Phase I studies.

In addition to the pharma companies listed in Table 11.5, other institutions active in clinical research in Indonesia include Indonesia University, Menzies School of Health Research, Wellcome Trust, National Health and Medical Research Council, Australia, National Institute of Health Research and Development, Indonesia, Showa University and the National Institute of Allergy and Infectious Diseases.

11.2.6 Challenges and future outlook

Currently the conditions required to conduct GCP compliance trials are much improved in Indonesia. It is now possible to carry out

Published by Woodhead Publishing Limited, 2012

quality clinical trials in Indonesia and the country could contribute significantly to global drug development. There are however challenges of insurance and indemnifications. Only a few local players offer clinical trial insurance, the liability cover for global clinical trials. There is a significant shortfall of trial monitors. The export of biological samples presents logistical challenges for sites participating in clinical trials. The stricter confidentiality and data protection guidelines do not prevail, although considerable awareness about their necessity is improving. A fear of publication still prevails and hence, good publishing practices need to be implemented in Indonesia. All the stakeholders understand the benefits of undertaking clinical trials in Indonesia and should cooperate with academia, implement good clinical practices, initiate GCP training and thus help the conduct of ethical research.

11.3 Clinical research in Vietnam

11.3.1 Background and history

Vietnam has a population of 85 million and represents a potential market for healthcare equipment and pharmaceutical products. Despite the government's efforts to upgrade medical facilities, its healthcare sector remains inadequate. The country has 150,000 beds in 1,200 hospitals nationwide, including 1,000 state-owned hospitals. The number of healthcare clinics and medical centres is increasing, and there are presently over 20,000 private healthcare clinics and 11,000 traditional medicine centres. Fifteen of Vietnam's hospitals and clinics benefit from foreign investment, most notably the Franco-Vietnamese Hospital in Saigon South and L'Hôpital français in Hanoi. Major clinics include the Family Medical Practice run by Dr Rafi Kot which runs clinics in Hanoi, Ho Chi Minh City and Da Nang; SOS International; and the Columbia-Gia Dinh joint venture.

Key hospitals in Vietnam include:

- 115 People Hospital;
- Da Nang Hospital;

Published by Woodhead Publishing Limited, 2012

328 Clinical Research in Asia: Opportunities and Challenges

- Cho Ray Hospital;
- Dong Nai Hospital;
- Kien Giang Hospital;
- Ho Chi Minh Heart Institute;
- Ho Chi Minh Oncology Hospital;
- UBHN Cancer Centre;
- Hue Central Hospital;
- K Hospital;
- National Institute of Hygiene and Epidemiology Hospital;
- Bach Mai Hospital;
- Viet Duc Hospital.

According to the Ministry of Health (MOH), 90 per cent of district-level healthcare centres have X-ray facilities and 70 per cent have ultrasound machines. However, most of them are in poor condition due to maintenance and training problems. A large budget has been allocated to upgrade the nation's medical equipment. During 1997–2000, $1 billion was allocated for the healthcare sector, of which $29 million was used for medical equipment. During 2005–10, $1.8 billion was spent on building 56 new hospitals, of which $1 billion was for equipment. The government budget accounts for only 20 per cent of the total expenditure. The remaining 80 per cent comes from official development assistance from the World Bank, the United Nations Development Program, the Asian Development Bank and other donors. Government hospitals, clinics and healthcare centres account for 80 per cent of the market share of medical equipment. Private clinics, medical schools and research institutes account for 10–15 per cent of the market share. Hanoi and Ho Chi Minh City are two major markets for medical products.

11.3.2 Pharmaceutical industry in Vietnam

Between 1995 and 2005, Vietnam's pharmaceutical industry grew more than 20 per cent. Total pharmaceutical sales increased from $260 million in 1995 to $817 million in 2005. Annual per capita drug consumption grew from $4.20 in 1995 to $10 in 2005.

Published by Woodhead Publishing Limited, 2012

By 2012, annual average drug consumption will be $12–15 per person. Local production accounted for 48 per cent of the market share ($380 million) in 2005; by 2012, local production will meet only 60 per cent of the local need. Vietnam has about 30 foreign-funded pharmaceutical projects, supplying products worth $40 million a year. There are over 10,000 registered pharmaceutical products on the local market, of which local production accounts for 35 per cent, and foreign imports 65 per cent. Vietnam has about 900 pharmaceutical trading companies, 30,000 pharmacies and 60 companies with direct import licences. The MOH plans to build three major pharmaceutical manufacturing units in the north, centre and the south. These plants will produce essential drugs and medicines for preventing epidemics. According to the plan, herb-based drugs will account for 30 per cent of all locally-produced medicines by 2015. Drugs and pharmaceuticals must be registered before they may be imported into Vietnam. The application should include details of the manufacturing process, product test reports, analyses of samples and product labels. All documents must be both in English with notarised copies and in Vietnamese. Although most distribution is conducted by local Vietnamese entities, the drug and pharmaceutical exporter must also obtain a company registration licence in Vietnam.

11.3.3 The regulatory environment

Due to the recent growth of clinical research in Asia, the Vietnam government has implemented several key regulations. One such regulation is Decision No. 2626/QD-BYT on the 'Promulgation of the Procedure for Organising and Functioning of Ethical Committees for Bio-medical Research, Mission 2008–2012'. The regulation on clinical trials was implemented in 2007. Decision No. 799/QD-BYT of the Minister of Health on the promulgation of the 'Guidelines on Good Clinical Practice of Clinical Trials' was implemented in 2008. Decision No. 23/2008/QD-BYT of the Minister of Health on the Promulgation of the 'Regulations on Utilisation of Vaccine and Medical Immuno-biological Products in Prevention and Treatment' was implemented in the same year.

330　Clinical Research in Asia: Opportunities and Challenges

There are several legal and regulatory provisions in Vietnam describing different aspects of the process by which a clinical research protocol should be submitted for approval and implementation. These laws also address evaluation. Before 11 January 2007, there were no laws regulating clinical trials. However, the Vietnam MOH is engaged in the process of developing inclusive operational guidance to meet the increasing demands in clinical research in Vietnam while ensuring adherence to strict technical and ethical requirements.

11.3.4 Regulatory approval

The protocol is sent to the MOH's Department of Science and Training (DST) for approval following review by the ethics and science committees. The DST coordinates the process of reviewing protocols, monitoring trial implementation, and evaluating trial results as well as providing guidance. As the majority of clinical studies are multicentre projects, the protocol must follow a standard MOH format, clarifying actual procedures and written in either Vietnamese or English.

The application should include the following documents:

- protocol;
- investigators' brochure;
- letter of interest (format provided);
- a clinical research contract between the sponsor and the principal investigator (format provided);
- trial design;
- curriculum vitae of principal investigator and co-investigators;
- a statement on ethical considerations;
- description of product(s);
- summary of findings from non-clinical studies;
- summary of findings from pre-clinical studies;
- summary of findings from clinical trials of previous phases;
- a report from the committee at the institutional level on scientific and ethical aspects of the trial;

Published by Woodhead Publishing Limited, 2012

- samples of trial product(s), provided in the smallest possible packaging unit;
- for protocol on Phase IV clinical trial, a free sales certificate or certificate of pharmaceutical product, and certificate of GMP must be included.

The MOH must respond within 60 working days of receipt of the completed protocol documents. Once approved, the contents of a protocol must not be changed or revised without prior approval from the DST.

Vietnam has recently moved to enhance its medical device regulatory system. While imported medical devices do not need to be registered in Vietnam to be marketed, they do require an import licence. First-time device imports that use a novel method of diagnosis or treatment must go through clinical trials in at least three government-designated hospitals in Vietnam before they can apply for an import permit. The Department of Medical Equipment and Health Works (DMEHW) will review the manufacturer's application for clinical trials. If approved, the DMEHW will allow a certain number of devices to be imported solely for clinical trials. Once the trials are over, the manufacturer's local representative can then submit trial results in the import permit application. The DMEHW may decide on a case-by-case basis whether certain devices require in-country clinical trials if they are deemed safe and are approved for marketing in another country.

11.3.5 Safety reporting in Vietnam

While strongly promoted in developed countries, adverse drug reaction (ADR) reporting, especially in clinical trials, has not been prominent in Vietnam. Since its establishment in 1994, Vietnam's National ADR Centre has only received reports for the post-marketing phase in trials and not for actual trial phases. The National ADR Centre operates as an independent institute and is totally dependent on foreign financial support. This makes it difficult for the centre to be actively involved in processing and making

332 Clinical Research in Asia: Opportunities and Challenges

decisions about reported ADRs. ADR reporting by pharmaceutical and other commercial companies has been compulsory since 2006 but there is no similar requirement for research and treatment facilities such as hospitals. The current approach to ADR reporting in clinical research in Vietnam is only to encourage investigators, and does not establish any legally enforceable responsibilities. Recommendations focus merely on situations when the investigated product may pose a clinically important or unexpected risk.

11.3.6 Clinical trials in Vietnam

Vietnam is participating in approximately 7–8 new industry-sponsored trials every year. Even with the global slowdown in 2009, the flow of new trials to Vietnam has been maintained. There were 142 trials already listed in the registry, out of which only 35 trials are active and recruiting. Of the 142 studies undertaken in Vietnam, only 62 trials are industry-sponsored trials, 50 trials are sponsored by individual investigators, local institutions or hospitals, universities and other organisations and 32 trials are sponsored by the National Institutes of Health or other US federal agencies.

Further analysis of publicly available industry reports suggests that several GCP studies in diverse therapeutic areas are being conducted in Vietnam. Almost 63 per cent of the trials undertaken in Vietnam are in Phase III, 17 per cent trials are in Phase II and 17 per cent trials are in Phase IV. The figures clearly demonstrate that the country is not ready to compete for Phase I studies.

Although a few global pharmaceutical sponsors, such as AstraZeneca and GlaxoSmithKline, are actively conducting clinical research in Vietnam (see Table 11.6), the country is yet to catch up with other countries in Asia. In addition to these companies, institutions active in clinical research in Vietnam include Gynuity Health Projects, Hanoi Medical University, Karolinska Institutet, National Institute of Allergy and Infectious Diseases, National Institute of Hygiene and Epidemiology, and the Vietnam and Southeast Asia Infectious Disease Clinical Research Network.

Published by Woodhead Publishing Limited, 2012

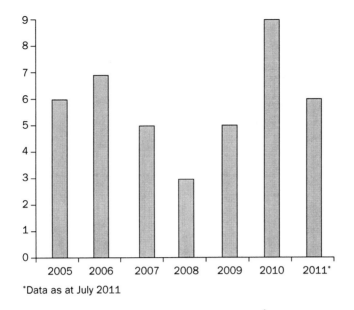

Figure 11.5 Growth of clinical trials in Vietnam
Source: www.clinicaltrials.gov (accessed July 2011)

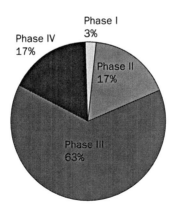

Figure 11.6 Clinical trials in Vietnam, by phase
Source: www.clinicaltrials.gov (accessed July 2011)

334 Clinical Research in Asia: Opportunities and Challenges

Table 11.6 Trials undertaken in Vietnam by major players

Industry sponsor	No. of trials
AstraZeneca	21
GlaxoSmithKline	8
Sanofi-Aventis	5
Bayer	4
Bristol-Myers Squibb	2
Novartis	2

Source: *www.clinicaltrials.gov* (accessed July 2011)

11.3.7 Challenges and future outlook

The MOH is in the process of developing guidelines for best practices in clinical trials and in training investigators and CRAs. The DST is also developing and piloting GCP standards and establishing a data management system in collaboration with the MOH's Drug Administration Department. In Vietnam, it is not always clear which MOH department is responsible for what, as some responsibilities do seem to overlap. While the DST is responsible for technical and ethical reviews, the Department of Finance is in charge of the financial aspects of protocols, and funding procedures are reviewed by the Department of Planning. This creates complicated and overlapping procedures for sponsors during the approval process. The MOH has been working to clarify responsibilities and the scope of review for each body.

Published by Woodhead Publishing Limited, 2012

12

Conclusions

Abstract: Clinical research business in Asia has its inherent strengths, weaknesses, opportunities and threats. In large part, the industry is subject to a number of environmental factors. This last chapter undertakes a detailed environmental analysis, highlighting the key macro-environments such as political, economic, socio-cultural, technological, legal and other environmental factors (PESTLE analysis). This will help in understanding the business environment of the CRO industry in Asian countries.

12.1 PESTLE analysis

Asia is a vast region, and home to almost 50 per cent of the world's population. While the clinical research business in Asia has its inherent strengths, weaknesses, opportunities and threats, it is predominantly controlled by environmental factors. In general terms, the environment for any business segment includes:

- the internal environment (e.g. staff/human resources);
- the micro-environment (e.g. competitors, external service providers, vendors, partners etc.); and
- the macro-environment
  - political environment;
  - economic environment;
  - socio-cultural factors;

Published by Woodhead Publishing Limited, 2012

336 Clinical Research in Asia: Opportunities and Challenges

- technological factors;
- legal environment;
- other environmental factors.

A useful model of analysis to understand the business environment of any industry is the PESTLE model. An analysis of the clinical research environment using the PESTLE model delves into various political, economic, socio-cultural, technological, legal and environmental factors in Asian countries.

12.2 Political environment

Clinical research is a highly regulated business and its success is dependent on health ministries championing a robust pro-global delivery mechanism. It is a scientific research model, requires people's participation and protects the safety and welfare of human beings. Favourable politics are essential as the business directly affects the public at large. The political environment of Asia is characterised by two emerging superpowers, namely India and China. No matter the political ethos, political systems in Asia are very bureaucratic. It has taken several decades for Asian countries to gain global acceptance with regards to their regulatory environment, intellectual property protection norms, confidentiality and data exclusivity and the management of clinical studies in their respective region. In spite of political backlash, terrorism and natural calamities, Asian governments have supported the growth of pharmaceutical research by providing ongoing assistance and incentives.

12.2.1 Regulatory environment

For a number of years, Asian countries have been demonstrating their capabilities with respect to the performance of clinical trials, yet there remain issues which discourage companies from bringing studies to the region. One such issue is the long approval process for clinical trials, as in some countries it can sometimes take longer than

Published by Woodhead Publishing Limited, 2012

six months for approval to be granted, which is understandably off-putting for sponsors. Nevertheless, thanks to the joint efforts of industry, hospitals and regulatory authorities, there has been a steady improvement in shortening these timelines. In some countries, institutional review board and regulatory submissions may now be done simultaneously, significantly improving the overall start-up timeline for new trials. In general, the approval timeline now is three to four months in most Asian countries except China where it still takes six to nine months. Table 12.1 summarises the average time to secure clinical trial approval in the Asian countries.

Regulatory bodies in most Asian countries are aware that the approval timelines need to be predictable and be further shortened without compromising the review mechanism. First-in-man studies

Table 12.1 Regulatory requirements in Asia

Country	Regulatory process	Approval timelines	First-in-man studies
Japan	Parallel	CTA 4 weeks EC 4–8 weeks	Permitted
India	Parallel	CTA 12–16 weeks EC 6–8 weeks	Not permitted unless the NCE is discovered in India
China	Sequential	CTA 16–36 weeks EC 4–8 weeks	Not permitted unless the NCE is discovered in China
South Korea	Parallel	CTA 8–12 weeks EC 4–8 weeks	Permitted
Taiwan	Parallel	CTA 8–12 weeks EC 4–8 weeks	Permitted
Singapore	Parallel	CTA 4–8 weeks EC 4–8 weeks	Permitted
Thailand	Sequential	CTA 4–8 weeks EC 8–12 weeks	Permitted
Malaysia	EC approval mandates CTA approval	CTA 8–12 weeks EC 8–12 weeks	Not permitted
Hong Kong	Parallel	CTA 16 weeks EC 4–6 weeks	Permitted
Philippines	Parallel	CTA 8–12 weeks EC 4–8 weeks	Permitted

Source: CTA; clinical trial application; EC, ethics committee; NCE, new chemical entity

Published by Woodhead Publishing Limited, 2012

are permitted in most countries except India, China and Malaysia. In India, first-in-man studies are permitted for new chemical entities discovered in India whereas molecules developed outside India are not permitted. Nonetheless, there is ongoing discussion between industry and regulators with respect to allowing first-in-man studies in India.

Restrictive regulatory requirements and regulatory differences across Asian countries affect the timing and cost of clinical trials. Some of the key regulatory requirements that may affect time and costs are:

- written clinical trial approval required for each trial;
- drug import licences required for each shipment;
- customs clearance during every consignment of drug import;
- annual renewal of import licence;
- export permission required for many Asian countries for export of biological samples to a central laboratory outside the Asian country;
- language requirements for documents (translations and certifications).

12.2.2 Intellectual property protection norms

Intellectual property protection is one of the most important concerns for global pharma companies undertaking studies in Asia. Prior to the implementation of patent laws, with the exception of a few countries such as Singapore, copying and reverse engineering was a major concern for pharma companies, especially those considering trials in India and China. To address these concerns, patent laws are now promulgated in many Asian countries in accordance with WTO standards. Nonetheless, global pharma companies are keeping a close eye on developments and treading cautiously when sharing critical product-related information with Asian countries. Measures have been taken to evaluate the implementation of the recently promulgated patent acts in letter and spirit. Now, with the WTO's agreement on Trade Related Aspects of Intellectual Property Rights,

Conclusions 339

member countries are required to establish minimum standards concerning the scope and use of intellectual property rights and the procedures for enforcing them. CROs in Asia are also enforcing stricter intellectual property procedures.

Confidentiality and data exclusivity, which in theory are binding in the West, are enforced in Asia, but there remains a question mark over the true spirit and accuracy over this enforcement, although the situation is improving. As such, when undertaking clinical trials in Asia, many sponsors move only non-critical functions to the country so that Asian offices do not need to handle critical information. Other companies undertake their critical outsourcing activities through their own legal entities or use a reliable global partner in these countries.

12.2.3 Improved infrastructure and processes

The majority of clinical trials in Asia are undertaken by public hospitals. The management of these hospitals, including the quality of their staff and infrastructure, is dependent on the political agenda of the respective country's government. Another major concern reported by pharma companies working in Asia is that the hospitals lack the infrastructure to support quality clinical research. This is certainly a legitimate issue in some Asian countries, but not Japan, Singapore, Hong Kong and a few others. In general, hospital facilities and the infrastructure for conducting studies and collecting/disseminating data are not equal to the high standard one might expect in a typically modern, high-tech hospital in the USA or Western Europe. However, quality is constantly improving and, in places, trial facilities and quality control are comparable with Western standards.

There is also concern about the unethical treatment of patients in countries without specific laws to protect participants. Many CROs claim to run facilities that are compliant with the ICH-GCP standards but in practice this is not the case. Many Asian countries are trying to regulate CROs and service providers. In India, the government is attempting to regulate CROs by registering them through the submission of proper documentation and controlling

Published by Woodhead Publishing Limited, 2012

340 Clinical Research in Asia: Opportunities and Challenges

them through periodic inspections. In India, China, South Korea and many other Asian countries, unless the CRO is officially recognised, they cannot obtain the necessary licence to conduct trials on behalf of the pharmaceutical sponsor in those countries.

12.2.4 Government incentives

Governments in Asia are encouraging R&D related investment directly or through public–private partnership. Governments across Asia have established a number of biotech/science parks and special economic zones. Some parks that are particularly well-adapted to medical R&D include Singapore's Biopolis; Taiwan's Kaohsiung Science Park; China's Zhangjiang High-Tech Park; and in India, Genome Valley in Hyderabad, and the Technology and Knowledge Parks in Mumbai, Bangalore, Ahmedabad and Pune. Most pharmaceutical research units and CROs operate from these special economic zones to take advantage of exemptions from tariffs and various tax and duty benefits. The government of India has exempted customs duty for the import of drugs and devices for clinical trial purposes. To promote clinical trial business, service tax is also not applicable.

12.3 Economic environment

12.3.1 Cost-effectiveness

Asia offers a significant time and cost advantage in terms of being able to recruit clinical trial patients quickly. Of all the Asian countries, Japan virtually offers no cost savings. The per patient cost for clinical trials in Japan is comparable or even higher than in USA and Europe. Because of these prohibitive costs, Japan's clinical research sector is not very mature. When global pharma companies conduct clinical trials in Japan, it is usually only to get the product approved for the Japanese market. China and India typically provide the most cost savings. The investigator fee in China and India is

Published by Woodhead Publishing Limited, 2012

Conclusions 341

often 30–40 per cent lower than that in the USA and Western Europe, while the cost of the clinical test and procedures is commonly 50–60 per cent lower than in the USA and Western Europe. Thus, the cost of conducting clinical trials in China and India is roughly one-third of what it would be in Western countries. Trials in Singapore and Hong Kong are costly but definitely cheaper than in Western countries. Countries such as Malaysia, Thailand, Taiwan and South Korea offer a lower level of savings than China and India, but generally have more sophisticated facilities and infrastructure as well as practitioners with more experience.

12.3.2 Human resources cost

Although most Asian countries (except Japan) have lower overall labour costs than the USA and Europe due to differences in the cost of living, India and China stand out. Both countries have extremely large, well-educated populations, with several hundred thousand science and engineering university graduates turned out annually in each country. Fresh graduates in these disciplines (i.e. without experience) can cost only $2,000 to $10,000 a year (varying widely by school and location). Qualified and experienced staff can earn a quarter of the salaries they would require in the USA or Europe.

Although the number of Asians trained in science and engineering fields is quite large, some may adapt poorly to working in a Western corporate environment. Thus, R&D personnel in Asia who have experience in Western firms are in high demand, and poaching is a significant risk. It is possible to get good results from fresh graduates if one's company finds good prospects and trains them comprehensively over time. However, if selection, training and retention programmes are not well thought out, the cost savings may not pan out.

The Westernised R&D talent available in Asia also is growing as Asians who have studied in Western universities return to their home countries to work. Some help local pharma companies grow. Some also return to their home countries to start their own companies, creating stronger Asian competition with Western companies.

Published by Woodhead Publishing Limited, 2012

342 Clinical Research in Asia: Opportunities and Challenges

12.4 Socio-cultural forces

Clinical research requires people's participation but must follow basic societal principles, i.e. the respect for the individual, beneficence, justice and protection of the subject's best interests. In some Asian countries, however, participation in clinical research is considered as a taboo subject due to people's poor socio-economic and cultural conditions. Much discussion has focused on the idea that impoverishment, illiteracy and social ills in Asian populations may have an impact on the ethical conduct of clinical trials. It is a commonly-held belief that impoverished people with limited education cannot decide of their own free will and may end up participating in a trial through socio-economic compulsion. Numerous other observers argue against this belief, however, pointing out the danger of generalisations. The potential subject may be poor and illiterate, but this must not be mistaken for a lack of common sense or intelligence; subjects should be capable of making decisions on their own. They may not comprehend the complicated statistical design of a clinical trial, but if the investigator engages them through proper counselling and provides them with adequate information, they can comprehend the situation and decide for themselves whether or not to participate in the trial. If they are not convinced, they will not participate. It must be remembered that such potential subjects have an equally strong commitment to their life and loved ones as the rich and more literate, hence one cannot take them for granted just because they are on the lower social strata.

Impoverishment is considered by many to be a compelling factor for potential subjects in Asia to become involved in clinical trials. But if one looks into the existing healthcare system, the majority of the impoverished population in India or China, in any case, depend on free or subsidised treatment from public hospitals and dispensaries as universal health insurance does not exist in Asia. As such, some subjects may see participating in a clinical trial as a means to ease their additional economic burdens in terms of medication and treatments. In a few studies, the trial design demands additional visits for tests and procedures. In such instances, the sponsor

Published by Woodhead Publishing Limited, 2012

Conclusions 343

provides compensation toward the conveyance, stay and loss of wages for the subject and other earning members of their family, as well as incidental expenses. This acts as a motivation and improves subject compliance and retention. Similarly, if the investigational product is temperature-sensitive, sometimes the sponsor may provide pool-refrigerators for use by the patients, either through a facility attached to the investigator's site or through their local physicians. These represent genuine compensation and logistical economic support for trial subjects, and would not be construed as an inducement or compulsion for enrolment.

At first glance, some of these costs appear to be additional burdens to the sponsor. However, such costs rarely represent a major expense and should be balanced against the fast recruitment potential and the increased subject retention. Furthermore, poor and illiterate subjects tend to be more compliant, as they are very sincere and follow protocol tests, instructed procedures and physician advice. To eliminate any concern regarding potential exploitation in developing countries because of illiteracy and poverty, it is in the interest of every pharmaceutical sponsor to maintain high ethical standards for clinical trials. However, where sponsors act with fairness and respect in equal measure, there can be no accusations of exploitation.

12.4.1 Language barrier

As most global pharma companies are headquartered in the USA and Western Europe, sponsor companies expect clinical research data and related documents to be generated in English. It therefore presents a great operational challenge if the study is to be conducted in Asian countries as each country has a number of different languages (Table 12.2).

In Asian countries, such as Japan, China, Korea and Taiwan, all essential documents must be translated into their local official languages as neither patient nor investigator is likely to have English as a first language. Although the official language of India is Hindi, as per the constitution, and most people understand Hindi (barring a few states in the southern region), the English language continues

Published by Woodhead Publishing Limited, 2012

344 Clinical Research in Asia: Opportunities and Challenges

Table 12.2 Languages in Asia

Country	Languages
Japan	Japanese
China	Mandarin, Cantonese
India	English, Hindi, Bengali, Oriya, Gujarati, Malayalam, Telugu, Tamil, Punjabi, Marathi, Gujarati
Indonesia	Bahasa-Indonesian, Sundanese
Malaysia	Malay, Chinese, Tamil
Singapore	English, Malay, Mandarin, Chinese, Tamil
South Korea	Korean
Taiwan	Standard Mandarin, Taiwanese, Hakka
Philippines	Philippino, English, Bicolano, Cebuano, Ilocano, Hiligaynon or Ilonggo, Kapampangan, Pangasinan, Tagalog and Waray-Waray
Thailand	Thai, Malay, Khmer

to be used for all official purposes. In India, the medium of higher-level science, medicine, pharmacy, nursing and alternative medicines education is English. Hence, although culturally India is a Hindi-speaking community, because of the educational systems, the physicians, nurses, monitors, and most literate subjects speak, write and understand English. Even India's judicial and governing institutions, health ministry, regulatory bodies and ethics committee use English as the medium for day-to-day communication and management. Nevertheless, it remains the case that many subjects in India are illiterate or have only a limited education and can read, write and speak only in their local language.

Hence, looking at the multilingual Asian culture, sponsors and other clinical research stakeholders must make every effort to ensure that essential documents are available in local languages so that they are easily understood by the patients, investigators and all concerned. What is essential in the Asian context is proper counselling and thorough guidance by the investigators, which may indirectly demand a lot of time spent mentoring the subjects to ensure recruitment and retention.

Published by Woodhead Publishing Limited, 2012

12.4.2 Ethnicity

Besides being multilingual, Asia offers multi-ethnic and multi-racial cultures. Ethnicity may affect trial results due to different metabolic rates and other genetic effects. The value of studies of Western subjects in Asian populations (and vice versa) is the subject of great debate.

Cultural differences in the practice of medicine may also affect trial execution and may affect trial results. For example, the concurrent use of traditional medicines in China or alternative medicines in India may be unreported, but can affect study results. Similarly, the standard practice of care in India, such as the use of physicians (not nurses) to take blood samples, may over-report the time spent by physicians in clinical research activities.

12.5 Technological factors

Technological advancement is rapidly changing the clinical trial environment. As just one example, web-based real-time data transfer has replaced paper-based data collection. In pursuit of gains in time and quality, the industry has moved from traditional methods of clinical trial management to electronic/digital options such as electronic data capture (EDC), digital pen and paper technology, interactive voice response systems (IVRS) and mobile phone technology. This requires the sponsor, CRO, investigators and site staff to invest not only in their technology infrastructure but also in training.

Yet while clinical research at the global level is migrating rapidly from paper-based data collection, Asia is still slow, and Asian sites and hospitals are still undertaking paper-intensive clinical research. Indeed, the infrastructure at many hospitals acts as a technological barrier; for example, many sites participating in EDC trials for the first time would need infrastructure such as laptops for the study. Sponsors must also reflect on sites' connectivity, speed of data transfer and data security-related issues. Many CROs and pharma companies have designated their Asian units as their global data-entry hubs for conducting low-end labour-intensive activities.

Published by Woodhead Publishing Limited, 2012

346 Clinical Research in Asia: Opportunities and Challenges

Asia offers a huge challenge for pharma companies to reach rural markets. The infrastructure and distribution network for sales of pharmaceutical products have less penetration in the rural market, while R&D is still concentrated in metropolitan cities such as Mumbai, Delhi, Beijing, Shanghai, Bangkok and Seoul. Rural healthcare lacks adequate infrastructure, connectivity, laboratory facilities and communication media. However, there has been significant growth in infrastructure in the last decade. India has become a world player in the provision of information technology services, and companies there have signed long-term contracts with global pharma companies for their clinical data management, pharmacovigilance, biostatistics and medical writing functions. China, Singapore and Hong Kong all have excellent laboratory and public transport infrastructure; their IT infrastructure is also well developed. Yet the number of EDC or IVRS service providers in Asia is very limited. That said, Asia will soon catch up with the advancements in clinical research technology.

12.6 Legal environment

The legal environment in Asia is very challenging due to bureaucracy in some countries, although many countries have improved their legal framework significantly. In many Asian countries such as Japan, India, China and Korea, pharma companies and CROs require a legal entity in order to undertake or support clinical research. In Asia, only the legal entity can apply for clinical trial permission and the drug import licence. Setting up a legal entity takes from two to three months in many countries in Asia; China is a notable exception, as the process can take from nine to 12 months. However, the process is very straightforward in Singapore and Hong Kong and setting up a legal entity can be done more quickly.

Other legal frameworks which are important for clinical research are the indemnification, insurance, patents and contracts and agreements, which are guided by global regulations and supported by country-specific laws. Legal interpretations are key as most of these laws have industry-wide coverage. Inevitably, the industry will face practical issues of how to handle legal challenges with regards to patents and copyrights, insurance claims and handling fraudsters or fraud.

Published by Woodhead Publishing Limited, 2012

Given the complexity of language, racial differences and multiple time zones in Asian countries, it is necessary to harmonise regulations at a regional level. While most countries have based their country-specific GCP on ICH-GCP, only time will tell whether we will have harmonised Asian GCP standards in the future.

12.7 Other environmental factors

Other factors that are important for clinical research business in Asia are the availability of potential subjects, qualified doctors, and CROs and other service providers.

12.7.1 Patient pool and doctors

Asia has more than 4 billion people (nearly two-thirds of the world's population), and many of these people are concentrated in large metropolitan areas. With the largest urban population in the world, Asia provides a large pool of treatment-naïve patients from multi-ethnic and multi-racial backgrounds. Asia hosts a wide spectrum of disease types and the treatment of major diseases is centralised in major hospitals, making patient access easier. Asia has a strong network of highly-qualified and Western-educated doctors practising modern advanced medicines who are inclined to work in global clinical trials. As a result, finding subjects with specific or rare diseases in populous countries such as China and India tends to take significantly less time than in the USA and Europe. Accelerating the product pipeline can be just as useful to the sponsoring company as lowering other overhead expenses.

Another important element in the success of clinical research in any territory is to find an appropriate and qualified CRO to manage the clinical trial. It is always a tough call whether to use a local CRO or a reputed global CRO that has offices in Asia. The global CRO may have excellent infrastructure and experienced resources in the USA or Europe, but its offices in Asia may not be staffed with the same quality of resources. Alternatively, the local CRO may have local knowledge and expertise better suited for certain clinical studies because it can devote more personalised attention to smaller projects.

Published by Woodhead Publishing Limited, 2012

348 Clinical Research in Asia: Opportunities and Challenges

12.7.2 Local partners

With the growth in Asian CRO business, many local players have also set up operations in this region. Most of them have operations in a single country, although a few have branched out to cover the Asia region. Table 12.3 provides a list of CROs local to Asia.

Table 12.3 Regional CROs in Asia

CRO	Country
EPS CRO	Japan, China, Singapore, Korea, Taiwan, Hong Kong
Protech Pharmaservices Corporation	Japan, China, Singapore, Korea, Taiwan, Hong Kong
Gleneagles CRC	China, Singapore, Indonesia, Thailand, Malaysia, Philippines, South Korea
China Clinical Trial Centre	China
Jinsite	China
PharmaResearch Corporation	China
Sundia Investment Group	China
RPS (Paramax)	China
Tigermed	China
Clinical Trial Concepts Limited	Hong Kong
Bridgetech Medical Technologies Research	Hong Kong
Biosafety Research Centre Japan	Japan
CMIC Co Ltd Japan	Japan, China, Singapore, Korea, Taiwan
CoreMed Corporation Japan	Japan
InCROM Institute Inc Japan	Japan
Mediscience Planning Inc	Japan
Maccine – Preclinical CRO	Singapore
Virginia Contract Research Organisation Co., Ltd.	Taiwan
PharmaCRO	Korea
Siro Clinpharm	India
Ercon Accunova	India
Dignosearch	India
Clininvent	India

Published by Woodhead Publishing Limited, 2012

Other service providers that contribute significantly to the growth of global clinical research business are as follows:

- huge IT and IT enabled services that support global data management, pharmacovigilance, statistics and medical writing services (e.g. Infosys, Cognisant, Satyam, Accenture, Tata Consulting Services and the like);
- central laboratories (India, China and Singapore have world-class central laboratory facilities);
- contract manufacturing and packaging facilities (India has the largest US FDA approved contract manufacturing facilities);
- couriers and cool-chain service providers;
- translation agencies;
- high-quality printers;
- insurance service providers.

Although many vendors provide services in each of these areas, only a few understand the full importance of confidentiality and the other security and documentation requirements of the global clinical trial business.

12.8 Strategic issues for the CRO industry

During the last two decades, while global pharma companies have increased their R&D investments in Asia, regional pharma companies both small and large have been increasingly considering Asia in their drug development initiatives. There has been a perceptible change in the Western mindset – from scepticism to acceptance – of the capability, skill sets and data quality of Asian clinical trials. In the last decade, Asia has been the centre of attention and the new emerging clinical research hub, charting a positive growth story for the contract research industry. The strategic issues that will shape the future of the CRO industry are explored below.

Published by Woodhead Publishing Limited, 2012

12.8.1 Organic growth vs mergers and acquisitions

After 1995, many global CROs entered Asia. Many of entered India first and then spread to China and other Asian countries. Most of them grew organically or through the acquisition of a smaller niche player in a related sector. As the industry grew, many global CROs with offices throughout the region based their regional headquarters in Singapore. Many CROs still focus their main operation in India or China (or both) and maintain additional offices in one or two other Asian countries.

Local CROs emerged out of the country-specific regulatory requirements for undertaking smaller bio-analytical and bioequivalence studies for the registration of generic products. Predominantly, these CROs were the off-shoots of local pharma companies or promoted by local entrepreneurs with experience in pharmaceutical or related business. A few local CROs branched out to multiple Asian countries. In the last five years, a few global CROs have acquired local CROs in order to scale up their business in the region more quickly. Mergers and acquisitions of CROs in Asia include the following:

- PRA International acquired Sterling Synergy, India, a Deepak Fertilizer Group company based in Pune and Mumbai;
- PPD acquired Excel PharmaStudies and Bioduro, both in China;
- Parexel acquired Apex International, Taiwan CRO, China;
- Accunova, Bangalore merged with Ecron, a German CRO;
- Pharmaron China acquired Bridge Lab, China;
- Jubilant Organosys, an Indian CRO acquired Target Research Associates, USA;
- Charles River acquired WuXi PharmaTech China.

Many others are pursuing organic growth and collaborating with strong local CROs as preferred service providers in the region. Looking at the potential of the CRO industry, many lease fund companies have also invested in local CROs.

Published by Woodhead Publishing Limited, 2012

12.8.2 Generic innovation

Over the last decade, generic pharmaceutical manufacturers in Asia have expanded their reach to market their products globally. While launching their me-too product in new territories, they are undertaking multiple new registration studies. As new technologies and bodies of scientific knowledge emerge, these generic companies are also being innovative and trying their molecules in newer indications, creating whole new sets of opportunities. Breakthroughs in science, innovation and technology continue to create novel opportunities for new products and processes. This has increased the pace of the CRO industry, and many generic companies that were not very effective in research are now being innovative and investing heavily in new product development.

12.8.3 Increased competition

For pharmaceutical company to launch a new product, it needs to undertake clinical research in a territory. Thus, competition starts even in the early phase when the team set up new product planning. Whether to include a region in clinical research is determined by whether the product is going to be marketed in the region. Even for the CRO, the country selection for a clinical trial is based on cost and the pharmaceutical company's objectives. The CRO industry is a people-oriented service industry. A major issue facing the industry is the intense competition on price. Due to varying standards of service providers, there is no standard price for global and local CROs. The industry has seen a legion of new market entrants, increased competition among key players and industry consolidation. Competitive advantage within the industry is being constantly redefined and to maintain their presence, key industry players are being forced to revamp their service offerings from full-service CRO to functional service provider to contract staffing models.

Published by Woodhead Publishing Limited, 2012

352 Clinical Research in Asia: Opportunities and Challenges

12.8.4 Competitive research

Clinical research in Asia is still concentrated in big hospitals and medical colleges in metropolitan cities. As such, there is strong competition among the pool of qualified investigators to recruit patients for global trials. Hence, when a pharma sponsor looks for CROs to submit bids based on feasibility, the CROs on the ground approach the same set of investigators for feedback. With the growth in economy, and advancement in science and technology, people are generally very well informed about the disease and standard of care. With varying understanding and increased purchasing power, it is always a great challenge to recruit patients in a clinical trial for new drugs when proven drugs are already on the market. As clinical research in Asia is a business with limited quality service providers, few experienced investigators exposed to a constant patient pool, where price and offerings are not standardised, it presents a great challenge in terms of competition for cost, timely recruitment and quality.

12.8.5 Western trial design

As most global clinical research outsourcing originates from USA and Europe, the clinical trial design is always based on Westernised disease management. In the current scenario, most trials are designed without proper consultation with Asian investigators. However, as Asia offers significant variance in racial, genetic and ethnic profiles, it is advisable for global pharma companies to design clinical trials to recognise ethnic diversity and ensure sufficient trials are conducted in other countries. Pharmaceutical companies are required to set up trial parameters to include a range of ethnicities consistent with FDA guidelines. Ethnic diversity may be an asset if future plans involve the sale of the product within the clinical trial country.

12.8.6 Changing geo-political environment

The global political environment has become a major factor. Due to the socio-political consequences of healthcare and medicines, the

Published by Woodhead Publishing Limited, 2012

Conclusions   **353**

pharmaceutical industry is facing increasing political pressure to reduce prices and control costs. In certain geo-political areas, particularly in developing economies, governments are increasing pressure on pharmaceutical firms and CROs to act in the interest of their countries, something that is likely to intensify in the future. For example, if the new molecule being tested is of significant interest for addressing tropical and infectious diseases in Asian countries, regulators even approve the first-in-man studies.

12.9   Future outlook

With steadily increasing drug development costs and significant time spent on clinical trials, outsourcing clinical trials in Asia has rapidly become an appealing option for many firms. Many companies have already successfully conducted many drug development global studies in Asia. With close clinical trial monitoring, Asian hospitals and investigators can perform high-quality GCP studies and can compete very favourably in terms of patient recruitment and costs with other centres in Europe, the USA and Latin America. Many Western companies are now outsourcing all phases of product development, including drug discovery, R&D and clinical trials to Asia as the medical communities in Asian countries continue to provide good-quality output with demonstrable cost reduction.

Although intellectual property protection issues still exist, it is prudent for all stakeholders to monitor intellectual property legislation and enforcement without relying on unsubstantiated information. Pharma companies should leverage CROs to understand the target country's customs, regulations and medical practices before establishing trials. As a risk mitigation strategy for pharma companies who are new in Asian countries, working with multinational and/or established local CROs with hands-on in-country experience is advisable. Pharmaceutical companies should develop partnerships, while maintaining healthy competition among vendors, and must develop detailed/practical contingency plans. It is advisable for global pharma companies to design clinical trials to

Published by Woodhead Publishing Limited, 2012

recognise ethnic diversity and ensure that sufficient trials are conducted in other countries. Global pharma companies should diversify their portfolio of clinical trial geographies to balance patient pool opportunities, cost efficiencies, expertise and regulatory risk.

Bibliography

Bhatt, A. and Sahoo, U. (2004) '2010 – Indian clinical research odyssey', available at: *http://saffron.pharmabiz.com/article/detnews.asp?articleid=20742&sectionid* (accessed 1 January 2010).

Bhuller, Rhenu (2010) 'Singapore shifting to a specialized CRO market', *Frost and Sullivan Market Insight*, 3 November, available at: *http://www.frost.com/prod/servlet/market-insight-top.pag?docid=213988299* (accessed 2 June 2010).

BioNet Asia Pacific (2008) 'Biotechnology industry overview, Taiwan', 9 September, available at: *http://www.bionetasiapacific.com/userfiles/files/IndustryOverview/taiwan.pdf* (accessed 15 September 2010).

Business World (2010) 'Death of a dream', 13 September, available at: *http://www.businessworld.in* (accessed 9 December 2010).

CDSCO (2005) 'GCP for clinical research in India', available at: *http://www.cdsco.nic.in/html/GCP.htm* (accessed 15 September 2010).

Clinical Trial Magnifier (2009) 'The University of Hong Kong, Clinical Trial Centre', *Clinical Trial Magnifier* 2(2), available at: *http://www.ctmagnifier.org/2009/M2009_2_02.aspx* (accessed 14 November 2010).

Clinical Trial Magnifier (2010) 'A case study: refining clinical research infrastructure', *Clinical Trial Magnifier* 3: 203–18, available at: *http://www.ctmagnifier.org/2010/M2010_3_03.aspx* (accessed 15 January 2011).

Data Monitor (2008) 'Online recruitment is streamlining clinical trials', available at: *http://www.datamonitor.com/store/News/online_recruitment_is_streamlining_clinical_trials?* (accessed 9 June 2010).

Ganguly, N. K. (2006) 'Biospectrumindia', available at: *http://www.biospectrumindia.ciol.com* (accessed 15 September 2010).

356 Clinical Research in Asia: Opportunities and Challenges

Gin, Beh Swan (2004) 'Singapore – the biopolis of Asia', *SMA News* 36 (11): 11–13, available at: *http://www.sma.org.sg/sma_news/3611/research_bsg.pdf* (accessed 1 May 2011).

Goldberg, Mark A. (2008) 'Japan's step towards global studies', *PharmaFocusAsia*, No. 6, available at: *http://www.pharmafocusasia.com/magazine/archives/issue6.htm#e* (accessed 18 February 2010).

Gonzalez, Joaquin L. III (1996) 'Evolution of the Philippine health care system during the last forty years of development administration', *Asian Journal of Public Administration* 18(2): 168–200.

Health Science Authority, Singapore (2003) 'Pharmaceutical Regulatory Information System (PRISM): Clinical Trial Certificate Module, User Manual Ver 1.1', available at: *www.hsa.gov.sg/...regulation/clinical_trials/.../HSA_CTC_Internet_Manual_v1.1_20_Aug_2003.doc* (accessed 12 September 2010).

IMS Health (2010) 'IMS Health market prognosis, 2010', available at: *http://www.imshealth.com/portal/site/imshealth/menuitem.a46c6d4df3db4b3d88f611019418c22a/?vgnextoid=4b8c410b6c718210VgnVCM100000ed152ca2RCRD* (accessed 12 September 2010).

Jacobs, Dianne (2005) 'In search of future leaders, Managing the global talent pipeline', *IVEY Business Journal*, available at: *http://wwwold.iveybusinessjournal.com/view_article.asp?intArticle_ID=547* (accessed 1 January 2010).

Japanese CRO Association (2010) 'Annual Report 2010', available at: *http://www.jcroa.gr.jp/* (accessed 15 September 2010).

Karlberg, Johan P. E. (2008) 'Industry-sponsored clinical trials in China', *Clinical Trial Magnifier* 1(8): 1–32, available at: *http://www.ctmagnifier.org/2008/M2008_1_08.aspx* (accessed 15 September 2010).

Karlberg, Johan P. E. (2008) 'Industry-sponsored clinical trials in South Korea', *Clinical Trial Magnifier* 1(9): 1–28, available at: *http://www.ctmagnifier.org/2008/M2008_1_09.aspx* (accessed 20 September 2011).

Karlberg, Johan P. E. (2011) 'Proficient clinical research city: What is the Hong Kong secret?', paper presented at The University of Hong Kong, Hong Kong SAR, 5 January.

Kelly, Edward J. (2007) 'Thailand's pharmaceutical industry – an update', *Thai American Business*, Vol. 4, available at: *http://www.amchamthailand.com/asp/view_doc.asp?DocCID=2806* (accessed 1 January 2010).

Published by Woodhead Publishing Limited, 2012

Bibliography 357

Kermani, Faiz (2004) 'Japanese R&D: Branching Out', *Applied Clinical Trials*, August, available at: *http://www.actmagazine.com/appliedclinical trials* (accessed 1 January 2010).

Kermani, Faiz (2005) 'A viewpoint on South Korean biotech', *Drug Discovery Today* 10(10): 685–8, available at: *http://journals2005. pasteur.ac.ir/DDT/10(10).pdf* (accessed 25 June 2011).

Kermani, Faiz (2005) 'Facing up to Japan's pharmaceutical future', *Pharma Chem*, April: 45–8.

Kermani, Faiz and Bonacossa, P. (2003) 'New ways to recruit trial subjects', *Applied Clinical Trials*, February, available at: *http://www.actmagazine. com/appliedclinicaltrials* (accessed 15 September 2010).

Kermani, Faiz and McGuire, S. (2003) 'Japan's ageing challenge', *Transpharma* 1(2): 34–7, available at: *http://www.chiltern.com/press/ Articles/TP02Japan.pdf* (accessed 15 September 2010).

Kulkarni, Narayan (2004) 'Data manager', available at: *http://www. bioinfo.ernet.in/datamanager.pdf* (accessed 11 July 2010).

Liu, Eva and Lee, Joseph (1998) 'Healthcare expenditure and financing in Taiwan', available at: *http://www.legco.gov.hk/yr97-98/english/sec/ library/08plc.pdf* (accessed 15 March 2010).

Liu, Jessica (2010) 'Demystifying the intricacies of Asian clinical trials', *Foresight*, available at: *http://www.incresearch.com/resource/foresight/ foresight_201001-demystifying-asian-trials.pdf* (accessed 17 July 2010).

Ministry of Economic Affairs (2009) 'Taiwan: introduction to biotechnology and pharmaceutical industries in Taiwan, Republic of China, available at: *http://www.bpipo.org.tw/download/pdf/2009/1009802416_en.pdf* (accessed 9 September 2010).

Ministry of Health, Malaysia (2004) 'Malaysian Guidelines for Good Clinical Practice', 2nd edn.

Mukherjee, Shoibal (2005) 'Pharmaceutical research and development in India', available at: *http://www.touchbriefings.com/pdf/1133/Mukherjee [1].pdf* (accessed 1 January 2010).

National Committee for Clinical Research (2010) 'Industry-sponsored clinical research in Malaysia: new chapter', available at: *http://nccr.gov. my/view_file.cfm?fileid=27* (accessed 23 June 2010).

National Pharmaceutical Control Bureau, Ministry of Health, Malaysia (2009) 'Guideline for application of clinical trial import license and clinical trial exemption in Malaysia', 5th edn (Version 3.1), available at:

Published by Woodhead Publishing Limited, 2012

http://www.crc.gov.my/guidelines/pdf/2%20Guidelines%20for%20the %20Application%20of%20CTIL.pdf (accessed 23 June 2010).

Organisation of Pharmaceutical Producers of India (OPPI) (2008) 'OPPI position paper – regulatory data protection, Mumbai', available at: *http://www.indiaoppi.com/OPPIpositionDataProtection.pdf* (accessed 15 September 2010).

Pharmaceuticals and Medical Devices Agency (2008) 'Annual report FY 2008', available at: *http://www.pmda.go.jp/english/about/pdf/2008/ annual_report_FY2008.pdf* (accessed 1 January 2010).

Polastro, E. T. and Little, A. D. (2004) 'Asia outlook: Chinese and Indian markets', available at: *http://conference.contractpharma.com/articles/ 2004/10/images/chinese-and-indian-markets.pdf* (accessed 26 November 2010).

Royal Danish Embassy (2006) 'Sector overview, the pharmaceutical industry in Thailand', available at: *http://www.ambbangkok.um.dk/NR/rdonlyres/ 4EC3899D-14E5-474D-B562-C5048792D722/0/SectorOverview PharmaceuticalIndustryJune2006.pdf* (accessed 21 June 2011).

Sahoo, Umakanta (2004) 'Laboratories and clinical trials in India', *The Monitor* 18(2): 25–7.

Sahoo, Umakanta (2004) 'Clinical trials in India', *The Monitor* 18(3): 33–6.

Sahoo, Umakanta (2005) 'India: clinical research careers looking up', *The Monitor* 19(4): 37–42.

Sahoo, Umakanta and Dipti, Sawant (2007) 'The clinical research profession in India', *The Monitor* 21(5): 51–5.

SFDA (2010) 'Provision for Drug Registration, SFDA (order No. 28) China', available at: *http://www.sfdachina.com/info/64-1.htm* (accessed 16 February 2011).

Thailand Pharmaceutical Update (2008) 'Lifesciences intellectual property review', available at: *http://content.yudu.com/A1engd/LSIPRannual2008/ resources/95.htm* (accessed 14 September 2010).

Varawalla, Nermeen (2006) 'Conducting clinical trials in Asia', *Applied Clinical Trials*, available at: *http://appliedclinicaltrialsonline.findpharma. com/appliedclinicaltrials/CRO%2FSponsor/Conducting-Clinical-Trials-in-Asia/ArticleStandard/Article/detail/334577* (accessed 15 September 2010).

Vietnam Ministry of Health (2007) 'Implementing clinical research in Vietnam', workshop proceedings, Hanoi, 12–13 July.

Published by Woodhead Publishing Limited, 2012

Bibliography

Virtual Asia (2001) 'The healthcare system in Philippines, special report', available at: available at: *http://www.philippinesforum.com/resources/research/files/health_ph.pdf* (accessed 5 September 2010).

Wang, Hui-Po (2003) 'Clinical trials in Taiwan, regulatory achievement and current status', available at: *http://www.cde.org.tw/Data/CDEDoc/Documents/Clinical%20Trials%20in%20Taiwan%E2%80%94Regulatory%20Achievement%20and%20Current%20Status.pdf* (accessed 9 June 2010).

Wong, Ellick (2002) 'Regulatory environment and clinical trials in South East Asia', available at: *http://www.scribd.com/doc/56220669/Regulatory-Enviroment-and-Clinical-Trials-in-South-East-Asia* (accessed 1 January 2010).

World Bank and International Finance Corporation (2010) 'Doing business in China', available at: *http://www.doingbusiness.org/~/media/fpdkm/doing%20business/documents/annual-reports/english/db11-fullreport.pdf* (accessed 9 December 2010).

World Health Organization (2002) 'Handbook of good clinical practice, a guidance for implementation', available at: *http://ori.hhs.gov/documents/WHOHandbookonGCP04-06.pdf* (accessed 1 January 2010).

World Medical Association (2008) 'Declaration of Helsinki: ethical principles for medical research involving human subjects', available at: *http://www.wma.net/en/30publications/10policies/b3/17c.pdf* (accessed 15 September 2010).

Wu, Yanrui (1999) 'The emerging healthcare market in Taiwan', Working Paper No. 92, University of Western Australia.

Young, Jack Lee (2009) 'Clinical trials in Korea: why Korea', available at: *http://www.lskglobal.com/pdf/Why%20Korea.pdf* (accessed 20 June 10).

Zabidi-Hussin, Z. A. M. H. (2007) 'Challenges in clinical research in Malaysia', *The Medical Journal of Malaysia* 62(4): 275–7.

Index

abbreviated new drug approvals (ANDA), 56
Adverse Drug Reaction Suffering Relief Fund, 32
Adverse drug reactions (ADRs)
in China, 139–41
in Vietnam, 331–2
Agency for Science, Technology and Research (A*STAR), 200
Asia
clinical research
background, 1–2
boom, 8–13
business, 5–7
cost-effectiveness, 340–1
country segmentation analysis, 15–17
economic environment, 340–1
environmental factors, 347–9
future outlook, 353–4
government incentives, 340
human resources cost, 341
improved infrastructure and processes, 339–40
intellectual property protection norms, 338–9
legal environment, 346–7
local partners, 348–9
patient pool and doctors, 347
PESTLE analysis of, 335–6
political environment, 336–40
regulatory environment, 336–8
regulatory requirements, 338
socio-cultural forces, 342–5
SWOT analysis of, 22–5
clinical trials in, 8–14, 17–19
US FDA inspection of, 19–22
contract research organisation
growth of, 13
strategic issues, 349–53
global pharmaceutical market, 2–5
health expenditure, 3–4

Belmont Report of 1979, 95–6
Bureau of Pharmaceutical Affairs (BPA), 185, 187
Business Registration Act, Singapore, 217

Central Drug Standard Control Organization (CDSCO), 73–5
Central Ethics Committee on Human Research (CECHR), 73–4
Centre for Drug Evaluation (CDE), 183–5, 187
certificate of approval (COA), 250

Published by Woodhead Publishing Limited, 2012

362 Clinical Research in Asia: Opportunities and Challenges

China
  clinical research in, 107–48
    ADR monitoring, 139–41
    economic environment, 132–4
    environmental analysis,
      130–46
    future outlook, 147–8
    new drugs, application and
      approval, 141–3
    pharmaceutical investments,
      109–11
    pharmaceutical market, 107–9
    political environment, 130–2
    regulatory environment, 134–5
    segmentation analysis, 16
  clinical trials in, 125–8
    accreditation of sites, 128–30
    active sponsors, 127–8
    by phase, 125–6
    for new drugs, 143–6
    international multicentre
      requirements, 141
    SFDA accreditation guidelines,
      128–30
  contract research organisations,
    122–5
  Drug Administration Law, 135
  good clinical practice, evolution,
    135–9
  healthcare delivery system,
    118–19
  healthcare system, 111–18
    ageing and healthcare,
      114–15
    disease burden, 116–18
    political situation, 115–16
    population factors, 114
  importance of traditional
    medicine, 120–2
  Ministry of Health, 134–5

  new drugs, application and
    approval of, 141–3
  pharmaceutical investments,
    109–11
  pharmaceutical market, 107–9
  regulatory environment, 134–5
clinical research
  country attractiveness index,
    12–13
  global growth of, 349
  in Asia *see also* Asia
    background, 1–2
    boom, 8–13
    business, 5–7
    economic environment, 340–1
    environmental factors, 347–9
    future outlook, 353–4
    legal environment, 346–7
    local partners, 348–9
    patient pool and doctors, 347
    PESTLE analysis, 335–6
    political environment, 336–40
    socio-cultural forces, 342–5
    SWOT analysis, 22–5
    technological factors, 345–6
  in China, 107–48. *See also*
  China
    ADR monitoring, 139–41
    economic environment, 132–4
    environmental analysis,
      130–46
    future outlook, 147–8
    new drugs, application and
      approval, 141–3
    pharmaceutical investments
      in, 109–11
    pharmaceutical market,
      107–9
    political environment, 130–2
    regulatory environment, 134–5

Published by Woodhead Publishing Limited, 2012

in Hong Kong. *See also*
Hong Kong, 293–313
background and history,
293–4
in India. *See also* India
cultural factors, 97–9
economic factors, 93–5
environmental factors, 101–3
evolution of, 61–73
future outlook, 105–6
government intiatives, 87–9
history, 60–1
legal factors influencing, 103–5
PESTLE analysis, 86–105
political factors influencing,
86–92
regulatory inspections, 85–6
socio-economic-cultural
factors influencing, 95–7
technology factors
influencing, 99–101
in Indonesia, 321–7. *See also*
Indonesia
background and history, 321–2
future outlook, 326–7
in Japan, 27–54. *See also* Japan
background and history, 27–9
clinical research industry,
29–32
future outlook, 54
in Malaysia, 269–91. *See also*
Malaysia
in Philippines, 315–21. *See also*
Philippines
background and history,
315–16
challenges and future
outlook, 320
in Singapore, 199–236. *See also*
Singapore

environmental analysis,
225–32
future outlook, 235–6
governing authority and
regulatory structure, 203–5
in South Korea, 149–73. *See
also* South Korea
compliance, 170–1
cultural barriers, 173
environmental analysis,
168–73
future outlook, 173
infrastructure, 169
pharmaceutical industry,
149–52
regional cooperation and
data acceptance, 170
shortage of skilled
professionals, 172
in Taiwan, 175–97. *See also*
Taiwan
future outlook, 196–7
in Thailand, 237–67. *See also*
Thailand
environmental analysis,
263–4
future prospects, 265–7
protocol approval, 244
in Vietnam, 327–34. *See also*
Vietnam
background and history,
327–8
future outlook, 334
Clinical Research Malaysia (CRM),
275
clinical trials
in China, 125–8. *See also* China
accreditation of sites, 128–30
active sponsors, 127–8
by phase, 125–6

Published by Woodhead Publishing Limited, 2012

364 Clinical Research in Asia: Opportunities and Challenges

for new drugs, 143–6
international multicentre
   requirements, 141
SFDA accreditation
   guidelines, 128–30
stages of clinical trials, 136–7
therapeutic areas, 128
in Hong Kong, 299–301, 309–11.
See also Hong Kong
in India 67–73. *See also* India
   approval of, 81–3
      export of biological
         samples, 82–3
      import permission and
         processing time, 81–2
   national and international
      collaborations, 70–1
   regulatory standards for
      phase 1 and phase 0, 84–5
   trials undertaken, 67–73
in Indonesia, 324–6. *See also*
Indonesia
in Japan, 44–6. *See also* Japan
in Malaysia, 286–8. *See also*
Malaysia
   challenges, 289
   environment, 274–5
   guidelines, 275
   permission, 277–80
   registration, 288–9
in Philippines, 319–20. *See also*
Philippines
in Singapore, 211–17. *See also*
Singapore
   challenges in, 232–5
   clinical trial certificate, 214–16
   hospitals/institutions, 212–13
   import of clinical trial
      material (CTMs), 216–17

industry-sponsored trials,
   211–13
pharma companies investing
   in, 208–9
study start-up timeline, 215
in South Korea, 154–5, 162–5.
See also South Korea
in Taiwan, 190–6. *See also*
Taiwan
   cultural barriers, 196
   environmental analysis, 194
   general clinical research
      centres (GCRCs), 192–4
   industry-sponsored trials,
      190–2
   infrastructure and facilities,
      194
   regional cooperation and
      data acceptance, 195
   reporting of SUSAR, 189–90
   shortage of skilled
      professsionals, 196
in Thailand, 261–3. *See also*
Thailand
   approval process, 256–7
   compulsory licensing, 254–5
   drug accountability/disposal
      report, 261
   final study report, 261
   insurance, 259
   interim report submission, 260
   investigational product
      requirements, 259
   IRB, documents for
      submission, 257–8
   marketing approval, for new
      drugs and generics, 254
   recruitment modalities, 260
   study start-up timeline, 257–9

Published by Woodhead Publishing Limited, 2012

Index

SUSAR report for
   investigational drugs, 259–60
   timelines, 256–7
in Vietnam, 332. *See also* Vietnam
pre-marketing, documents, 322–3
types of amendments, 82–3
Companies Act, Singapore, 217
contract research organisation (CRO)
   in Asia, 9–14. *See also* Asia
      growth of, 13
      strategic issues, 349–53
   in China, 122–5
   in Hong Kong, 300
   in India, 63–4
   in Japan, 29–32
   in Malaysia, 284–6
   in Singapore, 208–11
   in South Korea, 153–4
   in Taiwan, 180–1
   in Thailand, 242–5
   pharmaceutical market and, 7–8
   services of, 8
CRO. *See* contract research
   organisation
Cross-Strait Medical and
   Healthcare Cooperation
   Agreement, Taiwan, 195–7

Department of Medical Equipment
   and Health Works (DMEHW), 331
Development Centre for
   Biotechnology (DCB), 177
Drug Act of BE 2546, 239
Drug Administration Law, China, 135
Drug Control Authority (DCA),
   Malaysia, 272
   functions of, 276
   member composition of, 276
drug master filings (DMFs), 56–7
Drug Technical Advisory Board, 75

Drugs Controller General of India
   (DCGI), 82–3, 87–9

Economic Cooperation Framework
   Agreement, Taiwan, 175
ethics committee
   in Hong Kong, 306
   in Indonesia, 324
   in Philippines, 318–19
   in Singapore, 219–22
expedited safety reports, Malaysia,
   282–3

Forum for Ethical Review
   Committees in Thailand
   (FERCIT), 249–50
Forum for Ethical Review
   Committees in the Asian and
   Western Pacific Region
   (FERCAP), 250

good clinical practice (GCP)
   in China, 135–9
   in India, 74–81
      compliance rates of, 86
      member composition, 83–4
      salient features of, 75–81
         audit, 77
         communication with
            ethics committee, 78
         compensation, 76–7
         contract, 75–6
         ethics committee, 79
         ethics committee approval,
            80–1
         informed consent of study
            subjects, 79
         investigational product, 78
         investigator
            responsibilities, 77–8

Published by Woodhead Publishing Limited, 2012

366 Clinical Research in Asia: Opportunities and Challenges

monitoring, 77
review procedures, 80
role of foreign sponsor, 77
selection and recruitment, 78
sponsor responsibilties, 75
vs. ICH-GCP, 83–5
in Indonesia, evolution of, 323–4
in Japan
evolution of, 38–44
salient features of, 39–44
in Malaysia
clinical trial permission, 277–80
discontinuation/termination of trial, 283
drug accountability and disposal, 284
ethics committee approval, 280–1
evolution of, 276–84
final study report, 284
interim report, 283
regulatory approval, 280–1
safety reporting, 281–3
start-up timeline, 280–1
in Singapore
evolution of, 217–24
hospital ethics committee, 219–22
medical clinical research committee, 218–19
salient features, 217–18, 222–4
in South Korea
discontinuation/termination of trial, 161
drug accountability/disposal report, 162
evolution of, 155–62

final study report, 162
import, storage and labelling requirements of the IP, 159–60
IND review process, 156–7
insurance, 160
interim report submission, 161
IRB review process, 157–9
recruitment modalities, 161
safety reporting, 160–1
study start-up timeline, 159
in Taiwan
bridging study evaluation, 185
consultations, online application, 185–6
evolution of, 181–90
IND review process, 182–4
institutional review board, 186–7
recruitment modalities of, 190
regulatory approval process, 187–8
study start-up timeline, 188–9
SUSAR reporting, 189–90

Health Science Authority, Singapore, 215–16
healthcare system
in China, 111–18
ageing and healthcare, 114–15
disease burden, 116–18
importance of traditional medicine in, 120–2
political situation, 115–16
population factors, 114
in Hong Kong, 296–9
in Malaysia, 273
in Singapore, 205–7
in Taiwan, 178–80

Published by Woodhead Publishing Limited, 2012

Index

Hong Kong
 clinical research, 293–313
  background and history,
   293–4
  segmentation analysis, 16
 clinical trials in, 299–301, 309–11
 contract research organisation
  in, 300
 environmental analysis, 311–13
 future outlook, 313
 health insurance, 299
 healthcare system, 296–9
 pharmaceutical industry, 295
 regulatory environment, 301–9
  clinical trial insurance, 306
  ethics committees, 303
  import and export
   permission, 303–5
  progress report submission,
   309
  recruitment modalities, 308–9
  regulatory and ethics
   committee approval, 303
  safety reporting, 308
  study start-up timeline, 305–6

ICH-E5 (Taiwan), 185
ICH-E6 guidance (Taiwan), 182
ICH-GCP (International
 Conference on Harmonisation
 Guidelines for Good Clinical
 Practice), 39
 vs. Indian GCP, 83–5
ICMR, India, 85–6
IMS Health Quarterly ranks, 238
India
 clinical research
  BABE/Phase I and pre-clinical
   business, 64–5
  business, 63–4

centralised laboratory/ECG
 business, 66–7
contract research
 organisations, 63–4
cultural factors, 97–9
drug discovery and chemistry
 business, 62–3
economic factors, 93–5
environmental factors
 influencing, 101–3
evolution of, 61–73
future outlook, 105–6
government intiatives, 87–9
history, 60–1
IT and ITES life science
 business, 65–6
legal factors, 103–5
PESTLE analysis, 86–105
pharma partnerships, 58
political factors, 86–7
regulatory inspections,
 85–6
segmentation analysis, 16
socio-economic-cultural
 factors, 95–7
technology factors
 influencing, 99–101
training, 67
clinical trials, 67–73
 national and international
  collaborations, 70–1
 patenting, 103–4
 political factors, 86–92
 regulatory standards for
  phase 1 and phase 0, 84–5
 subject compliance, 97
 trials undertaken, 67–73
good clinical practice guidelines,
 74–5
 compliance rates, 86

Published by Woodhead Publishing Limited, 2012

salient features, 75–81
healthcare education
  infrastructure, 91–2
healthcare expenditure, 93–4
pharmaceutical industry, 55–60
regulatory environment, 73–81
Indonesia
  clinical research, 321–7
    background and history, 321–2
  clinical trials, 324–6
  ethics committee, 324
  good clinical practice, evolution,
    323–4
  regulatory environment, 322–3
Information Technology Act 2000,
  India, 105
informed consent, 265
institutional review boards (IRBs)
  in Hong Kong, 306
  in Singapore, 215
  in South Korea, 153–4, 157–9
  in Taiwan, 184, 186–7

Japan
  clinical research, 27–54
    background and history, 27–9
    future outlook, 54
    global clinical trials, 44–6
    good clinical practice (GCP),
      evolution, 38–44
    industry, 29–32
    pharmaceutical industry,
      30–1
    regulatory environment,
      32–7
  emerging outsourcing models,
    46–51
Japan Association for the
  Advancement of Medical
  Equipment (JAAME), 33

Japan CRO Association (JCROA),
  29–30
Joint Research Ethics Committees
  (JREC), 251–2

Malaysia
  clinical research centres, 285
  clinical research, 269–91
  clinical trial, 286–8
    environment, 274–5
    guidelines, 275
    permission for, 277–80
    registration, 288–9
    value proposition and
      challenges, 289
  clinical trial exemption, 277–80
  clinical trial import licence,
    277–80
  contract research organisation
    market, 284–6
  drug control authority, 272
    functions of, 276
    member composition, 276
  expedited safety reports, 282–3
  good clinical practice
    evolution of, 276–84
      clinical trial permission,
        277–80
      discontinuation/
        termination of trial, 283
      drug accountability and
        disposal, 284
      ethics committee approval,
        280–1
      final study report, 284
      interim report, 283
      regulatory approval, 280–1
      safety reporting, 272,
        281–3
      start-up timeline, 280–1

Published by Woodhead Publishing Limited, 2012

Index

healthcare systems, 273
medical research ethics
committee, 281
Ministry of Health (MOH),
272, 285, 288–9
National Medical Research
Register, 288–9
pharmaceutical industry,
269–71
regulatory environment, 275–6
Medical Clinical Research
Committee (MCRC), 218–19
composition, functions and
operations, 219
functions, 214–15
Medical Council of India, code of
conduct, 87
Medical Device Act of BE 2531,
239–40
medical research ethics committee
(MREC), Malaysia, 281
Medicines Act (Cap 176),
Singapore, 204
Ministry of Economic Affairs
(MOEA), Taiwan, 177–8
Ministry of Health (MOH), 328–31
in China, 134–5
in Malaysia, 272, 285, 288–9
in Singapore, 203, 205, 207
Ministry of Labour and Social
Security, China, 135

National ADR Reporting Centre,
Taiwan, 189–90
National Cancer Institute, India, 71
National Medical Research Council
(NMRC), Singapore, 207
National Medical Research
Register (NMRR), Malaysia,
288–9

National Pharmaceutical
Administration (NPA), 203–5
National University of Singapore
Academy of GxP Excellence
(NUSAGE), 228, 231
New Drug Act 2003, 239

Organization for Economic
Cooperation and Development
(OECD), 28–9, 115–16

PCHRD (Philippine Council for
Health Research and
Development), 316–17
Pharma Zone, Singapore,
199–200
Pharmaceutical Inspection
Cooperation Scheme (PICS), 231
Pharmaceuticals and Medical
Devices Agency (PMDA), Japan,
33–7
international strategies, 51–4
services, 33–6
Pharmaceuticals and Medical
Devices Evaluation Center
(PMDEC), 32–3
Pharmaceuticals Registration and
Import/Export Control Section,
305
Philippine Council for Health
Research and Development
(PCHRD), 316–17
Philippines
clinical research, 315–21
background and history,
315–16
challenges and future
outlook, 320
segmentation analysis, 16
clinical trials, 319–20

Published by Woodhead Publishing Limited, 2012

370   Clinical Research in Asia: Opportunities and Challenges

ethics committee, 318–19
institutional ethics review
  committees (IERCs) approval,
  318–19
regulatory environment, 316–18
Poisons Act (Cap 234), 231

regulatory environment
  in China, 134–5
  in Hong Kong, 301–9
  in India, 73–81
  in Indonesia, 322–3
  in Malaysia, 275–6
  in Philippines, 316–18
  in Thailand, 239–40
  in Vietnam, 329–30

Schedule Y, 73, 75, 84
SFDA (State Food & Drug
  Administration), China, 128–30,
  135
SGGCP (Singapore Guidelines for
  Good Clinical Practice), 217–18,
  222–4
Singapore
  A*STAR's Biomedical
    Engineering Programme, 227
  clinical research, 199–236
    environmental analysis, 225–32
    future outlook, 235–6
    governing authority and
      regulatory structure, 203–5
  clinical trial certificate, 214–16
  clinical trial resource centre, 224
  clinical trials, 211–17
    challenges, 232–5
    clinical trial certificate, 214–16
    hospitals/institutions, 212–14
    import of clinical trial
      material, 216–17

industry-sponsored trials,
  211–13
pharma companies investing
  in, 208–9
study start-up timeline, 215
contract research organisation,
  208–11
  clinical trials, by therapeutic
    area, 210
  market size, 208
  specialised therapeutics, 209–11
environmental analysis, 225–32
  political and economic
    environment, 225–6
  public–private partnership,
    226–9
  regulatory and legal
    environment, 230–2
  socio-cultural environment,
    229
good clinical practice
  evolution of, 217–24
  hospital ethics committee,
    219–22
  medical clinical research
    committee, 218–19
  salient features of guidelines,
    217–18, 222–4
Health Science Authority, 215–16
Health Services Research
  Competitive Research Grant, 207
healthcare system, 205–7
hospital ethics committee,
  219–22
  composition, functions and
    operations, 220
  responsibilities, 221
  role, 220–1
National Pharmaceutical
  Administration (NPA)

Published by Woodhead Publishing Limited, 2012

Index

adverse drug reaction
monitoring unit, 205
Chinese Proprietary Medicine
Unit, 204
Cosmetic Control Unit, 204–5
Drug Administration
Division, 203–4
Good Manufacturing
Practices and Licensing
Unit, 204
pharmaceutical industry
investments in, 200–2
overview of, 199–200
Trade Development Board, 216
Trade-Related Aspects of
Intellectual Property Rights
(TRIPS) Agreement, 210
translational and clinical research
flagship programme, 226
Singapore Clinical Research
Institute, 227–8
Singapore Economic Development
Board, 200
Singapore Guidelines for Good
Clinical Practice (SGGCP),
217–18, 222–4
Singapore Health Science
Authority, 290
Singapore-Stanford Biodesign
Program, 227
South Korea
clinical research, 149–73
compliance, 170–1
cultural barriers, 173
environmental analysis,
168–73
future outlook, 173
infrastructure, 169
language barrier, 172

pharmaceutical industry,
149–52
regional cooperation and
data acceptance, 170
segmentation analysis, 16
shortage of skilled
professionals, 172
clinical trial, 162–5
contract research organisation
market, 153–4
good clinical practice
evolution of, 155–63
IND review process, 156–7
IRB review process, 157–9
pharmaceutical industry, 149–52
standard operating procedures
(SOP), 41
State Drug Administration (SDA),
China, 128–30, 135
State Food & Drug Administration
(SFDA), China, 135
Strategic Initiative for Developing
Capacity in Ethical Review
(SIDCER), 250
suspected unexpected serious
adverse reaction (SUSAR), 189–90

TaiGen Biotechnology (Taipei), 178
Taiwan
biotech industry, 177–8
clinical research, 175–97
future outlook, 196–7
clinical trials, 190–6
cultural barriers, 196
environmental analysis, 194
general clinical research
centres, 192–4
infrastructure and facilities,
194

Published by Woodhead Publishing Limited, 2012

372 Clinical Research in Asia: Opportunities and Challenges

regional cooperation and data acceptance, 195
shortage of skilled professsionals, 196
SUSAR reporting, 189–90
contract research organisation (CRO), 180–1
Cross-Strait Medical and Healthcare Cooperation Agreement, 195–7
good clinical practice (GCP)
consultations, online application, 185–6
evolution of, 181–90
recruitment modalities, 190
regulatory approval process, 187–8
study start-up timeline, 188–9
SUSAR reporting, 189–90
healthcare system in, 178–80
institutional review board (IRB), 186–7
investigational new drug review, 182–4
pharmaceutical industry, 175–7
Taiwan-America Biotechnology Association (TABA), 178
Thai FDA, 239–40, 243–4, 250–1
Thai Ministry of Public Health (MOPH), 243–4
Thailand
clinical research, 237–67
environmental analysis, 263–4
future prospects, 265–7
protocol approval, 244
segmentation analysis of, 16
clinical trials, 261–3
approval process, 256–7
compulsory licensing, 254–5
conduction, 252–61

discontinuation/termination, 260–1
drug accountability/disposal report, 261
final study report, 261
industry-sponsored, 262–3
insurance, 259
interim report submission, 260
investigational product, 259
IRB documents for, 257–8
marketing approval, new drugs and generics, 254
recruitment modalities, 260
study start-up timeline, 257–9
SUSAR reporting, 259–60
timelines, 256–7
contract research organisation market, 242–5
clinical trial conduct, 243–5
major CROs operating, 243
patient recruitment, 245
demography of, 241–2
drug manufacturers, 238
Drugs and Cosmetics Act, 73
health insurance coverage, 245
hospital accreditation, 248
hospital systems, 246–52
biomedical research, 249–51
compliance with 21 CFR Part 12, 247
economic advantages, 247
ethical issues, 249–51
monitoring sites in Asia, 248–9
motivation for sponsors, 252
opportunities, 252
qualified site staff, 247–8
reduction in steps and resource loss, 251
therapeutic areas, 248

Published by Woodhead Publishing Limited, 2012

Index

world-class research standards, 251–2
pharmaceutical industry in, 237–8
pharmaceutical market in, 240–2
regulatory environment, 239–40
translational and clinical research (TCR), 226
Tuas Biomedical Park (TBP), 228

US Food & Drug Administration (US FDA), 20–2, 51, 53–7

Vietnam
adverse drug reaction reporting, 331–2
clinical research in, 327–34
background and history, 327–8
challenges and future outlook, 334
clinical trials, 332
key hospitals, 327–8
pharmaceutical industry, 328–9
regulatory approval, 330–1
regulatory environment, 329–30
safety reporting, 331–2

World Health Organisation (WHO), 28, 113–14, 273
World Trade Organisation, 338–9

Published by Woodhead Publishing Limited, 2012

CPSIA information can be obtained at www.ICGtesting.com
Printed in the USA
LVOW101506310113

318096LV00009B/237/P

9 781907 568008